Afghanistan: Transition under Threat

Studies in International Governance is a research and policy analysis series from the Centre for International Governance Innovation (CIGI) and Wilfrid Laurier University Press. Titles in the series provide timely consideration of emerging trends and current challenges in the broad field of international governance. Representing diverse perspectives on important global issues, the series will be of interest to students and academics while serving also as a reference tool for policy-makers and experts engaged in policy discussion. To reach the greatest possible audience and ultimately shape the policy dialogue, each volume will be made available both in print through WLU Press and, twelve months after publication, accessible for free online through the IGLOO Network under the Creative Commons License.

Afghanistan
Transition under Threat

Geoffrey Hayes and Mark Sedra
editors

Wilfrid Laurier University Press

Wilfrid Laurier University Press acknowledges the financial support of the Government of Canada through its Book Publishing Industry Development Program for its publishing activities. Wilfrid Laurier University Press acknowledges the financial support of the Centre for International Governance Innovation. The Centre for International Governance Innovation gratefully acknowledges support for its work program from the Government of Canada and the Government of Ontario.

Library and Archives Canada Cataloguing in Publication

Afghanistan : transition under threat / Geoffrey Hayes and Mark Sedra, editors.

(Studies in international governance series)
Includes bibliographical references and index.
ISBN 978-1-55458-011-8

1. Afghanistan—History—2001– . 2. Afghanistan—Politics and government—2001– . 3. Afghanistan—Economic conditions—21st century. 4. Afghanistan—History, Military—21st century. 5. Canada—Military policy. I. Hayes, Geoffrey, 1961– II. Sedra, Mark III. Centre for International Governance Innovation. IV. Series.

DS371.4A45 2008   958.104'6   C2007–906851–0

Co-published with the Centre for International Governance Innovation.

© 2008 The Centre for International Governance Innovation (CIGI) and Wilfrid Laurier University Press

Cover photograph © Department of National Defence, IS2004-2069a.jpg, 2004. Photo by Sgt. Frank Hudec, Canadian Forces Combat Camera. Cover design by Brian Grebow/BG Communications. Text design by Pam Woodland.

∞

This book is printed on Ancient Forest Friendly paper (100% post-consumer recycled).

Printed in Canada

CONTENTS

Afghanistan—Failing or Flourishing?

After a number of years of relegation to secondary strategic importance, Afghanistan is today back at the centre of global policy debates. At international conferences in Rome (July 2007), Tokyo (February 2008), Bucharest (April 2008), and Paris (June 2008), global leaders have committed themselves to addressing the difficult challenges that now loom before the Afghan people—a live insurgency, weak services and infrastructure, food insecurity, aid dependency, a consolidating narco-ascendancy, and poverty.

This rededication is welcome inside Afghanistan. In some quarters, it is considered overdue. But it holds the promise that for at least the next several years major donors and troop contributors will seek to resolve security and development challenges from the perspective of Kabul and Kunar, Sar-i-Pul and Farah, rather than view these issues through some of the more unhelpful lenses applied in the past.

The backdrop to this renewed attention is a sharp debate over whether efforts to bring stability and development to Afghanistan are gaining ground or are on the verge of "strategic failure." The latter view has particular currency with many outside Afghanistan, who see its conflict as "inevitable," "atavistic," even "perpetual." These observers argue that failure to produce an adequate "peace dividend" in the first years after the 2001 Bonn Agreement—combined with the taking root of impunity on a grand scale—is now dooming Afghanistan to another round of civil conflict. Their arguments draw richly on the mythology thrown up by the formative British and Soviet experiences in Afghanistan in the nineteenth and twentieth centuries.

This volume gives the case for both sides of this dispute. It is lucid on areas of under-investment. It enumerates areas of relative success. It questions the sequencing and coherence of international support and government decision making. It underlines the pivotal nature of decisions to accommodate, even appease, warlords, as well as the tragic future legacy of the Taliban's "strategic withdrawal" to safer ground in late 2001. The strategic challenges confronting us are clear. The shape of the transition to date—

its hard trend lines at the local level—are outlined but not treated in depth. For many outside Afghanistan, even those in the region, the "ground realities" in its thirty-four provinces and nearly four hundred official and de facto districts remain opaque—an impenetrable mystery, but the news is assumed to be generally bad.

These are important issues. Whether judgments are made from the eye of the terrorist storm in Kandahar or around a kitchen table in Lübeck, Germany, the global view of whether the UN, NATO, and scores of donors are succeeding or faltering in Afghanistan will be replete with consequence for Afghans, who have experienced the cold shoulder of neglect several times in their lifetimes. Afghans, of all people, know the cost of evaporating international will. Arguably the worst period of their epic thirty-year conflict came in 1992. A regime had fallen, and opportunity beckoned perhaps even more earnestly than in 2001. But the world was preoccupied with matters elsewhere.

In the streets of Kabul, it is difficult not to be inspired by the determination of ordinary Afghans to seize today's opportunity. They are skeptical, even dismissive, of their government—yet demand its services with fervour. They criticize the international community's performance but not its presence. They ask when, not whether, a regional approach will be taken to the security challenge facing Afghanistan—one studded by terrorist groups whose operatives pounce on Afghan life from camps and indoctrination centres beyond the reach of Afghan national security forces.

It is easy to dismiss the successive bargains between Afghans and the world over the past seven years for their obvious limitations. The Bonn Agreement was not a peace deal. The Afghanistan Compact was not a blueprint for nation-building. The Afghanistan National Development Strategy (ANDS) is not a plan for rebuilding the country.

But each one has delivered results. In the Istalif valley near Kabul, houses and orchards that were black with Taliban vengeance in 2001 are now green with new irrigation canals, bright with bulbs lit by micro-hydro. In the northwest, carpet weavers long exiled to Iran and Pakistan are returning to the trade in their tens of thousands. In Zabul province, farmers check the price of potatoes in Kabul and Kandahar over cell phones—now serving over 4.5 million Afghans. In Balkh province, the army and national civil order police are setting standards of discipline and patriotic service. In Garda Serai in Paktia province, the interprovincial highway being rebuilt through the home turf of Jalaluddin Haqqani is the centerpiece, tribal elders say, of "more reconstruction than under any previous king." In the rich fields around Lashkar Gah, the high price of grain has pushed even poppy bigwigs to plant wheat in quantity.

Afghanistan is recovering, but under a hail of continuing attacks that are far from being of its own making. It is a dynamic society—eager for change, preferably reform, and for the skills that bring employment. With sustained effort, institutions can take root that will withstand even stiffer challenges than today's pelting terrorist harassment and odd suicidal enormity. With visionary initiatives by an international community that truly seeks peace for South Asia—as it has successfully done in so many parts of Europe and Africa—Afghanistan can become an anchor for an even larger Asian project of growth-driven interdependence. For Afghans, this debate has only one correct outcome: make the land bridge at the heart of Asia a reality and a benefit for all.

Christopher Alexander, Deputy Special Representative of the
United Nations Secretary General for Afghanistan and
Former Canadian Ambassador to Afghanistan
(August 2003–October 2005)

As this volume is a collection of papers first presented at a workshop held in Waterloo, Canada, in December 2006, we would like to thank all of the workshop participants for the vibrant discussion that took place. It has greatly enriched the quality of the book. We are indebted to the Centre for International Governance Innovation (CIGI) for sponsoring the project and the Laurier Centre for Military Strategic and Disarmament Studies (LCMSDS) for co-organizing the workshop. We would also like to acknowledge the ongoing support of the Academic Council of the United Nations System (ACUNS). Thanks also to Brian Henderson, Rob Kohlmeier, and their team at Wilfrid Laurier University Press for their role in producing the book.

Special thanks go to our esteemed colleagues John English and Terry Copp for their vision and support; to Katherine Sage, who worked so hard to organize the workshop; and to Jonathan Goodhand, who not only provided a chapter but offered invaluable advice and guidance on the book. Of course this book could not have published without the chapter contributors, who produced superb work under great time pressure.

INTRODUCTION

Mark Sedra
Geoffrey Hayes

This collection of essays is the result of a workshop held near Waterloo, On-tario, Canada to examine Afghanistan's war-to-peace transition. Among the thirty-five participants were diplomats, academics, aid workers, sol-diers, and practitioners with extensive experience in Afghanistan. The wide-ranging and frank discussions revealed that the Afghan state building process actually comprises three separate transitions—political, economic, and security—which have in many respects been advanced independently.[1] This realization informed the structure of this book, which deconstructs each of the transitions separately while elucidating the interconnections that exist. The final section of the book offers an in-depth look at Canada's ex-perience in Afghanistan, covering both its multi-faceted activities within the country and the impact of domestic politics on its strategy and approach. With rifts emerging in the NATO alliance concerning the future of the Afghan mission, and popular support for the military deployment dwin-dling among member-state populations, understanding the policies, prior-ities, and political calculations of countries like Canada is critical. The in-sight gleaned from the Canadian case can help to understand the positions of other NATO member states and the critical role medium-sized donors play in countries like Afghanistan.

Afghanistan's political transition and in fact the entire state building process was born at the December 2001 Bonn conference, which assem-bled Taliban opposition groups and members of the international commu-nity under the auspices of the United Nations. But in this volume, Ali Jalali reminds us that, despite the tremendous amount of global attention devoted to the Bonn talks, the state building process "was an afterthought to the fight against global terrorism, and was driven by the desire to remove the threat to the United States emanating from Afghan territory." Donors like the United States were fixated on rooting out the Taliban and al-Qaeda, not consolidating a particular type of peace in Afghanistan. Both Jalali and William Maley note that there were considerable limits on who could come to the table at Bonn, with the Taliban and any sympathizers largely excluded from the political process. As a result, the agreement could be considered a "victor's peace" rather than a "grand bargain for peace," as it legitimized "a change of regime that involved handing over power to factional leaders that were on the 'right side' of the war on terror" (Goodhand and Sedra 2006, 35). Furthermore, it could be considered only a partial peace, as the losers, the Taliban, were not fully defeated and retained the capacity and will to challenge the new political order (ibid.).

The Bonn Agreement offered a blueprint for Afghanistan's political transition, outlining a series of benchmarks to be achieved. Among those were the convening of an Emergency *Loya Jirga* to choose an interim government, the holding of parliamentary and presidential elections, and the development of a new constitution. The process was enormously successful in meeting those benchmarks, but the manner in which it did had the effect of distorting, and, in some ways, undermining the post-conflict transition. To achieve the level of stability necessary to meet the Bonn milestones, the government endeavored to co-opt rather than confront armed powerbrokers, a form of "warlord democratization" (Rubin 2006; Goodhand and Sedra 2006). While the state gained legitimacy through the two elections, its accommodation of armed commanders under the government tent slowed reforms and bred public distrust of the state. More interested in preserving their power and autonomy then advancing Afghanistan's democratic transition, the bulk of these commanders would instrumentalize their positions within the state to advance their own parochial interests. The colonization of whole government institutions, most notably the police, by armed factions stunted Afghanistan's transition.

Although the Bonn process successfully met many of the primary criteria on the democratization checklist, it did so largely at the expense of the imperative of institutionalization. Roland Paris argues that institutionalization should precede political liberalization in cases of post-conflict peacebuilding. Successful democratization processes can be undertaken only when the state possesses the institutional capacity to provide basic public goods, notably security (2004). Ali Jalali notes that this sequencing was reversed in Afghanistan. Over two decades of civil war had destroyed the state's institutions, leaving a legacy of corruption and poor governance that was hardly a suitable foundation for democratization: "elections in the absence of effective state institutions hampered the development of the democratic process."

Nor did the Bonn process adequately integrate the development, security, and institutional transitions. In his chapter Mike Capstick says, "the Bonn Process succeeded in its aim of establishing the building blocks of statehood, [but] there was no agreed international strategy that linked the essential security, governance and development aspects of nation building until *The Afghanistan Compact* was approved at the London Conference in February 2006."

The Afghanistan Compact of 2006 certainly addressed many of the shortcomings of the Bonn Agreement. The Bonn process featured a loose set of exclusively political benchmarks with "enough ambiguities to allow both the Afghan government and the donor community to deviate from its designated path" (Goodhand and Sedra 2006, 5). By contrast, the Afghanistan Compact was at once more precise and broad-based. It offered more succinct benchmarks, outlining both donor and recipient responsibilities for achieving them, and touched upon all three elements of the "triple transition," encompassing the political, economic, and security spheres.

Although the compact gave the state building process the strategic direction and holistic outlook that was missing from Bonn, it still lacked the "teeth" necessary to push through sensitive reforms. The compact laid down the rules of the game, but it failed to identify consequences for both donor and recipient if those rules are transgressed. As Mark Sedra discusses in the context of the security sector, a lack of will to achieve the compact benchmarks in a timely manner is one of the greatest challenges facing the state building project.

There may be scope to utilize aid conditionality as a mechanism to overcome this political will problem and encourage greater adherence to reform objectives. Of course, any conditionality framework must be negotiated between Afghan and international actors for it to be effective and must hold both actors to account; the imposition of conditions on a recipient has been shown in other development contexts to be counter-productive. However, donors have been singularly unwilling to consider the use of conditionality, partially due to an empirically flawed perception that it is ineffectual in all circumstances, and partially due to an unwillingness to place any undue pressure on President Karzai, who is seen as the only viable political partner for the international community in Afghanistan. Accordingly, aid has largely been delivered in an unconditional manner, affording Afghan actors tremendous scope to resist painful reforms (Goodhand and Sedra 2006).

The provision of development assistance is at the core of the economic transition, as are efforts to stabilize the country's fiscal policy and encourage investment and private-sector growth. Given the otherwise sobering tone of our collection, it may seem surprising that William Byrd's economic scorecard for Afghanistan since 2001 is "reasonably positive." In macroeconomic terms, the country has maintained a stable exchange rate, controlled inflation, and encouraged economic growth. In his chapter, Byrd also acknowledges success in public finance management, where, for example, increasing domestic revenues will soon allow the Afghan government to cover its payroll. The Afghan government has developed a sound development plan, the Afghanistan National Development Strategy (ANDS), and has achieved significant gains in specific sectors like education, health, roads, and community development.

Nipa Banerjee would agree that Afghanistan has made significant headway in these sectors. Banerjee reserves special praise for the demining campaign and the National Solidarity Program (NSP), initiatives that have addressed the grass-roots needs of individual communities. Banerjee also notes positive results in micro-credit programs intended to empower and provide sustainable livelihoods for Afghan women.

But such economic gains are matched by enormous challenges that will take decades to overcome. Despite the country's macro-economic advances, poverty remains rampant, especially in rural areas, where over three-quarters of Afghans live. Basic services like water and electricity remain unreliable, even in Kabul. International donors continue to compete with each other and the Afghan government, rather than coordinating development efforts. Indeed, as Seema Patel notes in her chapter, "External donors such as nongovernmental organizations (NGOs), international private contractors, and the military provide more funds for service and reconstruction projects than the Afghan government."

Then there is the problem of poppy. Jonathan Goodhand questions basic assumptions about counter-narcotics in Afghanistan and conventional "supply-side interventions." In his assessment, the international community needs to rethink its strategy, which he says is dictated more by "Western countries' concerns about their own drug problems ... than the long-term needs and interests" of Afghans. He points to the gradual consolidation of the drug trade in Afghanistan in the hands of a handful of über traffickers as an adverse and unintended consequence of existing counter-narcotics programs. The mutually reinforcing relationship between counter-narcotics policy and state building may not be as clear as is commonly assumed: "There is a complex and ambiguous relationship between counter narcotics and state building, therefore, and heavy-handed eradication may have adverse effects and undermine the legitimacy and capacity of the central state with regard to local strong men." According to this logic, existing counter-narcotics policies undercut key elements of Afghanistan's political, economic, and security transitions. Goodhand explains that addressing the drug issue is a long-term and gradualist endeavor and will necessitate "policies and interventions in non-drug-focused spheres" such as socio-economic development and institution-building. More controversially, he questions the very "demonization" of drugs, calling for "transitional arrangements ...

that might involve providing amnesties for certain traffickers and incentives to encourage them to invest in the licit economy." While this may seem extreme to some, after six years of failed drug policies that have seen the industry grow to unprecedented levels, it is clear that unorthodox thinking and new approaches are needed.

The poppy problem plays a central role in the security sphere. According to the UN Secretary General's September 2007 report on the situation in Afghanistan, "criminal drug gangs ... enjoy a symbiotic relationship with anti-Government armed groups" (UNSG 2007). While, as Antonio Giustozzi indicates, it is unclear what level of funds the Taliban derives from the drug trade—accrued primarily through ad hoc taxation and the provision of protection for farmers—the Taliban have certainly benefited from the growing disaffection of farmers who have lost their livelihoods due to government eradication programs. Such programs have tended to target small farmers rather than large landowners with links to armed groups and influence in the government. As Giustozzi states, "the unpopularity of the government and what was perceived as the 'disrespectful' behaviour of the foreign troops, fuelled by a lack of understanding for the local culture, had the effect of dividing and demoralizing the opposition to the insurgents and creating some nostalgia for the time when the Taliban were in power."

"The Taliban as a movement does not exist any more." President Karzai uttered these words at a joint press conference with Donald Rumsfeld during a visit of the former US Defence Secretary to the Afghan capital in February 2004. Karzai attributed continuing violence to "common criminals" rather than organized insurgents and explained that "every act committed by a Kalashnikov is not an act done by the Taliban or al-Qaeda" (Associated Press 2004; Sedra 2004).[2] The Afghan president derisively pointed to a wave of appeals to the government from Taliban fighters seeking amnesty as evidence of the decline of the movement. "You would be surprised," he said, "how many approaches from the Taliban we have on a daily basis—individuals, groups coming to talk to us and let them back into the country" (Kitchen 2004).

Much changed in the three and a half years that followed. It was a far less confident President Karzai in September 2007 who was making peace overtures to a resurgent Taliban. Karzai raised the prospect of offering government positions to moderate Taliban leaders in exchange for the end of the insurgency, a proposal that would have been unthinkable in 2004. The confident Taliban soundly rejected Karzai's appeals on the grounds that no dialogue could take place as long as international forces remained in the country (Agence France Presse 2007). This episode is only one of many significant reversals in Afghan government policy in 2007 and 2008 that exemplifies the crisis surrounding the Afghan state building process and the country's fragile transition to stability and democracy.

Before you can build institutions, usher in sustainable development, and consolidate democracy, you must have a baseline of security. That minimum level of security is absent in much of Afghanistan today. Any discussion of Afghanistan's security transition will invariably focus on missed opportunities. What if the International Security Assistance Force (ISAF) had expanded across the country in 2002, when the Taliban had yet to recover, warlords had yet to consolidate their fiefdoms, and neighbouring states had yet to resume their proxy competition? What if security sector reform (SSR) was advanced more strenuously in the early stages of the state building process, with police and justice reform receiving commensurate levels of assistance to the Afghan National Army (ANA)? The final and perhaps most confounding question is what if talk of dialogue and reconciliation with moderate Taliban actors had taken place in 2001 and 2002 rather than 2007?[3] Maley argues that this was impossible to consider in the political and security atmosphere of December 2001, but a more nuanced policy toward the Taliban, balancing the use of force with more robust diplomacy and programs to advance reconciliation, may have paid dividends and helped to avert the present security morass. Such counterfactuals are impossible to answer definitively, but they help to explain the current security predicament in Afghanistan.

In his chapter on security sector reform (SSR), Mark Sedra ascribes particular importance to the failure of the international community to deploy a countrywide peace-support mission following the Taliban's fall.[4] William Maley observes that the decision in early 2002 by the United States to limit ISAF to Kabul signalled that the international community was not as committed to the long-term development of Afghanistan as the Bonn Agreement implied. In the absence of such a force, the onus fell on the SSR process to address the security gap in the country. This had the effect of distorting the process, producing a "slide toward expediency," as Sedra terms it, in which security-force operational effectiveness was prioritized over everything else (Sedra 2006). Quantity rather than quality dictated policy surrounding the development of the Afghan National Security Forces (ANSF); until 2005–2006 little attention was accorded to seemingly soft issues like human rights, security sector governance, and fiscal sustainability. The process had assumed the guise of a Cold War–era train-and-equip program, geared to churning out Afghan troops and police quickly in order to relieve pressure on coalition and international troops, rather than to produce rights-respecting and accountable security forces clearly subordinated to democratic civilian authority.

Each of the five pillars of the SSR process—military reform, police reform, judicial reform, demilitarization, and counter-narcotics—has stumbled. The main objective of the military reform pillar, clearly the success story of the process, is to create an effective and ethnically representative Afghan National Army (ANA). However, by 2008, more than five years into the process, the force continued to face significant problems of troop retention and equipment shortfalls, and could still only undertake limited operations without coalition support. Although the stated strength of the force in September 2007 was 40,360, only around 22,000 were combat-ready (UNSG 2007).

The Afghan National Police (ANP) is one of the most corrupt and dysfunctional institutions in the government, yet it is only in the past two years that serious effort and resources have been invested in remaking the force. As Sedra states, considering that the police form one of the "principal interfaces between government and society," this lost time has both undercut the legitimacy of the state and contributed to insecurity.

Another pillar that received little attention, to the detriment of the entire SSR process, was judicial reform, which only received a fraction of the resources allocated to its military and police counterparts. Although there is increased awareness of the centrality of the legal system to the functioning of the entire security apparatus, only in 2007 was the reform process endowed with a coherent strategy, and it still faces acute resource shortfalls.

Removing the remnants of war in the form of demilitarization is vital to consolidating a durable peace in Afghanistan and establishing the government's monopoly on the use of coercive force. Several initiatives have been undertaken under the umbrella of demilitarization, including a disarmament, demobilization, and reintegration program (DDR), a disbandment of illegal armed groups program (DIAG), a heavy weapons collections program, and an ammunition- and mine-destruction initiative. Some of these programs, particularly the DDR program and the ammunition- and mine-destruction initiative, have been quite successful, while others, such as the DIAG program, have stalled and even teetered on the verge of collapse. While these programs represent important first steps to address the issues of illegal weapons holdings and the existence of non-state militias, they have only scratched the surface of the problem.[5]

The exponential rise of the drug trade over the past six years clearly demonstrates the failure of counter-narcotics policies. The UNODC executive director, Antonio Maria Costa, referred to eradication efforts in Afghanistan, one of the main components of the counter-narcotics strategy, as "a farce" (John 7 September 2007). Similar adjectives could be used to describe other elements of the strategy, such as alternative livelihoods and interdiction. Billions of dollars of donor money have been invested in programs that have elicited few practical benefits.

What this overview shows is that it could take up to a decade more of international support before the Afghan security sector is effective, self-sustainable, and meets basic international standards. This is surely anathema to donors, growing weary of the elongated Afghan mission and facing other pressing international priorities from Darfur to Iraq. The May 2006 Kabul riots demonstrated better than any other single event the incompetence and ineptitude of the Afghan security forces. Any premature withdrawal of donor support would likely undermine any limited gains made and could catalyze the collapse of the sector.

International military forces, both NATO and the coalition, are convincingly winning the tactical battles against insurgents in the south and east; however, they do not have the resources to hold the territory after they have secured it. The ANSF, particularly the police, were to serve in this role but they have proved unable to do so. As soon as NATO leaves an area, the Taliban resurfaces. Communities are loath to support the government or international community, knowing that once they leave the Taliban will return. The UN Secretary General's Report aptly affirms that "a more comprehensive counter-insurgency strategy will be needed to reinforce political outreach to disaffected groups and address the security gaps that exist" (UNSG 2007, 3).

Any successful counter-insurgency strategy in Afghanistan will also have to engage Pakistan. As Husain Haqqani describes in his chapter, the Taliban movement was born in the Pakistani *madrassas* that straddle the border with Afghanistan, and the early support provided by the Pakistani government and its Inter-Services Intelligence Directorate (ISI) was instrumental in its rise to power. There is ample evidence, despite official denials from the Pakistani government, that some clandestine support continues to be provided to the Taliban by elements of the Pakistani government. As Haqqani states, "Pakistan's powerful security services, notably the Inter-Services Intelligence (ISI), never liked the idea of removing the Taliban from power."

It is widely believed that the leadership *shura* of the Taliban sits in Quetta, the capital of Pakistani Baluchistan, and that Taliban insurgents openly organize, train, and recruit in the Federally Administered Tribal Areas (FATA; see Hodes and Sedra 2007). Over the past two years, President Karzai has repeatedly accused the Pakistani government of not doing enough to rein in Taliban militants in Pakistani territory, a claim many Western nations involved in Afghanistan tacitly endorse. The mutual recriminations between the two governments placed the bilateral relationship in a deep freeze. While Pakistan could assuredly do more to crack down on Taliban militants, to say it has done nothing is an exaggeration. Over one thousand Pakistani soldiers have died over the past four years fighting Taliban militants, sympathetic tribes, and foreign jihadists (Jones 12 October 2007). The peace agreement that the Musharraf regime signed with the Pakistani Taliban in North Waziristan in 2006 was soundly criticized in Afghanistan and the West as tantamount to offering official sanctuary to terrorists. But it was driven by the realization that there is no military solution to the problem and that any effort to subdue the tribes by force would be deeply unpopular in the rest of Pakistan. Pacifying the largely lawless and mountainous region holding the 2,450 km Afghanistan–Pakistan border would be difficult for any army. When asked why al-Qaeda leaders were still "free to operate" in the border area, Musharraf retorted: "they are in the mountains and there are people who support them and hide them and these mountains are inaccessible ... even the British never went in" (*Times of India* 15 April 2007). By 2007, the North Waziristan peace accord had broken down, resulting in some of the most intense fighting since 2001. Along with a number of other political developments, such as challenges from the Supreme Court, the assassination of Benazir Bhutto and the defeat of Musharraf's party in the February 2008 parliamentary elections, Pakistan had been thrust into a state of crisis. The electoral victory of the Pakistani People's Party and the Pakistani Muslim League, who joined in a coalition to form the new government, raised hopes for an improvement in Pakistani–Afghan relations. Another result from the election that has encouraged the Afghan government and members of the international community was the poor showing of the Islamist parties, many of whom have expressed open support for the Taliban. Not only did Islamist groups fare poorly in the elections for the national legislature, but they lost control of the Northwest Frontier Province where a coalition of religious parties—the Muttahida Majlis-e-Amal (MMA)—was defeated by the Awami National Party (ANP), a secular, left-leaning Pashtun nationalist party. The elections represented both a referendum on the leadership of Musharraf, and a rejection of radical Islamism. Despite these encouraging signs, tensions between the two governments continued to grow by mid-2008, driven by rising cross-border attacks and terrorist violence in Afghanistan.

It is not just Pakistan that must do more to address cross-border terrorism and insecurity. The Afghan government's proclivity to blame the Pakistani "bogeyman" for all its security problems is counterproductive and intended to divert attention from its own domestic failings, such as its meek response to government corruption and its own homegrown security problems. There is a need for greater honesty about the nature and the roots of the Afghanistan–Pakistan security dilemma and enhanced co-operation to confront it.

It is worth noting that prior to the parliamentary elections in Pakistan, relations showed signs of thawing, particularly after the holding of a four-day Peace *Jirga* in August 2007, during which Presidents Karzai and Musharraf vowed to wage "an extended, tireless and persistent campaign against terrorism and further pledge that government and people of Afghanistan and Pakistan will not allow sanctuaries/training centers for terrorists in their respective countries."[6] The Peace *Jirga*, while a positive step, demonstrated the need to move beyond rhetoric and address some of the fundamental grievances that lay at the heart of relations between the two states, most notably their contested border, the Durand line. As Haqqani concludes his chapter: "Only when the international community addresses Pakistan's insecurity, and Afghanistan's concerns, in relation to the Durand Line will the two countries be able to find a basis for a stable, good neighbourly relationship." Considering the hardened and uncompromising positions of the two states, a resolution to this contentious issue remains far off, but it is nonetheless the key to lasting peace and security in the region.

Where does all this leave donor states like Canada? This volume ends with an assessment of the considerable Canadian contribution to Afghanistan. Before 2001, the Canadian presence in Afghanistan consisted mainly of humanitarian non-governmental organizations (NGOs). In the aftermath of the fall of the Taliban, a substantial Canadian military presence was closely followed by a large government-funded aid program and the opening of an embassy in 2003. By then the Canadian government was actively promoting its "3D" approach to Afghanistan, denoting an integrated strategy encompassing the government's defence, development, and diplomatic arms. Both Colonel Mike Capstick and Nipa Banerjee represented the Canadian government in Afghanistan, the former as head of the Canadian Forces' Strategic Advisory Team that continues to work in Kabul, the latter as head of mission for the Canadian International Development Agency (CIDA). Both agree that "lost opportunities" have only made the problems of Afghanistan that much more daunting.

Canadian armed forces personnel were in Afghanistan very soon after the American-led invasion of the country, and Canadian soldiers have served both under the US-led Operation Enduring Freedom (OED) and as part of the UN-mandated, NATO-led International Security Assistance Force (ISAF). Successive Canadian governments have committed troops to Afghanistan until 2011, making this mission the largest Canadian military operation since the Korean War. Since 2005, Canadian troops have been de-

ployed to the volatile southern province of Kandahar, the Taliban heartland and the key to restoring security and stability in the south.

As reports of Canadian casualties increased in frequency from 2006 to
2008—eighty-eight soldiers and one diplomat had died between 2002 and
July 2008—the Canadian public debate reflected a concern that Canada
was committed to military operations at the expense of ongoing development and diplomatic initiatives, a similar perception that surfaced in the
Netherlands surrounding its deployment of troops to southern Afghanistan.
Besides pledging $1.2 billion in development assistance to Afghanistan up
to 2011, Canada has also played a crucial political role in areas such as
election monitoring, heavy weapons cantonment, and mine action. Canada's
joined-up government approach has paid dividends, giving it a seat at every
important decision-making table in Kabul and wide international exposure
and prestige.

But, as Hayes outlines in his chapter, Afghanistan has emerged as a
highly charged political issue in Canada, driven by short-term political advantage and a longer-term confusion over just what the Afghanistan mission means to Canadians. Canada is just one of thirty-six countries making a military contribution to Afghanistan. Each has its own perceptions of
what it can and cannot do. With the state building process bogged down,
and the insurgency showing no end in sight, some have asked whether public opinion will accept Canada's continued engagement in Afghanistan.
Similar questions are being asked in the various capitals of NATO countries
currently committed to Afghanistan. What price will NATO member states
like Canada, Germany, the Netherlands, and Britain be willing to pay for
Afghanistan's successful transition and for how long?

In asking this question, Canadians have begun to re-evaluate why their
troops are in Kandahar. If the purpose of Canada's deployment to
Afghanistan was to restore international prestige, lessened by years of neglect of the country's military and a more timid foreign policy, it is achieving its goal. More importantly to Canadian policy-makers, it has healed a
damaging rift with the United States, caused by Canada's abstention from
the Iraq war. But such goals do not resonate with average Canadians, who
are suspicious of the US "war on terror" and inherently skeptical of military missions that do not fit the popular image of Canada as a peacekeeper.
Instead, the government has evoked the imagery of a humanitarian intervention meant to return children to school, restore women's rights and rebuild a war-shattered land. But if this is the reason, why Afghanistan and
not Darfur or the Democratic Republic of the Congo, countries whose
human suffering and poverty is equal to, or even more profound than that
of Afghanistan?

The Afghan government is monitoring the debate in Canada and other NATO countries very closely, because in many ways those debates will determine the fate of their transition from war to peace. President Karzai, like many Afghans, has expressed concerns that the international community may leave Afghanistan before the job is done, abandoning the country as the West did after the Soviet withdrawal almost two decades ago. The consequences then were over a decade of civil war and Taliban rule. To avoid a repeat of history, President Karzai has appealed to the Canadian government to maintain their military commitment beyond 2009: "The presence of Canada is needed until Afghanistan is able to defend itself and that day is not going to be in 2009…. Look around and see that the enemy is not yet finished; it is not yet defeated" (Canadian Press 2007). An independent panel appointed by the Canadian government to examine Canada's future role in Afghanistan, led by former foreign minister John Manley, agreed with the Afghan president, asserting that Canada's military contribution to Kandahar should not be tied to "artificial deadlines" but to the achievement of "real progress" on the ground (Government of Canada 2008, 32). The Conservative government of Prime Minister Stephen Harper would abide by the recommendation of the Manley report, formally extending the military mission beyond the 2009 deadline, not indefinitely, but by two years, until February 2011.

The impact of failure will not be limited to Afghanistan. Afghanistan has been a litmus test for NATO's efforts to find a new role in the world outside of Europe following the end of the Cold War, an effort embodied by the mantra oft cited by NATO leaders, "out of area or out of business." General Dan K. McNeil, the commander of all NATO forces in Afghanistan between February 2007 and June 2008, implied in October 2007 that wavering resolve in the NATO alliance over Afghanistan would not only threaten the mission but could put the entire Alliance at risk (Coghlan 2007).

As this collection goes to press in the spring of 2008, a palpable sense of pessimism has replaced the hope that permeated the state building process in the two years following the fall of the Taliban regime. It is a byproduct of a series of setbacks suffered by the government and international community over the past two years. Chief among them has been a sharp increase in insecurity, the unabated growth of the drug trade, the spread of corruption, and the slow pace of economic reconstruction.

In 2007, rates of insurgent and terrorist violence rose by 20% from 2006, resulting in a spike in civilian casualties (UNSG 2007, 2). Moreover, the insurgency is no longer geographically confined to the south and east of the country, with the emboldened Taliban's reaching into the heretofore-stable central and western regions.

The drug trade, and its concomitant economic and social ills, reached new heights in 2007. In its annual report on Afghanistan, the United Nations Office on Drugs and Crime (UNODC) documented a 17% rise in poppy cultivation from 2006 to 2007 and a 34% rise in production (2007). Not only does the trade provide a "tax base for insecurity" but it drives government corruption, supports the anti-government insurgency, feeds a growing domestic drug abuse problem, and crowds out legitimate economic activity. So dire is the situation that the government has reportedly begun to reconsider employing aerial spraying of herbicides to jumpstart eradication, a US proposal long dormant due to strenuous objections from the Afghan government (Semple and Golden 2007).

As corrosive as rising insecurity and the thriving narcotics trade have been for the state building process, the problem of corruption and weak governance, particularly at the sub-national level, has been just as debilitating. The inability of the government to deliver basic services to ordinary Afghans, many of whom are already innately suspicious of central authority, has engendered a growing crisis of confidence in the government and driven many to support non-state actors such as armed commanders or the Taliban. As the UN Secretary General's report states: "the State is extremely weak or non-existent throughout much of the countryside, while corruption is endemic in provincial centers" (2007, 3). Government efforts to combat the problem, such as the establishment of an Anti-Corruption Commission, have been largely ineffectual to date.[7]

Compounding the disaffection created by weak governance and corruption has been endemic poverty and underdevelopment. Large sections of the country continue to be deprived of development and humanitarian assistance due to insecurity. For instance, in September 2007, seventy-eight of Afghanistan's 364 districts were categorized by the UN as extremely risky and therefore inaccessible by UN agencies (UNSG 2007, 14). Many NGOs and donor agencies have completely halted work in the volatile southern provinces due to security concerns. The failure to provide the peace dividend emphatically promised by Afghan leaders and the international community to populations in insecure areas has created a level of alienation that has benefited spoiler groups. With Afghanistan emerging from a long civil war and featuring some of the worst development indicators on earth,[8] it will take decades to bring the country out of poverty. However, Afghans must see progress to improve their livelihoods and meet their imposing needs if they are to support the nascent state.

Although the prognosis for Afghanistan's transition appeared grim late in 2007, the government and international community can continue to point to a number of positive indicators to show that it remains on track.

The statistic most often trumpeted by Afghan and international leaders as a sign of the country's progress is the number of children going to school. By September 2007, 6.07 million children, 2.17 million of which were girls, were receiving an education and more than 670 schools had been built or refurbished (UNSG 2007).[9] Although education has been one of the success stories of the government, it has also become a target for its opponents. By June 2007, 412 of the 721 schools operating in the unstable south had closed due to insurgent attacks or intimidation (UNSG 2007, 15). Other indicators of Afghan government progress include the return of over 4.8 million refugees from Pakistan and Iran (IRIN 2007a; 2007b), the successful holding of presidential and parliamentary elections, and the promulgation of a new constitution.

Afghanistan has made remarkable progress in some areas, but too often these positive stories and statistics drown out debate on the profound threats that face Afghanistan's transition. For instance, rather than recognize the group's increasing strength, sophistication, and confidence, Afghan leaders and US military personnel tend to cite the rise of insurgent violence as evidence of the Taliban's "desperation." This type of "spin" has inhibited the emergence of honest debate on alternative strategies to combat the insurgency, particularly during the formative early stages of the state building process (Anderson 2007).

The main challenge facing Afghanistan today is not a lack of resources or capacity: it is a political problem. Three questions must be answered if Afghanistan is to successfully complete its transition to peace, stability, and democracy. First, does the Afghan government have the political will to implement the difficult reforms necessary to advance the state building process, combat corruption, and confront recalcitrant commanders? Do the Afghan and Pakistani governments have the political will to settle their simmering grievances and jointly confront their common security problems? Finally, will donor states like Canada have the political will to remain in Afghanistan long enough to see the job through, something that might take up to a decade? Much is discussed of the consequences of failure for Afghanistan—a return to repressive Taliban rule, the resumption of the civil war, and the re-emergence of a terrorist state exporting to the world. Each of these outcomes is possible, but what is clear is that the nascent state structures established since 2001 will collapse, billions of dollars in donor funds will have been wasted, hundreds of soldiers' deaths will have been in vain, and an unprecedented opportunity to stabilize the troubled country will have been squandered.

In spite of the many imposing challenges detailed in this collection, Afghan and international actors have been able to rely on one thing: the consent of the majority of the Afghan people. Unlike other post-conflict countries such as Iraq, where the majority of the population oppose the international presence, Afghans have steadfastly supported the internationally sponsored reconstruction process. This was demonstrated once again in the results of an October 2007 Environics Research Poll, conducted with the Canadian Broadcasting Corporation (CBC), in which 60% of Afghans surveyed approved of the presence of foreign troops in their country. Only 15% of the 1,600 people surveyed for the poll expressed a desire to see foreign troops leave.

As reliable as Afghan consent for the mission has been from 2002–2007, it is showing signs of vulnerability, as frustration with poor governance, corruption, insecurity, and rising civilian casualties from international military operations grows. An increasing number of Afghans across the country now assume the Taliban will return to power, not because they support the movement or approve of its ideology, but because of a perception that time and momentum is on their side. This perception above all else is the pre-eminent threat to Afghanistan's post-conflict transition. This collection, by examining the evolution of the state building process since 2001, seeks to understand the reasons for this growing pessimism and above all to suggest ways to arrest it.

Notes

1 The notion of the "triple transition" was first introduced by Marina S. Ottaway. See Marina S. Ottaway 2002, "Rebuilding State Institutions in Collapsed States." For a discussion of the triple transition in the Afghan context, please see Goodhand and Sedra 2006, *Bargains for Peace? Aid, Conditionalities and Reconstruction in Afghanistan*.
2 During the same press conference, Donald Rumsfeld declared that he did not see "any indication the Taliban pose any military threat to Afghanistan."
3 In 2005, the Government launched a Taliban reconciliation program that offered an amnesty to Taliban fighters who agreed to lay down their arms and pledge allegiance to the government. By June 2006, the Independent National Commission for Peace in Afghanistan, formed to oversee the program, had facilitated amnesties for over 1,500 Taliban fighters. However, the program, which has created deep divisions within the government, has not been accorded the resources or political capital it has needed to build on those gains (Gall 2005; Interview of Senior United Nations Assistance Mission for Afghanistan (UNAMA) official by Mark Sedra, Kabul, 17 June 2006).
4 For further discussion on SSR and the wider security environment in Afghanistan, please see: Cyrus Hodes and Mark Sedra 2007, *The Search For Security in Post-Taliban Afghanistan*.
5 For further discussion on the demilitarization process, see Michael Vinay Bhatia and Mark Sedra, *Afghanistan, Arms and Conflict: Armed Groups, Disarmament and Security in a Post-War Society* (New York: Routledge, 2008).
6 For the text of the Pak-Afghan Peace Jirga Declaration, see http://www.dailytimes.com.pk/default.asp?page=2007%5C08%5C13%5Cstory_13-8-2007_pg7_48.

7 Significant controversy was aroused when it came to light that Karzai's appointee to head the Afghan Anti-Corruption Commission was convicted for selling heroin to an undercover police officer in Las Vegas, US, in 1987 (Associated Press 2007).
8 Afghanistan ranked 173rd out of 178 countries surveyed in the 2004 United Nations Development Programme (UNDP) Human Development Index.
9 Under the Taliban, only 900,000 children were in school, and girls were prohibited from attending (UNSG 2007; Anderson 2007).

References

Agence France Presse. 2007. "Taliban will 'never talk' unless foreign forces leave." 30 September.

Anderson, John Ward. 2007. "Emboldened Taliban Reflected in More Attacks, Greater Reach." *Washington Post*. 25 September.

Associated Press. 2004. "Afghan President Says Taliban Defeated." 26 February.

———. "Afghan Anti-Corruption Chief Sold Heroin in Las Vegas in '87." 10 March.

Bhatia, Michael Vinay and Mark Sedra. 2008. *Afghanistan, Arms and Conflict: Armed Groups, Disarmament and Security in a Post-War Society*. New York: Routledge.

Brunnstrom, David. 2007. "Afghan army may fill key security role by 2009: NATO." Reuters, 24 September.

Canadian Broadcasting Corporation (CBC). 2007. "51% of Afghans feeling good about country's direction: poll." 18 October. http://www.cbc.ca/story/world/national/2007/10/18/afghan-poll.html?ref=rss.

Canadian Press. 2007. "Karzai Pleads Canada to Stay." 18 September.

Coghlan, Tom. 2007. "Afghanistan 'putting NATO's future in peril.'" *UK Telegraph*. 8 October.

Gall, Carlotta. 2005. "Afghanistan Offers Amnesty to Wanted Taliban Rebels." *New York Times*. 9 May.

Goodhand, Jonathan and Mark Sedra. 2006. *Bargains for Peace? Aid, Conditionalities and Reconstruction in Afghanistan*. The Hague, Netherlands: Clingendael Institute. August.

Government of Canada. 2008. *Independent Panel on Canada's Future Role in Afghanistan*. Ottawa: Government of Canada. January.

Hodes, Cyrus and Mark Sedra. 2007. *The Search For Security in Post-Taliban Afghanistan*. International Institute for Strategic Studies (IISS) Adelphi Paper No. 391.

Integrated Regional Information Network (IRIN). 2007a. "Afghanistan-Iran: Afghan refugees given repatriation extension." 27 February.

———. 2007b. "Afghanistan: Rate of refugee return slow ahead of winter." 10 October.

Islamic Republic of Afghanistan and the Islamic Republic of Pakistan. 2007. *Pak-Afghan Peace Jirga Declaration*. August. http://www.daily times.com.pk/default.asp?page=2007%5C08%5C13%5Cstory_13-8-2007_pg7_48.

John, Mark. 2007."Pressure for tougher Afghan anti-drugs drive—UN." Reuters, 7 September.

Jones, Owen Bennett. 2007. "Musharraf blames captured troops." *BBC News,* 12 October. http://news.bbc.co.uk/1/hi/world/south_asia/7042078.stm.

Kitchen, Michael. 2004. "Afghanistan/Rumsfeld." *Voice of America.* 26 February. http://www.globalsecurity.org/military/library/news/2004/02/mil -040226-32e7e750.htm.

Ottaway, Marina S. 2002. "Rebuilding State Institutions in Collapsed States." *Development and Change* 33(5): 1001–24.

Paris, Roland. 2004. *At War's End: Building Peace After Civil Conflict.* Cambridge, UK: Cambridge University Press.

Rubin, Barnett R. 2006. "Peace building and state-building in Afghanistan: Constructing sovereignty for whose security?" *Third World Quarterly* 27(1): 175–85.

Sedra, Mark. 2004. *Are the Taliban Really "Gone"?* Silver City, NM & Washington, DC: Foreign Policy in Focus. March 1.

———. 2006. "Security Sector Reform in Afghanistan: The Slide Toward Expediency. *International Peacekeeping* 13 (March).

Semple, Kirk and Tim Golden. 2007. "Afghans Pressed by U.S. on Plan to Spray Poppies." *New York Times.* 8 October.

Times of India. 2007. "Musharraf lashes out at Karzai." 15 April.

United Nations Development Programme (UNDP). 2004. *Afghanistan: National Human Development Report 2004—Security with a Human Face: Challenges and Responsibilities.* Kabul: UNDP.

United Nations Office on Drugs and Crime (UNODC). 2007. *Afghanistan Opium Survey 2007, Executive Summary.* Kabul & Vienna: UNODC.

United Nations Secretary-General (UNSG). 2007. *The Situation in Afghanistan and Its Implications for International Peace and Security,* A/62/345-S/ 2007/555. New York: United Nations. September 21.

ADF	Afghanistan Development Forum
AGE	Anti-Government Elements
AIA	Afghan Interim Administration
AICC	Afghan International Chamber of Commerce
AIHRC	Afghan Independent Human Rights Commission
AISA	Afghan Investment Support Agency
AL	Alternative Livelihoods
AMF	Afghan Military Force
ANA	Afghan National Army
ANAP	Afghan National Auxiliary Police
ANBP	Afghan New Beginnings Programme
ANP	Afghan National Police
ANSF	Afghan National Security Forces
ANSO	Afghan NGO Security Office
AREU	Afghanistan Research and Evaluation Unit
ARTF	Afghanistan Reconstruction Trust Fund
ASOP	Afghan Social Outreach Program
ASP	Afghan Stabilization Program
ATA	Afghan Transitional Authority
BPHS	Basic Package of Health Services
CAO	Control and Audit Office
CDC	Community Development Council
CF	Canadian Forces
CFC-A	Combined Forces Command - Afghanistan
CG	Consultative Group
CIDA	Canadian International Development Agency
CN	Counter-Narcotics
CND	Counter-Narcotics Directorate

CNPA	Counter-Narcotics Police of Afghanistan
CNTF	Counter-Narcotics Trust Fund
CPEF	Central Poppy Eradication Force
CSTC-A	Combined Security Transition Command—Afghanistan
CTC	Central Training Center
D&R	Demobilisation and Reintegration
DDR	Disarmament, Demobilisation and Reintegration
DEA	Drug Enforcement Agency
DFAIT	Canadian Department of Foreign Affairs and International Trade
DoD	US Department of Defense
DIAG	Disbandment of Illegal Armed Groups
EAG	External Advisory Group
EUPOL	European Policing Mission
FAST	Foreign-Deployed Advisory Support Team
FATA	Federally Administered Tribal Area
FDI	Foreign Direct Investment
HIPC	Heavily Indebted Poor Countries
IAB	Independent Appointments Board
I-ANDS	Interim Afghan National Development Strategy
IARCSC	Independent Administrative Reform and Civil Service Commission
ICARDA	International Centre for Agricultural Research in Dry Areas
ICG	International Crisis Group
ICRC	International Committee of the Red Cross
IDP	Internally Displaced Person
IED	Improvised Explosive Device
IAB	International Appointments Board
ISAF	International Security Assistance Force
ISI	Inter-Services Intelligence Directorate (Pakistan)
JCMB	Joint Coordination and Monitoring Board
KMNB	Kabul Multi-National Brigade
LICUS	Low Income Countries Under Stress
LOTFA	Law and Order Trust Fund for Afghanistan
MISFA	Microfinance Investment Support Facility for Afghanistan
MMA	*Muttahida Majlis-e-Amal* (United Action Front)
MoD	Ministry of Defence

MoI	Ministry of Interior
MRRD	Ministry of Rural Rehabilitation and Development
MTEF	Medium Term Expenditures Framework
MTFF	Medium Term Fiscal Framework
NABDP	National Area-Based Development Program
NATO	North Atlantic Treaty Organization
NDS	National Directorate of Security (*Amaniyat*)
NIU	National Interdiction Unit
NSP	National Solidarity Program
NWFP	North-West Frontier Province
ODA	Overseas Development Assistance
OEF	Operation Enduring Freedom
OMLT	Operational Mentor and Liaison Team
ONSC	Office of the National Security Council
PAG	Policy Action Group
PAR	Public Administrative Reform
PEFA	Public Expenditures and Finance Accountability
PFM	Public Finance Management
PRR	Priority Reform and Restructuring
PRT	Provincial Reconstruction Team
RC	Regional Command
RCMP	Royal Canadian Mounted Police
RTC	Regional Training Center
SAT-A	Strategic Advisory Team - Afghanistan
SME	Small to Medium Size Enterprises
SNTV	Single Non-Transferable Vote
SSR	Security Sector Reform
TA	Technical Assistance
TIP	Transition Integration Program
UNAMA	United Nations Assistance Mission in Afghanistan
UNCAC	United Nations Convention Against Corruption
UNDP	United Nations Development Programme
UNDSS	United Nations Department of Safety and Security
UNHCR	United Nations High Commissioner for Refugees
UNICEF	United Nations Children's Fund
UNOCHA	United Nations Office for the Coordination of Humanitarian Assistance

UNODC	United Nations Office on Drugs and Crime
UNSC	United Nations Security Council
UNSG	United Nations Secretary General
VCA	Vulnerabilities to Corruption Assessment

The Political Transition

William Maley

Looking Back at
the Bonn Process

On 5 December 2001, a range of Afghan political actors attached their signatures to the text of what was to become known as the Bonn Agreement. The product of a conference that brought together non-Taliban forces, it set out a path for transition to fresh political arrangements for a country that had endured decades of turbulence. The agreement prompted high hopes among ordinary Afghans that a new opportunity had emerged for them to escape from the miserable rut to which they had long been consigned. Furthermore, the endorsement of the Bonn Agreement by the United Nations Security Council in Resolution 1383 of 6 December 2001 appeared to anchor Afghanistan's transition firmly in the agenda of key issues confronting the international community, inspiring the conviction that Afghanistan would not be abandoned in the way that it had been following the completion of the withdrawal of Soviet forces from Afghanistan in February 1989.

More than six years on, the political situation in Afghanistan no longer seems promising, and the fears of the wider world that Afghanistan could become another Iraq are matched by the fears of the Afghans that they might be abandoned once again (Maley 2006a, 135–38). Insecurity plagues many parts of the country, and international forces deployed in the southern provinces of Afghanistan to assist the process of reconstruction are under frequent attack from well-armed, well-trained "neo-Taliban" (Giustozzi 2007; Tarzi 2008), whose operations from bases in Pakistan belie the high hopes of 2001 that Afghanistan had finally turned the corner. The government of president Hamid Karzai is increasingly beleaguered, and a whispering campaign against Karzai himself is being sedulously promoted in Kabul, in Islamabad, and in more remote capitals. Although Afghanistan is not yet the catastrophe zone that Iraq has become, ominous clouds now hang over its transition.

The aim of this chapter is to explore what factors have contributed to this slide. Was the Bonn Agreement defective, or did problems arise mainly in its implementation? Were Afghanistan's pre-existing problems simply too great for any intra-elite agreement to be able effectively to address them? The broad argument that I will advance is that there is some merit in each of these claims. The problems of Afghanistan are indeed awesome and defy easy solution. The Bonn Agreement was a bold and brave attempt to carry intra-elite negotiations to a higher level than had ever been attempted in Afghanistan, but it was nonetheless limited in what it could and did address. And many factors have complicated the process of creating an effective state structure to deal with the pressing needs of ordinary Afghans.

But the two greatest problems, I shall argue, lie outside the direct control of the Afghans themselves. The first is the relentless, compulsive drive of Pakistan to interfere in Afghanistan's affairs, a propensity that Western states have altogether failed to address in an effective manner. The other is the corrosive effect of the Iraq war in draining attention and resources from Afghanistan, where they could have been used to far greater effect. The net result has been a near-fatal loss of momentum in the Afghan transition, which leaves it now teetering on the brink of real disaster. The crisis in Afghanistan will not be resolved by mere rhetoric, or tentative steps, or half-measures: only a comprehensive and far-reaching re-evaluation of Afghanistan's needs and of the dimensions of international engagement holds out much hope of saving the situation.

The Afghan Context

The delegates who gathered at Bonn faced a daunting heritage from the years of strife that followed the communist coup of April 1978 and the Soviet invasion of Afghanistan in December 1979. These dramatic events had widespread ramifications for both state and society in Afghanistan (Bradsher 1999). The Afghanistan of the royalist and republican eras is no longer the Afghanistan of today, and the easy formulae that might have been used to underpin the practice of politics in the past no longer work well in this radically altered environment. Four particular factors lay at the heart of Afghanistan's dismal inheritance.

First was the substantial disintegration of the Afghan state. The Afghan state administration even before the 1978 coup was a ramshackle apparatus, blighted by corruption and nepotism, but relatively ubiquitous, although not especially strong in terms of its capacity to penetrate and regulate society or mobilize resources on a large scale. Its fiscal basis was weak, with Afghanistan's breakdown in the 1970s due in part to the state's excessive dependence on unstable revenue sources such as foreign aid and the sale of natural resources such as gas (Rubin 2002, 62–73). After the communist coup, and in particular after the Soviet invasion, this problem was greatly exacerbated. Resistance to the Soviets and their surrogates saw much of the countryside, and the Afghan population, slipping beyond the control of the Soviet-backed factions. The regime survived until 1992 on the strength of resources injected by the USSR, but when these funds were cut off at the end of 1991 following a US–Soviet agreement in the aftermath of the failed August 1991 coup attempt against Soviet president Gorbachev, the days of the regime were numbered, and it fell apart less than four months later. The consequence, however, was that the Afghan resistance (*Mujahideen*) parties inherited the symbols of a state—most importantly a capital city and seats in international organizations—but not resources on which the discharge of basic state functions depends. The re-establishment of a fiscal foundation for a collapsed state is no easy endeavor.

Second was the fragmentation of political elites, leading to the spread of a pervasive atmosphere of distrust. The Afghan *Mujahideen* were not a unified force but rather a loose agglomeration of groups and networks with divergent interests, a range of distinct ideological and political orientations, and differing social bases, as well as rival leaderships (Roy 1990). The ferocious struggle for control of Kabul after 1992, which saw the Pakistan-backed Hizb-i Islami of Gulbuddin Hekmatyar firing stockpiled rockets and artillery into the capital in order to prevent any other forces from exercising comfortable control over this symbolic prize, was simply one obvious manifestation of this fragmentation (Maley 2002a, 194–217). Beyond this, the Afghan population itself was and is marked by complex cross-cutting cleavages that lead ordinary Afghans to live simultaneously in a number of different social worlds, defined by factors such as gender, occupation, ethnic and *qawm*[1] affiliations, and sectarian identity. These are not inconsistent with an Afghan *civic* identity, but they do mean that there are many competing points of focus for loyalty other than the state, and that lines of conflict can readily crystallize if ethnic or sectarian entrepreneurs seek to activate them.

Third was the problem of massive social dislocation in Afghanistan. Out of a pre-war population estimated at 13.05 million, by 1990 there were 6.2 million Afghans living as refugees in Pakistan, Iran, and beyond. The consequences of this dislocation, and of internal population displacement, were acutely serious in a number of spheres. Forced migration detached a whole generation of Afghans from the skills on which they would need to depend in order to be able to pursue agricultural or pastoral livelihoods. This set the scene for high-level unemployment or under-employment in the event of the opportunity arising for voluntary repatriation. But more seriously, the disruption of society that forced migration entailed had the effect of exposing young Afghans to militant or radical strands of opinion to which they likely would have remained indifferent had it not been for the shredding of their life-chances. Specifically, the anti-modernist Taliban were very much a product of the breakdown of traditional society, rather than a simple outgrowth of traditional society (Maley 1998). The refugee experience exposed young men, mostly of ethnic Pashtun background, to the politicized and radicalized Deobandi madrassas in Pakistan, which became the venue for agencies of the Pakistan state to mold them into a fighting force (Nasr 2000, 179). Tragically, many of the Taliban were as much victims of what had happened to their homeland as were the other Afghans whom they were subsequently to harass.

Fourth was the exposure of Afghanistan to the manipulation and penetration of a range of external forces. Apart from the Soviet Union, the most important such force was undoubtedly Pakistan. During the 1980s, Pakistan was an impressively dedicated host for the world's largest refugee population but unfortunately derived from this the belief that it was entitled to determine the shape of future Afghan governments. Prior to 1978, its relations with Afghanistan had been poor, blighted by the so-called "Pashtunistan" dispute (Ganguly 1998, 162–92). This disposed it to favour, within the Afghan resistance, groups such as the radical Hizb-i Islami of Hekmatyar (Abou Zahab and Roy 2004; Hussain 2005), which preached a universalist brand of Islamism and might have seemed less likely to give emphasis in the future to past disputes of an ethnic or territorial nature. When the Hezb after 1992 proved incapable of holding or managing territory, Pakistan moved to promote the Taliban as an alternative. Its meddling through the agency of the Taliban amounted to a "creeping invasion" of Afghanistan, and as Barnett R. Rubin has noted, in the aftermath of the commencement of Operation Enduring Freedom in October 2001, Pakistan's reining in of its activities in Afghanistan came "in return for the safe evacuation of hundreds of Pakistani officers and intelligence agents from Afghanistan, where they had overseen the Taliban's military operations" (2007, 70). This history of manipulation explains why Afghan moderates, both Pashtun and non-Pashtun, tend to be profoundly wary of Pakistan and its wiles. They know their neighbour too well.

The Bonn Process: Aims and Achievements

The Bonn Agreement began a process of change that was concerned above all with developing the institutions of the state. Where the state has collapsed, the establishment of new state institutions may seem the obvious path to take, but that of course raises the question of exactly what it means to "establish" new institutions. There are at least two important stages in the process. The first is that of designing new institutions, that is, determining the shape they should take and the tasks they should perform. The second is that of endowing such new institutions with capacity and legitimacy. These two attributes are in significant measure related. *Legitimacy* signifies generalized normative support (Maley 1987; Saikal and Maley 1991), and institutions that enjoy such support may function more smoothly in at least some ways than those that are widely opposed. *Capacity* refers more specifically to the ability to perform relevant tasks and can depend on the availability of appropriate human and material resources, the organization of those resources in such a way as to contribute to effective performance, and the establishment of accountability mechanisms to guard against bureaucratic pathologies such as nepotism and corruption. Where Bonn went beyond previous attempts to craft an elite settlement was in recognizing that there was more to state building than simply endowing a collection of individuals with ostensible formal authority. Instead, it was envisaged that legitimacy would be built up through a range of measures: acquiring an attractive and charismatic leader in Hamid Karzai; securing for him the blessing of Afghanistan's long-serving former king; exploiting the traditional institution of the Great Assembly (*Loya Jirga*) both to boost Karzai's authority and then develop a new constitution; and, finally, using the mechanism of free and fair elections conducted with international support to select key officeholders for the future.

The Bonn process also embodied an attempt to bring together a diverse range of Afghan actors in a newly integrated political elite. This was to be achieved by allocating state offices to different groups in ways that would ensure the representation of the main social categories in the Afghan population: men and women, members of different ethnic groups, and Sunni and Shiite Muslims. Such a process could not be purely random, for inevitably those groups that had been most actively involved in resisting the Taliban in Afghanistan would demand and secure ministries that would reflect their salience on the ground. Nor was the process inclusive of all Afghan groups. The principal architect of the Bonn conference, Ambassador Lakhdar Brahimi, who had been reappointed as Special Representative of the UN Secretary-General for Afghanistan on 3 October 2001, has since argued that it was a mistake not to do more to draw the Taliban into the negotiation process. However, there were real limits on what could realistically be contemplated at the time. By November 2001, Taliban leaders such as Mullah Omar and Mullah Dadullah were fugitives, and much of what was left of the Taliban movement had melted back to their villages, fled to Pakistan, or in a few cases been transported to Guantanamo Bay. Furthermore, for the main anti-Taliban forces, an invitation to the Taliban to take part in Bonn would have been totally unacceptable (Chandrasekaran 2001), tantamount to inviting Pakistan's Inter-Services Intelligence Directorate to the table. They most likely would have boycotted the meeting themselves or acted as spoilers if forced to attend against their will. And it can also be argued that the re-emergence of the Taliban is not a consequence of their having been excluded from the Bonn process, in which it is unlikely that they would have been "good faith participants," but rather of other developments that caused the momentum of transition to flag and gave the Taliban and their backers a new opportunity to position themselves as actors in southern and eastern Afghanistan. Ultimately, the Bonn process and the Bonn Agreement reflected the political realities of the time.

Perhaps the greatest achievement of the Bonn process was that the specific benchmarks that had been set out in the agreement were ultimately met. An Emergency *Loya Jirga* did take place 11–19 June 2002, to convert the interim administration inaugurated on 22 December 2001 into a transitional administration, and while the surrounding politics were ferocious, notably around the future role of the former king, it finally passed off peacefully. A new constitution was then drafted at the constitutional *Loya Jirga* held from 14 December 2003 to 4 January 2004. Finally, elections were held with broad participation: for a president, on 9 October 2004, resulting in the election of Hamid Karzai with 55.4% of the vote; and then for the lower house (*Wolesi Jirga*) of a new bicameral national assembly, as well as for provincial councils, on 18 September 2005. These developments attracted a great deal of international attention and seemed to confirm that Afghanistan was well on the way to consolidating a new and civilized form of politics.

However, there were a number of things that the Bonn Agreement did not or could not do, which undermined the optimism that these developments inspired. First, the Bonn conference approached the issue of the structure of the future state in altogether too cavalier a fashion. It is very important at the outset of state building processes to reflect carefully on the kind of state that a country undergoing transition from severe disruption might require. Of course, the Bonn Agreement left some decisions of this sort to the constitutional *Loya Jirga*, recognizing that endorsement from a more broadly inclusive assembly than the participants at Bonn would be required if a new constitution were to have any legitimacy. It was thus in this later venue that key issues such as the relative merits of presidential and parliamentary systems, and unitary and federal models, were discussed (or not). However, some decisions taken at Bonn had significant ramifications for the future scope of government in Afghanistan. The most important of these related to the structure of ministries in the future state. The Bonn Agreement provided for an interim administration, which was to be "composed of a Chairman, five Vice Chairmen and 24 other members. Each member, except the Chairman, may head a department of the Interim Administration" (Maley 2002a, 271). The full implications of this were not grasped at the time, perhaps because the appointees were not initially described as "ministers." Without any root-and-branch evaluation of exactly what kind of departments or ministries Afghanistan might need, a new and complex structure was put in place, albeit reflecting Afghanistan's previous dysfunctional system of central administration. Three major problems flowed from this. One was that the functional responsibilities of departments within the interim administration were not effectively delineated, setting the scene for battles over turf control. Another was that with "departments" being handed out almost as prizes for the Bonn participants, the scene was set for departments to become fiefdoms under the control of particular factions. This did not occur uniformly, but the Independent Civil Service Commission that the Bonn Agreement foreshadowed as a brake on such personalization of administration proved—predictably—to be one of the weakest elements of the entire administrative structure. Finally, the approach at Bonn helped to lock in a model of state building in which the new Afghan state was substantially to mirror the structure and functioning of developed Western states, irrespective of whether this would prove sustainable in the Afghan context (Suhrke 2006).

Second, the Bonn Agreement did not effectively address the issue of transitional justice. When a society has undergone decades of disruption, it is a near certainty that multiple crimes will have been committed along the way, and highly likely that some of the perpetrators will be politically prominent figures. This is especially so if one subscribes to the rather strict notion of commanders' responsibility for subordinates' actions that was adopted after the Second World War by the US Supreme Court in the case of *In Re Yamashita* 327 US1 (1946). In Afghanistan, the inheritance at the time of the Bonn meeting was a singularly bloody one. While it is a severe exaggeration to suggest that the post-Soviet period was just as lethal as the era of Soviet occupation, a number of hideous episodes darkened the landscape after 1992, and ordinary Afghans had every reason to wish to see action taken to break with the past. But in the upshot, little was done. One blessing was the absence from Bonn of Gulbuddin Hekmatyar, whose participation had made a farce of several earlier attempts at elite settle-ment (Maley 1993), and for the most part those who participated in Bonn came with relatively clean hands, if not clean associates at home. How-ever, the Bonn process effectively turned a blind eye to the issue of ac-countability for past crimes. At two levels, one can argue that this was a re-alistic, although ultimately somewhat unhappy, outcome. If the pursuit of those with grim records prompted them to become "spoilers" (Stedman 1997), then the outcome might have been not the delivery of justice but rather the erosion of hopes for some kind of peace. This, it should be noted, did not represent the trumping of ethics by pragmatism but rather the bal-ancing of an ethic of consequences against an ethic of absolutes.

Furthermore, the institutions of justice in Afghanistan were themselves so enfeebled that the prospects of holding credible war-crimes trials were poor, something that became clear in 2006 when the prosecution of the (rightly-despised) former communist secret policeman Asadullah Sarwari degenerated into an embarrassing shambles (Human Rights Watch 2006b). Due process matters in giving effect to law, and the Afghan judicial sys-tem has fallen far short of the standards that an adequate system should em-body (Watson 2006a). Although there were plenty of demands from human rights activists (and others) that offenders from the past be excluded from political life, they overlooked the perils of attempting such exclusion in the absence of a trial process that had delivered defensible verdicts. But that said, the deferral to the future of the task of confronting Afghanistan's past, while understandable on practical grounds, nonetheless left a range of ob-servers with a real sense of disappointment.

Third, it was beyond the capacity of the Bonn Agreement to provide any direct or immediate solution to the problem of insecurity in Afghanistan. The idea of "security" is a complex and multidimensional one. Classically in studies of international relations, it referred to the threat that could be posed militarily by one state to another, but in recent years it has been used in more diverse senses. The vocabulary of threats to "human security" (Baj-pai 2003) has been employed to refer both to developmental problems of a kind that might previously have been described as "structural violence" (Maley 1985), and to the impact on ordinary people of the detritus of war. Such problems are by no means trivial, but they are distinct from the par-ticular form of security that can matter most to the citizens of countries that are emerging from prolonged periods of disorder, namely the threat of vi-olence at the local level, which can thwart their efforts to get their lives back on an even keel (Maley 2007). Such violence can emanate from crim-inal gangs, or militias, or from corrupt officials, or even from neighbours who have come to appreciate that power can grow from the barrel of a gun.

Here, the main solution comes in the form of a clean, capable, and adequately resourced police force linked to judicial organs that ensure that the rule of law replaces the rule of force. This, however, cannot be produced by decree, but rather depends upon the success of a state building process: Max Weber, after all, famously defined the state in terms of its ability to "monopolize the use of force" (Weber 1978, 56). One of the dilemmas that immediately confronted Karzai and his colleagues was that the security that ordinary people so desperately craved was not something that they were themselves in a position to deliver. For this, they looked to the wider world to bridge the gap through the deployment throughout Afghanistan of the International Security Assistance Force that the Bonn Agreement specifically foreshadowed. As we shall shortly see, this did not happen, and the disastrous consequences have now become all too obvious.

Factors Undermining the Optimism of Bonn

The high hopes of Bonn have been compromised by a range of developments in the period since December 2001. The task of making the Bonn process work was of course an exacting one, and no one should underestimate the scale of the problems involved (see Maley 2002b). The courage and achievements of President Karzai and a number of his colleagues should be recognized and celebrated, as should the commitment of countless ordinary Afghans. But at the same time, it is necessary also to recognize that the transition began to go astray quite early, and that what seems like a major slide in 2006 and 2007 reflects more the confluence of a number of threats and challenges that have long been obvious (see, for example, Maley 2003–2004; United States 2004; Johnson and Leslie 2004). The following paragraphs explore the more striking of these problems.

A critical blow to Afghanistan's transition was struck less than three months after the Interim Administration was inaugurated. This came in the form of a very public move by the United States, given public expression by vice-president Dick Cheney, to block the expansion of the International Security Assistance Force (ISAF) beyond Kabul (Sipress 2002). This decision, driven by a desire to conserve air-lift assets for use in a future campaign in Iraq, betrayed not only a serious ignorance of the fragile security situation beyond the Afghan capital, but a lamentable misunderstanding of the importance of *momentum* in transitions, and in Afghanistan in particular. In such circumstances, local power-holders are on perpetual watch to see from which direction the wind is blowing. In the immediate aftermath of the Bonn conference, it was vital to signal in every way possible that there would be no going back to the wretched experiences of the past, and that the wider world was committed to support the Afghan transition, robustly and for the long-run. The blocking of ISAF expansion seemed to signal the exact opposite. The importance of ISAF expansion was not military, but *symbolic*. This was fully appreciated by the Bonn delegates, by Ambassador Brahimi, and by independent observers such as the International Crisis Group (Olson 2002; International Crisis Group 2002). With the blocking of ISAF expansion, a golden opportunity to build stability in the outlying provinces of Afghanistan was lost. By the time the scale of this blunder was realized and the US acquiesced to the adoption of Security Council Resolution 1510 of 13 October 2003, which finally authorized ISAF expansion beyond Kabul, the seeds of future disorder in the south had been well and truly sown.

This was only one symptom of a wider problem, namely an unwillingness on the part of the wider world to commit to Afghanistan the kind of resources that the transition model built into the Bonn process required. While one can argue that that model was overly ambitious and faced real problems of sustainability (Ottaway and Lieven 2002; Suhrke 2006), it was what the Afghans had been led to expect they would experience. Perhaps out of a misguided fear that Afghans would automatically seek to combat any international presence, the force committed to Afghanistan in the post-Taliban era was a tiny fraction of that committed to Iraq. More seriously, the material resources committed to Afghanistan were relatively small as well. In documents prepared for a major conference held in London 31 January and 1 February 2006, the Afghan government estimated that over a five-year period Afghanistan would require US$18.865 billion to cover development needs; domestic revenue was anticipated to amount to only US$4.489 billion, less than the anticipated non-development recurrent costs of US$5.453 billion. As a result, US$19.829 billion, or approximately US$4 billion per annum over five years, would be needed in the form of international assistance (Afghanistan 2006, 61). The London Conference yielded no such pledges. Future donor commitments from March 2006 came only to US$10.5 billion, little more than half the figure Afghanistan required (Gardiner 2006). As Human Rights Watch pointed out, "reconstruction budgets in Kosovo, Bosnia and East Timor were up to 50 times greater on a per capita basis" (2006a). Again, the signal that this parsimonious approach sent to Afghans was deeply unfortunate.

Faced with the failure of the wider world to support ISAF expansion, Karzai was driven back to what one might call "Peshawar politics," based on the establishment of networks of patron-client relations. It is worth recalling that after his studies in India, Karzai worked for years in a very peculiar political environment, marked by the complete absence of anything like a state. The *Mujahideen* parties of course interacted with Pakistan's

Inter-Services Intelligence Directorate, whose orientations they came to appreciate all too well, but they controlled no instrumentalities of state-like character. Politics relied on deal-making, on the strategic disbursement of externally supplied funds, and on luring supporters away from other resistance parties. Translated to the post-2001 environment in Afghanistan, this approach has had deadly consequences. While Karzai's options in the south were severely limited by the blocking of ISAF expansion, the policy of giving state positions to potential spoilers has tarnished the image of the state and supplied the revived Taliban with a menu of popular grievances on which to draw. The most egregious example of this problem is to be found in the career of the Kandahari warlord Gul Agha Sherzai, who was initially foisted on Karzai by the US (Maass 2002), but who has continued to occupy state positions well after his failings have become obvious. Sarah Chayes, a long-time resident of Kandahar, has produced a damning account of the harm wrought by Gul Agha, and one can only guess at how much goodwill was squandered by the decision to rescue him from the oblivion into which he had appropriately slid during the Taliban period (Chayes 2006).

Allied to this has been an additional problem. The 2004 constitution created, on paper, a strong presidency. This gave rise to two difficulties. On one hand, in a heterogeneous society, the existence of a strong presidency risks leaving many groups with the feeling that they will be political losers (Saikal and Maley 2007). On the other hand, when a formally-strong presidency is allied to an occupant with little or no experience of state building, policy paralysis can result, and elite politics is likely to take the form of ferocious competition for the president's ear. This, sadly, has happened in Afghanistan, where elite politics since 2001 has been incredibly vicious, and belies the sentimental hope that in a society that has suffered so much, "leaders" would readily work together for the good of their country. These problems have been aggravated by Karzai's attempt to position himself "above" politics and his failure to use his authority to draw good people into a political party that reflects his own decent values (Ruttig 2006, 39–41).

Added to this is a further problem, namely a misreading of the implications of Karzai's easy victory in the 2004 presidential election. In consolidated democracies, it is broadly accepted that even a narrow election victory will position the victor to rule for the constitutionally-prescribed term, and to exercise the authority that derives from the office that he or she occupies. Thus president George W. Bush was able to exercise full executive authority after his inauguration in 2001 even though his opponent had won the popular vote in the November 2000 election. In countries emerging from years of civil strife, the situation is rather different. Since constitutional arrangements will typically not be fully institutionalized—in the sense of being widely accepted as representing the only way in which politics can be practised—the authority that a newly elected president exercises cannot be derived simply from occupying an office. In such a situation, the victor's electoral "mandate" is not a mandate to govern for a full term, but rather a mandate to attempt to meet the people's aspirations for security, employment, and other social goods. A failure to deliver can lead to a collapse of legitimacy. Those who argued that Karzai's electoral victory freed him to act with full discretion to promote his own agenda made the mistake of assuming that his electoral victory meant more than it actually could.

Unreal expectations also surrounded the September 2005 election. The fact that, as in 2004, an exercise of enormous logistical complexity was accomplished in a broadly peaceful manner led to understandable enthusiasm, but the practical political consequences of the election have not been as rewarding as one might wish. While the election of members to an elected legislature is symbolically positive, and the creation of political space for women members a particularly satisfactory outcome, the claim sometimes made in the US that "democracy" has now been brought to Afghanistan reduces the idea of democracy to a very simplistic level: stable and functioning democracies require much more than just the holding of elections (see Maley 1995). Furthermore, when one looks at the detail of how the new *Wolesi Jirga* was constituted, a number of troubling matters surface. Specifically, the use of the "Single Non-Transferable Vote" system to choose members of the chamber has not aided its functioning. This system, under which seats are allocated to provinces according to their estimated populations, voters simply vote for a single candidate in a province, and seats are allocated in order of the votes received, has potentially adverse consequences. If, in a province with ten seats, an attractive, moderate candidate wins 90% of the vote, he or she still only receives one seat, with the remaining 90% of seats being allocated among candidates who *in total* received only 10% of the votes. It is no surprise that the system is poorly regarded by specialists on electoral systems (see Bowler, Farrell and Pettitt 2005). Such a system makes it very difficult for parties to mobilize (which is why it appealed to Karzai and his cabinet), but it sets the scene for the promotion of ethnic solidarity to fashion manageable blocs of parliamentarians once the legislature actually meets. This has already happened in Afghanistan (Ruttig 2006, 43).

It is perhaps unsurprising given this mélange of factors that the new Afghan bureaucracy has proved to be a weak tool for the formulation and implementation of policy. Pathologies such as nepotism and corruption have flourished. This is not so much a product of moral failings as of incentives that make it rational for individuals to act corruptly or in a nepotistic fashion. The promotion of one's family or associates to bureaucratic positions makes sense in an environment in which anonymous trust is low (Maley 2003); and low salaries in the state sector, especially when compared with those available in international organizations to Afghans who have returned from abroad and are lucky enough to snare a position, provide a strong inducement for those with families to support to use their state positions in an extractive manner. Public offices become positional goods (Hardin 1995, 57). But this problem has certainly been compounded to some degree by the return to positions in the Afghan public sector of bureaucrats from the 1960s and 1970s, who in a number of cases have brought with them the very mindsets that contributed to the disastrous turn of events from 1978 onward. While some former officials have much to contribute, others seem determined to block any attempts at institutional modernization or innovation, since they are uncomfortable with new ways of doing things. This, and also the rush to recruit younger Afghans from Western countries, has marginalized to some degree the Afghans who worked for NGOs assisting the refugee population in Pakistan in the 1980s and 1990s, who with appropriate emphasis on capacity building could have formed the core of a genuine technocracy in Afghanistan. As a result, bureaucratic politics in the new Afghanistan has proved nearly as brutal as elite politics, and in recent months, a number of gifted and idealistic Afghans, drawn to Afghanistan not by the lure of high pay but by a genuine desire to serve their country, have quietly left, after concluding that the flaws in the Afghan administrative system prevented them from being able to add value.

As Karzai has grown more embattled, he has increasingly been surrounded by Westernized members of the Pashtun ethnic group. Notable among these are his Defense and Finance Ministers, and the Chair of the Independent Administrative Reform and Civil Service Commission. Although some of Karzai's advisors are very able, others are not, and a number of adverse consequences have flowed in recent times. Karzai's increased reliance on secularized Pashtuns of the sort who populated the upper echelons of the Afghan state in the 1960s and early 1970s has triggered alarm bells in Pakistan, whose military leaders are prone to see ghosts of the Pashtunistan dispute in every nook and cranny. More seriously, the predominance of such political figures has been at the expense of others to whom it is equally important to grant political space. One such group comprises traditional tribal leaders, who have been squeezed out of local power structures by the formally centralized structure of the state and by the role accorded in the south to disreputable potential spoilers. The other such group consists of those from non-Pashtun ethnic groups who provided the strongest opposition to the Taliban within Afghanistan between 1996 and 2001. All of the most senior associates of the late Ahmad Shah Massoud have now been excluded from the government, with the last to go being Foreign Minister Abdullah. The only Massoud associates left in significant political positions are Massoud's low-key brother Zia, who was one of Karzai's running mates in the 2004 election; Intelligence chief Amrullah Saleh; and Younos Qanuni, who established a distinct power base for himself as Speaker of the *Wolesi Jirga*. This drift from inclusiveness is potentially dangerous. Kabul is a largely Persian-speaking city, and the riots that hit Kabul on 29 May 2006 were widely read as a protest by supporters of the Massoud legacy against their increasing marginalization. Kabul is not at any grave risk of being overrun by the Taliban, but it could be rocked to its foundations by disaffection from within.

Without the involvement of Pakistan, southern and eastern Afghanistan might be unsettled, but it would not be afflicted with insurgency and terrorist strikes. In August 2007, Pakistani President Musharraf, speaking in Kabul, stated that "There is no doubt Afghan militants are supported from Pakistan soil. The problem that you have in your region is because support is provided from our side" (Shah and Gall 2007). Winston Churchill once remarked that the Germans had done enough for the history of the world (Fehr and Rehfeld 1970, 9). The same might be said of Pakistan, a deeply worrying state (Maley 2001; Grare 2007; Gregory 2007) with a history of supporting radical militancy in its neighbourhood and fomenting weapons proliferation more widely (Corera 2006). Its tribal areas provide a key base for radical extremists (International Crisis Group 2006b), and its meddling in Afghanistan is a decisive factor in the instability in the south and east of Afghanistan (Gall 2006c; Watson 2006a). As the French specialist on Pakistan Frédéric Grare has written, the "real question is not whether Pakistan is or is not supporting the Taliban, but why it is doing so" (2006b, 8). While President Musharraf presents himself as a liberal by Pakistani standards, he is locked into a destructive mindset in which the history of relations with Afghanistan, the perception of an existential threat from India, and the longstanding links between Islamist radicals and the Pakistan military come together to prompt a "forward" policy in Afghanistan using the Taliban as a surrogate and source of leverage. Baluchistan, according to the International Crisis Group, "has become a sanctuary where spokespersons and Taliban leaders brazenly operate" (2006a, 10; Watson 2006b), with the capital city of Quetta housing their principal headquarters (Cordesman 2006). Elsewhere in Pakistan, a 5 September 2006, "peace" agreement between the Pakistan government and Taliban militants in North Waziristan predictably led to more violent attacks in Afghanistan, starting with the assassination five days later of the respected governor of Paktia, Hakim Taniwal (Gall 2006a).

Western powers have been reluctant to apply pressure to Musharraf—in America's case through fear of a post-Musharraf regime with nuclear weapons, and in the case of the United Kingdom because of a perceived need for Pakistani police co-operation to address a threat from radicalized Muslim youth in the British Midlands (see Rashid 2007). But the danger in Pakistan is not so much a challenge to the military by Islamists, the risk of which Pakistan plays up for US consumption, but rather the use of radicals by the military itself for its own purposes (see Grare 2006a; Weinbaum 2006, 10–11). An overly indulgent approach to Pakistan by the West since 2001 has led to the rapid resurfacing of some of the most unappetizing features of the Pakistani military establishment, and Afghanistan and the Afghans have been the main victims. The new Pakistan government constituted after the February 2008 election will be best placed to prosper if it recognizes that the operations of the Afghan Taliban must be shut down, even if it is disposed to negotiate with its own Taliban radicals. This is not an issue on which the wider world can afford to compromise (Yaqub and Maley 2008).

Finally, the situation in Iraq has had grave effects on the Afghanistan transition. It hardly needs stating that the dire situation in Iraq (see Phillips 2005; Diamond 2005; Packer 2005; Ricks 2006; and Hashim 2006) has been a monumental distraction for Western leaders from the transition in Afghanistan, and while Afghanistan has not been wholly neglected or forgotten, it has certainly not received the attention that its strategic significance merits, and indeed has been held up as a success story when many problems have remained unresolved. Operation Enduring Freedom was one of the first victims of Operation Iraqi Freedom. The recognition dawned some time ago in Washington and elsewhere that scarce resources being deployed to minimal effect in Iraq might be much more gainfully employed in Afghanistan (Iraq Study Group 2006), but it remains to be seen whether this will ultimately result in concrete action on the ground, especially with the Bush administration committing itself to its troop "surge" in Iraq.

Paths Forward

The unravelling of the Bonn model confronts both the Karzai government and the wider world with significant challenges. At the outset it is necessary to note that because of the lapses that have cumulatively led to the present unhappy situation, it will not be easy to pull back from the brink, and even on the most optimistic of assumptions, it will take time to do so

(International Crisis Group 2006a). Four steps in particular are vital if the situation is to be salvaged.

First, it is imperative to avoid any words or actions that might lead to further loss of momentum. Too often, the political reality that words are bullets is overlooked by Afghanistan's ostensible supporters, who publicly canvas sensitive issues—for example, reducing the targeted strength of the Afghan National Army (Serchuk 2006), or cutting the diesel subsidy that helps the residents of Kabul survive the ferocious winter—without any apparent realization that this could be read as an indication of wavering commitment to the Afghan transition as a whole. Policies may of course need to be re-appraised to ensure that they are not lumbering the Afghans with unsustainable commitments, but the public sphere is no place in which to pursue the discussion.

But second, it is necessary to recognize that the administration headed by President Karzai has proved to be weak in a number of key respects, and to take this issue up in dialogue with the president. This should *not* be accompanied by thinly veiled threats to withdraw support for Karzai in favour of some other Afghans. Although Pakistan would doubtless like to see the back of Karzai and might even quietly promise to wind back the Taliban in exchange for the promotion of a pro-Pakistan leadership, it would be an act of staggering naiveté on the part of the United States and its allies to tread such a path, which could eventually reignite large-scale conflict within Afghanistan, from which only al-Qaeda and the narcotics industry would profit. Rather, recognizing that Karzai has many skills and talents, his external backers should emphasize that only through a clean and competent administration at both central and local levels can the Afghan state build its legitimacy. This will not come easily, but it is never too late to move in the right direction. Here, the crusading anti-corruption campaign of the new attorney-general, Abdul Jabbar Sabit, represents a promising start (Constable 2006). The benchmarks contained in the February 2006 Afghanistan Compact, which the UN Security Council endorsed through Resolution 1659 of 15 February 2006, should be used as starting points for enhancing state capacity, and it is essential that Western leaders deliver on their side of the bargain. The failings of Karzai's government are partly homegrown, but they owe much to both the dysfunctional model of a future state structure that emerged in Bonn, and to the culpable failure of the wider world to plug the security gap in Afghanistan from early 2002 onward.

Third, Pakistan should be pressured without mercy to smash the Taliban leadership networks that are operating on its soil. The simplistic alternative approach of conceding Afghanistan to effective Pakistani suzerainty while preserving a capacity to use military power against al-Qaeda "with whatever savagery is required to definitively destroy a barbaric enemy"

(Scheuer 2006, 119) would in the long run be a recipe for complete disaster for Afghanistan, for South Asian security, and for the United States and its people. It is intolerable that coalition troops and ordinary Afghans continue to die in Kandahar, Helmand, Uruzgan, and other parts of Afghanistan at the hands of extremists operating from sanctuaries in Pakistan. Pakistan has the capacity to address this problem, and its attempts to deny complicity deserve to be treated with scorn. Western governments should not hesitate to put such scorn on public display, not least out of loyalty to their own soldiers who are in the firing line.

In the past, attempts at quiet diplomacy have miscarried, for Pakistan has shown an unerring gift for seizing upon public praise and ignoring private pressure. To laud President Musharraf as a "superb partner," as US Deputy Assistant Secretary of State for South Asia John A. Gastright, Jr. did on the BBC *Newshour* program on 14 November 2006, is exactly the wrong approach to take. This is not to say that Pakistan should be confronted with negative sanctions only, but rather that much better behaviour on its part is required before the benefits of positive sanctions should flow any further. A transition from "rogue" to merely "roguish" behaviour is hardly sufficient. Nor is it to say that Afghanistan should not equally be pressured to consider recognizing the Durand Line as an international border and abandoning its hopeless, if fitful, advocacy of the cause of Pashtunistan. After all, as Barnett R. Rubin has accurately put it, "Islamabad will not respect a border that Kabul does not recognize" (2006, 14). But as past experience has shown, an unconstrained Pakistan is a dangerous actor, and those who treat the Pakistan military as a "good faith partner" normally get their fingers burned (Coll 2005; Gutman 2008).

Above all, the seriousness of the situation in Afghanistan must be properly grasped. While transitions are rarely straightforward (Maley 2002c; 2006b), the Afghans are well beyond the point where words alone will sooth their feelings (Gall 2006b). In his famous appraisal of the circumstances that led to the January 1986 *Challenger* disaster, the great physicist Richard P. Feynman concluded that for a successful technology, "reality must take precedence over public relations, for nature cannot be fooled" (Robbins 2001, 169). The same holds true for state building policy. There have been numerous wake-up calls in recent years about the situation in Afghanistan, but if robust action is not taken soon, Western leaderships may find themselves, as in Iraq, trapped in a nightmare from which there is no awakening.

Note

An earlier version of this chapter was delivered in 2007 as the Anthony Hyman Memorial Lecture at the School of Oriental and African Studies, University of London.

1 The *qawm* is a basic unit of social identity in Afghanistan and is based on family relationships, place of residence, and sometimes occupation. Hence, it may cross tribal and ethnic boundaries.

References

Abou Zahab, Mariam, and Olivier Roy. 2004. *Islamist Networks: The Afghan-Pakistan Connection*. London: Hurst & Co.

Afghanistan. 2006. *Afghanistan National Development Strategy: An Interim Strategy For Security, Governance, Economic Growth and Poverty Reduction*. Kabul: Islamic Republic of Afghanistan.

Bajpai, Kanti. 2003. "The Idea of Human Security," *International Studies* 40 (3): 195–228.

Bowler, Shaun, David M. Farrell, and Robin T. Pettitt. 2005. "Expert Opinion on Electoral Systems: So Which Electoral System is 'Best'?" *Journal of Elections, Public Opinion and Parties* 15 (1): 3–19.

Bradsher, Henry S. 1999. *Afghan Communism and Soviet Intervention*. Karachi: Oxford University Press.

Chandrasekaran, Rajiv. 2001. "Key Allies of Afghan Rebels Reject Future Taliban Role." *Washington Post*. 21 October.

Chayes, Sarah. 2006. *The Punishment of Virtue: Inside Afghanistan after the Taliban*. New York: Penguin.

Coll, Steve. 2005. *Ghost Wars: The Secret History of the CIA, Afghanistan and Bin Laden, from the Soviet Invasion to September 10, 2001*. New York: Penguin.

Constable, Pamela. 2006. "Top Prosecutor Targets Afghanistan's Once-Untouchable Bosses." *Washington Post*. 23 November.

Cordesman, Anthony H. 2006. *Winning in Afghanistan: How to Face the Rising Threat*. Washington, DC: Center for Strategic and International Studies.

Corera, Gordon. 2006. *Shopping for Bombs: Nuclear Proliferation, Global Insecurity, and the Rise and Fall of the A.Q. Khan Network*. New York: Oxford University Press.

Diamond, Larry. 2005. *Squandered Victory: The American Occupation and the Bungled Effort to Bring Democracy to Iraq*. New York: Times Books.

Fehr, Götz, and Werner Rehfeld. 1970. *Germany*. Munich: Bruckmann.

Gall, Carlotta. 2006a. "Suicide Bomber Kills a Governor in Afghanistan," *New York Times*. 11 September.

———. 2006b. "Afghans Losing Faith in Nation's Path, Poll Shows," *New York Times*. 9 November.

———. 2006c. "Pakistan Link Seen in Afghan Suicide Attacks," *New York Times*. 13 November.

Ganguly, Rajat. 1998. *Kin State Intervention in Ethnic Conflicts: Lessons from South Asia*. New Delhi: Sage.

Gardiner, Beth. 2006. "World Pledges $10.5B for Afghanistan Aid," *Washington Post*. 1 February.

Giustozzi, Antonio. 2007. *Koran, Kalashnikov and Laptop: The Neo-Taliban Insurgency in Afghanistan*. London: Hurst & Co.

Grare, Frédéric. 2006a. *Pakistan: The Myth of an Islamist Peril*. Washington, DC: Policy Brief No. 45, Carnegie Endowment for International Peace.

———. 2006b. *Pakistan-Afghanistan Relations in the Post-9/11 Period*. Washington, DC: Carnegie Papers No. 72, Carnegie Endowment for International Peace.

———. 2007. *Rethinking Western Strategies Toward Pakistan: An Action Agenda for the United States and Europe*. Washington, DC: Carnegie Endowment for International Peace.

Gregory, Shaun. 2007. "The ISI and the War on Terrorism." *Studies in Conflict and Terrorism* 30 (12): 1013–31.

Gutman, Roy. 2008. *How We Missed the Story: Osama bin Laden, the Taliban, and the Hijacking of Afghanistan*. Washington, DC: United States Institute of Peace Press.

Hardin, Russell. 1995. *One for All: The Logic of Group Conflict*. Princeton, NJ: Princeton University Press.

Hashim, Ahmed S. 2006. *Insurgency and Counter-Insurgency in Iraq*. Ithaca, NY: Cornell University Press.

Human Rights Watch. 2006a. *Afghanistan: Civilian Life Must Be Donor Priority*. New York: Human Rights Watch.

———. 2006b. *Afghanistan: Conviction and Death Sentence of Former Intelligence Chief Flawed*. New York: Human Rights Watch.

Hussain, Rizwan. 2005. *Pakistan and the Emergence of Islamic Militancy in Afghanistan*. Aldershot: Ashgate.

International Crisis Group. 2002. *Securing Afghanistan: The Need for More International Action*. Kabul/Brussels: Afghanistan Briefing No. 13, International Crisis Group. 15 March.

———. 2006a. *Countering Afghanistan's Insurgency: No Quick Fixes*. Kabul/Brussels: Asia Report No. 123, International Crisis Group. 2 November.

———. 2006b. *Pakistan's Tribal Areas: Appeasing the Militants*. Islamabad/Brussels: Asia Report No. 125, International Crisis Group. 11 December.

Iraq Study Group. 2006. *The Iraq Study Group Report*. New York: Vintage.

Johnson, Chris and Jolyon Leslie. 2004. *Afghanistan: The Mirage of Peace*. London: Zed Books.

Maass, Peter. 2002. "Gul Agha Gets His Province Back." *New York Times Magazine*. 6 January.

Maley, William. 1985. "Peace, Needs and Utopia." *Political Studies* 33 (4): 578–91.

————. 1987. "Political Legitimation in Contemporary Afghanistan." *Asian Survey* 27 (6): 705–25.

————. 1993. "The Future of Islamic Afghanistan." *Security Dialogue* 24 (4): 383–96.

————. 1995. "Peacekeeping and Peacemaking." In *A Crisis of Expectations: UN Peacekeeping in the 1990s*, ed. Ramesh Thakur and Carlyle A. Thayer, 237–50. Boulder: Westview Press.

————. 1998. "Interpreting the Taliban." In *Fundamentalism Reborn? Afghanistan and the Taliban*, ed. William Maley, 1–28. New York: New York University Press.

————. 2001. "Talibanisation and Pakistan." In *Talibanisation: Extremism and Regional Instability in South and Central Asia*, ed. Denise Groves, 53–74. Berlin: Conflict Prevention Network: Stiftung Wissenschaft und Politik.

————. 2002a. *The Afghanistan Wars*. New York: Palgrave Macmillan.

————. 2002b. "The Reconstruction of Afghanistan." In *Worlds in Collision: Terror and the Future of Global Order*, ed. Ken Booth and Tim Dunne, 184–93. London: Palgrave Macmillan.

————. 2002c. "Twelve Theses on the Impact of Humanitarian Intervention." *Security Dialogue* 33 (3): 265–78.

————. 2003. "Institutional design and the rebuilding of trust." In *From Civil Strife to Civil Society: Civil and Military Responsibilities in Disrupted States*, ed. William Maley, Charles Sampford, and Ramesh Thakur, 163–179. Tokyo: United Nations University Press.

————. 2003–2004. "The return of the warlords." *The Diplomat* 2 (5): 10–11.

————. 2006a. *Rescuing Afghanistan*. London: Hurst & Co.

————. 2006b. "Democratic Governance and Post-Conflict Transitions." *Chicago Journal of International Law* 6 (2): 683–701.

————. 2007. "Building State and Security." In *Building State and Security in Afghanistan*, ed. Wolfgang Danspeckgruber with Robert P. Finn, 3–18. Princeton: Liechtenstein Institute on Self-Determination, Princeton University.

Nasr, Vali R. 2000. "International Politics, Domestic Imperatives, and Identity Mobilization: Sectarianism in Pakistan, 1979–1998." *Comparative Politics* 32 (2): 171–90.

Olson, Elizabeth. 2002. "UN Official Calls for Larger International Force in Afghanistan." *New York Times*. 28 March

Ottaway, Marina and Anatol Lieven. 2002. *Rebuilding Afghanistan: Fantasy versus Reality*. Washington, DC: Policy Brief No. 12, Carnegie Endowment for International Peace.

Packer, George. 2005. *The Assassins' Gate: America in Iraq*. New York: Farrar, Straus and Giroux.

Phillips, David L. 2005. *Losing Iraq: Inside the Postwar Reconstruction Fiasco*. Boulder: Westview Press.

Rashid, Ahmed. 2007. "Britain 'out of step with NATO allies.'" *Daily Telegraph*.
6 January.

Ricks, Thomas E. 2006. *Fiasco: The American Military Adventure in Iraq*. New
York: Penguin Press.

Robbins, Jeffrey, ed. 2001. *The Pleasure of Finding Things Out: The Best Short
Works of Richard P. Feynman*, new ed. London: Penguin Books.

Roy, Olivier. 1990. *Islam and Resistance in Afghanistan*. Cambridge: Cambridge
University Press.

Rubin, Barnett R. 2002. *The Fragmentation of Afghanistan: State Formation
and Collapse in the International System*. New Haven: Yale University
Press.

———. 2006. *Afghanistan's Uncertain Transition from Turmoil to Normalcy*. New
York: Council Special Report No. 12, Council on Foreign Relations.

———. 2007. "Saving Afghanistan." *Foreign Affairs* 86 (1): 57–78.

Ruttig, Thomas. 2006. *Islamists, Leftists—and a Void in the Center: Afghanistan's
Political Parties and where they come from (1902–2006)*. Kabul: Kon-
rad Adenauer Stiftung.

Saikal, Amin, and William Maley. 1991. *Regime Change in Afghanistan: Foreign
Intervention and the Politics of Legitimacy*. Boulder: Westview Press.

———. 2008. "The President Who Would Be King." *New York Times*. 6 February.

Scheuer, Michael. 2006. "Clueless in Kabul." *The American Interest* 2 (1): 111–19.

Serchuk, Vance. 2006. "Don't Undercut the Afghan Army." *Washington Post*.
2 June.

Shah, Taimoor, and Carlotta Gall. 2007. "Afghan Rebels Find Aid in Pakistan,
Musharraf Admits." *New York Times*, 13 August.

Sipress, Alan. 2002. "Peacekeepers Won't Go Beyond Kabul, Cheney Says." *Washington Post*. 20 March.

Stedman, Stephen John. 1997. "Spoiler Problems in Peace Processes." *International Security* 22 (2): 5–53.

Suhrke, Astri. 2006. *When More Is Less: Aiding Statebuilding in Afghanistan*.
Madrid: Working Paper No. 26, Fundación para las Relaciones Interna-
cionales y el Diálogo Exterior.

Tarzi, Amin. 2008. "The Neo-Taliban." In *The Taliban and the Crisis of
Afghanistan*, ed. Robert D. Crews and Amin Tarzi, 274–310. Cambridge:
Harvard University Press.

United States. General Accounting Office. 2004. *Afghanistan Reconstruction:
Deteriorating Security and Limited Resources Have Impeded Progress;
Improvements in U.S. Strategy Needed*. Washington, DC: Report to Con-
gressional Committees, GAO–04–403, United States General Accounting Office.

Watson, Paul. 2006a. "In Afghanistan, money tips the scales of justice." *Los Angeles Times*. 18 December.

―――. 2006b. "On the trail of the Taliban's support." *Los Angeles Times*. 24 December.

Weber, Max. 1978. *Economy and Society: An Outline of Interpretive Sociology*. Berkeley & Los Angeles: University of California Press.

Weinbaum, Marvin G. 2006. *Afghanistan and its Neighbors: An Ever Dangerous Neighborhood*. Washington, DC: Special Report No. 162, United States Institute of Peace.

Yaqub, Daoud, and William Maley. 2008. "NATO and Afghanistan: Saving the State-Building Enterprise." In *The Bucharest Conference Papers*, ed. Robin Shepherd. Washington DC: German Marshall Fund of the United States.

2

Ali A. Jalali

Afghanistan
The Challenge of State Building

Diverging concepts underpinning the policies of domestic, regional, and global actors on the Afghan scene influence the process of state building in Afghanistan. International involvement in the state building process was an afterthought to the fight against global terrorism and was driven by the desire to remove the threat to the United States emanating from Afghan territory. The prime reasons for the US military intervention in Afghanistan were to destroy the terrorist network responsible for the 9/11 attacks and topple the Taliban regime. Although international efforts to stabilize post-Taliban Afghanistan are considered a strategic objective in the global war on terror, the operational exigencies of military action continue to cast a long shadow on the state building process in this war-devastated country. Local and regional allies picked by the United States for their counterterrorism schemes have their own agendas, and they often do not contribute to building peace and stability in Afghanistan. Additionally, the level of investment in reconstructing Afghanistan was initially determined not by the actual needs of the country but by the requirements of military operations—an inauspicious way to create a modern state. Increased donor contribution to reconstruction funds in recent years has often been supply-driven, not demand-driven. Afghanistan is the least resourced reconstruction program among recent international nation building efforts, such as those in the former Yugoslavia, Haiti, and East Timor. Afghanistan has been a low-cost military intervention and a cheap state building endeavour.

Following the ouster of the Taliban in 2001, Afghanistan scored notable achievements in rebuilding its state institutions, including adopting a modern constitution, holding peaceful presidential and parliamentary elections, creating national security institutions, improving women's rights, and expanding education institutions. And yet the country is faced with a revitalized Taliban-led insurgency, a record rise in drug production, deterioration of the rule of law, and a weakening grip of the national government over many districts in the south and southeast of the country. The principal reason for these setbacks is the failure to support the post-Bonn political dispensation with economic development, the rule of law, and national capacity building. The current troubles are a result of what was not done rather than what was.

The state building effort is complicated because it takes place amid a cycle of violence that has deep roots in Afghanistan's immediate past and in the region as a whole. Unlike many other cases of nation building, including Bosnia and Kosovo, state building in Afghanistan is conducted in an environment in which competing demands for a response to immediate security needs and the requirements of long-term priorities are often hard to reconcile, even though they can be mutually reinforcing. Further, the legacy of a turbulent history and a residual influence of recent war-instigated socio-political transformation continue to impact the process.

This chapter looks at emerging challenges and opportunities that face Afghanistan six years after the fall of the Taliban, and focuses on ways of building a modern state.

A Strong Nation and a Weak State

Nation building and state building are terms that are often used interchangeably in contemporary parlance. But the contrast between the two processes in Afghanistan is manifest. Despite experiencing a long period of instability and violence, nation building in Afghanistan is not an issue, but state building is a major challenge; Afghanistan has a strong nation and a weak state. In the recent past, the Afghan nation has shown surprising strength and viability, with no trace of secessionist calls, threats, or attempts. Even during the recent civil war and the breakdown of central government, the fighting factions were not interested in separatism but were fighting to gain control over Afghanistan. The nation is composed of different ethnic groups speaking more than one language and forced into physical remoteness by the rugged nature of the land, and yet it is united by common experience. Virtually all ethnic groups straddle the borders of the six neighbouring countries,[1] but they share more commonalities with their Afghan compatriots than their kinsmen across the border. This notion was further strengthened during the recent war, when millions of Afghans of different ethnic groups were forced to take refuge with their kinsmen in neighbouring states. It is based more on what Ernest Renan terms as "will" to persist together (cited in Gellner 1983) than on common ethnicity, language, or tribal affiliation.

The situation is different in many neighbouring countries. Pakistan is a strong state with a weak nation. As Hobsbawm writes, even a powerful religious identity, which created the foundation of the Pakistani state, can hardly constitute a nationalistic drive by itself. Even during the partition of India, "it is quite certain that the bulk of ordinary 'Indian' Muslims thought in communal and not in national terms" (Hobsbawm 1991, 70–71). Though Pakistan inherited strong state institutions, including 33% of the British Indian Army, it suffered from a weak sense of nationhood.

To the north, the newly independent Central Asian states also inherited strong state institutions, including armed forces, from the former Soviet Union. Yet they similarly had a paucity of strong national identity. As a region, Central Asia identifies with a distinct set of cultural and historical features that reflect its common experience through a long and momentous past. There exist different languages and numerous ethnic and locale-based cultures. However, the historical dynamism of what connects these communities is far stronger than the influence of what divides them into foreign-engineered separate states. Therefore, the major challenges facing the new independent states of Central Asia—which emerged as a by-product of the break-up of the Soviet Union in 1991—involve identity issues and nationalism as a means of legitimizing the colonial parceling out of the area into separate "Soviet republics"—a process known as "Razmizhevanie" (Khodorov, cited in Allworth 1994).

Located at the confluence of four regions (Middle East, Central Asia, South Asia, and the Far East through a border with China), it has been the destiny of Afghanistan to serve as a battlefield for imperial ambitions since the dawn of history. Reaction to foreign invasions has been the hallmark of Afghanistan's recent history. The country that long blocked military clashes between imperial Russia and British India was forced to fight both powers as the last century wore on. Joint reaction to foreign interventions solidified social and political ties between different ethnic and regional groups and unified them through common experience.

But the development of a modern state in Afghanistan has been extremely slow. Facing limited political, military, and financial resources, as well as geographic constraints, the central governments in Afghanistan historically exercised loose control over the country's regions and governed them through local leaders who either received special privileges from the state or were balanced against each other. This historical decentralization of governance has spawned a wide system of traditional power structures, norms, and practices that cannot be ignored in building a modern state in Afghanistan.

Until the eighteenth century, various states and empires dominated the territory of present-day Afghanistan, contributing to broad ethnic diversity that included Pashtuns, Persian speaking Tajiks and Hazaras, Uzbeks, and several other minority ethnic groups. In 1747, Pashtun leader Ahmad Shah Durrani founded an empire stretching from eastern Iran to northern India, which set the scene for the emergence of the modern state in Afghanistan. The empire started to decline at the beginning of the nineteenth century as British rule in India began to expand (Adamac 1974). During the nineteenth century, British and Russian rivalry for influence in central Asia drew Afghanistan into the "Great Game." This led to two Anglo–Afghan wars (1839–1842 and 1878–1880) in which the British armies tried unsuccessfully to occupy Afghanistan to check Russian expansion in central Asia (see Heathcote 1980). However, in the second half of the nineteenth century, the Great Game politics forced Afghanistan to embrace the state system under British suzerainty as a buffer against Russia. It was after World War I that Afghanistan won full independence following a third Anglo–Afghan war in 1919 (see Molesworth 1962).

King Amanullah's state building effort and an intensive reform program in the 1920s failed to create a major reform constituency. This shock therapy for modernization cost him his throne and plunged the country into civil war. Restoration of peace in 1929 ushered in a period of tight government control and a strictly measured modernization process.

A half-century of relative peace (1929–78) and foreign assistance helped Afghanistan build modern state institutions and economic infrastructure, both of which facilitated national integration and expanded the writ of the central government throughout the country. However, Kabul's lack of capacity and resources to respond effectively to the periphery's needs for good governance and public services left traditional power structures and informal conflict resolution institutions intact and functional. Kabul often sought to supplement these customary or traditional structures, which were particularly active in tribal areas, with formal institutions, avoiding competition or contradictions between them.[2]

The top-down democratic changes from 1963 to 1973, known as the "Decade of Democracy," paved the way for the expansion of civil society and the emergence of a new urban-based educated elite as the core of political opposition to the government. The new elite included both a pro-Soviet Communist block and a revolutionary Islamist movement. The rise to power of these new elites brought enormous violence and destruction to the nation. The fall of the old regime to a pro-Moscow Communist coup in

1978 opened a long period of violence that turned Afghanistan into a hotspot of the Cold War. The violence that began as an insurgency against the communist coup of April 1978 soon turned into a wider conflict. It led to the Soviet military intervention (1979–1989) and increased US-led western and Saudi support of the Islamic anti-Communist resistance forces, the *Mujahideen*. Once the superpowers drew back, neighbouring countries, other foreign states, and non-state actors moved in to pursue their competing strategic interests by engaging and supporting rival Afghan factions who were locked in a violent power struggle. The situation eventually brought the radical regime of the Taliban to power, a regime that hosted Osama bin Laden's al-Qaeda terrorist network.

The US-led coalition's war on terrorism in Afghanistan scored quick and spectacular military achievements, opening the way for Afghanistan to free itself from the grips of extremism and the scourge of international isolation. In less than two months, the Taliban regime was shattered, the al-Qaeda establishment broken up, and its leadership forced to run. But the struggle for peace proved to be much tougher than winning the war. More than two decades of violence and instability had destroyed the country's political and economic infrastructure and inflamed ethnic, sectarian, and regional divisions in the multi-ethnic nation.

Socio-Political Transformation

In addition to the enormous human loss and material destruction,[3] the long years of war and violence changed the fabric of the society and upset the traditional alignment of political forces in the country. No war in the past had ever caused so much social change in Afghanistan, as it ripped society apart in multiple ways. The breakdown of central authority during more than two decades of conflict and violence stimulated a socio-political transformation that vitalized regional patronage networks under the leadership of regional commanders who often invoked ethnic references to legitimize their leadership. This situation fueled ethno-regional competition for power and resource distribution.

Three interconnected domestic factors were responsible for the landmark transformation: a crisis of legitimacy, a failure to substitute destroyed state institutions with new ones, and a rise of sub-state powers. An unsuccessful struggle by successive governments to establish legitimacy became a major factor in destabilizing the state's authority. The traditional source of Afghan legitimacy, monarchy, ended with the overthrow of King Zaher Shah by his cousin Mohammad Daud in a bloodless coup in 1973. However, Daud's royal affiliation and his earlier prominent government positions provided for continuity with the country's monarchical past.

The bloody Communist coup of 1978 sparked a legitimacy crisis that continues to haunt the country's political scene. None of the ruling powers that succeeded the old regime managed to gain legitimacy. All of them, including the Communists (1978–1992), the *Mujahideen* (1992–1996), and the Taliban (1996–2001), based their legitimacy on ideology enforced by military power, which is alien to mainstream Afghan values. The regimes' efforts were challenged by religious/cultural resistance and hampered by factional splits, structural deficiency, economic failure, and foreign links.

None of these ideologies were able to escape factional splits that further weakened their legitimacy. Intra-party frictions and ideological instability and fragmentation were particularly pronounced at the subnational level where ethnic, linguistic, and sectarian differences undermined ideological solidity.

The failure to substitute the destroyed state institutions with new ones strongly influenced Afghanistan's socio-political transformation. The ideological governments failed to create viable political, social, and economic institutions to solidify their power. In their zeal to promote political agendas through ideology, Afghan leaders failed to set concrete objectives and to establish the concomitant programs to attain them. They used ideological rhetoric merely to mobilize supporters and undermine opponents. This lack of "structural legitimacy" contributed to the failures of the ideological approach. The "structural legitimacy" that Max Weber labeled as "rational-legal authority," is obtained when rules, supported by institutions to enforce them, underpin popular acceptance of government (1947, cited in Bill and Springborg 1990).

The impact of these transformations on the state–society relationship has been enormous. Traditionally, the central government served as a power broker within a conglomerate of ethnic groups and regional forces loosely tied together within the state. Under these conditions, political power emanated from the centre to the periphery. The collapse of state structure during the civil war led to the emergence of sub-state factions constituted around powerful regional–ethnic leaders who maintained militias and had access to domestic and foreign resources. The emergence and integration of ethnicized regional powers during the war reversed the traditional trend.

The Post-Taliban State Building Project

Afghanistan's transition from conflict to peace and sustainable development is a process of state building with its associated security, political, and economic dimensions. It involves the creation of a set of institutions, capacities, resources, and provisions for the rule of law. Governance embodies the use of institutions, structures of authority, and resources to manage society's problems and affairs. It entails control and coordination of activities. Therefore effective governance is underpinned by the legitimacy of the state, its long-term stability, and its capacity to deliver.

Both state building and governance in Afghanistan are troubled by diverging concepts that influence the policies of domestic, regional, and global actors on the Afghan scene. They are further hindered by a continued cycle of political and economic violence. In such an environment, competing demands for responding to these challenges are often hard to reconcile. Adopting and pursuing a much-needed comprehensive and integrated strategy, along with its coordinated implementation, is further exacerbated by the involvement of numerous domestic and international actors who come with an uneven level of commitment and different degrees of resources, procedures, and priorities. The resulting operational constraints inhibit strategic coordination in fighting the insurgency while building state institutions and good governance.

The Bonn Agreement served as the initial guide for the process of state building in post-Taliban Afghanistan. Adopted on 5 December 2001 by four Afghan political/ethnic groups at the UN-sponsored conference in Bonn, it called for the establishment of a six-month Afghan Interim Authority (AIA) to govern the country, beginning on 22 December 2001. This was to be in effect until an emergency *Loya Jirga* (Grand Council)[4] could select a broad-based transitional authority to lead Afghanistan, with the election of a fully representative government to occur within two years (Bonn Agreement 2001). Meanwhile, the UN Security Council authorized the deployment of a 4,500-strong International Security Assistance Force (ISAF) in Kabul.

From the outset, two contradictory concepts drove international intervention in Afghanistan. The country was described as the major front in the global war on terror, yet the intervention was a "light footprint" engagement. This light footprint continues to impair every aspect of reconstruction in Afghanistan.

Although the progress to date is notable, the current troubles are immense, and they are a result of what was not done rather than what was done. The Taliban were removed from power, but neither their potential to come back nor their external support was addressed. Alliances of convenience with warlords perpetuated the influence of the most notorious human rights violators. Competing demands for a response to immediate security needs and the requirements of long-term priorities were not balanced effectively, even though they reinforce one another. The failure to adopt a comprehensive and integrated approach to combat narcotics led to record increases in illicit drug production, which fuels corruption and funds terrorism and criminality. Inefficient use of insufficient funds, most of which are outside of Afghan government control, failed to create economic opportunities, good governance and the rule of law.

The Bonn Agreement gave the political process a timeline but failed to synchronize it with building indigenous institutional capacity in Afghanistan. The country had experienced more than two decades of war that destroyed the state bureaucratic institutions. In such an environment, building sustainable security institutions, establishing the rule of law, and creating economic opportunity need to be the prime focus of reconstruction. In Afghanistan, elections in the absence of effective state institutions hampered the development of the democratic process.

The first two years after the fall of the Taliban offered the best window of opportunity for reconstruction. The enemy was disintegrated, public support for the policies of the central government was overwhelming, and international military forces had the hearts and minds of the population. This opportunity was squandered. The United States' shift in attention and resources to Iraq came at a time when the global jihadists refocused their attention on a weak Afghan state. The Afghan government failed to act for long-term stability, opting instead for short-term deals with nonstate power holders who had their own interests. The result has been a weak government with incompetent security forces and a poor and corrupt justice sector. The Afghan government's failure to protect rural communities, to respond to the legitimate needs of the people, and to fight corruption has rejuvenated the insurgency.

The obsession over elections without sufficient investment in reconstruction undermined the legitimacy of the elections. The relatively early elections favoured warlords and militia leaders who influenced the polls with their money and guns. This significantly hindered long-term democratic practices, governance, and the establishment of the rule of law. Further, the quick elections helped sub-state power holders legitimize their networks by creating factional political parties that helped the civil war alignments to dominate the post-conflict political landscape. The situation delayed the emergence of national political parties, forcing the government to hold elections on a non-party basis, complicating the parliamentary functions. The fast-paced political process in Afghanistan was mostly influenced by the priorities of the international community and not the realities in Afghanistan. As the International Crisis Group stated, "The desire for a quick, cheap war followed by a quick, cheap peace is what has brought Afghanistan to the present, increasingly dangerous situation" (2006).

Although the new state building project opted for a top-down approach, the real political and military influence in the state remained a bottom-up trend. This was reflected in the post-Taliban political dispensation. Instead of Hamid Karzai, the Chairman of the AIA, appointing his cabinet, the cabinet of local power holders had to agree on his appointment. As the political process continued, the failure to build the institutional power of the centre perpetuated the influence of regional factions.

The absence of Afghan government control over development programs funded by a deeply divided international community disjointed development efforts, which were increasingly disconnected from the country's needs. In many cases strategic goals were overshadowed by pet projects that were popular to domestic constituencies of the donor nations. The slow pace of tangible reconstruction activity in the country caused public frustration.

Following the conclusion of the Bonn process, the Afghan government and the international community agreed on a shared vision for the long-term development of Afghanistan. The five-year Afghanistan Compact adopted on 31 January 2006 in London pledges continued international assistance to Afghanistan in the context of Afghanistan's Interim National Development Strategy (I-ANDS). The I-ANDS is the strategic framework for development over the next five years. It aims to enhance security, governance, the rule of law, human rights, and economic and social development. It also identifies efforts to eliminate the narcotics industry as a vital and cross-cutting area of work (Afghanistan 2006). The compact opens a new phase of partnership between Afghanistan and the international community, directed toward long-term capacity building.

The upsurge of violence in the spring of 2006 caught many by surprise. The Afghanistan Compact was focused primarily on socioeconomic development and based on the assumption that security had improved. With the deterioration of security in the south, however, the focus was shifted to military operations at the expense of programs designed to develop and improve governance. A rush to tactical military solutions and quick fixes derailed the strategic drive and integrated approach toward achieving the compact objectives. Now, it is imperative that a balance be struck between military operations and development projects.

Ending the Insurgency

The Taliban-led insurgency in Afghanistan is waged in a highly volatile sociopolitical environment. What drives people to fight is not merely the ideology but rather the unstable environment and the influence of existing networks of tribes, clans, criminal networks, and transnational organizations. There are many independent but interlinked actors challenging the Afghan government and its international allies for various reasons. It is quite different from the insurgency of the 1980s, when a multi-factional

Afghan resistance against the Soviet occupation was operationally fragmented, yet all groups fought for a common cause with uncompromising
determination.

The most serious problem in fighting insurgency is the absence of a coordinated strategy based on a shared vision and carried out through an
integrated military, political, and developmental effort. The US military
defines counterinsurgency as "military, paramilitary, political, economic,
psychological and civic actions taken by a government to defeat insurgency" (US Army and US Marine Corps 2006, 1). In Afghanistan, there is
little connection between tactical and strategic operations, between short-
term and long-term goals. Nor are military and non-military operations
coordinated and directed toward a common goal. Meanwhile, actions carried out by different partners, including NATO, the US-led Operation Enduring Freedom, the Afghan Government, regional partners (Pakistan in
particular), and others, are strategically fragmented.

NATO forces have won many battles against the insurgents in the south
since 2006 and 2007 but have seen little improvement in the strategic situation. A failure to consolidate military gains by holding and rebuilding
areas cleared from insurgents has blocked any strategic improvement. Afghan
security forces and allied contingents do not have sufficient forces to hold
ground, facilitate good governance, and protect the population (Ames 2007).
This situation hinders efforts to isolate the population from the insurgents
and win the hearts and minds of the people (*BBC News* 2007).

Because of an insufficient number of troops on the ground, military commanders tend to use heavy firepower as a force multiplier. Using long-range
artillery and air strikes against insurgents hidden among the population
has undermined counter-insurgency efforts. Despite this reality we have
seen a sharp rise in the use of air strikes by NATO and Coalition forces in
the past two years. The resulting collateral damage and civilian casualties
contribute to the insecurity and popular resentment exploited by the Taliban. Recently there have been demands for an additional ten thousand
troops to augment the forty-two thousand NATO troops in Afghanistan. In
January 2008, the United States announced the deployment of an additional thirty-two hundred marines to help foil the Taliban's expected spring
offensive. But the increase will have no major strategic impact unless other
elements of the counter-insurgency operations are carried out in a coordinated way. Additional troops and firepower will not help without good governance, sustainable security, and the establishment of the rule of law,
which are the most crucial elements of a successful strategy to defeat the
insurgency. In Musa Qalah, an area that was recently cleared of the Taliban,
one resident reflected the prevailing opinion that the people need security
more than they want schools and roads (Shafe and MacKenzie 2008).

There is also little connection between the military and non-military counterinsurgency efforts carried out by different partners. NATO military action typically targets terrorists and insurgents in order to dissuade, deter, and defeat them through combat action. But there is no clear owner either for the non-military part of the effort or for the overall strategy and campaign plan. Actions aimed at assuring, persuading, and influencing the populations, through the provision of human security, humanitarian assistance, basic services, infrastructure, institution building, and support for the rule of law are fragmented. It is a free-for-all sphere of action that spawns confusion, more problems, and more insecurity.

Negotiation with the insurgents has not been integrated into an overall strategy but pursued separately by different actors. Although there is wide support for peace talks with insurgents, there is little agreement among domestic and international actors on who to engage, what political price is acceptable in peace deals, and what is the vision for the end state. Recently there are growing suspicions in Afghanistan that certain members of the alliance favour a "colonial approach" to gain peace with the Taliban in the south. The approach allegedly entails granting local autonomy to reconciled Taliban leaders who will run local affairs but remain politically loyal to Kabul. This is seen as the creation of an Afghan FATA[5] or "Taliban light" enclaves. Such arrangements are doomed to failure in Afghanistan for several reasons. First, available opinion surveys indicate that despite the rise of violence, an overwhelming majority of the people view the Taliban negatively and do not favour their return to rule even locally (World Public Opinion 2006). A year ago, the level of Taliban sympathy in the south was estimated only at 11% (Charney Research and ABC News Poll, cited in USIP Briefing 2006). There is a strong inverse correlation between the strength of the government presence and the strength of support for the Taliban (ibid). Second, Pashtuns in Afghanistan are integrated into a multiethnic nation that has shown surprising strength and viability with no trace of calls, threats, or attempts at secession. Even during the recent civil war and the breakdown of the central government, the fighting factions were not interested in separatism but were fighting to gain control over Afghanistan. Third, such ethnic-based decentralization could generate a domino effect spreading across the country, including the stable areas, leading to a fragmentation of the country. At best it would be a tactical gain, but it would also be an immense strategic loss.

Negotiations with foreign-supported militants who want to overthrow the government and turn Afghanistan into a safe haven for global terrorism are out of the question. These militants need to either modify their beliefs or face the probability of being destroyed. Other insurgents, most of whom are not against the political system as an entity, but are opposed to the government, can be won over through a continuing process of national reconciliation. This will be possible only if these insurgents can be successfully isolated and protected from the radical elements within the insurgency. As long as instability persists in the south, Kabul will be in a weak position to achieve favorable deals through negotiations.

There is an urgent need for a consensus among the domestic and international partners on a unified strategy and campaign plan. The appointment of a new UN envoy to Afghanistan with more coordinating power is partly seen as a way to make up for the chronic lack of a coordinated strategy both in the military sphere and in the area of post-conflict or "in-conflict" reconstruction. However the challenge is much greater than simply coordinating the international effort. Harmonizing military operations and bringing them in line with a coordinated international effort is the main challenge. It is hardly expected that the new envoy will be able to preside over all international efforts and have influence over Afghan government decisions that could lead to a unified coordinated strategy. The alternative is to make the Afghan government the sole owner and coordinator of the overall strategy. However it is not likely to work until the Afghan government acquires the capacity to strategize and coordinate the overall efforts for stabilization and reconstruction.

A counter-insurgency strategy for Afghanistan is incomplete unless it also encompasses Pakistan, whose tribal border areas have become safe havens for the Taliban and al-Qaeda. Few insurgencies in the past have survived without a safe haven abroad. As long as the insurgents maintain a sanctuary in Pakistan it will be hard to defeat them in Afghanistan. The upsurge of religious militancy and violence in Pakistan and the Talibanization of the Federally Administered Tribal Areas (FATA), with increasing spillover to "settled areas," has aggravated the situation in Afghanistan. The Taliban have safe havens in Pakistan and receive technical and operational assistance from transnational extremists there.

The environment in the Pashtun belt has created psychological and political capital for the Taliban and transnational militants. Traditionally a moderate society, the Pashtuns have more than once been radicalized by outside influence and intervention in the past. Most recently, the empowerment of extremist elements by the Pakistani military and intelligence services, and their extensive support for the Taliban in Afghanistan during the 1990s, marginalized moderate political leaders and tribal chiefs in the region. The failure of Pakistan to deal with an expanding extremism in the tribal areas and the lack of an Afghan government presence in the Pashtun south and southeast have facilitated the rising dominance of extremist elements today.

The removal of sources of insurgency in the area requires a new regional approach involving combined military and political effort by the US, NATO,

Afghanistan, and Pakistan. The new approach should address several issues of legitimate concern to both Afghanistan and Pakistan, such as the development of the least educated and rural tribal areas on both sides of the Durand line, the promotion of democratic changes in Pakistan, the enhancement of governance capacity in Afghanistan, and the political integration of FATA. Looking at the larger picture, reducing the sources of transnational militancy and religious extremism in South Asia and fostering economic integration in the region needs to be part of the new approach.

Building National Security Forces

The development of Afghanistan's national security architecture continues in the form of the security sector reform (SSR) process, which comprises the creation of the Afghan National Army (ANA) and Afghan National Police (ANP) and the reform of the judicial system. SSR also encompasses the demobilization, disarmament and reintegration (DDR) program and counternarcotics efforts. Security sector reform has been the flagship of the Bonn process for rebuilding Afghanistan's security and law enforcement structures. With each of its five pillars (army, police, counter-narcotics, DDR, and justice) supported by a lead donor nation, SSR has developed unevenly.

Building a national army in Afghanistan has been a major challenge. This is the fourth time in 150 years of Afghanistan's turbulent history that the country is recreating the state military following its total disintegration caused by foreign invasions or civil wars.[6] The process of rebuilding has always been influenced by the prevailing political and social conditions in the country. The current attempt is not an exception.

Few of Afghanistan's armies have successfully monopolized the legitimate use of force. The Afghan army generally has not been the only military institution within a social system imbued with military pluralism. The country traditionally has relied on popular uprisings to fight foreign invasions, and has enlisted the aid of tribal levies to beef up the regular army to crush domestic rebellions (Jalali 2002). Despite the steady progress in modernizing and training the army and the development of the air force under King Zaher Shah (1933–1973), the Afghan military establishment failed to reach the level of professional maturity necessary to resist politicization.

Turning combatants into government soldiers is a daunting challenge that takes time, leadership, and state legitimacy. Traditionally, the primacy of tribal and local loyalty among the soldiers impaired the army's commitment to the government cause. The army was often crudely organized and led, inadequately armed, poorly trained, meagerly paid, and badly fed. Such an army was hardly capable of standing firm in the face of a determined foe. However, the same soldiers would fight with utmost determination with their kinsmen in their own region under the leadership of their local chiefs. A British observer of Afghan society, Edward Hensman, wrote in 1881: "The Afghan does not lack native courage, and in hill warfare he is unrivaled, so long as it takes the shape of guerrilla fighting. But once he is asked to sink his identity and to become merely a unit in a battalion, he loses all self-confidence and is apt to think more of getting away than of stubbornly holding his ground as he would have done with his own friends led by his own chief" (329).

Driven by operational demands to fight the insurgency and create an alternative to factional militias, the development of the ANA received a high priority. Since 2002, progress in building the US-supported Afghan National Army (ANA) has been remarkable. The ANA's strength reached fifty-five thousand by January 2008, and it is expected to attain its goal of seventy thousand by 2009. Organized in five Army Corps,[7] the ANA is deployed in brigades and battalions across the country. It also includes a small fleet of transport aircraft and helicopters. Despite the influx of US-donated vehicles, small arms, and other equipment in 2005–2006, the ANA suffered from insufficient fire power, the lack of indigenous combat air support and the absence of a self-sustaining operational budget. Therefore it continued to depend on military support from NATO and the Coalition forces and on the US to underwrite its costs.

Different from the draft armies of the past, the ANA is a volunteer professional military force composed of a career officer corps and contract enlisted men who have the option of reenlistment. It is more effective than previous armies but too expensive to be sustained by the current Afghan budget.[8] Given the prohibitive cost of maintaining professional forces, there is strong support in the country for the restoration of the national draft system that presumably also promotes national integration and civic education. However, the feasibility of the change depends on the level of sovereignty and control exercised by the government across the country.

The essential mission of building indigenous civilian police capacity in Afghanistan has been difficult. The national police had virtually ceased to exist after years of grinding civil war. With a main focus on fighting insurgency and militia-led violence, police capacity building was not the pacing element in the reform of the security sector; neither were broader rule of law considerations. Little international attention has been paid to the development of the Afghan National Police (ANP). Political decisions to reintegrate demobilized former factional combatants into the police force further undermined ANP development. In most cases, former factional commanders who are appointed to the police have loaded their offices with their unqualified supporters and corrupt cronies. Moreover, the nature of police functions makes it difficult to train policemen as units like army bat-talions and then deploy them where they are needed. The police need to be trained, deployed, and coached at the same time. The dominance of local loyalty and links with corrupt networks, along with poor training, low pay, and a residual culture of corruption, contribute to endemic corruption in the police force.

And yet the current exigencies have forced the Afghan police to operate at the forefront of the fight against terrorism, illegal border incursions, the illicit drug trade, warlords, and organized crime. Protecting reconstruction projects, including highways in the militant-plagued south, is another major challenge facing the ANP. As a result, the ANP has lost far more men than the ANA, coalition forces, and ISAF in fighting the insurgency and crimi-nal activity across the country during the past six years. Had the police been better trained, equipped, and armed, they would have suffered fewer casualties and made better contributions to stability operations.

The German-led development of the ANP has been slow, under-funded, and focused on long-term training. The goal was to build a force of sixty-two thousand civilian police including twelve thousand Border Police by 2008. Over the past three years, police capacity building and its coordina-tion with military forces have assumed a much higher priority among the US military and civilian agencies. However, increased US attention and investment in developing the ANP has been incremental.

The United States, through the State Department's Bureau for Interna-tional Narcotics and Law Enforcement Affairs (INL), began serious partic-ipation in Afghan police training in 2003 to reinforce the German-led pro-gram. The US established one central and seven regional training centres and supported massive short-term basic training of the police. However, the training, which is run by contractors, is mostly inadequate (two to four weeks), unsubstantial, and not effectively followed up through mentoring programs and on-the-job training.

The INL contribution to the police program was followed in 2004 by partial, and then, in late 2005, formal US military involvement with the Afghan police—including financial, personnel, and material inputs under the Combined Security Transition Command–Afghanistan (CSTC–A). The United States began a program to assist reform of the Afghan Ministry of Interior (MoI) in July 2004. Senior police advisors helped the MoI to de-velop standard operating procedures and community policing initiatives and began developing a plan for pay and rank reform.

In addition to these reforms, the United States and Germany have been training the Afghan Border Police. There are separate programs for the narcotics police, customs police, and highway police. Since the ANP are ac-tively engaged in counter-insurgency operations, the structure, training, and equipment of the police have been adjusted to the conflict environment. The Afghan police are organized into five regional commands, collocated with the five corps headquarters of the Afghan National Army. A new structure of the Ministry of Interior was adopted in 2006 that partly replicates the structure of the US-assisted Ministry of Defense. Counter-insurgency training for the Border Police and the Quick Reaction Force began in the spring of 2006 with eight units—one for each of the five regional commands, and three based in Kabul.

With increased Taliban-led insurgency activity in the south and east in 2005–2006, major changes were introduced in the Afghan police force. The authorized number of ANP was increased by twenty thousand to a level of eighty-two thousand, which includes an enlarged Border Police force of eighteen thousand and a nearly twelve thousand–strong "Auxiliary Police" force to be deployed in 124 high-risk southern and eastern districts threatened by cross-border insurgent attacks. The new ANP also includes civil order units for riot control in major cities and a five thousand–strong heavier Afghan National Police Constabulary (a *Carabinieri* and *Gendarmerie* type) designated to extend police/government influence to remote areas. Faced with an upsurge of insurgency activity, the Karzai government has sought to utilize some local and tribal communities to assist in fighting the Taliban. Kabul views the move as a way to mobilize local and tribal communities to assist in fighting insurgents. Critics see the move as contravening the program of disarming the militias. The project has faced many obstacles and, in most cases in the south, has ended in failure.

A 2006 US interagency assessment of Afghanistan's police program indicates that the ANP readiness to perform conventional police functions and carry out its internal security mission is "far from adequate." The assessment report, jointly prepared by the Inspector Generals of the Department of Defense and Department of State, points out that obstacles to establishing a fully professional ANP are formidable and include "no effective field training officer program, illiterate recruits, a history of low pay and pervasive corruption, and an insecure environment." Removing these obstacles requires "a comprehensive, integrated approach that encompasses leadership training, sustaining institutions and organizations, an oversight, and internal control mechanism." The report suggests that long-term US assistance and funding, at least beyond 2010, is required to institutionalize the police force and establish a self sustaining program (2006).

In January 2007, Washington pledged to provide $10.6 billion over two years to help Afghanistan strengthen its security forces and rebuild from years of war. A total of $8.6 billion dollars would be for training and equipping Afghan police and security forces, and $2 billion was earmarked for reconstruction. The money would be on top of $14.2 billion in aid the United

States had already given to Afghanistan between 2001 and 2006 (Cooper and Cloud 2007).

Meanwhile, the disarmament, demobilization, and reintegration (DDR) of militia forces remains a major security challenge. Although the DDR program succeeded in demobilizing over 63,000 factional militiamen and collecting over 57,000 small arms, while storing nearly all heavy weapons, reintegrating former combatants continues to be a major challenge. Nearly two thousand illegal armed groups in the country still pose threats to human security. The Afghanistan Compact had aimed at Disbandment of Illegal Armed Groups (DIAG) by the end of 2007, but most remained intact by the summer of 2008. Success of the program hinges on other aspects of development in the country. Breaking the war machines in the post-conflict period is a prerequisite for sustaining peace; however, failure to build attractive alternatives for former combatants could lead to a renewal of violence as well as a proliferation of criminal activity and banditry.

Governance

Good governance is hampered by a lack of state control over institutions and procedures that facilitate change in the country. Kabul is not in full control of institution building, security operations, and development choices. The basic functions of governance are performed by an array of state and non-state actors, including foreign militaries, international bodies, non-government organizations, and informal/traditional domestic power holders. The state has even deferred the "monopoly of legitimate use of force" to foreign actors in the face of an unstable security situation, in the hope that it can manage to rebuild the state under the security cover of foreign militaries. While such a pattern is not uncommon in post-conflict and developing states, the slow pace of state building in Afghanistan has inhibited efficiency in governance, security, and economic development. Consequently, without the state controlling a central role, public goods contributed by different actors tend to be uncoordinated, unstable, transient, and more supply-driven than demand-driven (see Nixon 2007, 12–14).

The Afghanistan Compact gives priority to "the coordinated establishment in each province of functional institutions including civil administration, police, prisons, and judiciary." Reforming the justice system is of prime importance. The compact aims at ensuring "equal, fair and transparent access to justice based upon written codes with fair trials and enforceable verdicts." Achievement of this hinges on a comprehensive "legislative reform of the public and private sector, building the capacity of judicial institutions and cadres, promoting human rights and legal awareness and rehabilitating the judicial infrastructure" (Afghanistan Compact 2006).

Building the sub-national government, including provincial, district, and municipal administration, is a major challenge facing state building in Afghanistan. The political vision as depicted in the Interim Afghanistan National Development Strategy (I-ANDS) includes the establishment of "effective, accountable, and transparent administration at all levels of government" within a unitary system (2006). It seeks to build a functioning physical and institutional justice framework that adequately protects the rights of the citizens in all provinces and districts and envisions the institutionalization of elected bodies at national, provincial, district, and village levels.

While the I-ANDS provides for the emergence of a representative and effective system of governance, detailed plans to achieve it are not clear. There are three major issues to be addressed before an effective government can be established at the sub-national level. These include the role of each level in service delivery, their required capacity for development planning, and the relationship between elected and appointed bodies (see Lester and Nixon 2006, 3–11).

The removal of existing perceptional and managerial distance between Kabul and the regions is essential for defragmenting administration. The key to this is bringing a balance between creating a strong and effective central government and ensuring a level of decentralization to secure equal distribution and participation. One of the challenges is the level of delegation of administrative and fiscal authorities to sub-national government. While resource allocation and staffing authority of sub-national administration continues to be limited, the specter of "federalism" and the lack of clear understanding about healthy decentralization methods continue to hinder the development capacity of sub-national government. Kabul's limited ability to delegate resources has put sub-national administration on autopilot.

Another key issue is the integration of formal, elected, and traditional governing bodies—including *maliks* (village chiefs), *khans/arbabs* (large land owners/tribal chiefs), *ulema* (religious figures), and traditional *shuras* and tribal *jirgas*. The establishment of elected bodies, including the national assembly, as well as provincial, district, and village councils further crowds the political landscape. The state needs to coalesce the traditional, local, provincial, and national government bodies into an integrated system of governance with clear roles, links, power, and resources for each element. Participation and inclusiveness lead to stability.

While national development is an incremental process, revitalization and regional coordination of three national programs can serve as vehicles for change and achieving good governance throughout the nation. These include the National Solidarity Program (NSP), the Afghanistan Stabilization Program (ASP), and the Provincial Reconstruction Teams (PRT). The NSP seeks to create and empower local governing councils to prioritize local reconstruction projects. It facilitates community development at the village level by providing the funds and technical assistance villagers need to conduct modest development projects of their own choice. The ASP aims to rebuild the physical infrastructure of over 360 district centres, to deploy well-trained, well-paid, and well-equipped police forces, and to establish an effective government with the capacity for service delivery. The PRT is a small military unit with civilian representatives, deployed in a province to extend the authority of the central government and to facilitate the development of security and reconstruction. Depending on conditions imposed by the troop-donating nations, PRTs operate in different ways— often out of control of the guiding bodies—and adopt unique balances between security and reconstruction activities. The imprecise pronouncement of the PRT mandate has opened the way for flexible discernment of its nature.

These programs share the concept of the so-called "ink spot" development scheme, which aims to create secure spots of development. Currently the NSP and ASP suffer from deficits in funding, weak management, lack of coordination, and inter-ministerial turf battles. The PRT impact is thwarted by non-standard practices and operational restrictions of the donor countries.

The Afghan government cannot expect to function effectively without expanding its revenue base through raising taxes and collecting state revenues. Afghanistan has almost the lowest rate of revenue to GDP in the world. Government revenue amounts to only 4% of the GDP; the rate for most developing countries is 10% and for developed nations over 30%. The Afghan government is critically dependent on international funding for recurrent costs. Such dependency is not sustainable. The medium-term goal (2006–2009) is for revenues to cover recurrent costs, making the government's recurrent budget fiscally sustainable. Kabul expects that reaching fiscal sustainability will be slow, since a number of items, including security costs that were financed by donors, were unexpectedly dumped on the government's core budget during the 2006–2007 fiscal year. Another challenge is building the capacity for a full budget execution. As of mid-2006, the development and operational budget execution rates were low at 33% and 59%, respectively. Low execution capacity means that even if money is available, it cannot be committed and used.

The Rule of Law

The rule of law is the heart of government legitimacy and a prerequisite for human security, involving the protection and empowerment of citizens. The dominance of security demands in an unstable environment has led to an over-securitization of the rule of law. This subordinates justice to security considerations and turns police into a tool primarily used in combating insurgency instead of protecting law and justice. Obviously there is a need to deal with security threats in a forceful way; however, the approach should not result in compromising the administration of justice, since the rule of law contributes to security in a major way.

In Afghanistan, security sector reform (SSR) also covers the reform of police and justice. While SSR and rule of law reform are conceptually interrelated, the dominance of security considerations tends to eclipse the objectives and focus of the rule of law.

Faced with an upsurge of insurgency activity, Afghanistan can hardly achieve peace merely by fighting and killing the insurgents. Neither are development projects alone likely to win the hearts and minds of the people as long as threats remain from militia commanders, drug traffickers, corrupt provincial and district administrators, and government incompetence. This also applies to the operation of coalition forces and ISAF in fighting terrorism and insurgency. Focusing on force protection at the expense of creating durable security; picking and choosing discredited allies in fighting terrorism; indiscriminate and unwarranted searches of peaceful villages without consideration for local culture; or detaining inhabitants who have no known connection with hostile armed groups are all actions often associated with international military forces that have provoked public resentment and indignant protest and have hindered stabilization. There is a need to adopt a status of forces agreement with the United States and NATO members who have deployed military troops in Afghanistan. Afghanistan and the United States signed a joint declaration of strategic partnership in May 2005, providing US forces "freedom of action," but that does not include an agreement reaffirming Afghan sovereignty and its national security interests with regard to relations with its neighbours and other states in the region.

Efforts to defeat the insurgents, to build peace, and to foster development should be sought through a rule of law system that guarantees human security. This means that security operations undertaken by international forces, the Afghan army and/or the police should be seen as a subset of the rule of law and not the other way around. As an American judge, Learned Hand, stated more than sixty years ago, "liberty lies in the heart of men and women ... when it dies there, no constitution, no law, no court can save it; no constitution, no law, no court can even do much to help it" (quoted in Chesterman 2005, 27). So security and peace are achieved through winning the hearts of the people, not through military operations.

Thus, insecurity in Afghanistan is also a question of access to health and education, to legal and political rights, and to social opportunities. The real security challenge is to provide services and jobs, and to protect human rights—especially in rural areas. Freedom from "fear" and freedom from "want" lead to human security and they require more than state security forces.

As Afghanistan takes steps toward building a stable, lawful, and democratic state, it faces the legacy of gross human rights violations committed during more than two decades of war and violence, casting a dark shadow over the peaceful and just coexistence of the people. National reconciliation is essential and should be geared not merely toward securing the state but toward the development of a stable political environment conducive to Afghans' coming to terms with their troubled past. Such an environment is unlikely to emerge as long as factional alignments from the civil war shape the political landscape of Afghanistan and a culture of violence, intolerance, and impunity survives. Human security requires a comprehensive strategy that ensures the establishment of good governance, the rule of law, the promise of development, and the protection of human rights. The basic institutions of civil society must be established and empowered to achieve lasting change.

A first step toward enduring human security is the Action Plan on Peace, Justice, and Reconciliation. Agreed to in the Afghanistan Compact, the Afghan government must implement the action plan by the end of 2008. The plan envisions the promotion of peace, reconciliation, justice, and the rule of law in Afghanistan, and the establishment of a culture of accountability and respect for human rights (Afghanistan 2005). The action plan is seen as a means of rebuilding trust among those whose lives were shattered by war, reinforcing a shared sense of citizenship and a culture of tolerance. A recent resolution by the Afghan parliament to reprieve warlords and others accused of war crimes—which could technically include the Taliban leader Mullah Omar and warlord Gulbuddin Hekmatyar—has been strongly opposed by the United Nations, human rights organizations, and many Afghans (Walsh 2007). The amnesty, which the Afghan lower house approved in February 2007, could hinder the national reconciliation process.

Justice reform efforts suffer from extremely inadequate human resources and infrastructural capacity. The court structure is outdated, many judicial personnel are unqualified, and corruption is deep-rooted. The period of violence in the country has destroyed the institutional integrity of the justice system and left a patchwork of contradictory and overlapping laws.

Although some progress has been made, particularly in law reform, no coherent and integrated strategy has been agreed upon for rebuilding the system. A functioning justice sector is vital to human security.

The rule of law that relates to counter-narcotics policies cannot be secured only through building the security forces; it also requires the development of the judiciary, the legal profession, civil society, and the expansion of free access to justice. Only balanced progress in security, good governance, justice, reconstruction, development, and the rule of law can provide human security in Afghanistan.

Conclusion

More than six years after the fall of the Taliban, Afghanistan faces major challenges in building state institutions. The Bonn process has laid the foundation for a modern state. The road map for consolidating the transition to democracy is the Afghanistan Compact. However, two years after its adoption, the country has yet to move from "compact to impact" (JCMB 2006). The country's transformation to an effective representative democracy with a prosperous private-sector-led market economy is still in an early stage.

In some areas the slow pace of development and reform is contributing to popular disaffection, and the ineffective implementation of the counter-narcotics strategy in turn hampers the fight against insecurity and insurgency. In such an environment, the underlying political and economic assumptions made about the pace of development may appear to be overoptimistic (2006). Further, as a recent report by the International Crisis Group argues, while "the growing insurgency is attracting increasing attention, long-term efforts to build the solid governmental institutions a stable Afghanistan requires are faltering" (2007).

Building a stable and effective modern state in Afghanistan requires a long-term commitment by the international community to address both short- and long-term needs. The strategy should aim to end the insurgency and to create effective governance systems capable of establishing the rule of law, providing human security and public services, and fostering economic development that can subvert the illicit drug trade with legal economic activities.

Long-term stability in Afghanistan requires that efforts be directed toward changing the divisive situation rather than adopting solutions solely to accommodate the existing fragmentation. Accommodation of traditional power structures and different ethnic groups has to be sought through democratic participation, political and economic integration, and the development of a civil society and private sector that mitigate the negative impacts of competing group interests.

Further, the legacy of a turbulent history and the residual influence of war-instigated socio-political transformation continue to affect the process. Neither adopting traditional structures as substitutes for modern state institutions nor an excessive decentralization of power are suitable responses to the current challenges. The state building process needs to reconcile these realities with the requirements of a stable state in Afghanistan. Removal of existing perceptional and managerial distance between Kabul and the regions is essential for the defragmentation of governance. The key to this is bringing a balance between creating a strong and effective central government and ensuring a level of decentralization to secure equal distribution of resources and participation.

Notes

1 For example: Pashtuns and Baluchs straddle the border with Pakistan; Persian speaking Afghans with Iran; Uzbeks, Tajiks, and Turkmens with Tajikistan, Uzbekistan, and Turkmenistan, respectively.

2 In 1968 I was personally involved, as a government official, in brokering a settlement between two feuding tribes (*Jaji* and *Mangal*) in Paktia Province using the influence of tribal *jirgas* and not the formal legal process of provincial judicial institutions. The long-standing dispute was over logging rights at the Migtoun Mountain shared by the two tribes.

3 An estimated 1.3 to 1.5 million Afghans, mostly civilians, were killed during the war and over half a million were disabled. See Ali Ahmad Jalali and Lester Grau, *The Other Side of the Mountain: Mujahideen Tactics in the Soviet–Afghan War* (Quantico, VA: US Marine Corps, 1998). Also see Asiaweek.com, November 28, 2002.

4 The *Loya Jirga* (Grand Council) is a traditional Afghan institution called into being by the state to make or endorse decisions of major national concern. It is an extrapolation from the model of the tribal and local Jirga or council that allows consensual decision making on community matters.

5 The Federally Administered Tribal Areas (FATA) stretches for 1,200 kilometers between Afghanistan and the settled areas of Pakistan's Northwest Frontier Province. The area is divided into seven Tribal Agencies: Bajaur, Mohmand, Khyber, Orakzai, Kurram, North Waziristan and South Waziristan Although part of Pakistan, the FATA functions as a semi-autonomous area where the state has a minimum presence. The area is administered through the office of the Political Agent (PA) who has both administrative and judicial authority supported by a locally recruited militia force (Khasadars). The tribes are subject to a British enacted law in 1901 known as the Frontier Crimes Regulations (FCR). The inhabitants of this underdeveloped and largely rural area do not enjoy political and legal rights as full Pakistani citizens.

6 In the 1870s Amir Sher Ali Khan recreated the Afghan army that disintegrated during the second Anglo-Afghan War (1878–80). In the 1880s Amir Abdur Rahman had to reestablish the army to unify the fragmented country. The army was remodeled under King Amanullah following the third Anglo-Afghan War (1919), but it met a fatal blow during the civil war of 1929. A new military establishment was created by

Nadeshah after his accession in 1929. The Soviet-sponsored reorganization and modernization of the Afghan army began in the 1960s and continued throughout the rule of the Moscow-backed communist rule. It totally disintegrated during the civil war of 1992–2001.
7 The corps are headquartered in Kabul, Kandahar, Herat, Mazar-i Sharif, and Gardez.
8 Meeting 70% of the year's revenue target by December 2006, Kabul collected $367 million of a targeted $532 million. Meeting the annual revenue target will raise the revenue to 6% of GDP and 57% of the recurrent budget.

References

Adamac, Ludwig. 1974. *Afghanistan's Foreign Affairs to Mid-Twentieth Century.* Tucson: University of Arizona Press.

Afghanistan National Development Strategy. 2006. Available on http://www.ands.gov.af/ands.

Ames, Paul. 2007. "Challenges Mount in Afghanistan." Associated Press, 4 September.

Asiaweek.com, November 28, 2002.

Associated Press. 2007. *International Herald Tribune.* 30 January.

BBC News. 2007. "UK's Afghan Gains May Be Lost." 28 September.

Chesterman, Simon.2005. "State Building and Human Development." Human Development Report 2005. Human Development Report Office, UNDP.

Cooper, Helene and David Cloud. 2007. "Bush to Seek More Aid for Afghanistan as Taliban Regroups." *New York Times.* January 26.

Gellner, Ernest. 1983. *Nations and Nationalism.* Ithaca, NY: Cornell University Press.

Hobsbawm, E.J. 1991. *Nations and Nationalism since 1780.* Cambridge: Cambridge University Press.

Heathcote, T.A. 1980. *The Afghan Wars.* London: Osprey.

Hensman, Edward. 1881. *The Second Afghan War.* London.

Inspectors General of the United States Department of State and Department of Defense. 2006. "Interagency Assessment of Afghanistan Police Training and Readiness." November. http://oig.state.gov/documents/organization/76103.pdf.

International Crisis Group (ICG). 2006. "Countering Afghanistan's Insurgency: No Quick Fixes." *Asia Report* 123. 2 November.

———. "Afghanistan's Endangered Compact." *Asia Briefing* 69. Kabul/Brussels. 29 January.

Islamic Republic of Afghanistan. 2005. "Action Plan of the Government of the Islamic Republic of Afghanistan on Peace, Reconciliation and Justice in Afghanistan." June.

———. 2006. Interim Afghanistan National Development Strategy. Kabul: Islamic Republic of Afghanistan. http://www.ands.gov.af/admin/ands_docs/upload/UploadFolder/I-ANDS%20Volume%20One%20_%20Final%20English.pdf.

Jalali, Ali A. 2002. "Rebuilding Afghanistan's National Army." *Parameters* (Autumn).

Jalali, Ali Ahmad and Lester Grau. 1998. *The Other Side of the Mountain: Mujahideen Tactics in the Soviet–Afghan War.* Quantico, VA: US Marine Corps Studies and Analysis Division.

James, Bill and Robert Springborg. 1990. *Politics in the Middle East.* New York: HarperCollins.

Joint Coordination and Monitoring Board (JCMB). 2006. "Implementation of the Afghanistan Compact." Bi-Annual Joint Coordination and Monitoring Board (JCMB) Report. November. http://www.a-acc.org/docs/JCMBBi-Annual ReportNov2006English.pdf.

Khodorov, I. 1925. *Natsional'noe Razmezhevanie Srednei Azii.* Novyi Vostok, No. 6/9, 68f. In *Central Asia: 130 Years of Russian Dominance, A Historical Overview*, 3rd ed., Edward Allworth, 256–57. 1994. Durham and London: Duke University Press.

Lester, Sarah and Hamish Nixon. 2006. "Provincial Governance Structure in Afghanistan: From Confusion to Vision." Afghanistan Research and Evaluation Unit (AREU). May.

Molesworth, Lt. Gen. George Noble. 1962. *Afghanistan 1919: An Account of Operations in the Third Afghan War.* London, Bombay: Asia Publishing House.

Nixon, Hamish. 2007. *International Assistance and Governance in Afghanistan.* Heinrich Boell Foundation Publication Series on Promoting Democracy Under Conditions of State Fragility, Volume 2. Berlin: June.

Shafe, Aziz Ahmad and Jean MacKenzie. 2008. Helmand and Kabul: Institute for War & Peace Reporting, ARR No. 279, 17 January.

Steele, Rachel Ray and Alexander Thier. 2007. *Hearts and Minds: Afghan Opinion on the Taliban, the Government and the International Forces.* United States Institute of Peace Briefing, August 16. http://www.usip.org/pubs/usipeace_briefings/2007/0816_afghan_opinion.html.

United Nations Assistance Mission in Afghanistan (UNAMA). 2001. "Agreement on Provisional Arrangements in Afghanistan Pending the Re-establishment of Permanent Government Institutions," Article 1. Bonn: UNAMA. December 5. http://www.unama-afg.org/docs/_nonUN%20Docs/_Internation-Conferences&Forums/Bonn-Talks/bonn.htm.

United States Army and United States Marine Corps. 2006. "Counterinsurgency." FM3-24, December. http//www.fas.org/irp/doddir/army/fm3-24.pdf.

Walsh, Declan. 2007a. "Afghanistan Approves Amnesty for Warlords." *Guardian Unlimited.* 1 February. http://www.guardian.co.uk/afghanistan/story/0,,2003941,00.html.

———. 2007b. "Afghan Amnesty Vote Angers UN," *Guardian Unlimited.* 2 February. http://www.guardian.co.uk/afghanistan/story/0,,2004391,00.html.

Wood, Sara. 2007. "Afghanistan Deployment Extended for 10th Mountain Division." American Forces Press Service. Army News Service Press Release. 25 January.

World Public Opinion. 2006. "Afghan Public Opinion Amidst Rising Violence." World Public Opinion Poll, 2–3. Fielded by D3 Systems and Afghan Center for Social and Opinion Research in Kabul. 14 December.

3

Jonathan Goodhand

Poppy, Politics, and State Building

Opium cultivation, heroin production is more dangerous than the invasion and the attack of the Soviets in our country, it is more dangerous than the factional fighting in Afghanistan, it is more dangerous than terrorism.... Just as some people fought a holy war against the Soviets, so we will wage jihad against poppies.

—Afghanistan president Karzai
(cited in Transnational Institute 2005, 7)

Following the fall of the Taliban regime, Afghan farmers began to replant their fields with poppy after the opium ban of 2000. The US focus on the war on terror meant that state building and counter-narcotics initially took a back seat. This prioritization has changed in the years between the Bonn Agreement in 2001 and the Afghan Compact of 2006. First, an international consensus has emerged on the need to prioritize state building in order to build long-term security in Afghanistan. Second, the growth of the opium economy, with record production levels recorded in 2007, has prompted growing concerns that the drug industry represents one of the primary threats to state consolidation. Although the pathways through which the opium economy induces state crisis/collapse are rarely defined precisely, it is assumed to do so by providing the tax base for insecurity and terrorism, distorting and corrupting political accountability, and impeding the emergence of a sustainable, licit (and taxable) economy. In this chapter I take a critical look at these three assumptions. After providing a short overview of the contemporary features of the drug economy and counter-narcotics efforts, I examine in turn the links between drugs and (a) security, (b) political consolidation and (c) development processes. I argue that the linkages between drugs and state building/state collapse are complex, multidimensional, and context specific—something that is rarely reflected in the discourse surrounding the "war on drugs." Second, counter-narcotics policies that are guided by questionable assumptions (and backed up with patchy data) are likely to promote, rather than counter, the dynamics they purport to address. Third, if peace building is the overriding objective, then other policy goals, including counter-narcotics, need to be made coherent with this.

Overview of the Drug Economy and Counter-Narcotics Efforts

Contemporary Dimensions of the Drug Economy

The quantity and distribution of poppy cultivation The global retail market for illicit drugs is estimated at $320 billion, a figure that is larger than the individual GDPs of nearly 90% of countries in the world (United Nations Office on Drugs and Crime (UNODC), cited in MacDonald 2007). Afghanistan's share in world supply increased from 42% in 1990 to 87% in 2005 (Martin and Symansky 2006, 26). The evolution of the drug economy during the war years has been dealt with elsewhere (Rubin 2000; Goodhand 2004; 2005), and this chapter focuses on the current situation. But Afghanistan's emergence as the global leader in opium production was based upon a "triple comparative advantage" of favourable physical, political, and economic conditions: a cultivation environment that produces opium poppies with a high morphine content; chronic insecurity and institutional weakness that have meant inadequate or non-existent forms of regulation; and poor infrastructure and rural poverty that prevent the development of alternative licit livelihoods. Over the years, Afghans have developed the know-how, expertise, and market connections to build upon these comparative advantages in order to survive, accumulate, or wage war.[1]

Opium cultivation rose by 59% between 2005 and 2006, reaching an all-time high of 165,000 hectares, producing 6,100 tons of opium (UNODC 2006). However, national figures mask considerable fluctuations in cultivation over time and diversity among provinces (Mansfield 2006, 49).[2] Currently, cultivation is concentrated in the south with the four southern provinces of Helmand, Uruzgan, Daikudi, and Zabul accounting for 92% of national production. According to UNODC (2007) figures, opium cultivation rose to 193,000 ha in 2007 and national production increased to 8,200 tons.

Clearly, poppy cultivation is deeply embedded in the rural economy and has significant macro- and micro-level economic impacts, which I expand on below. However, one should not exaggerate its pervasiveness and significance. Only 3% of Afghanistan's agricultural land is given over to poppy cultivation, while nearly half of the 364 districts in Afghanistan still report no opium poppy cultivation.[3]

The drug industry: actors, markets and dynamics At both the upstream and downstream ends of the value chain—Afghan farmers and drug consumers in the developed world—markets are characterized by numerous actors who are "price takers" (i.e., they do not set the price). But the number of actors at the intermediate stages is much smaller, and this is where price setting and price manipulation takes place (Byrd and Jonglez 2006, 136). This corresponds with other (licit and illicit) commodity markets in Afghanistan, in which there are low barriers to entry at the bottom but few actors and stronger forms of regulation further up the chain (Patterson 2006; Lister and Pain 2004).

Opium and its products dramatically increase in price along the value chain. The vast bulk of value added in the drug industry is generated outside Afghanistan (Byrd and Jonglez 2006, 130).[4] In 2005–2006, the total export value of opiates produced in Afghanistan equalled about 38% of non-drug GDP, down from 47% in the previous year due to growth of the non-drug economy. In 2006 the export value of drugs was $3.1 billion, compared to $2.7 billion in 2005. UNODC (2006) estimates that 76% of the income from narcotics goes to traffickers and heroin refiners (most of which is accrued to a limited number of bulk buyers and large-scale specialist traders), and 24% goes to farmers. In order to reduce risks, a significant part of revenue is spent on payments to "security providers" and government officials.

Farm gate prices of opium were low in the 1990s, but the Taliban edict banning opium production in 2000 led to a ten-fold increase. High prices of $300 per kilogram or above were maintained in 2002–2003 then declined progressively and stabilized around $150 per kilogram. This is still three times the levels of the 1990s, when cultivation was to all intents and purposes a licit activity. Since 2002, criminalization and law enforcement efforts have increased the "risk premium" charged by opium traders, which is reflected in higher prices. It is also important to note that there is substantial price volatility and considerable seasonal and spatial price variations. For example, as of 2006 the highest prices were in the eastern zones where eradication has been the most vigorously pursued. Moreover, the proximity of Herat, Farah, and Nimroz to the Iranian border explains high prices in these areas (Byrd and Jonglez 2006).

There is also significant stockpiling of opium stocks, which in 2006 reportedly amounted to six hundred tons, the equivalent of more than six months of exports, with a market value of $260 million (Martin and Symansky 2006, 29–30). A combination of inventory adjustments in Afghanistan and changes in purity downstream can be employed to help smooth price fluctuations. Although there is price volatility at the upstream end of the value chain, prices appear to be much more stable at the downstream end (Byrd and Jonglez 2006, 132).[5]

Although frequently described as a vertically integrated value chain, in practice the opium economy might better be conceptualized as a number of inter-connected but constantly mutating networks. There is no evidence to indicate the emergence of a hierarchically controlled, cartelized drug economy, although a recent UNODC/World Bank study reports growing market integration, with Helmand and Kandahar becoming centres of gravity that influence prices in other markets (Byrd and Jonglez 2006). On the other hand, a decreased integration between the Nangahar and Helmand/ Kandahar markets has been reported, influenced perhaps by the focus of counter-narcotics efforts on the former. With the demise (at least temporarily) of Nangahar as a major production centre, Helmand has emerged as a hub, drawing on its multiple "comparative advantages," which include proximity to the Pakistani border, easy access to Iran, lack of security, and limited central government control (2006). A further sign of the maturity of the industry is the increased amount of opium refined into morphine and heroin within Afghanistan[6] and the shift in quality and purity of heroin.[7] UNODC now estimates that 90% of the opium is processed in Afghanistan.

The principal trafficking routes are Iran (53%) and Pakistan (32%), followed by Tajikistan (15%) (UNODC 2006).[8] The drug industry is extremely flexible and responsive to changes in prices and control regimes. For example, Jalali, Oakley, and Hunter (2006, 4) report that between 2004 and 2005 there was a 20% shift in trafficking from the southern border with Pakistan to the western border with Iran, largely in response to the US troop presence in the south. Finally, as well as being an exporter of drugs, Afghanistan is experiencing a growing drug addiction problem. This has come, in large measure, with refugees returning from Pakistan and Iran, and there are reported to be more than 60,000 drug users in Kabul alone (MacDonald 2007, 22).[9]

Overview of Counter-narcotics Policies and Programs

In October 2002, the Afghan government established the Counter Narcotics Directorate (CND), which reported to the National Security Council. The CND was responsible for counter-narcotics (CN) strategy development and coordination. It was supported by the UK government, which was the lead nation for counter narcotics, one of five pillars in the security sector reform (SSR) strategy.[10]

Initial CN policies and programs, however, were either slow to get off the ground or were ill-conceived. For example a buyout scheme in 2002, which provided compensation of $350 per *jerib*[11] of poppy destroyed, in the end cost over $100,000 per hectare.[12] As well as being excessively expensive and not very effective, it stirred resentment in the south, where most farmers were not paid and the bulk of UK expenses were unaccounted for. At President Karzai's suggestion, a governor-led strategy was subsequently adopted, which involved working with local governors to lead eradication efforts. But this too was problematic because many of the governors were themselves involved with the drug trade.

The combination of early CN failures, the rapid growth of opium cultivation, and growing concerns about the related problems of terrorism and corruption have prompted two broad shifts in counter-narcotics strategy. First, there has been a widening of the CN agenda, a stronger focus on institution building, and more explicit links made with other sectors. Second, reflecting a trend in other pillars of SSR (such as policing), impatience with the rate of progress and perceived limitations of the lead nation concept have led the US to take on a more active role as funder and implementer of CN programs.

In 2003, the government adopted a multi-year CN strategy that aimed at reducing opium cultivation by 75% in five years and complete elimination within ten years. A range of key institutions were established, including the Counter-Narcotics Police of Afghanistan (CPNA) in the Ministry of Interior, which comprises investigation, intelligence, and interdiction sections. The Central Poppy Eradication Force (CPEF; subsequently renamed the Afghan Eradication Force) was established in May 2004, and in November 2004 the position of the Deputy Minister for Counter Narcotics was created within the Ministry of Interior to oversee and coordinate CN enforcement activities.[13] In December of that year, the Ministry of Counter Narcotics was established to coordinate and oversee counter-narcotics policies. In addition, a Counter Narcotics Trust Fund was created in October 2005 to coordinate financing and improve resource allocation.[14] Finally, steps have been taken to strengthen the CN regulatory framework. A new CN law was approved by the government that establishes penalties for corruption and bribery associated with drug trafficking; includes procedures for investigating and prosecuting major drug trafficking offences; establishes the Ministry of Counter Narcotics as the leading body to monitor, evaluate and coordinate all CN activities; and provides for the creation of new tribunals for drug traffickers and drug regulation commissions (Martin and Symansky 2006, 34–35). A Criminal Justice Task Force was also established and convicted 390 traffickers between May 2005 and 2007, while an $8 million CN Justice Centre will provide a one-stop shop for drug cases.

In parallel (and sometimes at odds) with this increased emphasis on institution building and a multi-pronged approach has been a dramatic expansion of the US involvement in CN. This has taken place at least partly in response to growing US concerns about the UK approach.[15] In 2004 the Drugs Enforcement Administration (DEA) and Department of Defence (DoD) announced the Kabul Counter Narcotics Implementation Plan. In 2005 alone, the US Congress earmarked $780 million for CN in Afghanistan. The DEA has deployed Foreign Advisory and Support Teams (FAST) to the country and has permanently stationed special agents and intelligence analysts to assist Afghan CN capacity in interdiction efforts. This has been part of the US-led Operation Containment, which involves bilateral investigations to dismantle drug trafficking and money-laundering organizations.

There has been an ongoing tension between what has been characterized as the UK position on CN, which emphasizes a long-term, multipronged approach, and the US position, which focuses on quick results in the eradication and interdiction spheres. Driven by concerns about the links between drugs and terrorism, the US has advocated "shock therapy," and immediately after George W. Bush's re-election, something tantamount to a Plan Afghanistan was announced. Then, in March 2007, the White House named Thomas Schweich as coordinator for CN and justice reform in Afghanistan.[16] Furthermore, the US Congress fenced off part of the 2007 aid disbursement pending certification by President Bush that Afghanistan was co-operating with US counter-narcotics policies. There has been growing US pressure for ground-based and subsequently aerial spraying.[17]

Counter-narcotics therefore rapidly moved up the policy agenda between 2002 and 2006, and this is reflected in its prominence in the Afghan Compact and the Interim Afghan National Development Strategy (I-ANDS). In London the eight pillars of the new CN strategy were launched: building CN institutions; public awareness; alternative livelihoods; eradication; law enforcement; criminal justice; international and regional co-operation; demand reduction and treatment of addicts.[18] And the I-ANDS emphasizes pro-poor CN policy that focuses initially on interdiction, law enforcement, institution building, and developing licit livelihoods while investing in infrastructure, protection of rights, and an enabling framework for private sector growth (Rubin and Hamidzada 2007, 21).

Drugs and the Political Economy of State Building

The opium economy was both a symptom and driver of the political economy of war, which evolved in the 1980s and 1990s and persists (indeed was re-invigorated) in the post-Taliban period. An examination of the political economy of drugs may provide an insight into the "real politics" of state building by illuminating underlying power structures and relationships, which mark the edges of, and lacunae in, state capabilities. A straightforward causal relationship between the drug economy and state building is commonly assumed; that is, more state building means fewer drugs and vice versa. Afghan actors including President Karzai and former finance minister Ashraf Ghani have skilfully played the "narco-terrorism" and "narco-state" card in the knowledge that drugs and terrorism are the keys to maintaining western funding and engagement in Afghanistan.

The chief policy implication of such a position is that counter-narcotics automatically represents a direct investment in state building. An alternative analysis is that the drug economy is a symptom of "distorted" governance and development, and as such is best addressed indirectly by targeting deep structural factors—for example through building the outreach and capacity of the state, strengthening the rule of law, and supporting anti-poverty programs. These two approaches—one emphasizing short-term eradication, and the other long-term structural solutions—represent two opposite ends of a policy continuum. Between these two extremes one can find debates related to questions of balancing and sequencing between eradication, law enforcement, and development measures (Koehler and Zurcher 2007; Mansfield and Pain 2006).

A more radical proposition given today's international drug control regime is to harness the institutional innovations and economic impacts associated with the drug industry in order to promote a gradual, though certainly conflictual transition from war to peace.[19] This represents a minority position, and one has to turn to historical experience, rather than current liberal orthodoxies (Paris 2004), to appreciate the rationale for this position. Thomas Gallant (1999), in a study of brigandage and piracy from a world historical perspective, makes a convincing case for the role played by illegal networks of armed predators in facilitating the spread and global triumph of capitalism. Bandits were deeply insinuated in the process of state formation and state consolidation. They facilitated capitalist penetration of the countryside by increasing monetization, encouraging marketization, and by providing a venue for upward economic mobility. Through a process of either co-opting or crushing rural outlaws in frontier regions, states experienced a "border effect" that strengthened their capacities. Put simply, "bandits helped make states and states made bandits" (Gallant 1999, 25).

Contemporary state builders may adopt similar tactics. For instance, the Burmese drug lord Khun Sa played a catalytic role in state formation by forcing Rangoon to impose control over its frontiers (McCoy 1999, 158).[20] Illegality and the state have been constant companions, and revenue from, and the control of, illicit flows may actually strengthen the state.

The above analysis should induce a level of skepticism toward the dominant discourse that assumes that the opium economy is akin to a "disease" that infects and corrodes governance relations and turns producer countries into "narco states" that threaten Western interests and security.

These different positions are explored in the next section, which examines critically the three propositions that drugs (a) fuel the insurgency and other forms of violence, (b) undermine the legitimacy and capacity of the state by corrupting government officials, and (c) prevent the emergence of a licit economy that will provide the basis for sustainable development in Afghanistan.

Drugs, Violence and the Insurgency

The US-led coalition's initial priority in Afghanistan was counterterrorism, and this resulted in several sins of omission and commission immediately following the fall of the Taliban—including the failure to extend ISAF's presence beyond Kabul, US financial support for regional strongmen, and turning a blind eye to poppy cultivation. As already noted, the opium economy flourished in the security vacuum that followed the fall of the Taliban.[21]

In the period following the fall of the Taliban regime, the combat economy has changed in response to external intervention, the emergence of a nascent state, and a new regulatory regime. In earlier phases of the conflict opium production was largely viewed, at least in the domestic context, as a licit activity.[22] The criminalization of poppy has meant that those involved have to look for protection beyond the state—and there is no shortage in Afghanistan of non-state "specialists in violence." In contexts where trust is fragile or completely breaks down, violence is a highly valued resource that is utilized to ensure contract compliance.

The specific functions of violence within the combat economy vary from one area to another. Broadly in the south and east, the combat economy sustains an anti-state insurgency, which has become increasingly intense and geographically widespread. In contrast, in the northern areas, the economy of violence revolves around controlling trade and reaching an accommodation with (rather than overthrowing or resisting) the state. In both cases different actors and forms of violence are involved and the role of drugs is different.

In the south, the drug economy appears to be fuelling (though not driving) a violent insurgency. Reports suggest growing links between insurgents, drug traffickers, local strongmen and tribal groups, all of whom have in interest in either overthrowing the state or keeping it at bay.[23] The long-standing links between the Taliban and the transport and drug mafias on the Afghan–Pakistan border have been well documented (cf. Rubin 2000; Goodhand 2004).[24] The Taliban's opium edict of 2001 severely strained this relationship, and the group's apparent collapse in 2001–2002 may partly be attributed to their deep unpopularity (especially in the tribal areas) as a result of the ban. But it is not surprising that these links were re-established once the Taliban had regrouped across the border following the coalition-led intervention. Just as the Taliban taxed the opium trade in the 1990s, insurgent groups are reportedly imposing transit and protection fees in the range of 15 to 18% on both drugs and precursor chemicals (Jalali et al. 2006, 2).[25] There are reports of a shift from opportunistic taxation toward a growing nexus in the south between the insurgency and the drug trade.[26] Opium has become an index of insecurity. Aid workers have increasingly noted that security is worse in places where people are growing poppies (Ramachandran 2003).[27] There has been a 121% increase in poppy cultivation in the southern region, and Helmand accounted for 42% (69,324 ha) of poppy cultivation in Afghanistan in 2006. It is reported that AGE (Anti-government elements) actively encourage and even threaten farmers to cultivate opium poppy (UNODC 2006, 4).[28] Many argue that poppy provides the tax base for the insurgency, but it appears likely that external resource flows are of a greater magnitude (see Giustozzi 2007b), though drugs may constitute a significant component of the Taliban's operating funds, enabling them to pay their fighters far more than government forces.[29] However, perhaps more important than its economic role is the opportunity the opium economy provides to the Taliban to generate political capital. Eradication campaigns in the south have created a situation whereby the Taliban can act as the protectors of the Afghan peasantry. Therefore the Taliban's apparent demise and then their re-insertion into Afghan society are linked to their relationship with drugs—but this is primarily a story of politics rather than economics.

In the north, conflict dynamics and the relationship with drugs are quite different. After the fall of the Taliban, local strongmen, with a *jihadi* background, consolidated their spheres of influence in the countryside and were able to maintain their autonomy by controlling or taxing the drug economy. Poppy provided them with a powerful fallback position and bargaining tool in relation to the emergent state and international actors. What followed has been described as a process of "warlord democratization" (Rubin 2006) in which, through a combination of inducements and coercion, there has been a selective incorporation of "specialists in violence" into the state structures. Shaw (2006, 196) argues that DDR programs have had a two-tier effect, first by inducing senior commanders to enter formal political processes and then by pushing lower-level commanders and their militias—who had few other "career" options—into a closer relationship with opium trafficking or the selling of protection.

In many parts of the north, a political equilibrium emerged, due in part to the stabilizing role of international forces, since warlords now have less to fear from an attack by rivals, but also because of the drug trade. Essentially this equilibrium is related to the emergence of embryonic mafia-type protection rackets, which have reached an accommodation with the state in return for a state policy of limited interference. The stability of this equilibrium varies from area to area,[30] but there is no automatic and straightforward relationship between the drug trade and violence. Violence is likely to be instrumental and limited, and is most frequently a consequence of market dysfunction and disorganization. Because it is bad for business, the default setting may be violence avoidance.

The links between drugs and more localized forms of conflict are complex and context specific. In a study of Laghman and Nangahar provinces, Koehler and Zuercher (2007) found that drugs may have indirect effects on violent conflict—for example by increasing the value of land, thus raising the stakes in the competition for scarce resources. And land conflicts themselves have a high propensity toward escalation of violence in the absence of effective conflict-processing mechanisms (ibid, 66). On the other hand, the authors found that the resources generated through poppy cultivation may have a "conflict dampening" role, and 79% of respondents in the study thought that money was the most important factor in addressing disputes (followed by patronage and physical force).

Therefore there is no privileged relationship between drug traffickers and the Taliban; all armed groups, of whatever ideological hue, are involved. Violence runs like a thread through the drug trade, but the above analysis questions the assumption that poppy inherently creates conflict. As explored below, the violence associated with the drug industry is at least partly linked to an increasingly militarized counter-narcotics control regime.

Counter-narcotics policies and conflict dynamics Initially, coalition forces adopted a "laissez-faire" policy toward drugs, born out of the strong tension between counter-insurgency and counter-narcotics objectives. Essentially geopolitical interests conflicted with the war on drugs (Labrousse 2005). Counter-insurgency efforts require good local allies, and intelligence and local warlords are unlikely to provide either support or intelligence to those who are destroying their businesses (Felbab-Brown 2005). Even in 2004, following a sharp increase in drug production, then US ambassador to Afghanistan Zalmay Khalizad stated in the run up to the parliamentary elections that "politics" dictated that it was necessary not to be "too harsh" on the question of drug eradication (cited in Labrousse 2005, 188).[31]

This approach changed as Western states began to draw a more direct connection between drugs and their own geopolitical and domestic interests. There has been a growing convergence between the war on drugs and the war on terror, to the extent that the former is seen as a proxy for the latter. The drug issue, like aid, has become increasingly securitized. It is now labelled as a security problem, which requires an urgent (and frequently militarized) response, beyond the purview of "normal" political processes. For example, paramilitary forces, trained by international security teams, have been created to work at the "sharp end" of eradication and interdiction operations. Eradication comes under the remit of the seven-hundred-strong Afghan Eradication Force (AEF), with the US private security company DynCorps contracted to provide the training and oversee implementation in the provinces, working with Poppy Elimination Programme (PEP) teams. While ISAF forces are not directly involved, PEP advisors are located within Provincial Reconstruction Teams (PRTs), and they also provide intelligence and logistical support. In many parts of the country, eradication efforts have met with violent resistance.[32] In the longer term, eradication may reinforce a new geography of (in)security in the provinces, in which the remote borderland regions become the main sources of cultivation and violent resistance to the state.

The UK-led Operation Headstrong in 2003 and 2004 focused on interdiction efforts by creating the Afghan Special Narcotics Force (ASNF), a British special forces–trained paramilitary group that operates within the Counter Narcotics Police of Afghanistan (CNPA). The ASNF conducts interdiction operations together with National Interdiction Units (NIU) and with the logistic support of Combined Forces Command-Afghanistan (CFC-A).[33] This has been paralleled by the US's DEA Operation Containment, which aims to identify, target, investigate, disrupt, and dismantle international heroin trafficking organizations in Central Asia (Zetland 2003).

ISAF's operating plan of 2005 explicitly stated that eradication of opium cultivation and processing facilities was not part of its mandate, but that it was willing and able to play a support role to the Afghan government. However Jalali et al. (2006) argue that ISAF forces should get involved in targeting labs, stockpiles, and trafficking routes, and there appears to be growing pressure from the government in this direction.[34]

Therefore at the "hard end" of the counter-narcotics-policy spectrum, there is a complex assemblage of military and paramilitary organizations, which have been created as a result of perceived deficiencies in the state. This parallels responses in other spheres, such as policing, in which security functions have been contracted out to tribal militias in the eastern and southern borderlands. "Inlaws" and "outlaws" are drawn from the same pool of actors—and often the same specialists in violence are simultaneously involved in providing protection for traffickers while selectively eradicating poppy. The distinction between militia and police, protection racket and state is therefore less clear than commonly assumed.[35]

In conclusion, while the relationship between violence and the drug economy cannot be denied, the linkage is far more complex, two-directional, and context specific than is recognized in current policy debates. Furthermore, counter-narcotics (and counter-terrorism) interventions themselves have contributed to the escalation of violence surrounding the drug industry—by prompting violent resistance, stimulating the market for protection, and boosting the profits of insurgents.

Drugs and the Emergence of Political Authority

Political Transition and the Shadow State The second proposition that I wish to explore is that the drug economy undermines state building—that poppy cultivation and trafficking expanded because of state breakdown, and their persistence impedes the re-emergence of a stable, legitimate state.[36] In parallel with the "official" political transition with its benchmarks of the emergency *loya jirga*, the constitutional loya jirga, and elections, there has been an "unofficial" transition in which power has coalesced around factions and groups who established a strategic edge in the war years and continue to have access to the means of protection and predation. Elections had the effect of entrenching power structures in the provinces, and real power in Afghanistan is closely linked to the capacity to generate money and patronage through the drug economy.[37]

This situation is partly due to the various sins of omission and commission of international actors mentioned earlier, which have accentuated the weakness of government as an autonomous actor. It is also partly of Karzai's own making; he is a product of "Peshawar politics" (Maley, this volume) with an inclination toward political brokering and deal making rather than to asserting strong leadership. He consequently tends to move problems rather than remove them (Jalali, this volume), including provincial governors and police chiefs who are known to be deeply involved in the opium economy.[38]

Because the central government is so weak and dependent on unreliable external patrons, power holders in the periphery have a level of autonomy and leverage. In the bargaining processes between central and peripheral elites, the latter calculate that it may not be safe to throw in their lot with the former, leading to the continuation of fluid political arrangements that take the form of "spot contracts" or constant "hedging" (Suhrke 2007). The nature of these brokered relationships varies from region to region, depending largely on the area's constellation of political and military actors and its potential for profitable extraction.

This dynamic is part of an age old "conversation" between centre and periphery, which can be conceptualized less as a struggle between an abstract state and sections of society like warlords, than a competition for control between different social forces (Giustozzi 2007a). States are never the totalities they claim to be, and in the Afghan case, governance arrangements involve a complex layering of new and old forms of authority (Lister 2007). There is a deep interpenetration of formal politics with informal structures of networks and factions, and as Mustaq Khan (2002) has shown in other contexts, internal political stability is not maintained through fiscal policy, but through largely off-budget and selective accommodation of factions organized along patron–client lines.

The Drug Economy and State Crisis War economies and shadow economies are frequently conceptualized as "subversive" phenomena that are located outside and in opposition to the state. Alternatively, they are seen to penetrate, corrupt, and corrode the state from within. The term "narco state" refers to states that have been captured by criminal drug networks and are no longer able to function independently of mafia interests. Koehler (2005, 77) posits two possible narco-state models. The first involves weak state institutions being captured by a powerful and well organized drug mafia, who effectively run a cartel economy. The second again involves a weak state, but this time with a highly decentralized and competitive criminal economy, which leads to a patchwork of detached local modes of governance (78). Arguably, contemporary Afghanistan more closely resembles the second model, though there are some indications that it is moving toward the first (which perhaps more closely fits the Tajik experience). Whereas during the Taliban period the state largely captured the drug business, perhaps now it is the other way around.

Poppy has several direct and indirect impacts on both the *degree* (capacity) of the state and the *kind* of state. It is widely believed to underwrite a parallel set of power structures, lubricate clientalist relations, and feed endemic corruption. The state has become the major avenue for accumulation and inter-factional competition, and the drug trade has increased the stakes and therefore the costs of appointments. For instance, an investigative report on the drug trade reported that a police chief in a poppy-growing area can expect to pay up to $100,000 in bribes for a six-month period to obtain and keep a salaried position that pays $60 per month (Baldauf 2006).[39] Highway police, until they were disbanded, were also believed to be heavily involved in facilitating and taxing smuggling; in fact drugs were reportedly smuggled using law-enforcement vehicles. In the same article, Afghan officials privately admitted that perhaps 80% of the personnel at the Ministry of Interior were benefiting from the drug trade. Furthermore, in a recent report from the Afghan Research and Evaluation Unit (AREU) on police reform, an interviewee described the Ministry of Interior as a "shop for selling jobs," confirming its reputation as one of the most corrupt ministries (Wilder 2007). It is reported that involvement in the selling of jobs and protection goes as high as the president's office, including the president's own brother Ahmad Wali Karzai (Giustozzi 2007a, 79).

Corruption is itself an expression of intense factional competition, and, arguably, early decisions in the state building process left unchecked the tendency for political struggles to follow factional fault lines. For instance, the focus on "good performers" meant that factionally dominated ministries like the Ministry of the Interior were left unreformed. Holding elections before solid institutions were in place led to "unruly" competition.[40] Democracy has not undermined patron–client relations. And the single non-transferable vote (SNTV) system created perverse incentives to vote along ethnic or factional lines rather than encourage the emergence of broader, more progressive alliances through political parties. As Giustozzi (2007a) argues, for such actors, the drug economy is a vehicle for accumulating power, and, furthermore, "political influence is never gained once and for all and has to be maintained, often at high cost and effort" (79). Political entrepreneurs higher up the chain who want to be seen as "legitimate" have a "remote control" engagement with the drug economy. They work through buffers lower down the chain.[41] A complex pyramid of protection and patronage has emerged, which provides state protection for criminal trafficking (Shaw 2006).[42] This assemblage of actors, networks, and institutions, like the opium economy itself, is extremely footloose and flexible. Patterns of capture and corruption can shift across ministries and other institutions in order to evade regulatory mechanisms (Byrd and Buddenberg 2006, 6).

The drug economy, therefore, provides a mode of accumulation that has enabled military and political entrepreneurs to "capture" parts of the state. The wholesale absorption of factional networks into the government administration at the national and local levels negatively affects the "degree" or capacity of the state—both in terms of its coercive and infrastructural power. Those who have risen to prominence during the war years and have used their strategic edge to enter the new Afghan state lack the administrative skills and know-how (unlike the technocrats) to work effectively with donors, manage projects, and deliver services to the population. Drugs, therefore have deprived the state of human resources and limited its financial resources, with the drug economy representing a huge quantity of untaxed income. Government revenue amounts to only 4% of GDP, which limits the service-delivery role of the state and increases its dependence on external resources. It is also important to note that these effects on the capacity of the state are not limited to Afghanistan, and the drug economy also has a corrupting influence on governance in neighbouring countries.

Drugs influence not only the capacity, but also the perceived legitimacy of the state. If the key challenge of post-conflict peace building is the construction of legitimate political authority, the widespread perception of corruption undermines the emergence of this authority. Corrupt officials are the face of government in the districts, and the discourse on corruption has been skilfully mobilized by the Taliban and anti-government elements.[43] A study by Integrity Watch Afghanistan, which interviewed 1,258 Afghans, found that 60% of respondents considered this administration more corrupt than any other in the past two decades (cited in Abrashi 2007). The courts and the Ministry of Interior were highlighted as particularly corrupt. This damaging perception of corruption also spreads into the international sphere and undermines the support for intervention among voters in Western countries. The more Afghanistan is represented as and perceived to be a "narco state," the more Western politicians find it difficult to justify the sacrifices involved with intervention. As President Bush has stated, he does not want to "waste another American life on a narco state" (cited in Risen 2007).

The drug economy is conventionally viewed as an index of state power, so that low-capacity regimes are more likely to have a "drug problem" than high capacity regimes. During the war years Afghanistan developed a strong global comparative advantage in illegality as a result of state collapse and the emergence of military entrepreneurs and transnational networks able to facilitate the trade. While this created an enabling environment for the initiation of the drug economy, different structural factors encouraged its consolidation and expansion. The most rapid expansion of the drug trade has coincided with two periods of state building—first during the Taliban regime when the number of opium-growing provinces grew from 10 to 23, and second during the Karzai regime when it grew from twenty-four to thirty-two provinces. One should not confuse correlation with cause, and many other (macro and micro) factors contributed to the spread of opium cultivation, but the common assumption that state collapse and warlordism are good for the drug trade is empirically inaccurate. As Gambetta (1993) and others argue, mafias need states to provide a level of stability and predictability in economic and political relations. The drug mafia supported the Taliban when they first emerged precisely because they could provide state-like functions in terms of security and law and order. Therefore the connection between state building and drugs is more complex than commonly assumed. One could hypothesize that rather than being a linear relationship that progresses from "low-capacity regime/high drug production" to "high-capacity regime/low drug production," the historical trajectory has been closer to an inverted "U," in which growing illegality is associated with the primitive accumulation of power and resources in the early phases of state building, followed by a decreasing reliance on shadow-economy activity in more mature, high-capacity regimes.

Counter-Narcotics Policies and State Building   The following section stresses two key points about the relationship between counter-narcotics policies and state building. First, the failure to prioritize and implement fundamental administrative reforms has limited the leverage and impacts of counter-narcotics policies. Second, counter-narcotics policies and programs have themselves had adverse impacts on efforts to build "good governance."

As highlighted above, there is a big gap between the (possibly unrealistic) aspirations outlined in Bonn of a liberal democratic state, and the reality six years later of a shadow state deeply penetrated by political factions and drug interests. Karzai's "big tent" approach, which prioritized stability over reforms, has enabled reform-resistant elements to consolidate their position and consequently act as spoilers within government. A whole raft of initiatives supposed to build accountability, transparency, and greater effectiveness have been blocked or diluted, in large measure because they challenge the interests of key actors in the central and provincial administrations. These include reforms of the police and judiciary, public administration reforms, and anti-corruption measures.[44]

The failure to confront drug interests through substantive reforms, also reflects the competing objectives of international players and leads to inconsistent policies, as highlighted earlier.[45] Karzai, particularly in relation to the drug issue, is caught in the dual legitimacy trap. Paradoxically, drug eradication may build Karzai's external legitimacy while simultaneously undermining his domestic standing. He has declared a *jihad* on drugs and like his predecessors, the Taliban, he has deployed notions of religious sin and collective shame to persuade farmers to desist from poppy cultivation. But illegality does not mean that such activities are regarded as illegitimate. Many Afghans view counter-narcotics policies as an externally driven, Western agenda, and criminalization/eradication could undermine internal government legitimacy—particularly when it cannot deliver on its part of the bargain by providing alternative sources of livelihoods/employment. Laws that lack legitimacy consequently require a greater reliance on coercion, and eradication efforts end up attacking farmers who voted for Karzai (Rubin and Zakilwal 2005). International forces are also de-legitimized by association in the eyes of many Afghans, who were initially supportive of coalition forces. CN policies may aggravate inter-ethnic and north–south tensions, since eradication efforts in the south accentuated the perception that the government was "anti-Pashtun."

In addition to their effects on the legitimacy of the state, CN policies have significant opportunity costs and may indirectly undermine state capacities. As Koehler (2005) argues, the "narco state" may be less of a threat to Afghan statehood than a "foreign steered counter-narcotics proxy state. The legitimacy of Afghan state building is running the risk of being sacrificed for a quick result counter-narcotics enforcement machinery" (70). Lister (2007) also highlights the adverse effects of externally driven CN policies at the provincial level: "Attempts to coordinate different ministries and create bodies which could deal with very large sums of provincial level funding to address the drugs problem were pushed forwards at breakneck speed, often ignoring existing provincial structures and government approaches" (8).

Therefore, even if CN efforts were successful in their own terms (which they are not), ultimately they run the danger of undermining the more fundamental goal of state building. First, the priorities and policies of external players, notably the UK and increasingly the US, have tended to override those of domestic actors. Second, the problem of weak domestic capacities has been addressed by importing capacity through foreign consultants or émigré Afghans and building parallel structures. Apart from the coordination problems this creates, it also has major opportunity costs—for example it could be argued that the resources spent on creating a separate ministry might better have been invested in reforming the core Ministries of the Interior and Justice. Third, too much money has been pushed too quickly through institutions and organizations that are ill-equipped to absorb and use it effectively (Surhke 2007; Lister 2007). This in turn has created enormous opportunities for rent seeking and corruption. Control regimes tend to reflect de facto power relations, and the state's involvement in counter-narcotics has generated perverse incentives for misgovernment. Eradication and interdiction have been used or threatened to undermine political enemies or extract resources, which has enabled producers to get rid of competitors and led to de facto consolidation of the drug industry.

Although some viewed "successful" eradication efforts in Nangahar province (where there was a 94% decrease in poppy cultivation in 2005 and only a limited rebound in 2006) [46] as a sign of the growing outreach and capacity of the state, the evidence suggests the opposite. Local strongmen were able to "turn off" production as a result of temporary bargains or "spot contracts" with the central state. The only real bargaining tool available to the state is to offer autonomy to warlords, which was the case in Nangahar—essentially rewarding "bad governance." Although there may be a growing understanding that being a warlord or *jihadi* commander is less secure and less lucrative than a position in the state bureaucracy (Koehler 2005), the process of co-opting or absorbing warlords paradoxically undermines the legitimacy and capacity of the state.

While opium cultivation in Nangahar significantly increased in the 2006–07 season, there has been a sharp reduction in Balkh, mirroring in some respects the political dynamics prevalent in Nangahar in 2005.

Provincial governor Mohammed Atta, a former warlord turned reformer/ statesman had hitherto consolidated his political power base partly through taxing and controlling the opium economy. By successfully enforcing a cultivation ban in 2006, he was able to simultaneously consolidate his power while also building his legitimacy and bargaining position vis-à-vis central government and international players (Pain 2007). As in Nangahar, however, this is best understood as a "spot contract," or a tactical ploy by local power holders rather than a durable solution to drug cultivation in the province. Rather than the borderland being swallowed up and pacified by the central state, the borderland may actually be penetrating and colonizing the state apparatus.[47]

Counter-narcotics efforts provide leverage to corrupt officials for extracting enormous bribes from traffickers and such corruption has attracted former militia commanders who joined the Ministry of the Interior after being demobilized (Rubin 2007a). While the Taliban have protected small farmers against eradication, very few high-ranking government officials have been prosecuted for drug-related corruption—not surprising given the role of the Ministry of Interior now plays in the drug industry. A greater focus on indictment since 2005 has led to several high-profile arrests, including a high-level Ministry of Interior official, Lt. Colonel Nadir Khan, who was sentenced to ten years in prison for stealing and selling fifty kilograms of confiscated heroin (Gall 2006). In New York in 2005 the Drug Enforcement Administration (DEA) arrested trafficker Bashir Noorzai, who had reportedly provided weapons and manpower to the Taliban in exchange for the protection of his drugs.[48] The overall aim of interdiction, complemented by other CN measures, according to Jalali et al. (2006), should be to turn opium cultivation and trafficking into high-risk activities in a low-risk environment. However, as the Transnational Institute (TNI) notes, the "choices about who and who not to indict, arrest or extradite seem to be arbitrary, irrational or highly politicized" (2005, 11).

Therefore, there is a complex and ambiguous relationship between counter-narcotics and state building, and heavy-handed eradication may have adverse effects and undermine the legitimacy and capacity of the central state with regard to local strong men. Combating drugs may not be synonymous with state building, and perhaps each should be viewed as separate policy objectives (Koehler and Zuercher 2006).

Drugs and Development

The Drug Economy as a Barrier to Development Poppy has penetrated the rural economy far more deeply than aid and with longer-term effects. For instance, the extension and dissemination work of those involved in the drug trade appear to have been far more effective than the equivalent activities of aid workers.[49] Poppy cultivation plays a multi-functional role (Mansfield 2001; Mansfield and Pain 2005), and for poor farmers it provides access to land and credit. Cultivation is less about profit maximization than negotiating short-term security in return for long-term poverty. Wood (2003) described this as the Faustian bargain of "staying poor but staying secure." Poppy represents a low-risk crop in a high-risk environment. Poppy cultivation is also an extremely labour-intensive crop, and around 12.6% of the population is involved in opium poppy cultivation, a total of 448,000 families compared to 309,000 in 2005 (UNODC 2006). In 2003, UNODC estimated that, on average, farmers retained slightly more than half of the gross revenue they accrued through opium production with the rest spent on production factors costs, taxes, and other levies including payments to local commanders. In 2006, the gross income of farmers was $780 million or 11% of GDP.

Owing to sustained growth of the licit economy, the size of the opium sector relative to the rest of the economy declined from 62% to 38% between 2002 and 2006 (Martin and Symansky 2006) However, opium-related demand and aid inflows are contributing to Dutch disease, in which prices of non-tradables and production factors get pushed up, and appreciation in the real exchange rate weakens competitiveness in non opium export markets and competes with imports (Byrd and Buddenberg 2006, 7).

Although in the short-term poppy is a low-risk crop for farmers, in the long term it may be high-risk because of the unpredictability of farm gate prices, which are subject to speculative manipulation and to the prospect of large-scale eradication. Furthermore, the opium economy has a negative impact on the investment climate, with few international businesses willing to make investments because of concerns about corruption and insecurity. In such a high-risk but high-opportunity environment, economic activity revolves around capturing rents associated with short-term, speculative activities. And a large part of opium-related savings are held in foreign-denominated assets.

Drugs and "Actually Existing" Development The literature on war economies shows that war is less about breakdown than about reordering and transformation (Keen 1998; Duffield 2001; Pugh and Cooper 2004). Paradoxically, war may create an enabling environment for development by boosting surplus appropriation and capital accumulation (Cramer 2006). War creates rent because it typically reduces the number of market competitors and increases risk—so the returns to those who take the risk are potentially very high (ibid., 193). In Afghanistan, war has been the catalyst both for processes of accumulation and immiseration, simultaneously generating profits and poverty (Bhatia and Gooodhand 2003). The Afghan wars have facilitated the penetration of capitalism into rural communities, with a range of attendant effects, including the increased differentiation of the peasantry, growing indebtedness and land scarcity, internal migration (with itinerant armies of labourers working on the poppy harvest and migration to cities), and migration out of the country.

Conversely, there is the story of rapid accumulation—of land, assets, and capital by local, regional, and national strongmen. If one places war-lordism and the drug economy in a historical and comparative framework, they may be seen less as symptoms of state breakdown than agents of, or catalysts for, state building and economic development. State building in-volves creating a national economy, and the drug industry is to some extent one of the few areas of economic activity integrated at the national level. The opium economy has had a stabilizing effect on the currency by having a significant net positive impact on Afghanistan's balance of payments,[50] though this is reduced by drug-related outflows of funds (including capital flight).

Although it is true that the bulk of the profits go to traffickers and those outside the country, the Taliban ban farmers' share in the profits have in-creased (final share price accruing at the farm gate in 2005 was around 16% compared to 13% before 2000),[51] and this final share is in relation to a considerably higher border price. Profitability of cultivation has increased, therefore, and reflects compensation for risks associated with stronger en-forcement (Byrd and Jonglez 2006, 132). In addition, income from the drug sector has been recycled into "licit" activities, particularly in relation to the construction industry; it has increased real estate prices, stimulated businesses, and improved daily-wage labour rates in cities and towns around the country. To a great extent, the urban economy depends on commercial activities taking place in the hinterland, especially along international bor-ders. Foreign exchange earned by narcotics exports finances the import of vehicles, durable consumer goods, and fuel, the customs duties on which constitute the government's main source of revenue (Rubin 2004, 6). In many respects, therefore, the drug economy contributes to "actually exist-ing" development (Duffield 2001); however, the effects of poppy are mixed and it is also important to note that there is a great deal of variation between contexts and actors at different locations within the opium economy (Mans-field and Pain 2005; Mansfield 2006).

At the micro level in poppy-growing areas there are visible signs of pros-perity in terms of house building, stimulation of local businesses, and con-sumer goods (Mansfield 2007a; Pain 2007). In Helmand, recent reports by the Institute for War and Peace Reporting (IWPR 2007b) show how the bumper crop for 2006–07 has improved the bargaining position of har-vesters. This is reflected in their demand of between one-fifth to one-half of the harvest, compared to their share of one-sixteenth in previous years.

Interestingly, landowners approached the government to resolve the dispute and a one-quarter share was brokered.[52] A prospective groom expressed satisfaction at the benefits of poppy, explaining, "It used to be that a young man would have to go to Pakistan or Iran to earn enough money to get married. By the time he came back, he was already old. Now we can make money from poppy, and we don't have to go away"(2007b).

Counter Narcotics and Development As argued earlier, policies in non-drug related areas have a significant impact on the potential efficacy of CN policies. Interventions in a range of areas from counterterrorism to regional tariff regimes, border controls, and rural infrastructure all have an influence on the structural conditions underpinning the drug economy and the incentives of the various actors involved.

On the counter-narcotics front, as Mansfield and others have argued, a composite, multi-stranded approach is the only one likely to succeed. This takes us beyond a rational actor, profit-maximizing farmer model, and the search for an elusive "magic bullet" crop (such as onions, saffron, or roses) that can out-perform poppy. Poppy plays a multi-functional role, and the decision to cultivate is tied up with questions of land ownership/tenure, indebtedness/rural credit, and rural employment. While some products may generate higher revenues, they require substantial multi-year investments and infrastructure that farmers cannot afford (Martin and Symansky 2006, 27). "Instant development does not exist" (TNI 2005, 12), and a sustainable transition from a war economy to a peace economy is contingent on the provision of a number of public goods, including improved security, better governance, and basic infrastructure (Mansfield 2007a).

Counter-narcotics objectives mapped out in Afghanistan's Millennium Development Goals and the Afghanistan Compact establish the benchmark of a sustainable reduction in the absolute and relative size of the drug economy. But there are different ways of working toward this goal. In a macro-economic simulation, different types of CN policies were found to have different macro-economic effects. It was also found that a strategy including eradication at early stages can lead to a contraction of the total GDP by nearly 6% (Rubin and Hamidzada 2007, 21). Although eradication tends to raise farm gate prices, interdiction lowers prices by reducing demand from traffickers. Essentially, it aims to increase the risk premium associated with opium trading. However, CN policies have tended toward eradication, with the metric of success being acreage destroyed and reduced aggregate production levels. The Good Performance Initiative, for example, is based on this set of metrics; that is, "good performers" are those provinces that have the strongest record in poppy reduction. Yet experience shows that eradication has a range of adverse effects, including higher prices that increase the value of opium inventory holdings of larger traffickers, increased opium-related debt, and the expansion of cultivation into new regions. Also, those whose crops are not eradicated will be better off (and consequently more able to bribe officials), so there are important distributional effects.

Eradication, therefore, leads to a net transfer of income from opium growers to drug traffickers, who then profit from the increased value of their stocks. As one trafficker, interviewed in Lashka Gah, Helmand this year, said, "I'll be very happy if the eradicators are successful. I have lots of poppy stored. If they don't destroy poppy, I'm afraid the price will come down" (IWPR 2007a). Eradication may also have the effect of driving farmers toward insurgents and warlords (Rubin 2007a).

Mansfield and Pain (2006) argue that eradication is based on the false premise that it can "inject risk into the system." But it cannot play this role in the most marginal environments as the poor literally have nothing to lose.[53] Also, those who bear the risks are not those who make the decisions (Rubin 2007b). And eradication brings major political costs for the government.[54] This is one of the main reasons why Karzai has been, until recently, unusually steadfast in resisting US pressure to conduct aerial or ground-based spraying.

There are strong arguments, therefore, for focusing on interdiction rather than eradication. Lower prices as a result of interdiction at the downstream stages would reduce price incentives to produce opium, lower the burden of opium-related debt, and reduce the value of opium inventory holdings (Byrd and Jonglez 2006, 138). However, whether eradication or interdiction is prioritized, it is clear that a shock-therapy approach, in addition to undermining the livelihoods of poor farmers, would have severe consequences for the economy at a macro level. A "decline in drug income would, at least temporarily, lead to a slowdown in real growth of the non drug economy and a deterioration in the balance of payments, putting downward pressure on the real exchange rate" (Martin and Symansky 2006, 37).

Hence efforts to shrink the illicit economy need to be balanced by initiatives that aim to grow the licit economy. Although alternative livelihoods (AL) are frequently touted as the quid pro quo for eradication, in practice AL programs have been under funded[55] and implemented in an ad hoc, piecemeal fashion; "a large number of interventions labelled as alternative livelihoods programs have been of a short-term nature, focus on a single sector ... and insufficiently coordinated geographically between donors" (Martin and Symansky 2006, 36).

A number of lessons can be drawn from the experience of counter-narcotics interventions in Nangahar and elsewhere. Not surprisingly, a sustainable reduction in cultivation has occurred in the most economically resilient areas; that is, those with access to markets and sufficient irrigated land and where there has been a significant investment in alternative economic activities. These conditions pertain, for example, in the areas within relatively easy reach of Jalalabad centre, and for the last three years there has been limited cultivation in this zone. But communities living in the more marginal borderland areas of Nangarhar are unable to reduce their exposure to the effects of eradication, leading to the distress sale of assets, increased indebtedness, and migration to Pakistan. It is estimated that the reduction in cultivation between 2004 and 2005 led to the loss of an estimated 9.8 million labour days, of which 3.4 million represented daily wage labour opportunities to the estimated value of $11.7 million (Mansfield 2004). By 2008, cultivation levels in these areas are expected to return to pre-2004 levels. Mansfield's (2007a) comparison of the Baharak and Jurm districts in Badakshan also points to the importance of subnational analysis. The success of the former in reducing cultivation compared to the latter was found to be the result of a combination of specific and localized factors, including the effectiveness of the state, the local security regime, access to markets, and changes in labour rates that have affected the profitability of opium cultivation relative to other crops.

Finally, an untried to date alternative to orthodox approaches is to work through market mechanisms in order to reduce or regulate opium production. The first of two such models is a "super buyer" program, which, it is claimed, would have the effect of disabling the market for cheap heroin (Zetland 2003). A second approach advocated by the Senlis Council, an international think tank, would be to buy up part of the Afghan poppy crop in order to address the world shortage of legal opiates for medicinal use. Senlis argue that this has worked in Turkey, one of the main sources of illicit opium and heroin in the 1960s before switching to legal production. However a number of factors are likely to militate against such an approach in Afghanistan. First, given the country's poor governance and security, there would be no effective control mechanism to force farmers to sell to legitimate buyers. In the absence of a strong state to police the scheme there would inevitably be leakage to illegal sources. Second, Afghan production would struggle to compete in the world market because of unit costs estimated at ten times those of the highly industrialized output in Australia. Third, it would send contradictory signals to farmers, which is one of the reasons why the scheme has been unpopular with the Afghan government.[56] Fourth, the demand for non-medicinal opiates will not disappear, and if the scheme were successful in Afghanistan, illicit production would simply migrate elsewhere.

Conclusions

War on Drugs or State Building?

> [A]*fter fighting five drug wars in 30 years at the costs of US$150 billion, Washington has presided over a [fivefold] increase in the world's illicit opium supply from 100 tonnes in 1970 to between 5000 and 6000 tonnes in the mid 2000s.*
> —McCoy 2003
> (cited in MacDonald 2007, 251)

There is ample evidence, globally and in Afghanistan, that supply-side interventions have failed to bring about a sustainable reduction in drug production. As well as not working on their own terms, drug policies are undermining higher policy goals related to security and governance. The war on drugs, to borrow the policy makers' jargon, is not an "evidence based" policy.

This chapter has examined the complex interconnections between drugs, (in)security, state building, and poverty/development, showing the ambiguous, two-directional, and contingent nature of these relationships. It has been argued that many of the negative epiphenomena associated with drugs—including terrorism, corruption, and impoverishment—may be exacerbated by, or even partly the result of, wrong-headed counter-narcotics policies. Perversely, the tightening environment against narcotics is also contributing to the consolidation of the drug industry around fewer more powerful and politically connected actors (Byrd and Buddenberg 2006, 6).

Rational, measured, and well-informed debate on the drug question is difficult. It is an emotive area and its demonization hinders a pragmatic, open-minded debate on the costs and trade-offs of different policy options. Ultimately, policy is driven by Western countries' concerns about their own drug problem, rather than the long-term needs and interests of the producing countries. The benchmark of success is overall production figures, and policies are aligned behind this goal, with a strong focus on eradication.

In Afghanistan, donor countries need to decide whether their priority is to implement global counter-narcotics policy or to build legitimate political authority in Afghanistan. As this chapter has shown, these are not the same thing and it is necessary to make choices. If peace building is the overriding objective, then other policy goals need to be made coherent with this. Just as development aid is now as a matter of course assessed in terms of its conflict/peace sensitivity, the same should apply to CN policies. All actors in the CN sphere should align their work behind the higher policy goal of peace building, and their work should be measured, and be held accountable, in these terms.

Peace building and drug policies clearly do overlap, but they overlap around the question of political conditions—the drug economy thrives because Afghanistan has a comparative advantage in illegality (Rubin and Guaqueta 2007). Drugs, somewhat like a mould, grow and expand in certain environmental conditions, the optimum conditions being weak regulation by the state and the international legal system. This means that ultimately CN is a political, rather than technical, task. And the reduction of opium production is likely to be the by-product of a political process, rather than being at the leading edge of this process. Furthermore it seems very unlikely that international actors can be successful in simultaneously waging war while attempting to eliminate poppy.

Thinking differently

Due to considerable research done over the years, there is already enough evidence on which to build more nuanced policy. However there is still work to be done on the analytical front and to ensure this analysis is incorporated more explicitly into policy.

First, it should now be clear that a rational-actor model that explains behaviour purely in terms of individual self-interest is wrong-headed, and we can only understand the opium economy by placing it within a wider political, social, and economic context. Although a substantial amount of work has been done on the production side of the opium industry, reflecting perhaps the obsession with eradication and the bottom end of the value chain, there is scope for more analysis further up the chain. Apart from Shaw (2006), few have written on the political effects of the opium economy. To my knowledge, detailed political ethnographies that examine the links between traffickers and governance arrangements have not been conducted—for understandable reasons, given the dangers involved—but could yield important information leading to more strategic interventions in the law enforcement and interdiction sides.

Second, more disaggregated analysis of the different actors involved could lead to more fine-grained policy. Clearly, motivations are not homogenous, and individualized packages of (dis)incentives may be more appropriate than off-the-peg rewards or sanctions. As Byrd and Jonglez argue, the "ultimate objective is to find weaknesses and vulnerabilities in the market and industry structure that can be exploited as part of the counter-narcotics strategy." Particular analytical challenges are to look at the "natural experiments" in which the opium market responded to major shocks. These include the Taliban ban, Nangarhar, and Balkh, since "analysis of these episodes can facilitate better understanding of the functioning of opium markets and the drug industry more generally" (2006, 118). Furthermore, studies of "new entrants" to cultivation will yield important insights into the transmission mechanisms. Finally, perhaps more systematic research is required on how counter-narcotics policies have effected other policy goals and programs and the complex tensions and trade-offs between them.

Acting Differently

Paradoxically, in order to tackle drugs there may be a need to deny this issue special status and instead treat it as a cross-cutting theme. Policies and interventions in non-drug-focused spheres ultimately appear to be far more important. Former narcotics producing countries such as Turkey and Thailand were only able to eliminate illicit opium production when socio-economic standards improved independently of drug-control policies.[57] Attempting to fast track institution building in the counter-narcotics sphere has great opportunity costs and arguably undermines the broader goal of building stable political authority. Therefore a greater focus should be placed on core state institutions, most notably the Ministries of Interior and Justice. This may mean a more conditional approach, particularly in relation to core reforms and appointments.[58]

As research on war economies shows, this problem has been a long time in the making, and timeframes need to be lengthened accordingly and a gradualist approach adopted. This does not mean that eradication has no role, but it has to be targeted on areas where sustainable alternatives exist and used carefully alongside other instruments.

Overall, there should be a focus on destroying value close to the top of the value chain through measures such as border controls and stronger interdiction. The benchmark for success should be less about absolute production figures than the reduction of the absolute and relative size of traffickers income (Rubin 2007b).

In the long term, countering the narcotics industry may mean that development actors need to rethink mainstream (neo-liberal) economic models. This would entail revisiting currently unfashionable Keynsian policies, including prime-pumping the rural economy through large-scale investments and public works in order to create on-farm and off-farm employment; subsidizing the agricultural economy; and offering protection to encourage nascent industries and significant expansion of national-level programs, such as the National Solidarity Programme (NSP) and other rural infrastructure projects.

Finally there may be lessons to be learned from the use of non-drug policy instruments in other war-to-peace transitions. Most successful transitions have involved a level of compromise between international best practice and pragmatic solutions for stability. The criminalization (and demonization) of drugs has made discussions on such compromises more difficult. But transitional arrangements might involve providing amnesties for certain traffickers and incentives to encourage them to invest in the licit economy or buy-back schemes as part of a bargaining process with rural communities. Rubin (2007b) has even argued for encouraging traffickers to transform themselves into becoming rural credit providers. Whether this last suggestion could work in practice can be debated. But the underlying assumption is valid and important—rather than criminalizing war economies there is a need to think more carefully about how to harness the energies of war in order to pay for peace.

Acknowledgments

This chapter is based on research that was funded by ESRC (Transformation of War Economies, Res. 223250071) and the Christien Michelson Institute. I am indebted to colleagues at CPAU in Kabul who supported elements of this research. I am also grateful to the following who provided valuable feedback on an earlier draft of the chapter: Antonio Giustozzi, David Mansfield, Adam Pain, Mark Sedra, and Andrew Wilder. Any errors or omissions are my own.

Notes

1 See Goodhand's (2004) typology of the combat, shadow, and coping economies that evolved in the course of the Afghan wars.
2 The post-Taliban period has seen the emergence of new areas of cultivation, including Bamyan, Nuristan, Khost, and Wardak provinces.
3 In 2006, six provinces were reported opium-free, eight cultivated less than 1,000 hectares, and twenty-eight cultivated less than 5,000 hectares.
4 Zetland (2003, 4), for instance, calculates that opium that costs $90 per kilogram at the Afghan farm gate becomes $2,870 per kilogram (refined heroin) in Pakistan, which in turn increases to $80,000 per kilogram in the US wholesale market and finally $725,000 at retail prices. The cross-border markup from Pakistan to the US is 2,400%, compared to the norm of 12% for most agricultural products.
5 In spite of a major increase in production in 2006, prices at the downstream end have remained fairly stable. One reason for this may be that traffickers have stockpiled surplus opium as a hedge against future price shocks (see Costa 2007).
6 In 1995, 41% of opiate-based exports were in the form of heroin, but by 2002 this had risen to 72%.
7 Different opiates do not have the same purity, and their prices depend on their quality and characteristics. At the low end of the spectrum is "brown sugar," and at the high-quality end is China White with a level of heroin chlorhydrate reaching up to

98%. A global conversion ratio of between 6 and 10 to 1 is used to calculate the quantity of opium required to produce heroin and morphine. In Afghanistan a 7-to-1 ratio is commonly used.

8 It should be noted that these figures are based on seizures and do not distinguish between opium, morphine, and heroin. At best they should be viewed as rough estimates.

9 This figure is based on a UNODC study conducted in 2003, which represented 23,995 hashish users, 14,298 users of pharmaceutical drugs, 10,774 opium users, 7,008 heroin users, and 6,568 alcohol users. MacDonald notes that the total figure was likely to constitute a substantial underestimate.

10 The others pillars were the Afghan National Army (US), police (Germany), judiciary (Italy), and DDR (Japan).

11 A *jerib* equals one-fifth of a hectare of land.

12 Perversely, an up-front cash payment created an incentive to grow poppy.

13 This position was filled by General Dauod, who was previously Commander of the Sixth Army Corps in Kunduz.

14 As of November 2006 it held $84 million.

15 After the 2004 harvest, Robert B. Charles, US Assistant Secretary of State for International Narcotics and Law Enforcement Affairs, made it clear that the issue of eradication was a point of disagreement. In testimony in April 2004 before a US Congress subcommittee hearing under the pointed title, "Are the British Counter Narcotics Efforts Going Wobbly?" he said, "if there is heroin poppy there which needs to be eradicated, we shouldn't be picking and choosing, we shouldn't be delaying, we shouldn't be making it conditional upon providing an instant and available income stream" (cited in TNI 2005, 6–7).

16 In February 2007, senior Republicans on the House Foreign Affairs Committee, led by the ranking member, Rep. Ileana Ros-Lehtinen, Florida Republican, wrote to Defence Secretary Robert M. Gates and Secretary of State Condoleezza Rice, asking for the appointment of "a high-level coordinator of overall Afghan narco-terrorism policy." The bluntly worded letter said interagency rivalry and US policy failures in Afghanistan risked allowing it to slide back into chaos. "The open and public dispute with our British allies on opium-eradication methods, along with the many different and often conflicting views of NATO, our Department of Defence, the Drug Enforcement [Administration], and other US agencies on how best to handle the narcotics challenge does not bode well for success," the letter said (cited in Waterman 2007).

17 It is noticeable that although the Afghan government has followed the US lead in almost every policy area, on the question of aerial eradication they have stood their ground and robustly argued against such a policy.

18 At the London conference the UK pledged £270 million for 2006–2008.

19 The Senlis Council's proposal for legalized production of opiates for medicinal use, which is explored later, in some respects falls into this final category.

20 Arguably, if one views the Taliban as proto state builders (cf Cramer and Goodhand 2002), their control and taxation of the poppy economy was a factor that enabled them to extend their control over the country and concentrate the means of coercion.

21 A range of micro and macro factors contributed to the re-emergence of the drug economy. First, the Taliban's opium ban had the twin effect of pushing up prices and increasing opium-related debt in rural areas. Poor farmers had little choice but to grow poppy in order to repay their debts, while for the more wealthy, high prices created strong incentives to allocate land to poppy. These factors were reinforced by the end

of the drought that meant an increased availability of wheat and a freeing up of internal and external markets (Mansfield 2007b). Second, the CIA's policy of providing millions of dollars to commanders also played a role because these dollars were quickly recycled into loans to farmers to finance the next spring's poppy crop.

22 A manifestation of this perceived licitness was the cultivation of poppy on prime agricultural land in easily accessible areas.

23 It should be noted however, that hard data on the drugs–insurgency nexus is difficult to come by, and what does exist is highly conjectural.

24 Some argue that, ultimately, "criminal involvement" is likely to affect the motivational structure of originally ideologically motivated groups (Cornell 2006). However the Taliban's symbiotic relationship with Pashtun entrepreneurs in the shadow economy in the 1990s appeared to have little effect on their conservative ideology.

25 It is difficult to get reliable figures on this, and they probably vary from area to area. Others report a 10% tax on farmers and 15% from laboratories and 15% as a transit fee.

26 In Nimroz Province the Taliban reportedly demanded that traffickers provide $4,000 a month and a Toyota Land Cruiser to support ten-man fighting units, according to UN officials (cited in Risen 2007). Furthermore, Giustozzi (2007b, 88) cites reports of alliances between the neo-Taliban and traffickers being cemented by marriage.

27 According to UNODC only 20% of farmers in areas with good security now grow opium, whereas 80% do so in areas where security is poor. The latest UNODC survey shows a growing north–south divide, with 80% of farmers in poppy-growing areas in the south being involved in opium cultivation, whereas the national proportion is only 13%.

28 For example, the Taliban reportedly send out night letters that instruct peasants to grow poppy and in return they will receive protection. If they refuse they will be killed.

29 In Kunar, Korenegal Valley, young men are paid up to £2,600 for every IED attack on American soldiers (Walsh 2006).

30 See Mansfield (2007a), who contrasts the level of stability in Baharak district with that of Jurm in Badakshan province and relates this to the particular configuration of political and military players in each locale and their relationship to provincial authorities.

31 According to Risen (2007), there were repeated clashes between the State Department and the Pentagon over drug policy, with the latter refusing to take action against the drug trade, while the CIA and military also turned a blind eye to drug-related activities.

32 For example, in May 2005 national staff members of Chemonics were killed in Helmand and Zabul provinces. In April 2005 in Maiwand district of Kandahar, eradication campaigns were suspended after clashes between farmers and the Central Poppy Eradication Force (CPEF). Protestors blocked the main road between Kandahar and Herat and villagers threw stones and fired shots at the CPEF.

33 Between 2005 and 2006, interdiction increased sharply with the seizure of 86.6 tons of opium and 7.7 tons of heroin, which constituted about 3.4% of opium output. This compares with 0.4% for 2002 and 2003.

34 For example, government officials in Kabul were incensed when British psychological operations teams put out radio broadcasts in April 2007 that announced that British soldiers would not destroy poppy crops because they knew people had a

livelihood to earn. The Afghan government is putting growing pressure on troops to provide more active support in the area of interdiction and trafficking (Coghlan 2007). However, coalition interventions that target villages in paramilitary fashion and conduct house searches under suspicion of hiding opium stocks generate a great deal of resentment (Koehler 2005).

35 See Tilly (1985) on states and protection rackets and Giustozzi's (2004) critique of the assumed distinction between "good state" and "bad warlord."

36 Defined here as the capacity of the state to perform its core functions of providing security, representation, and wealth/welfare (Milliken and Krause 2002).

37 For example, the Afghan Independent Human Rights Commission, after the parliamentary elections, reported that an estimated 80% of the candidates in the provinces and 60% in Kabul maintained contacts with armed groups and drug traffickers (IRIN 2005).

38 For example, Jan Mhd in Uruzgan and Akhunzada of Helmand, who were removed from office in 2006 after extreme pressure from international actors using the leverage of PRTs to pressurize Karzai. Akhunzada, however, was moved to the senate, from where he continues to exert influence on events in his home area. Perversely, Karzai also removed the governor of Nangahar and replaced him with the governor of Kandahar, Gul Agha Sherzai, thus swapping someone with the best record of poppy reduction with someone who had the worst.

39 Pay grades have subsequently changed, and a provincial police chief is now paid between $500 and $600 per month.

40 See Paris (2004) on the dangers of liberalization before institutionalization in postconflict contexts.

41 For example, in Jurm district of Badakshan a local commander has reached an agreement with a parliamentarian who has close links to the president's office—the commander, in return for delivering votes and the ongoing support of the population, receives the parliamentarian's patronage, who then turns a blind eye to poppy cultivation.

42 For example, one former *Mujahideen* commander, Din Muhammed Jurat, became a general in the Ministry of Interior and is widely believed to be a major figure in organized crime (Rubin 2007).

43 For example, the Taliban recently introduced their own "code of conduct," which aims to set standards of professionalism and behaviour in contrast to the perceived corruption of government (Schuster 2006).

44 The Afghan government recently published its "Anti-Corruption Roadmap" and established a US-backed Criminal Information Unit within the Ministry of Interior to reduce corruption by strengthening internal affairs and accountability mechanisms. But Afghanistan's anti-corruption chief, Izzatullah Wasifi, has a troubling past, and a recent Associated Press investigation found he was convicted two decades ago for selling heroin in the United States (Pennington 2007).

45 In 2005, DEA agents and Afghan counterparts found nine tons of opium in the office of Sher Muhammad Akhundzada, governor of Helmand, but the CN team was blocked from taking any action against the governor, who had close ties to American and British military intelligence and diplomatic officials (Risen 2007).

46 But there has been a major increase in poppy production in 2007.

47 As Mansfield notes (2007a, 27), in Jurm, one of the most conflict-ridden districts in Badakshan, "there was a perception that the commanders had absorbed the government rather than the other way around."

48 Few in the media pointed out that Noorzai had previously been arrested by the US in late 2001 because he was a major player in the illicit drugs business in the south working closely with Taliban leaders. He was released because he was a useful intelligence asset and willing to collaborate in return for impunity (TNI 2005, 11).

49 The combination of credit, access to land, extension services, cash income, and security guarantees from local power holders cannot be matched by either the government or aid agencies.

50 The stable value of the new currency has been an important factor in the popularity of the government and a source of national pride (Rubin 2004, 6).

51 Though this was down from the figure of 35% in 2003 (Byrd and Jonglez 2006, 132).

52 One harvester said, "I have no other way of making money, so I go off and do 15 days' harvesting. I might make 10,000 to 12,000 afghani [$200–240]. That could solve my problems."

53 This argument resonates with Hirshleifer's (1994) point that the poor may have a comparative advantage in violence as they have less to lose.

54 The riots in Kabul of 2006 reportedly involved a large number of young, unemployed men, highlighting perhaps the critical links between livelihoods/employment, government legitimacy, and security.

55 Only 1% of the funding from the Counter Narcotics Trust Fund and the Good Performance Initiative had been disbursed by June 2007.

56 Senlis continues to operate in the country despite the decision of the Afghan Senate of May 27, 2006, ordering closure of Senlis Council's offices in Afghanistan.

57 Though in both cases worldwide production was not affected, as it moved from Turkey to Iran and Afghanistan and from Thailand to Burma (Armenta et al., cited in Zetland 2003).

58 See Goodhand and Sedra (2007) for a discussion on the scope for conditionalities.

References

Abrashi, Fisnik. 2007. "Afghan Bomber Hits U.S. Embassy Convoy." *Washington Post*. March 19.

Baldauf, Scott. 2006. "Inside the Afghan drug trade." *Christian Science Monitor*. 13 June.

Barnett, Michael and Christoph Zuercher. 2007. "The Peacebuilder's Contract: How External State-building Reinforces Weak Statehood." Discussion draft for research partnership on postwar state building. http://statebuilding.org.

Bhatia, Michael and Jonathan Goodhand, with Haneef Atmar, Adam Pain, and Mohammed Suliman. 2003. "Profits and Poverty: Aid, Livelihoods and Conflict in Afghanistan." In *Power, Livelihoods and Conflict: Case Studies in Political Economy Analysis for Humanitarian Agencies*, ed. Sarah Collinson. London: Humanitarian Policy Group (HPG) Report, 13.

Buddenberg, Doris and William Byrd, eds. 2006. *Afghanistan's Drug Industry: Structure, Functioning, Dynamics and Implications for Counter-Narcotics Policy*. UNODC and World Bank.

Byrd, William and Doris Buddenberg. 2006. "Introduction and Overview." In *Afghanistan's Drug Industry. Structure, Functioning, Dynamics and Implications for Counter-Narcotics Policy*, ed. Doris Buddenberg and William Byrd. UNODC and World Bank.

Byrd, William and Olivier Jonglez. 2006. "Prices and Market Interactions in the Opium Economy" in *Afghanistan's Drug Industry. Structure, Functioning, Dynamics and Implications for Counter-Narcotics Policy*, ed. Doris Buddenberg and William Byrd, 117–154. UNODC and World Bank.

Coghlan, Tom. 2007. "Smash Our Trade in Opium, Afghans Tell British." *Daily Telegraph*. 27 May.

Cornell, Svante. 2006. "The Interaction of Narcotics and Conflict." *Journal of Peace Research* 42 (6): 751–60.

Costa, Antonio Maria. 2007. "An Opium Market Mystery." *Washington Post*, http://www.csdp.org/news/news/post_costa_042507.htm. 25 April.

Cramer, Christopher. 2006. *Civil War Is Not a Stupid Thing. Accounting for Violence in Developing Countries*. London: Hurst.

Cramer, Christopher and Jonathan Goodhand. 2002. "Try Again, Fail Again, Fail Better? War, the State, and the Post-Conflict Challenge in Afghanistan." *Development and Change* 33 (5): 885–909.

Duffield, Mark. 2001. *Global Governance and the New Wars: The Merging of Development and Security*. London: Zed Books.

Felbab-Brown Vanda. 2005. "Afghanistan: When Counternarcotics Undermines Counterterrorism." *Washington Quarterly* 28 (4): 55–72.

Gall, Carlotta. 2006. "Opium Harvest at Record Level in Afghanistan." *New York Times*. 3 September.

Gallant, Thomas. 1999. "Brigandage, Piracy, Capitalism, and State Formation: Transnational Crime from a Historical World-Systems Perspective" in *States and Illegal Practices*. Josiah McC. Heyman and Alan Smart, eds., 25–62. Oxford: Berg.

Gambetta, Diego. 1993. *The Sicilian Mafia: The Business of Private Protection*. Cambridge: Harvard University Press.

Giustozzi, Antonio. 2004. "Good State vs. 'Bad' Warlords? A Critique of State-Building Strategies in Afghanistan." Crisis States Programme, Destin, LSE, Working Paper Series No. 1.

———. 2007a. "War and Peace Economies of Afghanistan's Strongmen." *International Peacekeeping* 14 (1): 75–89.

———. 2007b. *Koran, Kalashnikov and Laptop: The Neo-Taliban Insurgency in Afghanistan 2002–7*. London: Hurst.

Goodhand, Jonathan. 2004. "Afghanistan in Central Asia." In *War Economies in a Regional Context: Challenges for Transformation*, Michael Pugh and Neil Cooper with Jonathan Goodhand, 45–89. London and Boulder, CO: Lynne Rienner.

————. 2005. "Frontiers and Wars: The Opium Economy in Afghanistan." *Journal of Agrarian Change* 5 (2): 191–216.

Goodhand, Jonathan and Mark Sedra. 2007. "Bribes or Bargains? Peace Conditionalities and 'Post Conflict' Reconstruction in Afghanistan." *International Peacekeeping* 14 (1): 41–61.

Hirshleifer, Jack. 1994. "The Dark Side of Force." *Economic Inquiry* 32: 1–10.

Integrated Regional Information Networks (IRIN). 2005. "Afghanistan: Rights Body Warns of Warlords' Success in Elections." 18 October.

Institute for War & Peace Reporting (IWPR). 2007a. "Helmand Heads for Record Poverty Harvest" ARR 241. 9 February.

————. 2007b. "Harvest in Helmand." ARR 250. 12 April.

Jalali, Ali, Robert Oakley, and Zoe Hunter. 2006. "Combating Opium in Afghanistan." Strategic Forum, Institution for National Strategic Studies, National Defence University, No. 224. November.

Keen, David. 1998. *The Economic Functions of Violence in Civil Wars*. Adelphi Paper 320. Oxford: Oxford University Press for the International Institute of Strategic Studies.

Khan, Mushtaq. 2002. "Fundamental Tensions in the Democratic Compromise." *New Political Economy* 7 (2): 275–77.

Koehler, Jan. 2005. "Conflict Processing and the Opium Poppy Economy in Afghanistan." Jalabad: GTZ Project for Alternative Livelihoods in Afghanistan.

Koehler Jan and Christoph Zuercher. 2006. "Statebuilding and the Opium Economy in Afghanistan. A View from Below." Unpublished draft. 18 January.

————. 2007. "Statebuilding, Conflict and Narcotics in Afghanistan: The View from Below." *International Peacekeeping* 14 (1): 62–74.

Labrousse, Alain. 2005. "Drugs: The Major Obstacle to Afghan Reconstruction?" In *Trouble in the Triangle: Opium and Conflict in Burma*, ed. Martin Jelsma, Kramer, and Pietje Vervest, 175–92. Bangkok: Silkworm Books.

Lister, Sarah. 2007. "Understanding Statebuilding and Local Government in Afghanistan." Crisis States Research Centre, Working Paper 14.

Lister, Sarah and Adam Pain. 2004. "Trading in Power." Kabul: Afghanistan Research and Evaluation Unit (AREU).

MacDonald, David. 2007. *Drugs in Afghanistan. Opium, Outlaws and Scorpion Tales*. London: Pluto.

McCoy, Alfred. 1999. "Requiem for a Drug Lord: State and Commodity in the Career of a Khun Sa." In *States and Illegal Practices*, ed. Josiah Heyman and Alan Smart, 129–68. Oxford: Berg.

————. 2003. *The Politics of Heroin: CIA Complicity in the Global Drug Trade*. Chicago: Lawrence Hill Books.

Mansfield, David. 2001. "The Economic Superiority of Illicit Drug Production. Myth and Reality." Paper for the International Conference on Alternative Development in Drug Control and Cooperation, Feldafing, Germany.

————. 2004. "Diversity and Dilemma: Understanding Rural Livelihoods and Addressing the Causes of Opium Poppy Cultivation in Nangahar and Laghman, Eastern Afghanistan." Report for the Project for Alternative Livelihoods (PAL) in Eastern Afghanistan.

————. 2006. "Responding to the Diversity in Opium Poppy Cultivation." In *Afghanistan's Drug Industry. Structure, Functioning, Dynamics and Implications for Counter-Narcotics Policy*, ed. Doris Buddenberg and William Byrd, 47–76. UNODC and World Bank.

————. 2007a. "Governance, Security and Economic Growth: The Determinants of Opium Poppy Cultivation in the Districts of Jurm and Baharak in Badakshan." Report for GTZ/AKDN. February.

————. 2007b. "Beyond the Metrics: Understanding the Nature of Change in the Rural Livelihoods of Opium Poppy Growing Households in the 2006/7 Growing Season." Report for the Afghan Drugs Inter Departmental Unit of the UK Government. May.

Mansfield, David and Adam Pain. 2005. "Alternative Livelihoods: Substance or Slogan?" AREU Briefing Paper. September.

————. 2006. "Opium Poppy Eradication: How Do You Raise Risk Where There Is Nothing to Lose?" AREU Briefing Paper. September 2006. Kabul: AREU.

Martin, Edouard and Steven Symansky. 2006. "Macroeconomic Impact of the Drug Economy and Counter-Narcotics Efforts." In *Afghanistan's Drug Industry. Structure, Functioning, Dynamics and Implications for Counter-Narcotics Policy*, ed. Doris Buddenberg and William Byrd, 25–46. UNODC and World Bank.

Milliken, J. and K. Krause. 2002. "State Failure, State Collapse, and State Reconstruction: Concepts, Lessons and Strategies." *Development and Change* 33 (5): 753–76.

Patterson, Anna. 2006. "Going to Market: Trade and Traders in Six Afghan Sectors." Kabul: AREU.

Pain, Adam. 2007. "Water Management, Livestock and the Opium Economy: The Spread of Opium Economy Cultivation in Balkh." Kabul: AREU.

Paris, R. 2004. *At War's End: Building Peace after Civil Conflict*. Cambridge: Cambridge University Press.

Pennington, Matthew. AP. 2007. "Afghan anti-corruption chief is a convicted heroin trafficker," *USA Today*. March 9. http://www.usatoday.com/news/world/2007-03-09-afghan-corruption_N.htm.

Pugh, Michael and Neil Cooper, with Jonathan Goodhand. 2004. *War Economies in a Regional Context: Challenges of Transformation*. Boulder, CO: Lynne Rienner.

Risen, James. 2007. "Poppy Fields Are Now a Front Line in Afghan War." *New York Times*. May 16.

Ramachandran, Sudha. 2003. "Afghanistan's opium wars." *Asia Times*. December 9.

Rubin, Barnett R. 2000. "The Political Economy of War and Peace in Afghanistan." *World Development* 28 (10): 1789–803.

———. 2004. "Road to Ruin. Afghanistan's Booming Opium Industry." New York Centre for American Progress/Centre on International Cooperation, New York University.

———. 2006. "Peace Building and State-Building in Afghanistan: Constructing Sovereignty for Whose Security?" *Third World Quarterly* 27 (1): 175–85.

———. 2007a. "Saving Afghanistan." *Foreign Affairs*. January/February: 57–78.

———. 2007b. "Transitional Counter-Narcotics in Afghanistan Using Capacity from the Opiate Industry." Unpublished paper. 16 June.

Rubin, Barnett R. and Humayun Hamidzada. 2007. "From Bonn to London: Governance Challenges and the Future of Statebuilding in Afghanistan." *International Peacekeeping* 14 (1): 8–25.

Rubin, Barnett R. and Omar Zakhilwal. 2005. "A war on drugs or a war on farmers?" *Wall Street Journal* (Eastern ed.). 11 January.

Schuster, H. 2006. "The Taliban Rules." *CNN*. 12 June. http://www.cnn.com/2006/WORLD/meast/12/06/schuster.12.6/index.html.

Shaw, D. 2006. "Drug Trafficking and the Development of Organised Crime in Post Taliban Afghanistan." In *Afghanistan's Drug Industry. Structure, Functioning, Dynamics and Implications for Counter-Narcotics Policy*, ed. Doris Buddenberg and William Byrd, 189–214. UNODC and World Bank.

Suhrke, Astri. 2007. "When More Is Less: Aiding Statebuilding in Afghanistan" Discussion draft for Research Partnership on Postwar State-Building. http://state-building.org.

Tilly, Charles. 1985. "War Making and State Making as Organized Crime." In *Bringing the State Back In*, ed. Peter Evans, Dietrich Fueschemeyer, and Theda Skocpol, 169–91. Cambridge: Cambridge University Press.

Transnational Institute. 2005. "Downward Spiral. Banning Opium in Afghanistan and Burma." Drugs and Conflict Debate Papers, no. 12. June. Transnational Institute, Netherlands.

United Nations Office on Drugs and Crime. 2006. *Afghanistan Opium Survey*. http://www.unodc.org/pdf/execsummaryafg.pdf.

———. 2007. *Afghanistan Opium Survey 2007*. http://www.unodc.org/pdf/research/Afghanistan_Opium_Survey_2007.pdf.

Walsh, Declan. 2006. "In the heartland of a mysterious enemy, US troops battle to survive." *Guardian*. 5 December.

Waterman, Shaun. 2007. "Afghan Drugs Post Created." *United Press International*. 28 March.

Wilder, Andrew. 2007. "Cops or Robbers? The Struggle to Reform the Afghan National Police." Afghan Research and Evaluation Unit, Issues Paper Series, Kabul. June.

Wood, Geof. 2003. "Staying Secure, Staying Poor: 'The Faustian Bargain.'" *World Development* 31 (3): 455–71.

Zetland, David. 2003. "Markets for Afghan Opium and US Heroin. Modelling the Connections." Social Science Research Network. http://ssrn.com/abastrct=668761.

The Economic Transition

4

William A. Byrd

Responding to Afghanistan's Development Challenge

An Assessment of Experience and Priorities for the Future

Introduction and Background

Since the fall of the Taliban regime, Afghanistan has faced a highly un-usual, and in many respects unique, set of development challenges—in particular the combination of extreme poverty and underdevelopment, very limited human capital, severe loss of state legitimacy and capacity, lack of rule of law, and the burgeoning illicit, mainly opium economy. Facing these challenges has been a reconstituted, internationally and to a large extent domestically legitimate Afghan government, together with the international community that has made a sizable political, military, and financial com-mitment. Afghanistan has thus become a demanding test case of the effec-tiveness of the international community's interventions in conflict-affected low-income countries suffering from state disintegration. This chapter as-sesses policies and performance over the past five years in responding to Afghanistan's development challenge, and, based on the lessons from ex-perience, looks toward the future.

After outlining the enormity of the development challenge faced by Afghanistan as well as some positive aspects of the situation, the chapter provides background on the economy and on key development issues and structural problems. It then assesses what has happened on the economic and development fronts over the past five years, covering economic man-agement, public sector management and governance, development man-agement, and economic performance and state building. It delves a bit more deeply into the dynamics of the evolving situation and then discusses Afghanistan's development prospects, issues, and priorities for the future. The chapter closes with further reflections on the state building agenda.

The Challenge

Devastated by nearly a quarter-century of protracted conflict, Afghanistan at the end of 2001 faced a daunting challenge in reconstruction. However, as one of the poorest and economically most backward countries in the world even prior to the onset of conflict in the late 1970s, Afghanistan also faced enormous development issues, which were inseparable from the reconstruction agenda. In particular, restoration of the status quo antebellum would not have been an acceptable strategy, for a number of reasons:

First, the dislocations of war over a very long period of time—destruction of traditional livelihoods, displacement of people, massive population growth, urbanization (including long stays in refugee camps or cities of neighbouring countries), large-scale monetization of the economy, growth of informal and illicit economic activities, and environmental degradation—meant that a return to the pre-war economy was not possible.

Second, although it had a high degree of self-sufficiency, the pre-war Afghan economy could not have been a springboard for economic development. It was a subsistence economy albeit with some traditional exports (dried fruits and nuts, carpets) at the margin. Moreover Afghanistan was not self-sufficient fiscally, relying on external aid to finance its public investments.

Third, the conflict had gone on for so long, and too much had happened globally during that period, for it to be viable to go back to the pre-war economy. Key developments included, among others, greater globalization of agriculture (including higher non-tariff barriers and quality standards even in traditional Afghan markets like India), the communications revolution, developments in transportation, and more generally an increasingly globalized economy.

Fourth, the pre-war Afghan state had only a veneer of modernity, did not reach out much beyond Kabul and a few other cities, and was oriented toward keeping the peace much more than service delivery, transformation, or development. Expectations of what the state can and should do have become far higher.

Finally, "reconstruction" without development would have left the country very poor and facing major vulnerabilities and risks of renewed conflict. This would have defeated the purpose of the international intervention in Afghanistan that has taken place since 2001.

Thus, overall, Afghanistan faced a situation in which reconstruction by itself made little sense, but there was a massive development agenda—for the country to steadily raise average per-capita incomes and move up from being a very poor low-income developing country (near the bottom of global development rankings) toward the higher end of the low-income range and eventually toward lower middle-income status. Pursuing this agenda was greatly complicated by the rapid rebound of the drug economy in the two years following the effective but short-lived Taliban ban on opium poppy cultivation in 2000. This ban had meant that economic development would have to occur in the context of reducing, and over time phasing out, the country's leading economic activity.

Background on the Economy

The economy that Afghanistan inherited in late 2001 was shaped not only by the pre-war legacy but by the long period of conflict, during which destruction of limited pre-war economic institutions occurred and illicit and conflict-related economic activities and behaviours became entrenched (Rubin 2000). According to available data and estimates, the Afghan economy stagnated (amid severe fluctuations) during the period from the late 1970s until the end of the century, with little or no growth of real gross domestic product (GDP) (Guimbert 2004). Not surprisingly, given that institutions and modes of doing business tend to persist, the impact of the "conflict economy" on recent economic development has been profound. Some key stylized facts about the Afghan economy are outlined below:

Afghanistan's economy is dominated by the informal sector (including illicit activities). It has been roughly estimated that 80 to 90% of total GDP (including opium) is accounted for by the informal sector (World Bank 2005b). As can be seen from Figure 1, not only is the informal sector dominant in agriculture as would be expected, it is also very important in mining, manufacturing, construction, trade, and infrastructure. This reflects not so much excessive government regulation and red tape (although corruption by all accounts is widespread and increasing) but a lack of basic rule of law and a poor investment climate resulting from state erosion and lack of capacity, infrastructural and financial constraints, and insecurity. The informal economy encompasses a wide spectrum of activities ranging from those that are fully legal (although perhaps evading registration requirements and/or tax liabilities) to those that are illicit in the way they are conducted (not necessarily in themselves) and, at the extreme, those that are outright illegal (notably narcotics).

Weak state capacity and lack of rule of law combine with the large informal/illicit economy to generate an "informal equilibrium," whereby incentives for development of formal sector businesses are weak, and instead the incentives to stay informal tend to be dominant (World Bank 2005b). Breaking out of this vicious cycle is a critical element of the overall development

FIGURE 1 **Rough Estimates of the Informal Economy**
in Different Sectors

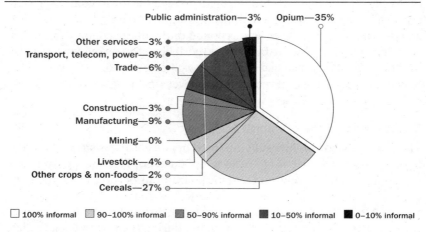

Source: Based on World Bank (2005b, 7).
Note: Percentage figures refer to the share of each sector in total GDP. Shadings are very rough estimates of the percentage of the informal economy in the sector concerned.

agenda, leading to sustained growth of economic activities in the formal sector and associated employment growth.[1] Dynamic trends related to the informal equilibrium are analyzed later in this chapter.

Afghanistan's human capital has been severely depleted by destruction, loss, and, most important, dismally low investment in human capital during the past thirty years. Correcting this will take several decades. In this context, high albeit temporary demand for some forms of labour (including from the international community in Afghanistan) does not seem to translate into sustained high employment growth but rather into high wage rates that even attract skilled labour from neighbouring countries.

This is manifested strikingly in weak government capacity, despite some improvements in recent years. Although structures and civil servants are in place, the effectiveness of government by all accounts is limited in most respects. Moreover, corruption is becoming very widespread and is perceived by firms as one of the main obstacles they face in the business environment.

The country appears to be suffering from "Dutch Disease," whereby extraordinary financial inflows support the balance of payments and thereby result in the appreciation of the exchange rate in real terms. This situation makes the economy less competitive because of higher costs. In the case of Afghanistan, this reflects large inflows of drug proceeds, aid, and possibly remittances, as well as the scarcity of literate, trained, and professionally qualified labour. Thus wages for skilled and professional labour are very high, and unskilled wages are driven up by the labour-intensive opium economy. Trends in the foreign exchange rate for the Afghani up to 2005 very much reflect the symptoms of Dutch Disease, and trends in the relative price of non-tradables to tradables have been similar (see IMF 2006, 11). With domestic inflation running higher than global inflation and the exchange rate holding fairly steady against the US dollar, Afghanistan's currency has been suffering from overvaluation. Although most of the appreciation in the real effective exchange rate occurred during the first several years post-2001, such appreciation is likely to have continued after 2005, albeit much more slowly given the sharp reduction in domestic inflation (although it is still above global inflation rates). International experience demonstrates that chronic overvaluation of the exchange rate is not good for economic growth.[2]

Reflecting a combination of Dutch Disease, investment climate problems, the dominance of opium production (for which the country has a strong comparative advantage), and other issues, Afghanistan's economy does not produce a sustainable gross domestic product with strong growth potential. Past export markets have been eroded or lost, or in some cases shifted into the informal sector with lower levels of quality and value. Import substitution is occurring to a much more limited extent than might have been expected given the high levels of imports of goods that have been produced in the past in Afghanistan, are relatively easy to produce with low levels of investment, or are transport-protected due to high weight–value ratios, and so on.

Overall, this is a high-cost, high-risk economy for investment, employment, and growth in the formal sector. Despite high demand, and with some notable exceptions (e.g., mobile telecommunications), expansion of the formal sector has been more limited than the overall growth of the economy would imply. The informal economy has exhibited dynamism (e.g., in propelling Afghanistan to become the dominant opium producer in the world and in smuggling and other trade) and plays an important role in absorbing excess labour in informal activities. But the informal economy itself does not provide a solid foundation for future economic growth and employment generation. It is not conducive to technological modernization and productivity improvements; incentives to invest in training are limited; size of business enterprises tends to be severely constrained; sustained export development is hard to generate (quality standards, getting around non-tariff barriers, insurance, etc.), and the learning by doing associated with formal sector activities does not occur, nor is there strong demand for required business services.

Amid these problems and constraints, there are some positives. First, Afghanistan has an entrepreneurial population—the long period of conflict and the refugee experience of many Afghans have tended to make people even more entrepreneurial. This characteristic, combined with the vibrant informal economy, enabled most Afghans to survive, and in some cases thrive, in an extremely difficult environment. The refugee population also built up significant human capital, comprising a valuable resource that can be brought to bear.

Second, Afghanistan by and large maintains a market-oriented and unrestricted policy environment for the private sector. This includes in particular relatively low import tariffs, few non-tariff barriers, relative ease of establishing new enterprises, sensible laws and regulations, and so on. Macroeconomic stability provides an important cornerstone for private sector development and employment growth. However, it must be recognized that despite this overall policy environment, at the level of the government bureaucracy—in particular at lower levels and in day-to-day transactions—and individual business firms, there tends to be hostility and corruption rather than neutrality, let alone productive co-operation. Businessmen complain about widespread bribery, harassment, and red tape, whereas government officials tend to see private businesses as having a mindset overly oriented toward short-term profits as opposed to longer-term investment and employment and, in the case of corrupt officials, as sources of cash to be exploited.

Third, as demonstrated in Afghanistan's Investment Climate Assessment, rigid labour laws are not a significant constraint on economic activity and employment generation in the private sector (as opposed to in the public sector, where there are de facto and de jure limits on labour adjustment).

Fourth, the informal sector itself could be a source of great economic dynamism, if it is harnessed through appropriate incentives and faces a conducive business environment for "formalization." It is important to transform the entrepreneurship, flexibility, and responsiveness to shocks demonstrated by Afghanistan's informal economy into sustained growth drivers in the formal sector.

Fifth, economic growth has been high, at well into double-digit rates over the last five years (see later discussion and also Figure 2). Even though this includes a large element of recovery and is based to a considerable extent on one-time or unsustainable growth drivers, such growth provides an environment of high demand that should be conducive for employment growth and business enterprise development. However, as growth settles down to lower levels, this window of opportunity will phase out.

This mélange of stylized facts and weaknesses, combined with some potential opportunities, makes overall for a highly unusual, in many ways virtually unique economy with formidable challenges. This calls for well thought-out, innovative, effective, and flexible economic policies and development approaches in response.

Key Development Challenges and Structural Issues

As in any country, the medium-term growth agenda is critical for Afghanistan to generate productive employment, raise per-capita incomes, and reduce poverty in a sustained manner. Maintaining rapid economic and employment growth will be all the more important because it is expected that a large, dynamic, and labour-intensive component of the economy—the opium sector—will decline and be phased out over time (Afghanistan and International Agencies 2004). At the same time, the forces driving recovery in the early post-Taliban years are expected to weaken. Thus new, sustainable "growth drivers" need to emerge. Intimately related to the challenge of sustaining economic growth is the need to build the competitiveness of Afghanistan's economy, not least so that exports can over time replace aid and opium as sources of foreign exchange for the country's balance of payments.

A second key development challenge is state building. Afghanistan will not achieve sustained development without a functioning, effective, accountable state. This in turn requires strong institutions, financial resources (ultimately through domestic revenue mobilization to pay for core state functions), adequate human capacity, and sound processes and management, including maintaining a reasonable degree of integrity. State building is a tall order, but it will be essential for the overall success of Afghanistan's development. In particular, complementary public inputs (infrastructure, regulation, rule of law and security, etc.) are prerequisites for sustained private-sector-based economic growth in the formal sector. And effective service delivery will be critical for building Afghanistan's human capital.

The profile of poverty itself is a challenge for poverty reduction, an ultimate development objective. Based on available household survey evidence, Afghanistan's poor are overwhelmingly illiterate, suffer from very low health indicators, have limited assets, are often highly vulnerable to shocks and to seasonal patterns of income, and must juggle marginal income-earning opportunities to make ends meet. Moreover, Afghanistan's poverty profile includes some difficult geographic pockets of poverty (e.g., remote rural areas with poor water and other resources) and confirms that education and health indicators are negatively correlated with poverty. Although income inequality in Afghanistan appears not to be very high, it is not clear what the trends have been; even limited inequality at very low levels of income can reflect extreme deprivation for the poorest.

These development challenges are made far more difficult by the continuing and expanding insurgency, chronic insecurity and lack of rule of law,

and problematic politics. These in turn are related to the lack of state func-
tionality mentioned above, the multi-faceted issues associated with the
opium economy, the expanding insurgency in the south, and to a lesser extent in the east, and political normalization, which has made a great deal
of progress on paper but also appears to have entrenched conflict-related
elites and political practices.

A Preliminary Assessment of the Past Five Years

It has now been more than five years since the political agreement reached
at the Bonn conference in December 2001, since the preparation of an initial reconstruction needs assessment and the Tokyo conference on
Afghanistan's reconstruction in January 2002, since the World Bank and
other international agencies came in with their first round of reconstruction assistance, and since the Emergency Loya Jirga established the transitional administration in July 2002. Thus there has now been sufficient
time to allow a meaningful review of economic and development management, policies, and performance, and to come to an initial assessment, even
if still preliminary.

As an effort to distill such an assessment into convenient summary form,
a rough "scorecard" is presented in Table 1. This inevitably simplifies a
much more complex, detailed, dynamic, and nuanced picture, but it may
be useful in identifying the areas where Afghanistan has done well and
those where serious problems and blockages have been encountered. The
discussion below fleshes out the scorecard and draws out key findings and
lessons.

Economic Management and Growth

Macroeconomic management has been a success story for Afghanistan,
starting early on with its highly successful currency reform and a strong commitment to avoid domestic budget deficit financing (i.e., all spending exceed-
ing domestic revenues to be covered by external assistance). This latter
commitment has been adhered to, and in combination with prudent monetary policy has resulted in a stable exchange rate and progressive decline
of inflation from initially high rates (hyperinflation in the 1990s) to single-
digit levels in the past two years (see Figure 2).

In other areas of economic policy the picture has been somewhat more
mixed. Financial sector reforms—in particular the establishment of a sound
regulatory framework—have encouraged a number of private banks to establish themselves in Kabul. However, there has been only limited progress
in restructuring the half-dozen state-owned banks, most of which appear
to be financially unviable. Moreover, the private sector in Afghanistan still

TABLE 1 **Economic and Development Policies, Management and Performance—A Rough Scorecard**

Category	Policy/ Mgmt. Score	Out- come Score	Comments
Economic Management			
Macroeconomic Management	+	+ +	Sound macro policies targeted at low inflation; successful currency reform provided foundation for price stability; inflation has come down to single digits; concerns about "Dutch Disease," high-cost economy
Fiscal Policy	+	+ +	Avoidance of domestic financing of the fiscal deficit; strong efforts to mobilize domestic revenue (although rate of revenue growth slowing); prudent control over total expenditure but increasing pressures
Trade Policy	+	0	Major rationalization of tariffs (which are low in regional context), with few non-tariff barriers; however, recent pressures for protection; trade facilitation is weak and problematic; export performance has been poor
Financial Sector Policy	0	–	Reforms have resulted in several private banks getting started, but the private sector still does not have much access to financial services, and limited progress has been made in restructuring state-owned banks
Private Sector Enabling Environment	0	–	Afghanistan maintains pro-private sector policy environment on paper, but there are obstacles of corruption and red tape, lack of access to finance and land, electricity, etc.; progress in formal sector development limited
Policies for Economic Growth	–	+	Growth policies have been fragmented and do not comprise an effective growth strategy; double-digit economic growth so far, but serious doubts about sustainability and what factors will drive future growth
Public Sector Management and Governance			
Public Finance Management	+ +	+	Major improvements in budgetary process; credible fiduciary standards and financial controls; but improvements dependent to a large extent on temporary external capacity; PFM in line ministries remains weaker

TABLE 1 *(continued)*

Category	Policy/ Mgmt. Score	Out- come Score	Comments
Public Sector Management and Governance, continued			
Public Administration Reform and Capacity Building	+	0	Significant progress through asymmetric reforms and development of a comprehensive PAR program, but limited success, sustainability of capacity building efforts; implementation of pay and grading reform will be key
Security Sector Reform	–	–	Good progress with Afghan National Army, but very slow reform of police; no national security strategy, and security has deteriorated in many areas
Justice Sector Reform	–	–	Lack of a sound sector strategy; little progress overall; institutions not functioning well, but recent improvements in leadership of some of them
Anti-Corruption Strategy and Policy	–	– –	Strong, consistent Government public commitment against corruption, and some progress in PFM, etc., but institutional disarray, and corruption by all accounts is widespread and has been increasing
Counter-Narcotics Efforts	–	– –	Sensible National Drug Control Strategy but fragmented and inconsistent CN activities; opium production has soared in recent years; signs of increasing consolidation and strength of drug industry
Political Normalization and State Building	+	0	Political progress in line with the Bonn Agreement of December 2001, but signs of dysfunctional political practices, "capture" of parts of the state via corruption associated with the drug industry, etc.
Development Management and Outcomes			
Development Strategy and Poverty Reduction	+	+	Compelling Government strategy documents since 2002, but need for prioritization, more consultations, and Government-wide ownership; currently working on ANDS to address these issues
Government Leadership	+	0	Strong Government efforts to exert leadership, but hindered by limited capacity, poor leadership in some sectors and line ministries, and donor practices and (in some cases) lack of donor buy-in

TABLE 1 *(continued)*

Category	Policy/ Mgmt. Score	Out- come Score	Comments
Development Management and Outcomes, continued			
Aid Management	+	0	Government attempting to take the lead and to instill Paris Declaration approach, but limited success in improving the cohesion of off-budget aid or in shifting large amounts of aid on-budget
Donor Aid Practices	0	–	A minority of aid can be said to follow "good practice"; however, most aid flows through bilateral channels without meaningful government leadership; recently signs that military concerns are distorting some aid
Development Communication	–	– –	Very limited efforts and poor outcomes in development communication within Government, at political level, with civil society, with public, and by donors; expectations have been raised and not well managed
Sector Policies and Performance			
Education	0	+	Tremendous expansion of primary enrolment (including girls) but still a very long way to go; major quality issues at all levels of education
Health	+ +	+	Successful adoption of cost-effective Basic Package of Health Services, with expanding coverage; numerous problems in the hospital system
Roads	+	+	Rehabilitation of Afghanistan's highway system nearly complete, but often at high cost; much construction and repair of rural roads; concerns about meeting maintenance requirements
Telecoms	+	+ +	Major progress in mobile telecommunications based on competitive private sector with regulation
Irrigation, Water, and Other Infrastructure	–	–	Some progress with rehabilitation, e.g., in irrigation, but lack of major investments, very few credible feasibility studies, and in many cases weak progress toward sector strategies; enormous agenda for the future

TABLE 1 (*continued*)

Category	Policy/ Mgmt. Score	Out- come Score	Comments
Sector Policies and Performance, continued			
Energy	–	– –	Modest improvements in power supply, power master plan prepared; but limited progress in Kabul has been a source of popular discontent; institutional weaknesses, modest investments, sustainability concerns
Agriculture	– –	–	Agricultural recovery from drought and some growth, but need transformation, agro-processing, and export development; weak institutions and need to bring in private business sector more
Community Development	+	+ +	National Solidarity Programme now covers most villages and effectively delivers small-scale rural infrastructure; questions about the institutional dimension, sustainability, future roles of Community Development Councils
Social Protection	0	+	Significant relief efforts and public works employment programs, which have achieved moderate success; limited progress toward developing an effective, broad-based, and sustainable social protection strategy

Source: Author's assessments.
Note: + + highly positive (very major progress); + positive (substantial but uneven progress, remaining problems); 0 neutral (neither positive nor negative, or mix of progress and setbacks); – negative (on balance); – – very negative (little or no progress at all or even backsliding).

does not have much access to financial services, and lack of access to finance constitutes one of the main obstacles perceived by private businesses as constraining their activities (World Bank 2005c).

Turning to trade policy, Afghanistan maintains a relatively liberal trade regime by regional standards, as a result of a major tariff rationalization in 2004. But there are signs of increasing pressures for a more protectionist approach. And export performance falls far short of what is needed to eventually overcome the dependence on inflows of aid and drug proceeds. Trade facilitation is weak and apparently suffers from widespread corruption. Although data on Afghanistan's balance of payments—like most other economic data on the country—are weak and have serious problems, the over-

FIGURE 2 Macroeconomic Indicators

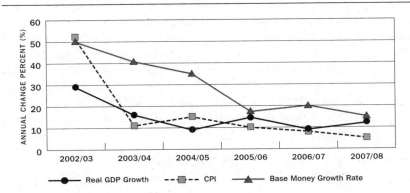

Source: IMF, Afghanistan Central Statistical Office.
Note: 2007/08 figures are projections.

FIGURE 3 Trade and the Balance of Payments

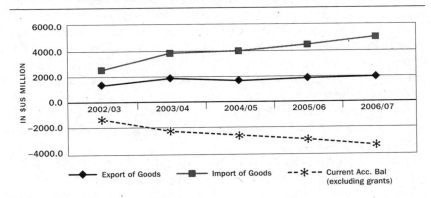

Source: IMF estimates.

all trade trends shown in Figure 3 accurately convey the anemic growth of exports and rapid growth of imports. The growing current account deficit has been financed largely by aid inflows.

Economic growth has been high over the last five years (Figure 2), averaging well into double-digit rates (excluding opium). Rapid growth has helped facilitate progress on the whole range of reconstruction, political normalization, and development agendas. However, the growth spurt appears to reflect primarily one-time (recovery at end of major conflict, from an extremely low base), temporary (influx of aid, population, remittances), and undesirable (stimulating impact of the opium economy) factors. Moreover, while Afghanistan has striven to develop a pro-private sector- and market-oriented policy environment, these efforts have achieved only mixed success, and a coherent, effective approach to sustaining economic growth, accompanied by the key required policy instruments, has not yet emerged.[3] Progress in developing a conducive enabling environment for private-sector development has been mixed, and the economy remains dominated by the informal (including illicit) sector. The growth issue will become increasingly important in the future as the initial growth spurt diminishes, and new, sustainable growth drivers will be needed. Another, related aspect is employment.

Public-Sector Management and Governance

Among the various dimensions covered under the umbrella of this broad topic, by far the greatest progress has been made in public finance management (PFM). Success in PFM improvements encompasses the broad fiscal aggregates as well as building better systems and processes to achieve positive outcomes. As can be seen in Figure 4, domestic revenue has been steadily increasing as a ratio to GDP, nearly doubling between 2002/03 and 2006/07. Operating expenditures are toward the lower end of the normal range for low-income countries. However, development expenditures include very substantial amounts of recurrent spending (see World Bank 2006a, chapter 6). Substantial progress has been made in covering an increasing proportion of operating costs from domestic revenues, and Afghanistan will soon be in a position to cover the government payroll from its own revenues. Maintaining revenue growth and continuing to progress toward a more sustainable fiscal situation will require continuing strong efforts and political will.

While a sound budget process (now including a nine-month formulation cycle) has been put in place and is functioning well for the operating budget, effective prioritization of the development budget has proven more difficult. In recent years the aggregate development budget target has far exceeded the actual out-turn of actual spending by year-end, which reflects several factors: (i) weak sector planning and inclusion of many poorly prepared or unprepared projects in the budget; (ii) uncertainty and unpredictability of funding; (iii) difficulties in cutting the proposals of ministries, even if based on past performance it is clear that they are wildly excessive; and (iv) issues related to multi-year funding commitments and ensuring that budget allocations do not hinder spending on large or lumpy projects. There have been improvements in the ratio of actual spending to the development budget target, especially in 2006/07, a sign that absorptive capacity is progressively increasing. However, prioritization continues to be a weak point in the budget process.

FIGURE 4 Budget Aggregates

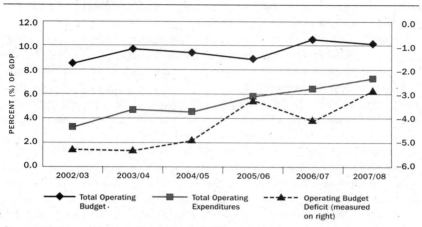

Source: Ministry of Finance, Government of Afghanistan.

Turning to PFM systems and processes, starting from an extremely low base, Afghanistan has made impressive improvements in all areas—from budget formulation to ex post accounting and auditing. An assessment of Afghanistan's PFM system based on the internationally developed Public Expenditure and Financial Accountability (PEFA) indicators found that Afghanistan had largely achieved levels comparable to other low-income developing countries: "This assessment generally portrays a public sector where financial resources are, by and large, being used for their intended purposes as authorized by a budget which is processed with transparency and has contributed to aggregate fiscal discipline. The expenditures and financial position of the government are reported regularly in an understandable format. Performance regarding the allocation of spending across programs and agencies and the efficiency of operations is not as good, however." (World Bank 2006a, v).

Overall this is a major accomplishment, considering the starting point in 2001. As noted, there continue to be weaknesses in prioritization and in enhancing the efficiency of resource utilization. A more general issue is that these accomplishments have been based to a considerable extent on external support to PFM operations. Hence the key challenge will be to further improve—or at least maintain—PFM performance ratings as the external capacity is phased out over time and replaced by sustainable domestic capacity.

In national capacity building and public administration reform, performance has been considerably weaker than in the PFM area. Nevertheless, some significant progress must be acknowledged. At the start, the

government was largely ineffective, and civil servants were paid only sporadically and at extremely low pay levels (due to hyperinflation in the 1990s).
The difference between the pay of the lowest grades and that of top officials
was only 10–20%—almost certainly the most compressed civil service pay
structure in the world.[4] Payment of civil servants was regularized, and most
civil servants are now paid in a reasonably timely manner. Significant albeit
still very modest decompression of pay has occurred (through a very large
percentage increase in base pay). However, the tendency in the pay increases so far has been to increase the cash allowance across the board, as
this does not have any implication for pension liabilities.

The asymmetric Priority Reform and Restructuring (PRR) program was
launched in 2004, under which key departments and in some cases ministries, in return for modest restructuring and merit-based recruitment for
designated positions, could temporarily pay those staff at much higher
salary scales on a temporary basis. The experience with PRR has been
mixed, but initial results were good in some ministries and agencies. An effort at wholesale expansion of PRR (reflecting in part political pressures and
equity concerns) severely diluted quality—the restructuring in many cases
was only pro forma, and merit-based selection for positions frequently was
observed in the breach, with incumbents being highly favoured.

During the past two years the focus in public administration reform has
shifted toward designing more comprehensive civil service reforms, including most notably pay and grading reform that would raise and sharply de-
compress pay levels for civil service positions, with a vetting process to
move existing civil servants onto the new pay structure based on their qualifications and explicit position requirements. This ambitious reform raises
many questions: about the fiscal cost and sustainability of the new pay
structure; whether and to what extent organizational restructuring should
precede the exercise (it makes little sense—and would be very costly—to
move staff onto the new pay structure in departments that would ultimately
be abolished or merged); how to ensure reasonably effective implementation (and in particular avoid the risk of a wholesale rush to move everyone
onto the new pay structure without concern for qualifications or whether
there is a need for them); implications for pensions and pension costs; sequencing and timing of implementation, and so on. Such reform efforts
have more often than not failed in other developing countries, including those
starting out from a much better position than Afghanistan. Nevertheless,
the government has moved ahead with the design of this program, and implementation is expected to start shortly.

Capacity building remains a central issue that has not been well addressed, except in a fragmented and not fully sustainable manner in some
ministries. Much capacity has been "bought in" at high cost but has not re-

sulted in the building of sustainable core capacity in government. There are widespread concerns about the quality, cost, management, and sustainable capacity building impact of technical assistance (TA) for Afghanistan, which according to rough estimates amounts to several hundred million dollars per year (see World Bank 2007).

Despite the serious problems with public administration reform and capacity-building efforts, other dimensions of governance improvements have fared far worse by comparison. Corruption has increased progressively and has spread widely since the downfall of the Taliban, especially in recent years. Anti-corruption efforts have been undermined by institutional disarray, limited political will, and the sheer magnitude of the problem (including notably drug-related corruption). Corruption, a symptom of poor governance, is a cancer eating away at Afghanistan's state, economy, and society. Although corruption is found in all countries, its adverse impact is magnified in Afghanistan by (i) the loss of the state's capacity, effectiveness, and legitimacy during a quarter-century of conflict; (ii) the entrenchment of an illicit/informal economy during the conflict—especially the opium economy; (iii) the large amounts of funds potentially available for corrupt purposes, including from drugs and aid; (iv) pressures to spend money quickly at the expense of sound monitoring and financial controls; and (v) the fragility of the political situation and the political normalization process.

The government has strongly and consistently stated its commitment to fight against corruption, and there have been promising initiatives and progress in some areas. Examples include:

- The prominence given to the anti-corruption agenda in government public statements and documents—going all the way back to the Tokyo Conference at the beginning of 2002 and including the I-ANDS and the ANDS;
- Substantial progress in developing and implementing basic fiduciary controls to limit the risk of corruption in Afghanistan's Core Budget, and more generally improvements in public financial management which play an important role in preventing corruption;
- Assessments of vulnerabilities to corruption (VCAs) that are underway in a number of sectors/areas, conducted in close collaboration and consultation with government agencies (examples include revenue administration, the civil service appointment process, energy, roads, and underground resources, etc.); and
- An anti-corruption roadmap paper prepared with the assistance of international partners, which was presented by the government at the 2007 Afghanistan Development Forum Meeting.

Nevertheless, these areas of progress pale against the magnitude of the challenge. If nothing is done about corruption, Afghanistan's development prospects will be severely threatened and undermined, not only because of the associated direct losses of resources and distorted behaviour but also because corruption attacks the legitimacy of the government in the eyes of both the Afghan people, whose buy-in and support is essential, and the international community that provides financial and military assistance as well as political backing. Corruption is profoundly inimical to state building, a core element of Afghanistan's overall reconstruction and development agenda.

Counter-narcotics efforts have not succeeded in reducing opium production, which on the contrary has soared to record levels; moreover, they have inadvertently contributed to a consolidation of the drug industry around fewer, powerful, and politically connected actors (Buddenberg and Byrd 2006). Opium production has increased sharply, especially in 2006 and 2007; it has shifted around the country, spreading to most provinces and more recently becoming more concentrated in the insecure, insurgency-ridden province of Helmand. Initial successes in reducing production have turned out to be unsustainable, and the drug trade has become more organized and consolidated, as noted above.

Justice sector reform and investments in the justice sector have lagged far behind improvements in security services (especially the Afghan National Army), as discussed in World Bank (2005a, Volume V). This imbalance reflects weak and fragmented government leadership and weak donor support. Lagging justice sector reform has adverse ramifications for other important parts of Afghanistan's overall development agenda, including among others private sector development.

Development Management and Outcomes

A sound development strategy is essential for good development management. Since 2002 the government with external support has produced a series of high-quality development strategy documents, including most notably a draft National Development Framework in April 2002 (Afghanistan 2002), the *Securing Afghanistan's Future* exercise and report of January 2004 (see Afghanistan and International Agencies 2004), and the Interim Afghanistan National Development Strategy (I-ANDS) produced in early 2006 (Afghanistan 2006). In addition, although the Bonn Agreement of December 2001 did not deal extensively with development issues, the Afghanistan Compact, agreed upon with the international community at the London meeting in January 2006, includes major clauses and a number of benchmarks covering development aspects.[5] There have also been numerous strategy documents produced dealing with individual sectors and topics, albeit of varying quality. The government has been preparing an ambitious full-scale ANDS, which will also serve as Afghanistan's Poverty Reduction Strategy Paper to be submitted to the World Bank and the International Monetary Fund (as the I-ANDS served as its I-PRSP). Overall, Afghanistan has not lacked for high-quality development strategy documents, so this has not been a constraint on progress.

Two issues have adversely affected development strategy formulation, however. There was extremely limited consultation and dissemination for the earlier strategy documents. The National Development Framework was never translated into national languages and was disseminated little outside donor meetings. *Securing Afghanistan's Future* did not have full buy-in from within the government and was a quick exercise that again did not include a significant consultation component. Although there were more extensive consultations around the I-ANDS, neither it nor the Afghanistan Compact were presented to or discussed in parliament, even though the latter included certain benchmarks requiring parliamentary ratification.

Second, these strategy documents tended to reflect a "needs assessment" approach and did not embody a resource envelope (except as constructed *ex post* by adding up the requirements) nor explicit prioritization and sequencing or even some principles that might guide prioritization.[6] A needs assessment approach probably made sense at the outset and was less problematic in the early years when absorptive capacity was more limited, the budget process was rudimentary, and available funds could not be fully spent (de facto prioritization was determined under such circumstances by the disbursement rates for spending on different activities). However, beyond a certain point (certainly reached in the last several years), both improvements in the budget process and increasing absorptive capacity meant that meaningful prioritization became much more essential, and the lack of prioritization in government strategy documents became a very serious disconnect and constraint. This lacuna has been recognized, and the full ANDS is intended to include a much greater focus on costing and prioritization. However, as prioritization is fundamentally a political process, and given the nascent and difficult politics currently in Afghanistan—within the cabinet as well as vis-à-vis the legislature—effective prioritization in both development strategy and the annual budget process is likely to be difficult and to take time to instill.

Turning to government leadership, in addition to the strategic documents discussed above, the government has attempted with some degree of success to take leadership of the development agenda and development management (including aid management, discussed later in this section). By the end of 2002, a heavily donor-driven and donor-led mechanism—the Afghanistan Reconstruction Steering Group—was replaced by a government-led consultative group process. Subsequently, in a variety of ways, the government demonstrated a considerable degree of leadership with respect to the development agenda and development management, including through regular annual Afghanistan Development Forum meetings, organizing and taking the lead on major development strategy exercises, and also strongly emphasizing key elements of the aid effectiveness agenda, based on the Paris Declaration on Aid Harmonization.

However, government leadership has encountered limits and has fallen well short of what would be desirable. This relates in part to political fragmentation and difficulties encountered in the political normalization process, as well as to a clash between traditional and conflict-induced modes of doing business and more "modern" modes of interaction. The difficulties also reflect inherent, as well as more fixable, tensions resulting from Afghanistan's extraordinarily high dependence on aid and the modalities of aid delivery. Fundamentally, there is a contradiction between government leadership and high aid dependence—the "State Building Paradox" referred to in Nixon (2007)—that needs to be well managed to avoid prolonged aid dependence detracting from government leadership.

The situation and progress of aid management is also very much related to the challenges faced by the government in trying to exert leadership and is worsened by the following factors. First, there are an enormous number of donors active in providing assistance to Afghanistan—according to the government, as many as sixty-two, including various non-governmental donors. Second, a substantial number of these donors—a half-dozen or more—are major players in terms of the amount of assistance they provide and/or as actors on the world stage. Unlike in many other post-conflict countries, there is no natural dominant or "lead" donor in the development sphere (although the US has played that role on the military side).[7] In addition, although there has never been a UN government or trusteeship in Afghanistan, the UN system, the United Nations Assistance Mission in Afghanistan (UNAMA) in particular, plays a very important role, led by a special representative of the UN Secretary-General. This includes the overall coordination of the closely interlinked political, security, and development agendas.

While in part a reflection of the extremely limited capacity in government that was discussed earlier, this relates very much as well to problems in the modalities of aid to Afghanistan. Roughly two-thirds of total assistance to Afghanistan (more in the early days) has been channelled bilaterally and outside the government budget and control systems, with very little coordination and even limited information sharing. Although some donors provide most of their aid through the Afghan national budget, several very large donors go off-budget with the bulk of their assistance.

The deleterious effect of this aid-flow pattern on efforts by the government to take leadership in development management, as well as on the state building agenda more generally, must be emphasized. While in most developing countries much if not most aid tends to be off-budget, the damaging effects are more limited in a context where the government has enough domestic revenue to cover most of its core recurrent expenditures and part of development spending as well. In Afghanistan, on the contrary, a "business-as-usual" approach to aid is much more damaging. In addition to the very serious difficulties such a pattern of aid poses for government leadership in aid management, it is also highly distortionary in terms of prioritization, lack of predictability, and competition for very scarce qualified human resources, which are recruited by off-budget projects, preventing them from working in the government or otherwise building core government capacity. Much of Afghanistan's very limited pool of professional and managerial talent is employed in this "second civil service."

In 2006 the international community and the government of Afghanistan subscribed to a comprehensive Afghanistan Compact with five-year benchmarks, and associated with it are a monitoring and dialogue process overseen by the Joint Coordination and Monitoring Board (JCMB). Despite undoubted benefits, this process appears to be rather burdensome (not least in terms of the number and varying locations of meetings) and mechanically process-oriented. Hence its results in terms of improving aid coordination appear to have been limited so far and don't offset the deficiencies related to off-budget aid that were mentioned earlier.

Development communication is another problem area in development management. Positive messages about the progress made have not been emphasized strongly enough or repeated often enough to have a commensurate impact on perceptions. At the same time, already inflated expectations have been exacerbated by high-profile meetings, numerous visits, and public announcements of large amounts of assistance available or pledged. This area has not received sufficient priority from either the government or donors, and communication has been fragmented, with little coordination for the most part. As a result, not only have positive benefits been limited but disappointed expectations among the populace are increasingly becoming a political issue with possible adverse ramifications for security as well.

At the sector level, development performance has been decidedly mixed, covering the full range of ratings used in Table 1. The greatest progress has been achieved in the health sector (through widespread implementation of the Basic Package of Health Services (BPHS) implemented mainly by non-government providers) and in community development through the National Solidarity Programme (NSP). Progress has been poor in the energy sector and also in most other infrastructure.[8] Rehabilitation and construction of roads has achieved significant progress albeit at relatively high costs in highway rehabilitation,[9] and there has been considerable social protection provided through sizable humanitarian assistance, but without a strategy or effective government programs for this purpose. Education has seen a tremendous increase in access and enrolments, with elementary school enrolments reaching unprecedented levels, far above any seen in the pre-war period (especially for girls). However, there are serious concerns about the quality of education that is being delivered (which would need to be confirmed through achievement tests). And education is being delivered almost entirely through the traditional highly centralized service delivery model, with all teachers having the status of civil servants in the national government, which raises a number of questions on fiscal, accountability, and efficiency grounds.

Although radically different models of service delivery and the role of the state have been used in the various sectors, the most important determinant of performance appears to have been the strength and cohesion of Afghan leadership at the level of line ministries. Ministries either led by the minister him- or herself, or through a competent, cohesive, and empowered leadership team just below the minister level, that have developed and implemented a sound approach to the sector concerned, have achieved a considerable and even surprising (in the Afghanistan context) degree of progress. On the other hand, ministries that have lacked leadership and a cohesive team at the top have struggled and often have achieved much less, if any, progress toward sector objectives.

This cursory review of sector development management and performance raises an important question as to whether the performance of lagging line ministries (and the sectors they are responsible for) can be raised to the level of the better-performing ministries, which would have a strong positive impact on sector and overall development performance. Given that a major factor in this regard would appear to be leadership, lagging line ministries' Afghan leadership teams need to be strengthened and made more coherent. This would certainly be possible in terms of the Afghan human capacity available for such leadership positions, but there are probably political constraints affecting the selection of cabinet members, and even if change efforts are focused on the level immediately below the minister, issues related to empowering competent ministry management teams would need to be addressed.[10]

Turning to development outcomes, these have been driven in the positive sense by rapid economic growth over the past five years and increasingly effective programs and service delivery in a few sectors like health. However, even after a substantial rise in recent years, Afghanistan's per-capita income remains very low, and its social indicators are among the worst in the world despite some significant improvements. Employment in the formal sector, like formal-sector development as a whole, has not made much of a dent in the growing labour supply, and although the informal sector can and does mop up unemployment, it undoubtedly includes much low-wage underemployment and seasonal employment (the latter most notably in opium poppy cultivation).

Finally, poverty reduction is the ultimate and quintessential development outcome, and the revival of economic activity and growth undoubtedly has had a positive impact. Poverty, however measured, remains widespread and deep (in terms of the gap between the poor and the poverty line).

Overall Assessment and Some Caveats

Overall, this assessment of development policies and performance, based on a composite picture of the last five years, is reasonably positive. If we step back from day-to-day engagement and think about the five-year picture in relation to the starting point, it is clear that despite the enormous challenges and constraints, much meaningful progress has been made. The situation after five years would have been much worse, if not for the currency reform and macroeconomic stability; rapid economic growth and associated rises in incomes; payment of civil servants' salaries on an increasingly regularized basis; the expansion of service delivery in some sectors (health, education); and a highly successful community development program (NSP). In many other areas progress has been less dramatic but nevertheless significant in many respects.

There are, however, some areas where the lack of progress has been striking. In economic management, the broader enabling environment for private business in the formal sector is still quite weak. This also includes aspects of financial services and to a lesser extent, especially with recent backsliding, trade policy. There are very serious problems with the governance agenda (other than PFM), including stumbling justice sector reforms, widespread and increasing corruption, and counter-narcotics efforts that have failed to stem a large increase in opium production and inadvertently have contributed to the consolidation of the drug industry. On the development management front, there are serious problems despite considerable progress: the aid system remains to a large extent fragmented and chaotic, most aid goes outside government channels, efforts by the government to exert leadership have not been fully successful, and so on. At the level of sectors, there has been poor progress in major infrastructure development (other than highways) and especially mobile telecommunications.

Lack of electricity, water, and other essential services in many urban areas is not only a serious development issue but also foments discontent. At a fundamental level, the lack of security in many parts of the country, and limited rule of law, are critical issues that are discussed in other chapters of this book.

In addition to the uneven progress across different parts of the development agenda, there are a number of important caveats affecting this assessment as a whole or parts of it, which must be taken into account and which temper the level of optimism.

First, the assessment of progress has been against the starting point in late 2001 and against a reasonable yardstick of significance and importance. While this is undoubtedly useful, what is relevant for Afghanistan's future prospects is whether progress has been adequate in relation to what the country needs in order to escape from the "conflict trap" of the 1990s and move forward on the path of sustained development.[11] There is considerable doubt as to whether progress in most areas has met this more demanding standard; only in a few can this be said to have definitely occurred.

A second, related caveat is that the progress and accomplishments, however real, are running far behind expectations—on the part of the population, politicians, donors, and among government officials. Expectations were unrealistically high at the outset, and they were excessively fuelled by a number of factors, including numerous and often high-level donor meetings, politicians' promises (from both Afghans and international actors), the large pledges and commitments of aid announced with much fanfare, smaller but nevertheless substantial amounts of aid funds reported as disbursed, and the comparison of all these with the reality that public services, infrastructure, and even basic government functioning are still in a poor state in many respects and in much of the country. This clash of expectations with reality is not only a problem in itself, but it also adversely affects Afghanistan's prospects through the popular discontent fuelled, which can have political and, at the extreme, even security implications. In addition to inherent problems of managing expectations in such a volatile environment, where after a quarter-century of conflict expectations inevitably were high, this lack of progress is also attributable to poor development communications.

A third important caveat is that a five-year composite picture does not do justice to changing trends and dynamic developments within this fairly long period of time; in particular, the most recent trends may diverge from earlier progress. In some areas there was important progress during the first two to three years, followed by slowdown, drift, or even backsliding—seriously affecting prospects in the immediate future as well as over the medium term. In the economic sphere, such an adverse pattern of developments within the five years has been limited to a couple of areas, most notably trade policy. In public sector management and governance, it is possible that the situation with respect to corruption has worsened more rapidly in recent years. Clearly the role of the drug industry, particularly its interactions with the state, has evolved adversely. The role of parliament (including in the budget process) is still relatively new and continues to develop. On the other hand, recent improvements in leadership in the justice sector may open up opportunities for reform that did not exist earlier.

A fourth caveat is that irrespective of the progress (or lack thereof) in the areas covered by this chapter, new or growing problems emanating from outside these areas may be increasingly impinging on Afghanistan's development prospects. In any case, the broad elements of Afghanistan's agenda are closely interlinked, requiring strategic integration in thinking and approaches. The insurgency in the south and east of the country, in particular, poses serious threats to the development and state building agenda, especially if it continues at a high level of intensity. A second set of issues relates to politics. Even though the political benchmarks of the Bonn process were met and all of the institutions of a democracy are now functioning in Afghanistan, at least in rudimentary form, political normalization can be problematic in an environment characterized by lack of rule of law, entrenched power-holders from the protracted conflict situation, weak norms of democratic political behaviour, and a growing insurgency. Although it is too early to assess these trends, there are grounds for some concern. A prominent example is the Amnesty Bill recently passed.

With all these caveats, the undoubted achievements of the past five years are put into perspective against the magnitude of the challenge and the apparent drift and the backsliding in some areas in recent years. It is clear that what has been done so far is not enough, and the question of which areas require more intervention will be taken up in the concluding section.

Changing Dynamic Patterns and Trends

This section delves a bit more deeply into the changing dynamics of Afghanistan's state building challenge and its interlinkages with other key dimensions, including most notably the drug industry.

State Building, Formalization, and Security

The need for strategic integration of the different elements of Afghanistan's development agenda—security, reconstruction, economic growth, governance and state building, and counter-narcotics—has been repeatedly emphasized (World Bank 2005b, especially chapter 3; McKechnie 2003). The conceptual framework of a "vicious circle" or low-level "informal equilibrium" was developed by the World Bank (2005b, chapter 1) to analyze the forces at work during the conflict period and immediately after, which mutually reinforce each other and contribute to keeping Afghanistan poor, dominated by the informal sector, weakly governed, lacking rule of law, and subject to chronic insecurity. Developments since 2001 have brought major changes to the scene, but the underlying dynamics and power structure are still very important. The discussion below briefly summarizes what is inevitably a complex topic.

As emphasized earlier in this chapter and as discussed in more detail in the World Bank report (2005b, chapter 1), Afghanistan's economy is dominated by the informal sector. The "informal equilibrium" that prevailed in 2001 and shortly thereafter is depicted in Figure 5. As the failed government cannot ensure security around the country, local powers (warlords) take over this role, but they undermine the rule of law and have limited incentives to provide public goods. Instead, they have incentives to develop profitable illegal activities to finance their armed forces (see Rubin 2000). Entrepreneurs have little or no incentive to become formal in this situation, and as a result they do not pay taxes, preventing the government from being able to acquire resources to provide security or other services. Thus this "vicious circle" is self-perpetuating and creates a strong constituency that is hostile to the strengthening of the central government.

Breaking out of the informal equilibrium and moving to a "formal equilibrium," which is much more conducive to medium-term economic growth and state building, would require strong actions on a number of fronts.[12] As indicated in Figure 6, when the government builds its capacity it is more able to provide public goods and enforce the rule of law, which changes the incentives for private businesses so that at least some of them move into the formal sector. This in turn results in more tax payments to the government, enabling it to further build its capacity; the incentives to go formal are thereby further enhanced, and so on. A key (albeit probably unrealistic) ingredient of this scenario is that warlords are removed from the scene by disarming their militias and encouraging them to operate increasingly through legitimate political channels. External assistance is envisaged to play an important role by providing additional resources to the government to help it strengthen the rule of law, provide public services, and enhance its own ability to collect revenues. Foreign investment can facilitate formalization and private sector development. The informal sector can become a source of entrepreneurs and businesses that move into the formal sector. It must be recognized that this is a longer-term scenario, but nevertheless it shows the desirable direction of change and the end-point.

FIGURE 5 The Informal Equilibrium

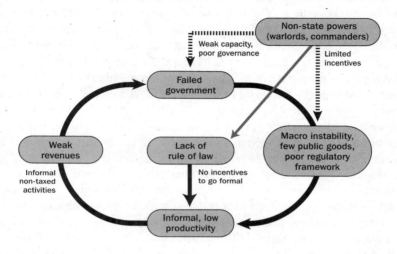

Source: Adapted from World Bank (2005b, 10).

FIGURE 6 Moving toward the Formal Equilibrium

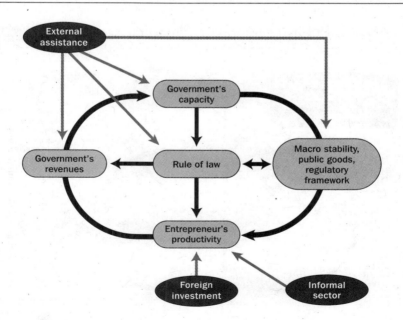

Source: Stephane Guimbert (personal communication), based on World Bank (2005b, 31).

Despite the superficial attractiveness of the "formal equilibrium" scenario, it is becoming increasingly clear that although there has been some progress in this direction (e.g., macroeconomic stability and rising domestic revenues), dynamic trends are far from universally positive. Figure 7 attempts to illustrate some of the recent trends that are of concern. Under this scenario, warlords and commanders have not disappeared but in many cases have successfully entered politics, becoming members of parliament or provincial councils.[13] This may have undermined efforts to build the rule of law (an example is the recent Amnesty Bill approved by the parliament). In addition, the environment for formalization has not improved as markedly as might have been expected, and progress on the private sector development agenda has lagged. Although some aid has directly and indirectly supported the state building agenda (as illustrated in Figure 6), most external assistance has been channelled outside the national budget and treasury, and therefore has not been supportive of building sustainable government capacity. And the growing insurgency is undermining state building and formalization, not least by shifting attention toward conflict-related and short-term issues. The consolidation of the drug industry also is playing a very important role in undermining the government, rule of law, and formal private sector development, including through political corruption funded by drug proceeds.

FIGURE 7 **The Evolving Informal Equilibrium**

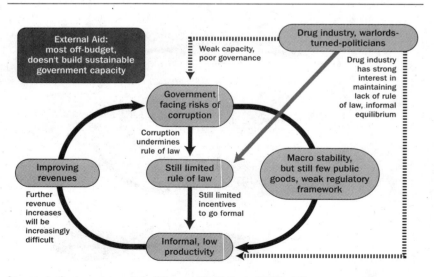

Source: Author's assessment, building on World Bank (2005b, 10).

What Figure 7 suggests overall is that some key aspects of the state building and formalization agenda are going off-track, and that overall progress is being threatened by (i) the evolving politics in which former warlords, commanders, and conflict-generated political groupings are playing an important role; (ii) the linkage of the state and politics with the consolidating drug industry; (iii) the continuing and expanding insurgency; and (iv) the modalities by which most aid is delivered and the disappointing results achieved by much of the aid. State building in this context risks being distorted by corruption and political practices and also by interest groups formed during the long period of conflict.

Drug Industry Dynamics

Afghanistan's drug industry has been evolving since 2001–03. Figure 8 depicts a vicious circle involving the opium economy, warlords, and insecurity—broadly reflecting the situation as opium production rebounded in the first two years following the downfall of the Taliban. In this situation, payments from the opium economy strengthened warlords, who in turn undermined the state, while drug-related corruption also undermined the state directly. In return for payments, warlord militias helped provide the enabling environment (often including armed protection) for the opium economy to operate. The weak government was unable to provide genuine security or rule of law, and this created a good environment in which the opium economy could continue to thrive.

What this vicious circle suggests is that a multi-faceted strategic framework would be needed to effectively address the opium economy and the problems it causes for the rest of Afghanistan's development agenda. Counter-narcotics efforts (narrowly construed) alone would be unlikely to prove successful. In a World Bank report (2005b, chapter 7), a strategic framework for a more comprehensive approach to fighting drugs in Afghanistan was put forward (see Figure 9). In addition to reducing the size of the drug economy through effective counter-narcotics measures more narrowly construed, this framework included (i) curbing warlords' powers by stopping payments and other support to them, DDR to take away their militias, and co-opting them into the government as appropriate; (ii) building government capacity and effectiveness a well as resources; and (iii) security sector reform and capacity building.

However, not enough improvement at the broader strategic level was achieved, and counter-narcotics efforts have failed to prevent further growth of the opium economy or the consolidation of the drug industry (Shaw 2006). As a result, both the opium problem and its adverse impacts on the state building and development agenda have become worse. As depicted in Figure 10, the transformation of warlords into politicians working in

FIGURE 8 The Vicious Circle of the Opium Economy

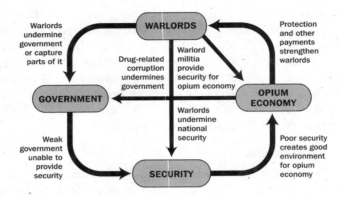

Source: Adapted from World Bank (2005b: 120).

FIGURE 9 Strategic Framework for Breaking Out of the Vicious Circle

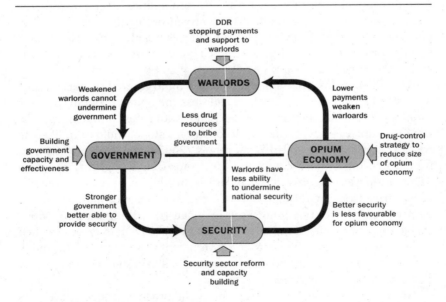

Source: Adapted from World Bank (2005b: 127).

FIGURE 10 **Consolidation of the Drug Industry**

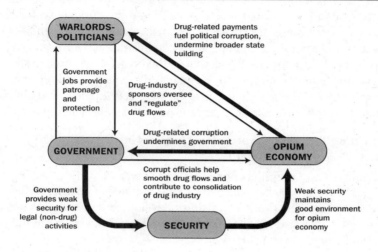

Source: Author's assessment; drawing on analysis in Shaw (2006).

the political and governmental sphere has been accompanied by the compromising by drug industry interests of parts of some government agencies like the Ministry of Interior and the police. The triangle between drug interests, their political and other sponsors, and parts of the government reflects the fact that—primarily through widespread corruption in their implementation—counter-narcotics efforts have inadvertently contributed to drug industry consolidation. Security forces, most notably the police, are in part facilitating activities of the drug industry rather than countering it.

Priorities for Action

The changing dynamics of the situation in Afghanistan are troubling in several respects. The interactions between the evolving politics and state building could be seriously detrimental to the latter; the insurgency is, in addition to its direct threat, distracting attention from the broader and longer-term development agenda and distorting priorities. The drug industry continues to fuel corruption and to undermine important parts of the government, widespread and growing corruption is seriously harming the government's credibility and legitimacy in the eyes of the people, and there is increasing discontent about the slow progress of reconstruction.

This section of the chapter focuses on priorities for action in several critical areas of the development agenda. It does not discuss the political process or the insurgency, although as emphasized earlier these impinge greatly on Afghanistan's development prospects. First, some options on how to respond to the challenge of sustaining robust private sector-based economic growth are put forward. Then the governance agenda is discussed, including anti-corruption, public administration reform, and (related to both) public accountability, as well as the progress required in the area of development communication. Elements of a "smart" counter-narcotics strategy also are discussed, and priorities for development and aid management. At the close, the chapter returns to the state building agenda.

Sustaining Economic Growth and Supporting Private Sector Development

Sustaining (non-opium) economic growth, never easy under any circumstances, will be especially challenging in the circumstances discussed above, with central elements of Afghanistan's development agenda progressing more slowly than is desirable, distorted by some of the trends in the politics, insurgency, and drug industry. Nevertheless, there appear to be opportunities to move forward. First, however, it is very important to keep in mind directions and policies that, based on international experience and conditions in Afghanistan, are not likely to work and therefore should be avoided. Some examples are listed in Box 1.

Taking a more positive perspective, some options for action to help stimulate private sector–based economic growth are put forward below.

First, at the macro level, a more active exchange rate policy (i.e., depreciation of the Afghani) may help offset the adverse impact of the Dutch Disease and make production of tradables (exports and import substitutes) more attractive, thereby promoting private sector development and associated employment growth. As noted earlier, international experience suggests that an overvalued exchange rate is inimical to longer-term economic growth in developing countries. An option worth serious consideration would be to pursue a more active exchange rate policy vigorously, but not beyond the point where it significantly increases inflation and threatens macroeconomic stability.

Second, turning to the more micro level, there may be ways to break through barriers related to the investment climate by means of "enclave-type" approaches in the short run—most notably by scaling up and maximizing the effectiveness of industrial parks. While bringing about overall improvements in the investment climate nationwide inevitably will be a medium- to longer-term endeavour, it should be possible within the contained areas of industrial parks to alleviate the main bottlenecks for potential investors—security, access to land, corruption and red tape, and infrastructure (power, water, convenient transport). It should also be possible,

BOX 1 **What Is Not Likely to Work in Promoting Economic Growth**

International and Afghan experience suggests that some common approaches to promoting sustained growth are very unlikely to work. The following are examples of approaches that should be avoided:

- **Highly complex schemes** Schemes requiring capacity, effective discretionary action, and an unrealistic level of integrity in the government bureaucracy are unlikely to work well.

- **Protection of domestic economic activities via high import tariffs or quantitative restrictions** Aside from the anti-export bias, lobbying tendencies, and the weakening of efficiency incentives, etc., that are associated with protective trade regimes, Afghanistan's porous borders and the widespread availability of the smuggling option mean that tariff protection or non-tariff barriers are most unlikely to be effective. The fact that even heavily transport-protected activities are not taking off suggests that trade barriers would not be very effective in promoting import substitution. Moreover, the critical imperative to build competitiveness through export development would not be served by a protective trade regime.

- **Blanket subsidy schemes** Although attractive in principle as a means of offsetting certain disadvantages (e.g., high cost of labour, barriers to exports), blanket subsidy schemes carry numerous distortions and problems, especially in the Afghan context. Moreover, the fiscal costs of subsidies would be high and very difficult to manage given the low revenue–GDP ratio, limited donors' support to the operating budget, and their aversion toward subsidies. Thus, ways need to be found to achieve some of the desirable effects of subsidies (e.g., making labour and exports more attractive for business) without large direct fiscal costs.

- **General tax breaks** A related point is that general tax breaks are unlikely to be very effective and would carry high costs in terms of foregone revenue, which Afghanistan can ill-afford. These are in effect subsidies delivered through the tax system and have similar problems to direct subsidies.

- **Developing state-owned enterprises** Based on international experience, state-owned enterprises are not an effective or efficient way to increase the pace of economic and employment growth.

continued

BOX 1, *continued*

- **Boosting aggregate demand to stimulate economic growth** will not work well in the Afghan situation. Economic growth has been relatively high during the past five years. Further stimulating aggregate demand probably would have adverse inflationary consequences, would most likely contribute to greater wage inflation, and would probably not result in significantly higher growth.

with an appropriate micro-level legal and regulatory framework, to enhance access to finance through collateralization of land and facilities located on industrial parks. Business support services and training (e.g., for preparing credible proposals and bids) also could be anchored in industrial parks. International experience with industrial parks, which has been decidedly mixed, indicates that in order to be successful, they need to be managed on a commercial basis, preferably by the private sector under competitive contractual arrangements. A quick review of the experience so far with industrial parks in Afghanistan, bringing in lessons from international experience, could serve as the basis for improvement and scaling up of industrial parks to better meet investors' needs. It may also make sense to extend the industrial park concept to include export zones. This could be part of a broader export promotion policy. While the experience with such zones internationally has been mixed, combining the benefits of industrial parks in the Afghanistan context (as outlined above) with an export orientation would be worth exploring.

Competitive contracting of international or regional firms could be pursued to develop "value chains" that would result in the production and export of goods from Afghanistan (with exports being the contractual target). Rather than trying to develop the value chain through fragmented public investments and support to the private sector in different parts of the value chain (which carries a serious risk that actual exports will not materialize in the end due to other constraints becoming binding), the private sector itself could be made responsible for developing the entire value chain (with public support as needed). By demonstrating clear results in the form of exports, such an approach might generate more widespread knowledge and confidence in the private sector to move forward.[14] If this kind of approach seems promising, the concept needs further thought and development; in particular there would need to be careful design of contracts (based on performance, encouraging employment generation, a focus on areas of Afghanistan's perceived comparative advantage, but not too narrow—i.e., not trying to "pick winners"), and a robust competitive process (to avoid potential governance issues).

There may also be other effective ways to encourage export development and international competitiveness. Examples could include, among others, complementary investments (e.g., in cold stores for fresh produce, developing standards and quality testing, provision of some form of incentive-compatible export subsidy, export finance, insurance, etc.). Serious efforts also need to be made to establish Afghanistan as a significant brand name, at least in some niche markets. The opportunity created by the country's having a certain degree of global visibility should not be lost.

Privatization could be another vehicle for stimulating private sector development. Many existing state-owned enterprises are defunct, and few of them have very high levels of staffing. Making the facilities, land, and real estate of SOEs available for development and utilization by the private sector may well stimulate the development of the latter.

A whole range of business development and support services are needed, including thorough training of the requisite human capital. For example, the government could contract a firm that would provide (as a fee-based service) support to Afghan businesses to write proposals and bid for public procurement contracts. Businesses' accounting could be supported, justified by the externalities of enabling tax assessment and helping with the deepening of the financial sector. There are also more conventional services like insurance. Perhaps a scheme could be considered whereby designated services could be accessed through vouchers given to firms that pay taxes, as a way to maximize the impact on the formalization of the economy (and making sure that the system is demand-driven).

Containing corruption and reducing red tape (discussed in the following section) are important elements in improving the business climate. From the perspective of private sector development, the most urgent priority may be to focus on streamlining the enormous number of laws, regulations, licensing rules, fees, etc., currently on the books. A possible approach might be to ask ministries to quickly prioritize the laws and regulations that are important to them (with appropriate technical guidance) and then cancel the rest. This kind of "guillotine" approach puts the onus on those who want to retain laws and regulations to provide a justification and to prioritize them.

A focus on the construction industry as a source of employment growth would make sense. For the foreseeable future, the construction industry will be a major and possibly dominant private sector employer in urban areas. How can its robust development be encouraged? Are there other industries or activities that would be potentially strong sources of increased demand for labour in the future?

Enterprise development can be pursued as a means of expanding business activity and livelihoods in Afghanistan's rural areas. Links between farmers and competitive private agro-processing facilities could be very important in enhancing the value addition from Afghan agriculture and stimulating employment. An effective interface is needed for such linkages to work well, and in a context of small-scale farming some kinds of associations among farmers would be essential. The social capital built up through the National Solidarity Programme may provide a sound foundation to build upon. Rural enterprise entities, farmers' associations, and a variety of other arrangements in the countryside could interact to provide agricultural production (including associated labour supply) to entrepreneurs engaged in agro-processing. A variety of models exists, some of which could be explored and experimented with to find those that are most suitable in the context of rural Afghanistan.

Can short-term vocational training programs make a difference? International experience suggests that such programs are not likely to improve the situation very much unless tied to dynamic, growing sectors and businesses. In a context of high growth (which Afghanistan currently enjoys in several sectors), how could such programs be organized for maximum effectiveness and responsiveness to labour market demand? Maybe training programs organized by private companies themselves and meeting their needs could be subsidized in some appropriate way.

Quality of education is a critically important determinant of productivity and private sector development over the medium term. The importance of education is likely to continue to grow, since by all indications technological progress globally has been and will continue to be biased toward skilled labour (i.e., increasing demand for educated labour and reducing demand for unskilled labour). Even though the impact takes much time to be felt, it is important to make improvements in education in a timely manner. It is in particular very important to focus on the quality of education at higher levels—there is no point in sharply increasing the numbers of university graduates if the quality of their education is so low that they become virtually unemployable (unable to compete for higher-end jobs but unwilling to do jobs with low skills requirements and/or requiring manual labour). Innovative, demand-driven, and commercially managed approaches to vocational education also need to be developed. There is already considerable market demand for well-educated people in a variety of fields, which the education system needs to respond to in a more effective manner.

There is much concern in Afghanistan about generating employment, which over the medium term will be achieved only by robust private sector–based economic growth. However, in the short run there may be a role for public works employment programs to provide temporary employment and incomes for the poor. There may also be a role in the short run for measures that reduce (or at least slow the increase of) labour supply in Afghanistan, thereby lowering unemployment and/or raising market wage rates. In this context, Afghan labour responds to and flows in regional labour markets, most notably Pakistan and Iran but also farther away in places like Dubai. Moreover, Afghan labour employed in regional markets generates flows of remittances into Afghanistan. Over the medium term the bulk of employment for Afghans will need to be generated in Afghanistan itself. But in a situation where unemployment is currently a very serious problem, a strong case can be made that in the short run the "safety valve" of regional employment for Afghans should not be closed. In particular large flows of people and labour back into Afghanistan, ahead of employment opportunities, should be avoided. This is an issue with important regional implications, and it needs to be taken up with key regional partners. At the higher end of the labour market, it is important that the quality of higher education in Afghanistan be adequate to meet the needs of private sector development. Thus it would be desirable to avoid sharply increasing the supply of university graduates until the quality of their education can be improved.

Finally, and more generally, it is clear that results-oriented productive co-operation between the public and private sectors can help improve the business climate and facilitate the removal of bottlenecks. While mind-set changes and co-operative attitudes need to be fostered, it is important to keep some kinds of interactions off the table—lobbying for firm-specific benefits, corruption, etc. Far higher priority needs to be given to the private sector development and employment agenda by both government and donors. While avoiding pitfalls mentioned earlier and not going for "crash programs" that are likely to prove counterproductive from a medium-term perspective, the economic growth and private sector development agenda clearly requires much more attention from policymakers and donors, as well as substantially more resources.

Strengthening Governance

Governance problems (broadly defined) threaten to undermine the effectiveness, credibility, and legitimacy of the Afghan state and thereby the entire reconstruction and development agenda. Short-term priorities in this broad area include making headway against corruption, pursuing difficult yet critically important public administration reforms, strengthening public accountability, and making further progress in improving public financial management. Strengthening accountability—through external audit, to the legislature, and to the public and civil society—comprises a very important, and hitherto relatively neglected, component of all three priority areas.

Anti-Corruption   As emphasized earlier, corruption appears to be widespread, expanding, and becoming increasingly entrenched. Realism is called for in considering how much can be done about corruption, and how fast. This does not mean inaction, but rather focusing efforts on achieving meaningful progress and avoiding empty rhetoric that leads to disappointed expectations. Prevention and other elements (including awareness raising and external accountability), not just investigation and prosecution, will be crucial in the fight against corruption. This in turn will require developing systems, processes, capacity, and integrity mechanisms that help prevent corruption.

There are a number of critical issues that hinder the fight against corruption. One is the need for government-wide ownership of the anti-corruption agenda. A related issue is the need to demonstrate—through actions not just words—genuine high-level government commitment in the fight against corruption. The government's anti-corruption roadmap paper (Afghanistan 2007) puts forward a short-term action program with a number of meaningful yet feasible measures. These include, among others, follow-up on the Control and Audit Office's audit findings related to fraud and corruption, implementation of the constitutional provision for public asset declarations by top government leaders, effectively implementing the agreed-upon vetting process for high-level political appointments, parliamentary ratification of the United Nations Convention Against Corruption (UNCAC), and reviewing and adjusting key national laws so that they are consistent with UNCAC.

The institutional framework for fighting corruption needs to be clarified. Corruption is a quintessential cross-cutting issue, and a wide range of government agencies are involved in various aspects of the anti-corruption agenda. The following is a list of recommendations:

- There needs to be high-level inter-institutional oversight of the anti-corruption effort; no one agency can take the lead on all parts of the agenda. In this context the formation of the government's high-level Inter-Institutional Committee on anti-corruption has been a positive step. However, arrangements for effective inter-institutional oversight of the anti-corruption effort beyond the Inter-Institutional Committee's report need to be made clear.
- The government agencies concerned need to co-operate with each other; far too much attention seems to be focused on fighting over which agency

is "in the lead" rather than working together to achieve results against corruption. In particular, the phenomenon of different agencies each preparing their own "anti-corruption strategies" in isolation from each other and from development of the national anti-corruption strategy must stop.

- More specifically, the role of the specialized anti-corruption agency (GIAAC) needs to be reconsidered and narrowed. GIAAC needs to have a more focused mandate in line with its limited actual and potential capacity, and it should be bringing agencies together rather than competing with them.
- Leadership is critical. In this context, the leadership of an anti-corruption agency and other organizations involved in the fight against corruption must rise to the highest ethical and professional standards.

Turning to next steps, as discussed in the Afghan government's anti-corruption roadmap paper (2007), priorities for action include:

- clearly expressing the government's commitment against corruption, through promulgation of a credible action program with meaningful yet feasible steps demonstrating such commitment—otherwise the government will lack credibility in addressing corruption;
- clarifying the institutional framework for anti-corruption;
- understanding better the context, problems, actors, and dynamics of corruption in Afghanistan, so as to better inform anti-corruption strategy and policies;
- assessing vulnerabilities to corruption in key sectors, agencies, and functions—through preparation of Vulnerabilities to Corruption Assessments (VCAs) and corruption risk mitigation plans, taking appropriate actions, and monitoring progress in anti-corruption efforts at the sector, agency, and function level;
- resolutely pursuing key cross-cutting reforms, including public administration reform, judicial reform, counter-narcotics efforts, and strengthening external accountability (through parliament, media, civil society);
- developing a national anti-corruption strategy, as part of the ANDS process; and
- fostering support from the international community around a harmonized approach, while ensuring that leadership is firmly in government hands.

Public Administration Reform The public administration reform (PAR) agenda is complex and difficult yet extremely important. Despite significant progress there is still a very long way to go before the objective of a lean, effective, and accountable civil service can be achieved.

The comprehensive pay and grading reform has undergone extensive design work, and implementation is expected to start soon. There has been much analysis of the fiscal cost of the new salary structure, and adjustments have been made in the interest of fiscal sustainability. If Afghanistan's domestic revenue continues to grow rapidly, and the core budget is not overwhelmed by shifts of recurrent expenditure liabilities to it from the external budget, the cost of the new salary structure should be manageable.

However, sharply raising pay levels in the civil service without other necessary changes will not result in improved effectiveness, better service delivery, or even greater integrity. One critical prerequisite for success is a certain level of basic restructuring of government ministries and agencies around their main objectives and to rationalize outdated and unnecessary structures. For example, some ministries have been formed through the amalgamation of several ministries and agencies, and in the absence of any real restructuring still have, for example, as many as three administration departments. Even if restructuring will be a continuing exercise, basic anomalies like this example should be resolved before implementing pay and grading reform. There is no point in going through this reform, resulting in large numbers of staff being shifted to the new position structure with much higher pay levels, when whole units or parts of them should be abolished or otherwise restructured.

A critical element that will influence the effectiveness and success of the pay and grading reform is the handling of civil servants who lack the qualifications for corresponding positions in the new structure, and/or are surplus to requirements (e.g., in some of the lower-grade positions). Presumably many may be qualified for positions at a lower grade level in the new structure (and minimizing sensitivities in this regard, the new structure has fewer grades and does not map one-to-one vis-à-vis the existing structure), but if the exercise is carried out properly there are bound to be a number of staff who are not qualified for positions or end up being surplus to requirements at lower grade levels. Although this is recognized, there is not yet clarity in how these staff will be dealt with. It is clear, however, that moving them to the new pay structure must be avoided. Options include (i) continuing their employment for a designated period of time, or until retirement in the case of older employees, but on the old salary structure; (ii) early retirement for those who are fairly close to the retirement age (the average age of the civil service is relatively high, with a great many in their 50s); (iii) involuntary retrenchment (but this would most likely involve extra payments whose levels would need to be carefully considered to provide appropriate incentives while containing the fiscal cost.

Another important issue related to the pay and grade reform is the implications for pensions. Pension benefits after retirement for those moved to the new salary structure will be substantially higher, which will need to be factored into the medium-term fiscal scenario. Moreover, the transition arrangements and how time served under the old salary structure will be treated need to be specified in a fiscally responsible manner. And finally, whatever the approach taken to dealing with staff who do not move to the new pay and grade structure, it should be made clear that they will receive pension benefits according to the old, not the new system.

In terms of sequencing, it must be recognized that if implemented right—and particularly taking into account that at least some basic restructuring will need to be done—the pay and grade reform will take a considerable period of time, on the order of four to five years at least. The government plans to proceed on two tracks: accelerating the implementation of the pay and grade reform for the most senior civil servants and moving ahead on a ministry basis (depending on which ministries are most ready in terms of restructuring, mission statements, etc.) for the rest.

Finally, the quality of implementation will be critical for the success of the pay and grading reform. While expectations should not be excessively high in the Afghanistan context, there is no point in going through the exercise, and ending up with a considerably more costly civil service, unless merit-based procedures are followed adequately in the process. For senior civil servants, it is imperative to employ a practical approach that works and to avoid cronyism with its risks of corruption. This will set an example for the lower grades. Although a properly implemented credible process will be essential, especially at the higher level, it is also important to minimize the disruptions to government and civil service functioning that result from the exercise.

Although the pay and grading reform dominates the near-term landscape of PAR, other critical areas cannot be neglected, and indeed will have important implications for the success of pay and grading reform. The appointment process for senior civil servants, which is handled by the Independent Appointments Board (IAB) under the Independent Administrative Reform and Civil Service Reform Commission (IARCSC), is critical. The progress made in instituting a regularized and at least nominally merit-based process for selecting senior civil servants (grades 1 and 2 under the existing structure) must be recognized, particularly in the context of Afghanistan, where appointments based on relationships and political affiliations, if not outright corruption, have been the norm. However, there are numerous problems with the merit-based appointment process, including shortcomings in the process itself, but also more importantly related to the quality of IAB commissioners (who lead the process), IAB's support capacity, relatively limited attention to pre-screening and other preparatory efforts, and consequent over-emphasis on the interview, etc. The IAB and IARCSC have recognized these problems and have devised an action program, including a variety of short-term and medium-term measures, to improve the merit-based selection and appointment process. One critical point is that the capacity needs and quality concerns related to this process must be kept in mind. In the short run a sharp increase in the number of merit-based appointments of senior officials would not be desirable and should not be expected until efforts to improve the quality of the process start bearing fruit. Appointments of civil servants below the top two grades are handled by line ministries, with the IAB playing a monitoring role.

More generally, the capacity and profile of the IARCSC will need to be enhanced if it is to play its designated role both in the pay and grading exercise and more generally in PAR. In addition, capacity for civil service processes (appointment, performance review, human resources, etc.) in line ministries needs to be strengthened.

An extremely important area of PAR, particularly from the perspective of service delivery, is at sub-national levels (provinces and districts). Although Afghanistan has a unitary state, which (with the important exception of municipalities) sub-national units are part of, sub-national levels of government are very important, serving as the "face" of the state vis-à-vis most ordinary citizens and playing a primary role in delivery of most public services (ranging from local security to education and health).

Public Financial Management   In the area of public financial management (PFM), the priority is to maintain the momentum of earlier progress and to further strengthen PFM, including through progressively building sustainable capacity in government to handle core PFM functions. The PFM Action Program and Ministry of Finance reform plan, both of which have received high-level approval, need to be effectively implemented. This is a broad agenda, but it is based on a good platform to build upon given the substantial progress so far.

At the broad level, maintaining Afghanistan's progress toward fiscal sustainability will be crucial but will become increasingly challenging. Absorptive capacity is catching up with resource availability, necessitating hard decisions on prioritization (discussed further in the next section). Further increasing domestic revenue mobilization will be essential but increasingly difficult as the "easier" revenue sources get exploited. With the formation of parliament as well as provincial councils, political pressures—both to increase expenditures and to avoid difficult measures to raise more revenues—can be expected to intensify. Managing such pressures will require a strong budget process that brings in key stakeholders earlier rather than later and makes explicit fiscal trade-offs to promote buy-in and ownership for budgetary decisions. It is also very important to strengthen the buy-in and ownership of the cabinet in the budget formulation process and in decisions made during budget formulation. The budget formulation process needs to be government-wide with the entire cabinet and all ministries buying into it.

Turning to more specific areas of PFM, key priorities include the following:

- improving procurement by implementing the Procurement Law and building capacity for this purpose, including both in the Procurement Policy Unit (located in the Ministry of Finance) and procurement capacity in key line ministries;
- operationalizing the integration of the recurrent and development budgets (an important reform underway), in particular by further developing and expanding the program budgeting initiative that has been piloted in three ministries;
- taking forward the provincial budgeting initiative, while fully recognizing its limitations in the context of Afghanistan's unitary state structure, and using it as an opportunity to increase funding for non-salary expenditures at sub-national levels of the government administration, which has been neglected;
- strengthening the internal audit function, led by the Ministry of Finance, both in that ministry's Internal Audit Department and in the line ministries;
- expanding individualized and computerized salary payments for civil servants to more line ministries and provinces; and
- further improving the budget formulation process by
  - fully implementing the longer nine-month budget preparation cycle announced by the Ministry of Finance,
  - ensuring that the Medium-Term Expenditure Framework (MTFF) and preliminary annual aggregate and sector budget ceilings (which need to be made available early in the budget process) are used to force difficult trade-offs and prioritization decisions to be made, and
  - encouraging wider stakeholder participation in the budget process, including regular consultations with parliament.

Monitoring progress in the reform and strengthening of PFM are important priorities. The first assessment of Afghanistan's PFM performance according to the PEFA indicators was conducted in mid-2005, and it is being followed up by a second assessment to evaluate subsequent progress and remaining problem areas.

External and Public Accountability A critically important element of both anti-corruption strategy and PAR, as well as PFM, is external or public accountability. This is critical for getting other branches of government (the legislature) and civil society actively involved in pursuing both agendas.

A first priority in this regard is to develop and make full use of the existing external financial accountability mechanisms. This involves continuing to build the capacity of the Control and Audit Office (CAO) and to strengthen its regular audit function. Review of audit reports by parliament and follow-up actions by the government, as well as monitoring of follow-up by parliament, are critical for making the external audit function meaningful and effective.

The role of parliament in the budget formulation process needs to be systematized and brought forward earlier in the process—both in the interest of improving the budget process itself, as discussed earlier, and to enhance the accountability of the budget process. Another important element of external accountability is parliamentary review of budget outcomes and policy discussions on the budget.

A final issue related to parliament is the need to promote the accountability *of* parliament, not just accountability *to* parliament. There are concerns about vulnerabilities to corruption in the activities of parliament itself (for example, confirmation of ministers), and even more in terms of pressures from representatives on individuals and agencies in the executive related to hiring, contracts, etc.

Public accountability of the executive, as well as parliament, ultimately depends on the public, both organized civil society institutions and, through the press and media, the public at large. Helping civil society institutions strengthen themselves and build capacity to become more effective is important, but transparency, information sharing, and public communication by the government also will be essential. Development communication, one of the obvious weak points in experience so far (see Table 1 earlier in the chapter), is discussed later.

Responding to the Challenge of the Opium Economy

The drug industry lies at the heart of the challenges Afghanistan faces in state building and governance. Responding effectively requires, first, clarity about objectives and the time horizon. The objectives from an Afghanistan-centric view would be to reduce the country's economic dependence on opium on a sustained basis over time (i.e., not just year-to-year fluctuations), and to contain and reduce the threat from the drug industry to the country's state building agenda.

A second critical aspect is the need to learn from the rich experience with counter-narcotics efforts in Afghanistan as well as elsewhere. The following lessons are elaborated on in Box 2: (1) blanket eradication of opium poppy does not work beyond the short-run successes achieved, which are vitiated by shifts of cultivation to other places and/or a subsequent rebound in the area where it was eradicated; (2) short-term alternative livelihoods programs are costly, wasteful, and unsustainable; and (3) inevitable corruption in the implementation of counter-narcotics law enforcement measures results in distortions and can backfire (see also the earlier discussion on the dynamic trends around the drug industry).

BOX 2 **Some Lessons from Experience with Counter-Narcotics Efforts in Afghanistan**

Experience with counter-narcotics efforts in the face of difficult challenges in Afghanistan, particularly since 2001 but also with the Taliban ban in 2000–2001 and earlier efforts in the 1990s, provides rich lessons which should fully inform the counter-narcotics strategy and specific approaches. Three examples of such lessons are summarized below.

1 **Blanket eradication of opium poppy fields does not work, as it is not sustainable over time or at a national level.** The two most prominent examples of apparently successful eradication are the near-complete Taliban ban on opium poppy cultivation in 2000–2001 and the 96% reduction in cultivation in Nangarhar Province (at the time one of Afghanistan's largest opium producers) in 2004. Within two to three years afterward, opium poppy cultivation had rebounded in both cases. Moreover, even at the time of the respective bans, cultivation increased sharply in areas outside the bans' purview—in Northern Alliance-controlled areas in the case of the Taliban ban, and in Helmand and other provinces at the time of the reduction in Nangarhar.

Eradication is economically unsustainable, except in better-off localities where people already have viable alternative livelihoods—based on access in particular to water, land, and commodity and labour markets. Otherwise, eradication can exacerbate poverty and paradoxically increase dependence on opium, especially through the impact on opium-related debt. There are cases reported of farmers whose opium poppy fields have been eradicated several times but who still continue to cultivate opium poppy because this is the only way they can manage (and have any hope of servicing) their opium-related debts. Beyond the debt dimension, by reducing the incomes of poorer farmers, forcing asset sales, etc., eradication can reduce coping capacities and resilience and make it more likely that such farmers turn again at the first opportunity to opium poppy cultivation.

continued

Eradication is also politically difficult to sustain. The unpopular Taliban ban undermined political support for the Taliban in some key Pashtun heartland areas, possibly making it easier for the Taliban regime to be overthrown in late 2001. The campaign against drugs in 2004–05, which achieved by far its greatest success in Nangarhar Province, also carried significant political costs for the government, especially in that province.

And finally, from a more technical standpoint, eradication is chasing a moving target. As opium poppy is an annual crop, cultivated on less than 10% of Afghanistan's irrigated area, it can easily shift locations—opium traders, wage labourers, and even farmers have exhibited considerable mobility in response to changing counter-narcotics priorities.

2 A second lesson from experience relates to so-called "alternative livelihoods" programs intended to mitigate the reduced incomes suffered by rural households that exit from the opium economy. Experience in Afghanistan amply demonstrates that **short-term alternative livelihoods programs tend to be very costly in relation to their benefits as well as unsustainable.**

The quintessential alternative livelihoods projects provide cash-for-work or agricultural inputs. First, it should be noted that these are only designed to replace (temporarily) some of the income foregone by not cultivating opium poppy; the bulk of such programs do not attempt to deal with the issues related to dependence on the opium economy for access to assets like land, water, credit, etc. as well as markets. A more comprehensive approach to alternative livelihoods, which then becomes akin to longer-term rural development, takes much more time. Second, the pressure to spend money quickly tends to increase waste and open up opportunities for corruption. And finally, "rapid" alternative livelihoods programs inevitably raise people's expectations, resulting in subsequent disappointments and thereby undermining the credibility of the government and external actors involved. Thus there is no substitute for effective and fairly comprehensive longer-term rural development to provide viable alternatives to opium.

3 A third lesson from experience is that, **in Afghanistan's environment of weak governance and lack of rule of law, corruption in the implementation of counter-narcotics enforcement efforts (both interdiction and eradication) is inevitable, and that such corruption leads to distortions and undermines the objectives of the counter-narcotics strategy.**

continued

BOX 2, *continued*

More specifically, such corruption has inadvertently contributed to the consolidation of the drug industry—around fewer, powerful, and politically connected actors (see earlier discussion). Moreover, corruption in implementation tends to result in the adverse impact of counter-narcotics actions being felt disproportionately by poorer farmers, who typically do not have financial resources to pay bribes, or suitable connections with local power-holders to exploit. Also, corruption in implementation profoundly undermines the credibility and perceived legitimacy of the state, both in terms of counter-narcotics efforts and also more generally.

Note: For further exploration of issues associated with counter-narcotics efforts in Afghanistan, see chapter 3 by Jonathan Goodhand in this volume.

These and other lessons from experience provide ample grounds for concern and for exercising caution in use of traditional counter-narcotics instruments. However, inaction or neglect is not a viable alternative given the profound threat posed by the drug industry to Afghanistan's entire state building and development agenda. Action is required, but there is a need to fully take into account the lessons from experience and the pitfalls encountered hitherto and factor them into the design of counter-narcotics policies and measures. In other words, there is a need to develop a "smart" strategy against drugs (see Buddenberg and Byrd 2006, chapter 1). Fundamentally, there is a need to recognize that counter-narcotics instruments inevitably are blunt, unwieldy, and distortionary in responding to a very nimble and powerful adversary. This calls for care and a strategic approach in deploying such instruments.

A sound principle is to focus efforts against those parts of the drug industry that pose the greatest danger to the nation and its development agenda—i.e., the larger drug traffickers and their sponsors who threaten to undermine state building through political corruption and the compromising of state agencies, like the police and Ministry of Interior.

A second principle is the need to take fully into account the adverse side effects and distortions induced by counter-narcotics instruments, which could undermine or even negate any beneficial effects. A prime example is corruption in the implementation of counter-narcotics policies. There is no point in designing a plan that may work well if there is no corruption when it is obvious beforehand (and based on experience) that there will be corruption in implementation.

It also needs to be kept in mind that the drug industry is by no means a static target but rather will respond dynamically (and effectively) to actions against it. For example, as discussed in detail in Shaw (2006), counter-narcotics actions have inadvertently contributed to the drug industry evolving into a more concentrated form. Senior police appointments have become a vehicle for managing and smoothing the flow of drugs. During the past several years, the drug industry has responded effectively to reform of the Ministry of Defense (by shifting its focus to the police and Ministry of Interior); to DDR and political "normalization" (by less open and more distant interactions with warlords-turned-politicians; and to eradication efforts (by first spreading more widely across the country and then, when eradication also started to cover these areas, taking advantage of the growing insecurity in Helmand and other southern provinces and concentrating more opium production there).

Another issue that needs to be factored into the equation is avoiding perverse incentives. If, for example, counter-narcotics assistance (including, in particular, support for alternative livelihoods activities) is concentrated in the major opium-producing areas, other (non-cultivating) areas are likely to resent this and may even weaken their efforts to keep out the opium economy. More generally, it would be advisable not to focus overly on the major current opium producing areas but rather include as an objective in the short run "containing" the opium economy through measures discouraging its spread to non-dependent provinces and localities.

Based on these principles, the following recommendations are put forward:

- Focus eradication efforts on better-off opium poppy cultivating areas and also areas that are new to poppy cultivation. Experience suggests that eradication efforts can be beneficial and sustainable in such areas.
- When a locality is targeted for eradication on this basis (the province is usually too big a unit for this purpose, but the district or sub-district level would be more appropriate), go for complete rather than partial eradication in that locality—this will minimize the risk of corruption in implementation and associated distortions.
- Recognizing the political difficulties involved, do focus interdiction efforts against medium and larger drug traffickers and their sponsors. This will set a positive example for counter-narcotics efforts at lower levels.
- Given the weakness of the judiciary and the difficulties in successfully prosecuting major drug figures (although progress has been made in operationalizing special counter-narcotics courts and in training personnel), actors associated with the drug industry should at least be removed from their positions in government, which can have a surprisingly strong im-

pact in the Afghan context. Aside from any direct benefits, this will send a strong signal of credibility for the counter-narcotics strategy.
- Do not throw money into short-term alternative livelihoods programs but rather support sensible rural development, recognizing that this will take much time.
- As emphasized earlier, don't concentrate efforts and resources too much in the main opium producing areas, but rather consider a kind of "containment" strategy to progressively close off large parts of the country from vulnerability to becoming dependent on opium.
- Mainstreaming of the counter-narcotics dimension into development programs is very important and will help in scaling up meaningful efforts on the development side. However, mainstreaming should not be approached mechanically but rather in a flexible albeit results-oriented manner.
- Equally important is the need to mainstream the development dimension in counter-narcotics strategy and actions. Given the importance of the opium economy from a development and governance perspective, "mainstreaming" these considerations in decisions, policies, and instruments for fighting against drugs makes very good sense and could help avoid future problems.

Improving Development Management and Aid Effectiveness

This area will be critical to the success of Afghanistan's development agenda and to attracting, allocating well, and utilizing effectively the large amounts of international assistance that the country is expected to continue to require.

At the outset, the importance of the time dimension in Afghanistan's overall agenda, and in development management and aid coordination, must be emphasized. All stakeholders need to take the long view. From the military standpoint, a conventional war is typically an all-out effort of limited duration. However, Afghanistan now faces an expanding insurgency (as well as more general insecurity and limited rule of law), and counter-insurgency tends to be a much longer-term effort, stretching out over many years and even decades. In fact, the time horizon for a successful counter-insurgency effort is on the same order as that for other main elements of Afghanistan's overall reconstruction and development agenda—state building, capacity development, building and strengthening institutions, security sector reform, and so on. This implies that all elements need to be working to a long time horizon and making choices about prioritization and sequencing within that. Both military and aid practices need to be aligned with the longer time horizon and adjust their thinking and procedures accordingly. The understandable tendency toward focusing mainly on short-term solutions needs to be avoided, while making sure that what all actors are doing in the short run is both substantial enough in relation to the challenges and leading toward longer-term objectives.

Development Management A first priority in improving development management is strengthening the leadership of ministries whose development performance has been lagging. As emphasized earlier, Afghanistan's experience over the past five years indicates that progress at the sector level depends on having a competent, cohesive, empowered Afghan team of leaders running the sector ministry. This can be achieved in several different ways, and it is not essential (although often desirable) that the minister personally take the lead (although at a minimum, the ministry leadership team just below the level of the minister has to be empowered by the minister). But a strong initiative is needed to break through or get around any political constraints. Based on experience, ministry leadership is a critical necessary condition and almost constitutes a sufficient condition for progress, since once a leadership team is in place, it will actively seek to alleviate other constraints that are impeding ministry performance. While Afghanistan is severely constrained by its limited human capacity, there is ample talent, including a good degree of ethnic balance, to provide a total of a hundred or so good leaders to provide strong leadership in all of the main ministries.

A second key priority is to continue to enhance the budget process and use the budget as the central instrument for policy and reform as well as public sector resource allocation. This will be critical for attracting more donor funds through national budget channels and thereby improving the coherence of a fragmented set of aid programs and projects by donors working outside the national budget.

In this regard, two key elements are strengthening the medium-term orientation of the budget and prioritization. The Medium-Term Fiscal Framework is a good start but needs to be taken further, and moreover the links between the MTFF and the annual budget process need to be strengthened. Over time, in particular as planning and medium-term budgeting at the sector level improve, the MTFF can be progressively transformed into a Medium-Term Expenditure Framework (MTEF), which will provide a stronger foundation for sector expenditure envelopes. However, the key priority in the short run is to promote the use of the MTFF as a policy instrument for discussions and decisions on the budget. In particular, the medium-term consequences associated with decisions—on staffing (notably in the security services), revenue mobilization, public investments, size of service delivery networks, and more generally the role of the state—need to be fully factored into and appropriately affect the decisions concerned.

A key medium-term objective is progressing toward fiscal sustainability, which can be defined in the context of Afghanistan as reaching a situation where domestic revenues are basically sufficient to cover budgetary operating expenditures. The MTFF and associated medium-term fiscal planning should continue to work toward this objective despite challenges on both revenue and expenditure sides.

Prioritization is difficult both politically and technically, but it is increasingly important. In the early days, when the government's absorptive capacity was very limited in relation to the large aid flows coming in, explicit prioritization was less important. The allocation of expenditures (i.e., de facto prioritization) was determined by the ability of different ministries and agencies to get programs going and to attract and disburse funds. As absorptive capacity has progressively increased over time (major progress that should be recognized), the need for and importance of explicit prioritization also has increased. For some programs, most notably the National Solidarity Programme, absorptive capacity is already outrunning the availability of funds, and such cases will only increase in the future. This puts more pressure on the prioritization aspect of the budget process, which has not worked very well so far. In this regard, providing at least rough ceilings for sector development budgets early in the budget process, based on past performance as well as adjustments in overall national priorities, would be helpful. It is also extremely important that the Afghanistan National Development Strategy (ANDS) provide clear broad directions of prioritization, even though specific annual allocations will need to be worked out as part of the budget process.

Aid Management and Coordination In the context of Afghanistan, which is so heavily aid-dependent, aid management and coordination forms a critical, even dominant component of development management. Unfortunately there is much that needs fixing in this area, and it is of particular concern that lessons from the experience of the past five years (as well as international experience) appear not to be getting absorbed; on the contrary there are some signs of reversion to practices that have already shown that they could not work well during the early period of Afghanistan's reconstruction.

Turning to the national development strategy, the ANDS preparation is moving forward with the objective of finalizing it in the first half of 2008. As noted earlier, the shortcomings of previous strategy formulation exercises, in terms of lack of prioritization and limited consultation in particular, have been recognized, and the ANDS process emphasizes these aspects, with a key objective of developing costed, prioritized strategies at the sector level. An articulated and extensive consultation process has been under way.

However, there are some issues with the interface of the ANDS process with aid coordination, in particular the process for monitoring the implementation of the Afghanistan Compact and the Joint Coordination and Monitoring Board (JCMB) which was set up for this purpose. The rationale for combining the oversight, organizational structure, secretariat apparatus, government/donor groups (eight consultative groups, two umbrella groups, twenty-six working groups, etc.), meetings, and follow-up for the Afghanistan Compact, ANDS, and monitoring the compact benchmarks was to ensure that the compact and its implementation remain fully consistent with the ANDS and that there is overall national leadership. The envisioned synergies have not materialized, however, and the heavy meeting load and still rather mechanical monitoring of compact benchmarks may well be distracting from and interfering with preparation of the ANDS.

Moreover, in addition to the JCMB/ANDS structure, there are other forums for coordination of international assistance to Afghanistan. These include the Afghanistan Development Forum (ADF), the Policy Advisory Group (PAG), the External Advisory Group (EAG) for the ANDS, a recently constituted group of development donors chaired by the World Bank, and the ARTF Donors Committee. Listed below are some changes in direction that may be necessary to ensure timely completion of the ANDS with adequate quality as well as better results from aid coordination:

- While ensuring that the essential elements are there, the ambitiousness of the ANDS needs to be tempered by the time and resources available. The focus should not be on the quality of the ANDS document, but rather on preparation of a pragmatic, doable, and prioritized strategy, underpinned by diagnostics that are available from existing data, reflecting meaningful consultations and broad government buy-in and ownership, and aligned with the budget.
- With respect to the JCMB/compact monitoring process, monitoring of compact benchmarks needs to be guided by ANDS sectoral strategies and focus on their substance, rather than being driven by timetables and process. The overall objective that the compact seeks to promote—the development of Afghanistan—should not be lost through mechanical monitoring of indicators.
- Oversight of implementation, monitoring, and follow-up with respect to the ANDS once it is completed should be the responsibility of regular institutions of government, not through a separate, parallel structure.
- There is a need to streamline what has become a rather burdensome, meeting-intensive, and mechanical process of donor coordination. The number of meetings held under the JCMB/compact monitoring process

should be drastically reduced. There is no need to hold a meeting of every consultative group (CG) to monitor the implementation of each compact benchmark. Instead, informal meetings can be held regularly at the technical level.

• The approach should be much more problem-solving in nature, with problems identified by the JCMB Secretariat and perhaps discussed at a single problem-solving meeting, before being taken up by the JCMB meeting as needed.

• Turning to aid coordination, in general it would benefit from much more focus on implementation, complementing the strategy work under the ANDS.

• The number of meetings devoted to aid coordination could be considerably reduced. One option would be a monthly meeting between the government (at a senior level) and the donors, which would be a forum for thematic discussions as well as an opportunity to bring up specific problems encountered. Other than this, meetings at the sector level would be based on the concrete needs.

• Where there are bottlenecks in the line ministries, the focus should be on making necessary changes in them, rather than trying to cover the gap through aid coordination meetings as frequently occurs with notable lack of success.

Technical assistance (TA) refers to analytical, advisory, and operational support to the government and its programs and projects, provided by outside firms or individuals. TA comprises a critical component of development and aid management. There is an urgent need for drastic improvements in the organization and management of TA. Although data are poor, very large amounts—certainly in the hundreds of millions of dollars per year— are being spent on TA, with little in the way of oversight, management, coordination, sustainable capacity building, or monitoring for results. There are widespread concerns that TA is not achieving results or supporting outcomes commensurate with the financial and human resources being applied. In particular, most TA appears more likely to be self-perpetuating rather than helping develop the domestic capacity that will obviate the need for continuing external TA. Problems are aggravated by the very limited supply of professional and managerial Afghan talent, and the typically high reservation wages of such persons, which makes it difficult for them to be attracted directly into the government.

Although the problems associated with TA reflect issues in the wider aid system and cannot be solved overnight, there are some practical options for improving the situation in the short run. First, what should *not* be done: TA should not be thrown at a problem in an ad hoc manner; under such circumstances it is likely to worsen the situation or indeed become part of the problem, rather than (part of) the solution. If not well-managed and coordinated, TA is most likely to be less than the sum of its parts. Thus more TA can easily have negative value added—not least in the form of greater coordination problems. Less is often better than more. In particular, TA should not be seen as a substitute for adequate government leadership particularly at the line ministry level. TA works far better when there is effective government leadership in the institution concerned; the two are much more complements than substitutes.

From a more positive perspective, TA desperately needs a medium-term perspective. Typically TA contracts are of very limited duration, on the order of one to two years. This means that they are suitable only for certain types of TA, for example, discrete pieces of advisory TA work, and not for other tasks like longer-term capacity building. With relatively short contracts, overheads and learning curves become relatively costly. A way to ease these problems, in a fluid situation where demands change, could be to engage in longer-term contracts or framework agreements with particular firms.

Having clear objectives, both for TA overall and for specific TA activities, is essential. Much TA comes into Afghanistan with vague, unrealistic, inappropriate, or virtually no objectives. While objectives, particularly with respect to capacity building, need to be realistic and achievable, they also need to be meaningful, linked to the national strategy and its objectives, and monitorable.

With clear objectives, monitoring of the performance of TA—essential for achieving meaningful results, becomes possible. While the government should be the focal point of monitoring efforts, donors also need to monitor the performance of the TA they finance or provide, particularly in the case of TA not financed through the budget.

As highlighted earlier, government leadership is essential, and TA will have limited or even negative value added in the absence of at least a certain level of government leadership. Where this precondition is in place, TA must follow the government's lead and allow itself to be guided and coordinated accordingly. There are various options for improving the management and coordination of TA under government leadership, which are outlined in Box 3.

Finally, an important element of development management, which also relates closely to aid coordination, is public communication on development aspects, both by the government and on the part of donors. This has been a serious problem area since 2001, particularly in the excessive fuelling of the already high expectations of the Afghan public as well as to some extent the donor countries, and in the failure to communicate adequately

BOX 3 **Options for Improving the Management, Coordination and Financing of Technical Assistance (TA)**

There are various specific options for improving the management and coordination of TA, including the following (in decreasing order of ambition, difficulty, and likely effectiveness):

- **Pooled funding** of TA for a ministry or agency, with the TA contracted through government channels. This kind of financing mechanism fully reinforces an effectively coordinated approach to TA.
- **A single TA provider** for the concerned government ministry or department, which reports to the Afghan leadership of the ministry or department. This option, which is possible (as long as there is coordination and a sensible division of labour among donors) is applicable even without pooled funding or funding through the budget.
- **A lead provider designated by the government** that coordinates and oversees all the TA to the unit, with the full agreement and cooperation of the other TA providers.
- **A lead individual advisor designated by the government,** who provides oversight and guidance to all TA, for and on behalf of the government.
- **Coordinated planning by multiple TA providers,** under government leadership and guidance.
- **Continuation of present practices but with stronger leadership, management, and oversight** by the government ministry or agency that is recipient of the TA.

The best option is likely to vary with the conditions in different ministries and agencies.

the real achievements and progress made, exacerbating the problem of disappointed expectations. These issues call for urgent attention to enhancing development communication. This effort must be led by the government, but donors' support, co-operation, and staying on-message will be essential for achieving greater success in communication than in the past.

Concluding Remarks

All of the priorities discussed above relate to the state building agenda, but, as emphasized earlier, state building in the context of Afghanistan appears to be at serious risk of going in directions that may well be harmful for national objectives. Put most bluntly, *state building loses much of its*

lustre and raison d'être if it involves building a state that becomes se-
verely undermined by corruption. State corruption could include being
beholden to the drug industry or other criminal and anti-state interests on
the one hand, and being awash in petty corruption on the other, to the
detriment of service delivery, rule of law, and other national objectives, but
most notably the credibility and legitimacy of the state. In this context, the
accelerated move toward normal political institutions as per the December
2001 Bonn Agreement, although fully achieved in terms of meeting the
benchmarks and, at least broadly, the timetable set in the Bonn Agreement,
has also brought significant problems and side effects. This is not surprising in a deeply conflict-scarred context, where the rule of law is largely
lacking in many parts of the country, government capacity remains very
weak on the whole, political power is still to a large extent based on past
conflict-induced patterns, and there has been a failure to address the difficult legacies and human rights violations of the turbulent final two decades
of the twentieth century in Afghanistan.

Moving forward with building a legitimate, effective, and accountable
state—a central element of Afghanistan's overall development agenda—
will require close attention and careful adjustments to reduce the risk,
which is already materializing, that what comes out of the process is a corrupt state that does not effectively promote national development or provide services and has lost its credibility with most Afghans. Any expectations that Afghanistan will be able in the near future to build a state that
meets developed-country standards in most respects are unrealistic and
should be abandoned. But it is essential to achieve adequate progress and
reasonable minimum standards in terms of security and rule of law, good
governance, and increasingly basic service delivery. This will be critical to
keep the Afghan people on board. Although the state building effort is
falling short in crucial respects, the more positive experience in specific
areas like public finance management (PFM), for example, does provide
some grounds for hope.

To complement "top-down" state building, i.e., building the institutions,
processes, capacity, and accountability of state institutions (including very
importantly at the sub-national level), there is a need for "bottom-up" approaches and for generating meaningful public accountability. For example,
the Community Development Councils (CDCs) under the National Solidarity Programme are promising yet fragile institutions and, if properly nur-
tured and sustained, can become the focal point for grass-roots development
prioritization and monitoring.

In conclusion, this chapter has attempted to summarize the very real
progress achieved, the problems and constraints encountered, and the priorities for Afghanistan as it faces a highly unusual, in many respects virtu-

ally unique, set of development challenges. The progress achieved provides a platform for further progress in many areas. The areas where progress has been slow or negligible, and recent adverse trends in some areas, provide grounds for concern, however.

Especially under the difficult conditions faced in Afghanistan, development and state building inevitably will be a long-term effort. However, much needs to be done in the short run, and we are left with the question of whether the effort as a whole, including responses to the growing challenge of the insurgency, for example, is adequate in relation to the challenges faced.

While more realistic expectations are called for on the part of all stakeholders than in the heady days immediately after the downfall of the Taliban, it also seems clear that the sum total of current efforts, *as they are being implemented now*, is insufficient to make continuing steady progress over the medium term—toward Afghanistan's legitimate national objectives or toward the international community's goals for the country. There is in the absence of substantial changes a significant risk of some combination of drift, slow progress, and backsliding. Since it cannot be taken for granted that international military forces will stay in Afghanistan indefinitely (and moreover that would not be desirable), nor that international financial assistance will be maintained at current levels indefinitely, such a scenario would carry grave risks over the medium term. In particular, in the absence of a great deal of further progress, withdrawal of many international troops and/or a sharp cut in international financial assistance would have severely harmful consequences.

Thus, some combination of additional resources (including military as well as financial) and much better deployment and use of available resources will be essential to improve development performance sufficiently so that Afghanistan moves toward being in a sustainable position—financially, capacity-wise, and in terms of the government's legitimacy and credibility. This chapter has laid out some priorities for action in the development field (broadly construed). Similar rethinking and, as needed, bold moves (while maintaining a medium-term perspective), will be required in other key areas, including on the security front and in the political patterns.

William A. Byrd is Adviser, Poverty Reduction and Economic Management, South Asia Region, World Bank. The views, findings, interpretations, and conclusions expressed in this paper are those of the author in his personal capacity and should not be attributed to the World Bank, its Executive Board of Directors, or the governments they represent.

Notes

1 The informal sector exists in all countries, although at high levels of average per-capita income it tends to be relatively small as a share of GDP. What is missing in Afghanistan, for the most part, is the existence of a significant, dynamic formal sector.

2 The Dutch Disease and real exchange rate movements for Afghanistan are analyzed in IMF (2006, 7–23). For a recent analysis of real exchange rate trends and determinants in the context of post-conflict aid, see Elbadawi, Kaltani, and Schmidt-Hebbel (2007). Several sources cited in this paper assess the relationship between exchange rate overvaluation and lower economic growth.

3 Some elements of a possible strategy for sustaining economic growth were discussed in World Bank (2005b).

4 The marked compression of pay in Afghanistan's civil service reflected the severe erosion of base pay (which was reasonably differentiated) by hyperinflation, combined with across-the-board allowances to ameliorate the effect of inflation. This resulted in a situation where the bulk of pay was in the form of cash allowances which were the same for all civil servants. See Evans, Manning, Osmani, Tully, and Wilder (2004) for a detailed discussion of pay and other conditions in the Afghan civil service.

5 This reflected in part a widespread impression that the Bonn Agreement's explicit political benchmarks had been successful in encouraging and enforcing a remarkable degree of progress, and that the same approach could be applied with respect to the development agenda.

6 See World Bank (2006a, chapter 5) for a discussion of prioritization at different levels and options and approaches for this purpose.

7 The USA is by a large margin the biggest aid donor to Afghanistan. However, the European Commission, Japan, the UK, and several other European countries are also major donors to Afghanistan. The World Bank and Asian Development Bank both provide several hundred million dollars per year in support of Afghanistan's reconstruction. For many of the smaller donors, Afghanistan is their most important aid recipient or one of the most important. The fact that some smaller countries contribute significant numbers of troops to the International Security Assistance Force (ISAF) in Afghanistan adds further complexity to the situation.

8 A notable exception is mobile telecommunications, which have been provided entirely on a private/regulated basis. This is by a very large margin the most successful infrastructure-related sector in terms of rate of expansion, quality of service, and also (among all sectors) in attracting direct foreign investment into Afghanistan.

9 The unit costs of highway rehabilitation are discussed in considerable detail in World Bank (2005a, Volume IV, chapter 5).

10 In this context it should also be noted that in the absence of at least some degree of line ministry leadership, external consultants and TA can aggravate rather than ameliorate problems. Multiple, uncoordinated TA providers, different policy views and competition among them, advisors possibly reflecting the views of donors funding them as much as or more than Government interests, low quality and supply-driven nature of TA—all of these problems can become unmanageable in the absence of effective line ministry leadership. See also Michailof (2007) for a detailed assessment of TA and capacity building.

11 An example of this kind of criterion is the analysis of economic growth in the *Securing Afghanistan's Future* exercise (see Afghanistan and International Agencies 2004, chapter 1), where "required," "feasible," and "projected" rates of growth were calculated and discussed.

12 The formal equilibrium does not mean that there would no longer be a substantial informal sector; all countries have sizable informal sectors and there is little sign that the share of the informal sector in the total economy substantially declines until relatively high levels of development are achieved. What is meant by the formal equilibrium is that the business climate and enabling environment are conducive to the emergence and dynamic growth of a significant formal sector. See World Bank (2005b, chapters 1 and 3).

13 As has occurred all along, some important power-holders have also been brought into the executive or other senior state positions. While this has been seen as a means of co-opting them into the state building agenda, these figures have maintained their networks and have tended to continue with their earlier approaches to Afghan politics. Thus there is a salient question as to whether these persons have been co-opted by the state or, at least in part, have co-opted parts of the state.

14 A model might be, in the case of agricultural products, the practice of "contract farming" whereby large corporations (e.g., grocery chains in Europe) contract sizable farms (or farmers' associations) in developing countries to produce certain goods of an adequate quality standard for sale on their shelves, with the corporation providing a whole range of inputs and quality control to make this happen. Such corporations would not normally engage in this way with Afghanistan, but might be willing to do so if the process is appropriately subsidized by the aid community.

References

Buddenberg, Doris, and William A. Byrd, eds. 2006. *Afghanistan's Drug Industry: Structure, Functioning, Dynamics, and Implications for Counter-Narcotics Policy.* Kabul, Afghanistan: United Nations Office on Drugs and Crime and World Bank.

Elbadawi, Ibrahim, Linda Kaltani, and Klaus Schmidt-Hebbel. 2007. *Post-Conflict Aid, Real Exchange Rate Adjustments, and Catch-Up Growth.* Washington, DC: World Bank Policy Research Working Paper no. 4187 (April).

Evans, Anne, Nick Manning, Yasin Osmani, Anne Tully, and Andrew Wilder. 2004. *A Guide to Government in Afghanistan.* Washington, DC, and Kabul: World Bank and Afghanistan Research and Evaluation Unit.

Guimbert, Stephane. 2004. *Structure and Performance of the Afghan Economy.* World Bank South Asia Region PREM Working Paper Series, no. SASPR-1 (May).

International Monetary Fund. 2006. *Islamic Republic of Afghanistan: Selected Issues and Statistical Appendix.* IMF Country Report no. 06/114 (March).

Islamic Republic of Afghanistan. 2002. *(Draft) National Development Framework.* Kabul, Afghanistan (April).

————. 2006. *Interim Afghanistan National Development Strategy*. Kabul, Afghanistan (January).

————. 2007. *(Draft) Anti-Corruption Roadmap for the Islamic Republic of Afghanistan.* Paper presented at the Afghanistan Development Forum and Joint Coordination and Monitoring Board meetings (April).

Islamic Republic of Afghanistan and International Agencies. 2004. *Securing Afghanistan's Future*. Kabul, Afghanistan.

McKechnie, Alistair J. 2003. *Humanitarian Assistance, Reconstruction and Development in Afghanistan: A Practitioner's View*. World Bank Conflict Prevention and Reconstruction Papers, Social Development Department, no. 3 (March).

Michailof, Serge. 2007. *Review of Technical Assistance and Capacity Building in Afghanistan*. World Bank discussion paper for the Afghanistan Development Forum.

Nixon, Hamish. 2007. *Aiding the State? International Assistance and the State-building Paradox in Afghanistan*. Afghanistan Research and Evaluation Unit, Briefing Paper Series (April).

Rubin, Barnett. 2000. "The Political Economy of War and Peace in Afghanistan." *World Development* 28 (10): 1789–1803.

Shaw, Mark. 2006. "Drug Trafficking and the Development of Organized Crime in Post-Taliban Afghanistan." In Buddenberg and Byrd (2006), chapter 7.

World Bank. 2005a. *Afghanistan: Managing Public Finances for Development (In Five Volumes)*. World Bank Report no. 34582–AF–34582.

————. 2005b. *Afghanistan—State Building, Sustaining Growth, and Reducing Poverty (A World Bank Country Study)*. Washington, DC.

————. 2005c. *The Investment Climate in Afghanistan: Exploiting Opportunities in an Uncertain Environment*. Washington, DC.

————. 2006a. *Afghanistan: Managing Public Finances for Development*. Washington, DC (glossy-cover main report).

————. 2006b. *Treating the Opium Problem in World Bank Operations in Afghanistan: Guideline Note*.

————. 2007. *Service Delivery and Governance at the Subnational Level in Afghanistan*. World Bank Report (July).

5

Seema Patel

Laying Economic Foundations for a New Afghanistan

Over thirty years of war had wreaked havoc on Afghan institutions, resources, and people. Rule of law collapsed, giving way to massive political violence, human rights abuses, and social trauma. Afghanistan experienced the erosion of economic foundations, mass flight of skilled human and other capital, environmental degradation, market inefficiencies, and the breakdown of government, basic services, private production, and infrastructure. Many lost their livelihoods, and while some lived on the margins, others sought refuge in other countries.

It was clear in the early days of reconstruction that the recovery would be particularly challenging and would require a significant amount of resources, efforts, and patience. While institutions were re-established and rebuilt, laws debated and drafted, and a new government elected and installed, the security of the Afghan people would need to be protected, and new sources of income would need to be created to counter poverty and violence, and build confidence in the new state. The government of Afghanistan with the support of the international community has been working to achieve these goals for the past seven years. There have been some achievements. Yet there still remains a palatable popular discontent with the pace of progress, new security challenges from a resurgent Taliban and criminal elements, pervasive corruption, poor social services, and a systemic lack of income opportunities for ordinary Afghans.

An Assessment of Economic Recovery

Any retrospective assessment of economic recovery efforts and results in Afghanistan since 2001—even after recognizing the enormity of the task, the complexity of Afghan society, the weakness of government structures, the scarcity of resources, and the fragility of the security environment—will be mixed. For the economy to rebound in Afghanistan, the approach must be comprehensive, and multi-pronged, advancing on multiple fronts or pillars simultaneously: (1) ensuring good governance, (2) developing a legal market economy, (3) combatting poverty traps and unemployment, and (4) rebuilding human capital.

Ensuring Good Governance: Macroeconomic Stability and Public Finance Management

Afghanistan's national systems and institutions for managing public finances and developing fiscal and monetary policies deteriorated during the country's many years of war. The government was unable to responsibly and systematically collect, regulate, and spend money to deliver critical services or develop new economic opportunities for its population. Checks to ensure transparency and accountability to the public and limit the opportunities for corruption and exploitation broke down. The Afghan state has historically been a rentier state, or, dependent on the largesse of outsiders to cover its own expenses. During the years of war, this assistance often came at the price of intrusive political actions by donor states and groups, further fuelling, as it often does, with insecurity and instability.

The government of Afghanistan, under pressure from the international community, particularly the Breton Woods Institutions, prioritized establishing macroeconomic stability. Central Bank reforms, the introduction of a new currency, and a disciplined monetary policy held the exchange rate steady during the first years of reconstruction at approximately 50 afghani per dollar. The Central Bank, Da Afghanistan Bank, meanwhile increased its foreign currency reserves from virtually zero to almost $2 billion (IMF and Afghanistan 2007, 34). The reforms were a success. They kept the country's currency balances but were not so stringent that they stifled economic growth and expansion. Fiscal reform under the auspices of then Minister of Finance Dr. Ashraf Ghani and various international technical advisors also began early in the reconstruction process. From 2002 to 2005, the Ministry of Finance was turned into a modern institution, and the country's budget process was rationalized. New laws for customs and tax collection caused domestically generated revenue to increase almost 500% from 2003 to 2007 (ADB 2006, 157). Computerization and the hiring of officials more honest and professional than their predecessors also improved oversight of government monies.

Despite these successes, however, securing sufficient revenue to administer basic functions—the development of infrastructure, provision of social services, protection of national security, and expansion of the economy—remains a large hurdle for the government. Afghans remain dependent on the international community to fund operations through the Afghanistan Reconstruction Trust Fund (ARTF) and the Law and Order Trust Fund for Afghanistan (LOTFA) or through donor assistance programs (IMF and Afghanistan 2007, 15). Alternative government structures at the local and tribal levels as well as pervasive corruption siphon off the central government's funds. The majority of the population is unaccustomed to paying taxes and is distrustful of the government's commitment to providing positive improvements in return. Most market transactions occur in the informal economy, and tax evasion is common, limiting the level of revenue the government can expect from taxes on trade and business.

The government must also be able to administer its national budget to cover the recurrent operating costs of state institutions and services through the operating budget and invest in new national development projects to improve the lives of its citizens through the development budget. The government has become more effective at managing its operating budget, spending approximately 60% of its available funds on critical inputs such as civil servant salaries and office expenses for the ministries and provincial governments (IMF and Afghanistan 2007, 2). As for the development budget, the government is currently able to convert only 43% of its available cash into infrastructure and social services projects. Bottlenecks and corruption in the line ministries and provincial governments, over-centralized practices, low capacity to manage reconstruction and development projects, and deteriorating security prevent implementation of the bulk of government development funding (ADB 2006, 156). This is especially true outside major urban centres, where government officials are few and far between. The National Solidarity Program, which provides funding directly to local communities to undertake development projects, is a notable exception. It has enabled the government to implement development projects, such as roads, wells, clinics, and microhydro systems in inaccessible and insecure rural areas. External donors such as nongovernmental organizations (NGOs), international private contractors, and the military provide more funds for service and reconstruction projects than the Afghan government.

Although economic stability and institutional improvements should be celebrated, the state is far from being self sufficient, and costs are rising. A new national army, police force, and parliament have all added to the government's operating costs. Thousands of civil servants, teachers, doctors, and judges are still being hired to provide the people with desperately needed services. The state must move to diversify its funding sources. It should encourage economic activity that can easily be taxed, such as trade and local and foreign business operations, while planning in the long term for a general population taxation system. The state must move much more quickly to increase oversight and reduce the corruption that is limiting the government's legitimacy and effectiveness. Most importantly, the state needs to prove it can raise the living standards of ordinary Afghans by implementing projects faster in remote locations, and in partnership with local communities. For stability to prevail in Afghanistan, where people have historically been skeptical of central government, the state must prove that it can responsibly manage public finances and positively impact people's lives.

Fostering Private-Sector and Rural Development

Before the Soviet intervention in 1979, Afghanistan's economy was underdeveloped and stagnant, with little access to global markets, few comparative advantages, and many market inefficiencies. During the 1960s and '70s, the growth rate averaged only 2–4% per year (Afghanistan, ADB, UNDP, IMF, and WB 2004, 6). The years of war meant the destruction of infrastructure, human capital, and other factors of production, while the framework of rules and rights governing transactions became defunct, and prospects for mobilizing capital toward investment in productive assets became doubtful. Industry and trade all but disappeared as a result. Most international and local businesses pulled out or shut down, markets emptied, and agricultural production scaled back to subsistence farming. Informal, illicit, and violence-based markets expanded and eventually dwarfed the formal, legal economy.

The process of developing a high-growth, modern, market-based, formal economy based on legitimate goods and services began in 2001, following improvements in the security environment. Private markets were the first to reappear, and received a boost from the millions of Afghans who returned to their homeland with capital and entrepreneurial ideas. Government reforms, including legislation to improve financial, commercial, and trading markets; privatization plans; and institutional promotion and support of the private and rural industrial sector went a long way toward fostering increased production and trade. Regionally, Afghan goods are still comparatively expensive, but previously existing trade agreements have been renewed, and new agreements have been negotiated and enacted in order to increase opportunities for Afghan producers (US Foreign and Commercial Service and Department of State 2006). A more permissive security environment, a better business regulatory environment, and foreign assistance investment in infrastructure, such as roads, telecommunications, irrigation, and power, have all helped to increase industrial and agricultural productivity. Afghanistan's GDP has grown by an average of 16% during the past five years (IMF and Afghanistan 2007, 15), and according to the International Monetary Fund, this growth should continue, albeit at a slower rate, into the future (IMF and Afghanistan 2007, 25).

A few large international firms, including DHL, Coca-Cola, Siemens, British Petroleum, First Microfinance Bank, Roshan, and Afghan Wireless have established profitable operations in Afghanistan (AISA Investment Fact Sheet 2007a). New institutions such as the Afghanistan International Chamber of Commerce (AICC) and Afghanistan Investment Support Agency (AISA) have been instrumental in encouraging foreign and diaspora investment, reducing business registration red tape, and advocating for pro-market policies, such as an improved regulatory environment, more tax incentives, and new customs codes to reduce duties in several sectors. The stability of the currency and the central bank's discipline has comforted investors from Turkey, China, the United Arab Emirates, Iran, and the United States, among others, that the afghani will maintain its value over time. Yet, there are still significant stumbling blocks to foreign direct investment (FDI). Corruption, high taxes, confusion over land titles and rights, and the recent deterioration in security have once again increased the cost of operations and undermined the confidence of international and diaspora investors; some have even been persuaded to withdraw completely.

Afghan farmers, businesses, and traders are less easily discouraged by problems in security and regulatory environments, but they have their own set of constraints. In most areas of Afghanistan, operating costs of the private industrial and agricultural sectors are extraordinarily high due to a lack of available and affordable infrastructure, such as irrigation systems, reliable power sources, communication networks, and roads. The recent construction of the country's main highway, the Ring Road, facilitates the transit of thousands of dollars' worth of goods between Afghanistan's major urban centres—Kabul, Mazar-i Sharif, Herat, and Kandahar—and across the borders with Pakistan, Iran, Uzbekistan, and Tajikistan. Still more secondary and farm-to-market roads are needed. A number of roads promised to other provincial centres have barely been started. The people in these provinces remain cut off from the centre's markets, jobs, social services, and reconstruction programming, subsequently fueling perceptions of inequities. Also, insecurity in the south and east and unofficial "taxes" collected by local commanders, militias, and police have made it dangerous for many Afghans to use the new roads, thereby discouraging access and undermining economic activity.

The ability to communicate and conduct business from remote and dispersed locations generates market efficiencies. The pro-market policies of the Ministry of Communications have facilitated the dispersal of communication technologies to districts and villages across Afghanistan. As a result of rapid expansion of private cellular services, the government, individuals, and businesses all have increased access to market information and connectivity to suppliers, distributors, and customers. More market transactions are conducted as a result.

In Afghanistan, the lack of electricity is the most significant barrier to investment. The Ministry of Power and Water is barely able to offer two hours of electricity per day to Kabul (Zucchino 2006), while roughly 93% of the country remains unconnected to any electrical source (Islamic Republic of Afghanistan 2007a, 1). Plans are underway to establish a national power grid, combining imported and domestically generated power, with priority being given to economic hubs such as Herat, Kabul, and Kandahar. It is likely to take years before the grid is fully operational and able to meet private-sector needs (Islamic Republic of Afghanistan 2007a, 1). In the interim, some businesses are providing for themselves with privately owned and run generators, but, given the high cost of fuel, these are expensive to sustain. Most businesses remain subject to unforeseen power outages with concomitant negative effects on productivity and operations stability.

Horticulture in Afghanistan requires irrigation. Unfortunately, a 2002 study conducted by the International Center for Agricultural Research in the Dry Areas (ICARDA) estimated that 30% of the country's irrigation systems were damaged due to conflict, and another 15–20% in disuse due to abandonment, neglect, and lack of maintenance (ICARDA 2002). Although many small-scale projects are underway to deepen canals and rehabilitate more than one thousand broken irrigation systems, Afghanistan is far from implementing a holistic water-management system for irrigation and hydropower. Programs have been focused on near-term crisis management to stem the devastation of floods and droughts rather than on long-term improvement in agricultural yields.

In addition, local entrepreneurs lack access to investment capital at a reasonable cost. Failure to finance its burgeoning industrial and agricultural sectors has caused chronic harm to Afghanistan's economic recovery. The commercial banking industry has grown rapidly to include thirteen banks with branches in provincial capitals outside Kabul (Basharat 2006). The banks service many ordinary Afghans and are starting to provide mid-size entrepreneurs with the capital they need for startup activity, but business loans of $50,000 to $250,000 are not yet widely available; when they are, they often come at the high price of 15–20% interest rates on a short-term (1–2 year) basis.[1] Borrowing against the coming harvest is a critical mechanism for farmers, giving them access to credit to sustain their families during the winter months and to invest in equipment, seeds, fertilizer, livestock, and other necessary, productivity-enhancing inputs. Other than microfinance programs that cover the most needy entrepreneurs, small to medium players have no formal mechanism to extract capital, and instead must rely on informal systems, such as *Hawala* dealers, kinship networks, diaspora sources, and in some cases local commanders and drug traders.

Despite these constraints, a number of small- to medium-sized enterprises (SME) of $1 million or less, particularly in the construction, carpets and textiles, and mining industries, have emerged (AISA 2007d). In the agribusiness industry, however, private investment during the past three years declined by 12.6% (2007d), despite foreign aid to encourage the development of value-added alternatives to illicit poppy production. New industrial parks in Herat, Bagram, Mazar-i Sharif, and Kandahar offer a creative solution to infrastructural deficiencies, with clear land titles, electricity and water, roads, buildings and maintenance, and security for factories in designated zones (AISA 2007b; 2007c). Countless small and nimble informal traders and service-providers have opened their doors, taking advantage of short-term opportunities. In fact, according to the World Bank, informal transactions constitute nearly 80–90% of the country's economic activity (World Bank 2004, 5). Yet, the government of Afghanistan has taken no concrete action to capitalize on its citizens' ingenuity and entrepreneurship by formalizing the economy. Another ongoing concern for the health of the private sector is the tendency of the state, the NGO community, and international donor projects to crowd economic space, undertaking activities that might be more efficient and sustainable under private ownership.

Agriculture remains the predominant sector of the Afghan economy, representing roughly one-third of gross domestic product (GDP), excluding opium, and accounting for nearly two-thirds of employment (ADB 2006, 146). It remains the source of greatest potential for broad-based, long-term economic growth. Co-operative arrangements, improved trade regulations, and new roads have facilitated the movement of foodstuffs to markets where they can be sold, but the slow growth of the agribusiness industry has hampered the development of high-value, marketable agricultural products and brands for international trade. Meanwhile, opium continues to be a source of economic growth and macroeconomic health, contributing to the GDP, increasing the purchasing power of Afghans, and generating large aggregate demand. Yet, the poppy trade injects massive corruption and instability into the economic and security environment. Although poppy cultivation declined by 21% in 2005, this trend reversed in 2006, with land under cultivation increasing by 59% (UNODC 2006, 2). Horticultural products, particularly if processed and packaged, represent a credible alternative to poppy. Limited access to markets, poor irrigation infrastructure, and insufficient credit continue to discourage investment, however, and prevent the growth of licit, value-added agricultural production. On the positive side, revenue from opium as a share of GDP has surprisingly declined from 62% in 2002–2003 to 38% in 2005–2006. That this occurred despite rising poppy production and drug exports reflects steady and sustained growth in the licit economy (Martin and Symansky 2006, 27).

Jump-starting the growth engine in Afghanistan requires creating a favourable environment for the private sector, rural development, and improved trade. A rational regulatory environment and new institutions that promote and support the private sector and reduce risks must be established to increase investor confidence and operational and marketing capacity. The backbone of business—infrastructure, access to capital in a fair and transparent banking sector, and human skills and knowledge—also need to be developed. Opportunities to sell products and services in both domestic and international markets should be cultivated through trade agreements and safe and efficient local distribution networks. Some of this work has begun in Afghanistan, but it needs to be sustained, and in some cases accelerated, to help increase licit economic activity and decrease the country's dependence on international assistance and illicit income.

Combatting Poverty Traps and Unemployment: Basic Needs and Livelihoods

Years of war have left Afghanistan's families plagued by unsteady or non-existent income streams, caught in cycles of debt, and without access to land, financial capital, and physical assets. Some families lost their main bread-winner to the violence, while for others the dependents considerably outweigh the wage earners. Access to even the most basic needs, such as food, clean water, and shelter, is patchy in most Afghan communities and especially among populations at risk, such as returnees, ex-combatants, orphans, and female-headed households.

The international community responded early to the challenge of devastating poverty with humanitarian efforts to deliver basic goods and protect the groups most at risk. Short-term job-creation programs that employ targeted groups of Afghans by the day, week, or month to build roads and execute other reconstruction projects have generated some new jobs and some local private-sector activity, but donors' large-scale procurement practices still favour international development contractors over the local private sector. The majority of Afghans, and not just at-risk populations, are caught in poverty traps poorly understood by the international community. While international programs typically develop little more than short-term solutions for targeted groups, the Afghan government and indigenous businesses remain unable to support broader-based employment, and the majority of Afghans continue to suffer from debilitating unemployment.

The benefits of high economic growth, steady inflation, trade balances, and pro-market reforms have yet to trickle down to the ordinary Afghan. Despite positive economic indicators, according to a survey by Altai Consulting in 2006, only 3% of Afghans indicated that economic growth has been the most important accomplishment of the central government in the past two years, while 32% of respondents indicated a lack of jobs or slow economic growth has been the most important failure (Altai Consulting 2006). Although domestic markets are bustling with entrepreneurial Afghans who have set up their own small businesses, and countless farms are productive, government estimates put the unemployment rate at 33% of the working-age population (Gardesh 2006). More importantly, of employed Afghans, only 13.5% reported a steady and secure stream of income in a survey conducted by the Afghanistan Independent Human Rights Commission in 2006 (AIHRC 2006, 8). Despite new payroll accounting and delivery systems, many Afghans working for the government—from public officials and judges, teachers, and doctors, to police, and army officers, for example—do not receive their paycheques. Approximately 23 million Afghans, or 77% of the Afghan population, live in rural areas where the agriculture sector is predominant (World Bank 2007b), and the majority of trade is conducted in-kind. Opportunities to earn hard currency are limited, as are opportunities to diversify income sources. Most adults get by on short-term employment and day labour, seasonal migration, income from their children's labour, and illicit or informal support systems. In drought years, when harvest yields are low, Afghans are forced to aggregate excess debt and sell off physical assets to make ends meet. As a result of these pressures, 80% of rural Afghans are estimated to be vulnerable to extreme poverty (World Bank 2005, 12).

Since families are unable to earn sufficient income to keep their households afloat, they rely on aggregating debt to respond to economic shocks and crises (AREU 2006). According to the Afghanistan Independent Human Rights Commission's (AIHRC) survey on Economic and Social Rights, 63.5% of respondents stated that their household is in debt, at an average level of $1,150 per family (AIHRC 2006, 8). With an average annual per capita income of $270, this is a major source of vulnerability (World Bank 2007a). The traditional unregulated *hawala* system of dealers, who provide informal banking services in lieu of the commercial system, continues to be the primary mechanism for managing financial assets. Debt is also accumulated with nefarious actors such as drug traders and local strongmen, who charge exorbitant rates and are likely to use violence against defaulters. The Microfinance Investment Support Facility for Afghanistan (MISFA) has helped the most vulnerable, and the growing commercial banking sector has provided alternative sources for credit and loans to the upper-middle class, but neither program is aggressive enough to reach the majority of Afghans (MISFA 2007).

The lack of clear ownership of land and property aggravates the sense of economic insecurity for Afghans. Initiatives to clarify property titles and undertake land reform have been met by some resistance and even apathy. Property and land theft is commonplace, yet the formal justice system has been incapable of preventing and punishing these crimes on behalf of rightful owners. The influx of international organizations, meanwhile, has caused rents and prices to soar, particularly in urban areas, inflating the cost of living (IMF 2005, 34). In response, Afghans have resorted to a combination of coping mechanisms including short-term renting, shifting to more inexpensive residences, and relocating to live with extended family members.

Improvements made since 2001 in providing access to vital infrastructure and basic needs have minimized the vulnerability of ordinary citizens to economic and social shocks and increased their chances of achieving productive livelihoods. Shelter, water, and food are more readily available in urban areas due to the tireless work of NGOs, international, and local institutions. In smaller rural communities, informal safety nets such as familial, clan, and *qawm* groups; access to communal and tribal networks; and religious charities fill gaps for most Afghans while they wait for the state to build new systems to deliver basic goods.

The return of more than 4.2 million refugees to Afghanistan between 2002 and 2005 (UNHCR Statistical Yearbook 2006) indicates a positive step for peace. However, many Afghans, hearing about improved conditions at home, returned from Pakistan and Iran only to discover they have fewer services and lower incomes than abroad (UNHCR 2005). The influx of people has further strained already stretched urban and rural management, resources, and services. Internally displaced person (IDP) and refugee populations have critical humanitarian needs and are in need of programs that encourage long-term resettlement.

The state is currently unable to meet basic humanitarian needs on a large scale, particularly in emergency cases. Natural disasters, such as droughts and floods, as well asand ongoing conflict, continue to create new at-risk populations. In 2006 alone, 30,000 people required emergency assistance or were displaced or evacuated as a result of floods (Emergency Disasters Database). Concomitantly, renewed violence from both insurgency and counterinsurgency military operations led to the displacement of between 110,000 and 130,000 people in the southern conflict-ridden provinces of Kandahar, Uruzgan, and Helmand (UNCHR 2007). International and local authorities were required to respond anew with humanitarian assistance to meet requests for food, water, and shelter for a growing number of affected people.

Women and children face distinct economic risks. Although many women express a desire to have a job, they are often under-educated or face social obstacles preventing them from working outside the home. They are vulnerable to sudden shocks, such as divorce or widowhood, which leave them without a source of income on which to survive. Sometimes extended family members are able to absorb the imperiled women and their children, but more often than not, they are forced into destitution and must resort to begging. Approximately 37,000 children are estimated to be working on the streets of Kabul as labourers and beggars to supplement family income (UN OCHA 2007). Nearly seven million children, almost half the total in the country, do not have access to an education, and approximately six million suffer from malnutrition (Oxfam 2006, 3, 17). International programs to protect women and children have been addressing these issues aggressively, but deep-rooted gender biases and social constraints continue to hamper progress.

Poverty and unemployment are forcing Afghans to turn to the illicit economy to survive, fueling insecurity and undermining governance. Police, judges, and government officials accept bribes to subsidize their low salaries, which jeopardizes fair judicial processes and the legitimacy of the state. The narcotics industry, another lucrative income source for Afghans, undermines the formal, legal economy, good governance, and security. As many as 2.9 million people, or 12.6% of the Afghan population, are involved in poppy cultivation (UNODC 2006, iv). Although the benefits are radically skewed toward traffickers and their partners, a large majority of Afghan farmers in the rural parts of Kandahar, Helmand, and Badakshan rely on the credit system and income derived from the rising farm-gate value of poppy. Alternative livelihoods programs, which have been implemented to discourage cultivation, have not adequately addressed the complex poverty constraints afflicting the Afghan farmer. A majority of farmers indicate a willingness to grow alternatives while the international community is providing support, but they often return to the illegal crop once benefits stop. Eradication creates additional economic insecurity and fuels frustration with the government. Farmers whose fields have been eradicated are unable to feed their families, pay back loans collateralized with future poppy harvests to dealers, or develop alternative income streams fast enough to protect their families from ruin (UNODC 2006). Many turn to even more dangerous solutions as a result, including joining the Taliban and the private militias of local commanders. Ex-combatants also need economic alternatives to discourage them from returning to former commanders and other violent activities, yet thousands of former militia members are jobless. Incomplete reintegration, due to poor economic prospects or insufficient follow-up, is undermining the demobilization process and has added another dimension of instability to Afghanistan's economic woes.

Growth-oriented policies are not sufficient to combat chronic poverty and the sense of marginalization and exclusion existing among various groups and at-risk populations in Afghanistan. Humanitarian action, although necessary early on, is not a long-term or sustainable solution to protect the poor. Instead, the population at large must be targeted for long-term poverty reduction solutions and economic empowerment. A fundamental shift in the development approach is needed to increase access to and protection of financial assets and personal property. Reforms of the country's financial and legal institutions are also needed, but most Afghans will not see tangible benefits from such reforms for many years. Market-oriented solutions that leverage the economic activity of thousands of small and medium enterprises from the informal market to deliver employment with reasonable and predictable incomes will reduce the vulnerability of Afghans in time. Until then, in the short term, the donor community must respond by providing more emergency resources and rebuilding community safety nets.

Rebuilding Human Capital: Education and Health

Another legacy of the war years and Taliban rule is the erosion of human capital. The emigration of the most educated and skilled class of people and the crippling of the domestic health and education systems has meant that the country has had to rebuild its labour force. International donors eagerly developed initiatives to reconstruct health and education services, delivering visible projects to the Afghan people. Between 2002 and 2006, 4.3 million Afghan children—more than 30% of whom were girls—returned to school, more than 1,750 schoolhouses were rehabilitated (UNICEF 2005), and major universities were reopened. Access to basic healthcare and clinics improved from 7% of the population in 2001 to almost 80% in 2006 (Islamic Republic of Afghanistan 2007b), and hospitals increased their bed capacity. However, most international investment in these sectors has been used to build infrastructure rather than to develop a sustainable, holistic system.[2] Presently, there is a shortage of qualified teachers and doctors (particularly for female students and patients, respectively), educational materials, medicines, and medical equipment. Access is also limited, due to distance and a deteriorating security environment. Curricula and services at hospitals reflect outdated practices and need modernization and reform. In some cases, teachers and doctors have been trained and would be able to provide services, but their salaries are so low and paid so infre-quently that they refuse to work. In other cases, fear of being targeted by the Taliban in reprisal for providing services has driven trained providers underground. Even in urban areas where teachers and doctors are more readily available and willing to practice, meeting the demands of a rapidly growing population has been a challenge.

Programs that train and educate Afghan adults to become more mar-ketable and productive in the new economy, would bolster the labour sup-ply and empower a new cadre of entrepreneurs and future employers. Vo-cational training has generally been limited to skills like carpentry, weaving, and driving, or other specific skills sought by international NGOs. This training has not sufficiently extended to areas such as computer use, account-ing, civil service administration, and management. Extending training along these lines could increase Afghan employability in both the government and private sector, where demand for professional skills is high. The re-turning diaspora has helped fill some skills gaps, but also has created labour competition, which has solidified income inequalities between the com-paratively better-educated returnees and Afghans who did not leave the country.

An educated and healthy population with a new class of entrepreneurs, civil servants, traders, and leaders is needed to sustain the new economy. Building human capital is a long-term initiative, and the impact of a health-ier, more educated labour force on economic recovery will take time to ma-terialize. Steps should be taken today to develop the necessary inputs to en-sure a holistic system is in place. Educators and medics must be prepared and paid to undertake their work. Local communities and civil society must have a stake in the reform and protection of these services, so they continue to function over time and can endure fluctuating security conditions and wavering international support.

A New Economic Agenda

In sum, sound macroeconomic policies and structural reforms have been implemented, ensuring economic stability during the tumultuous political and social transition from war. State revenue has increased, while the ca-pacity of the government to manage public finances has improved. Some of the basic foundations for trade and commerce have been put into place, such as new roads, communication systems, education and health facilities, and regulatory institutions.

However, improvements made at the macro level have not yet had much impact on ordinary Afghans. The majority of Afghans are still vulnerable to extreme poverty and suffer from unsteady employment, and few safety nets are available in times of crisis. Poverty is fuelling anger and frustration toward the central government and international donors, and inadequate incomes are being supplemented through illicit sources, such as opium production and graft. Young men are joining the fighting ranks of the Taliban-led insurgency, criminal gangs, or local militias to earn cash, undermining progress made on the battlefield by national and international armed forces.

Even with full international support, sound policies and programs, and sustained economic growth, the new state will continue to face a number of chronic challenges. The central government will struggle to retain legitimacy, to collect revenues for the sustenance of its military, bureaucracy, and development programs, to eliminate corruption, to deliver social and judicial services, and to extend its presence to the whole country. Pockets of territory will remain or fall under the influence of local strongmen, and Afghans will rely on local and tribal institutions to fill the vacuums left by the state and to provide safety nets in times of socioeconomic crises. Afghanistan is in a volatile region, and its neighbours will continue to meddle in the domestic economy and politics. Before the war the country was poor and underdeveloped. Long after the international community loses interest in Afghanistan's development, it is likely to remain poor and underdeveloped. Providing sufficient jobs with steady income for Afghan families to rise out of chronic poverty is likely to take decades.

In the short to medium term, economic initiatives and reforms will not be able to mitigate all of Afghanistan's challenges, but they can at the least improve lives and help locals become less vulnerable to economic shocks. Most importantly, they reduce the incentives for Afghans to seek alternative and illicit means of survival, including a reversion to violence-based employment. Progress is possible, and people's livelihoods can be protected if both international and local expectations are realistic. The primary goal should be a stable Afghanistan. Reforms in the economic and human development sphere should be carried out to promote that stability, by reducing the negative impact of the war economy and providing the majority of Afghans the opportunity to rebuild their lives. Increased employment, equitable distribution of income, and the development of safety nets to protect the poorest citizens can reduce the incentives for war and should be considered in tandem with macroeconomic reforms and humanitarian action.

After decades of neglect by local leadership and governments, Afghan communities have become largely self-reliant and resourceful, skilled in navigating and moving resources and information around the country, and adept at dispute resolution and reconciliation, providing security, and governing locally. From *shuras* to private businesses, micro-hydro projects, *hawala* traders, micro-credit, and development zones, Afghanistan has demonstrated the value of local ownership. The National Solidarity Program (NSP) empowers ordinary Afghans to make choices according to the needs and interests of their specific community, while delivering benefits to a large portion of the population outside of Kabul and the provincial centres. These successful structures are small scale and dynamic, decentralized, and derived from traditional mechanisms.

The government of Afghanistan and the international community must support more initiatives that mobilize communities, engage, and empower private citizens to participate in reconstruction and development programming. The Afghan government and international assistance providers must move away from a centralized model where large development projects are administered and run by international NGOs and private contractors. They must learn to operate in more entrepreneurial and agile ways by delivering resources directly to the local level through a process that has momentum and is difficult to derail despite insecurity and corruption. Projects are more likely to be sustainable and efficient if they are built from already functioning systems that engage people to own, manage, and maintain their stake from the outset.

Afghanistan is at a critical point in its recovery—momentum is being lost, expectations are too high, and many Afghans are losing confidence in the new government and the international community. A revised agenda for economic recovery should be considered. An optimal approach in Afghanistan today would employ more innovative and flexible solutions to protect livelihoods better and deliver economic security faster to ordinary people.

Notes

1 Interview with Azarakhsh Hafizi, Chairman, Afghanistan International Chamber of Commerce, September 2006.
2 Interview with government official, USAID Afghanistan Mission, September 2006.

References

Afghanistan Independent Human Rights Commission (AIHRC). 2006. *Economic and Social Rights Report*. Kabul: AIHRC. http://www.aihrc.org.af/rep_economic_socail_may_2006.htm.
Afghanistan Investment Support Agency (AISA). 2007a. *AISA Investment Fact Sheet*. http://www.aisa.org.af/Data%20&%20Research/Basic-Data.htm.

———. 2007b. "Invest in Afghanistan." Afghanistan Industrial Parks Development Authority. http://www.aisa.org.af/ipda/.

———. 2007c. "Invest in Mazar-e-Sharif." Afghanistan Industrial Parks Development Facility. http://www.aisa.org.af/ipda/mazai.html.

———. 2007d. *Small and Medium-sized Enterprise (SME) Fact-sheet.* http://www.aisa.org.af/Data%20&%20Research/Basic-Data.htm. Altai Consulting. 2006. "ANDP Afghan National Development Poll: Survey 3." Kabul: Altai Consulting.

Asian Development Bank. 2006. *Asian Development Outlook 2006.* Hong Kong: ADB. http://www.adb.org/Documents/Books/ADO/2006/documents/afg.pdf.

Basharat, M. 2006. "Private Bank Opens Office in Kabul." *Pajhwok Afghan News.* June 13. http://www.a-acc.org/c/news/news_private_bank.html.

Dobbins, J., J.G. McGinn, K. Crane, S.G. Jones, R. Lal, A. Rathmell, R. Swanger, and A. Timilsina. 2003. *America's Role in Nation-Building: From Germany to Iraq.* Santa Monica, CA: RAND Corporation.

Emergency Disasters Database. 2006. *Country Profile: Afghanistan.* http://www.em-dat.net.

Gardesh, H. 2006. "Jobless Face Grim Future." *Institute for War and Peace Reporting.* July 13. http://www.iwpr.net/?p=arr&s=f&o=322263&apc_state=henh.

International Centre for Agricultural Research in the Dry Areas (ICARDA). 2002. Seed Unit/Future Harvest Consortium to Rebuild Agriculture in Afghanistan. "Seed and Crop Improvement Situation Assessment in Afghanistan." http://www.icarda.org/Afghanistan/NA/Full/Physical_F.htm.

International Monetary Fund. 2005. "Islamic Republic of Afghanistan: Fourth Review Under the Staff-Monitored Program,".Washington, DC: IMF. http://www.imf.org/external/pubs/ft/scr/2005/cr05237.pdf.

International Monetary Fund and Islamic Republic of Afghanistan. 2007. "First Review Under the Three Year Arrangement Under the Poverty Reduction and Growth Facility: Staff Report." IMF Country Report No. 07/130. Washington, DC: IMF.

Islamic Republic of Afghanistan, in collaboration with the ADB, the UNDP, the IMF, and the World Bank. 2004. "Securing Afghanistan's Future: Accomplishments and the Strategic Path Forward." http://www.adb.org/Documents/Reports/Afghanistan/securing-afghanistan-future-final.pdf.

Islamic Republic of Afghanistan. The Ministry of Water & Power of Afghanistan. 2007a. Power Sector Strategy for the Afghanistan National Development Strategy (draft). Kabul: Government of Afghanistan.

Islamic Republic of Afghanistan. Embassy of Afghanistan: United States Mission. 2007b. "Frequently Asked Questions." http://www.embassyofafghanistan.org/faqs/faqsociety.html.

Martin, E., and S. Symansky. 2006. "Macroeconomic Impact of the Drug Economy and Counternarcotics Efforts." In *Afghanistan: Drug Industry and*

Counter-Narcotics Policy. Washington, DC: World Bank. http://go.world
bank.org/ZTCWYL49P0.

Microfinance Investment Support Facility for Afghanistan. http://www.misfa.org.af/.

Oxfam International. 2006. *Free, Quality Education for Every Afghan Child*.
London: Oxfam.

Schuette, Stefan. 2006. *Searching for Security: Urban Livelihoods in Kabul*.
Afghanistan Research and Evaluation Unit (AREU). http://www.areu
.org.af/index.php?option=com_docman&Itemid=&task=doc_download
&gid=326.

United Nations Children Fund (UNICEF). 2005. *Afghanistan Education Fact
Sheet*. http://www.unama-afg.org/news/_pr/_english/UN/2005/UNICEF-
Education%20Fact%20Sheet.pdf.

United Nations High Commission for Refugees (UNHCR). 2005. "Afghan New
Year signals new returns, new challenges." March 21. http://www.unhcr
.org/cgi-bin/texis/vtx/afghan?page=news&id=423edda54.

———. 2006. *UNHCR Statistical Yearbook: Country Datasheet*. New York:
UNHCR. http://www.unhcr.org/cgi-bin/texis/vtx/country?iso=afg&
expand=statistics.

United Nations Office for the Coordination of Humanitarian Affairs (OCHA)
IRIN News. 2007. "Children work the streets to support families." January 16. http://www.irinnews.org/report.aspx?reportid=64363

United Nations Office on Drugs and Crime (UNODC). 2006. *Afghanistan Opium
Survey 2006*. New York: United Nations. http://www.unodc.org/pdf/exec
summaryafg.pdf.

United National Development Program. 2006. *UNDP Country Programme for
the Islamic Republic of Afghanistan 2006–2008*. New York: UNDP.

United States Foreign and Commercial Service and US Department of State.
2006. *Doing Business in Afghanistan: A Country Commercial Guide for
U.S. Companies*. http://www.export.gov/afghanistan/pdf/afghanistan_ccg
_2006.pdf.

World Bank. 2004. "Afghanistan: State Building, Sustaining Growth, and Reducing Poverty: A Country Economic Report." Washington, DC: World Bank.
http://siteresources.worldbank.org/INTAFGHANISTAN/News%20and
%20Events/20261395/AfghanistanEconomicReportfinalversion909.pdf.

———. 2005. *Poverty, Vulnerability and Social Protection*. http://www-wds.world
bank.org/external/default/WDSContentServer/WDSP/IB/2005/03/22/000
012009_20050322100004/Rendered/PDF/296940AF.pdf.

———. 2006. "World Bank Says Drugs Now Afghanistan's Economic Lynchpin."
Washington, DC: World Bank. http://findarticles.com/p/articles/mi_kmafp/
is_200503/ai_n13269241.

———. 2007a. *Doing Business: Economics*. http://www.doingbusiness.org/
ExploreEconomies/EconomyCharacteristics.aspx.

———. 2007b. *WDI Online: Afghanistan*. http://devdata.worldbank.org/data
online/old-default.htm.

Zucchino, D. 2006. "In Afghanistan, Yesterday's Warlords are Today's Diplomats." *Los Angeles Times.* November 29. http://seattletimes.nwsource.com/html/nationworld/2003452568_afghanwarlords29.html.

The Security Transition

6

Antonio Giustozzi

The Neo-Taliban Insurgency
From Village Islam to
International Jihad

Who Are the Neo-Taliban?

Although relatively few of the "old Taliban" rushed to join the new jihad, they initially accounted for all of the 10–12 top leaders of the Leadership Council based in Quetta. It is therefore not surprising that the "ideology" of the Neo-Taliban derives to a large extent from that of the "old" Taliban: a mix of the most conservative village Islam with Deobandi doctrines, with a stress on the importance of ritual and modes of behaviour (Dorronsoro 2005, 299–301, 310–11; Maley 1998, 15; Roy 1998, 210–11). At the same time they seem to have absorbed from their foreign jihadist allies a more flexible and less orthodox attitude toward imported technologies and techniques, disregarding, for example, the alleged Islamic ban on the representation of human figures. Venturing into the world of video production, they made large-scale use of documentaries, interviews and footage of speeches in propaganda VCDs and DVDs. The insurgents carried video cameras with them to the battlefield to film the fighting and used the footage for the production of propaganda material (Mir 2005; Shahzad 2006c). The content of the propaganda suggests that, since 2001, the Neo-Taliban have become much more integrated into the international jihadist movement, their rhetoric stressing concepts such as "global Christian war against Islam" and solidarity with other jihadist movements around the world, which are clearly perceived as part of the same struggle.[1]

The middle and low ranks of the Taliban are largely composed of new recruits. Few "old Taliban" actively joined the insurgency in its early days, although a larger number did so later. Others might have contributed to spreading pro-Taliban feelings among the population without actively fighting (Ansari 2003a, 2003b; Burke 2003; Nivat 2006, 80–93; Rubin 2006a; Shahzad 2001; Ware 2002; Zabriskie and Connors 2002).[2] From 2002 to 2007, Pakistani madrasas continued to provide an inexhaustible flow of new recruits, and the "madrasa boys" provided the hard-core fighting force of the Taliban. From 2003, the ranks started filling with village recruits too, mobilized with a whole range of different motivations. Some of these local recruits were opportunistic and were marginal elements, particularly during the early stages of Taliban penetration in a particular area. These groups were not politicized, and their activities were low-scale, but nonetheless they were contributing to the creation of insecurity outside the Taliban's core areas. Although it would be inappropriate to describe them as mercenaries, financial incentives likely played an important role among their motivations, and they were disinclined to take serious risks (Gall 2006a; Wright 2006b).[3] A certain number of these "mercenaries" (possibly 10–20% of the total force) do seem to have fought on the Taliban side, but their role appears to have been marginal. The Taliban sometimes paid villagers cash (reportedly US$15–55 a day) to harass foreign and government troops with occasional rocket attacks and shooting, probably because it was more practical than maintaining teams of trained and committed guerrillas around each enemy military base (Clark 2006; Collett-White 2003; Morarjee 2006; Sand 2006). Core members were paid indemnity for the families too, allegedly ranging between $100 and $350 a month, but they were not mercenaries and often fought to the last man.

Elements of the population influenced by the clergy, whose members often sympathized with the Taliban, provided a larger and more important source of recruitment.[4] By the early twenty-first century, the strict beliefs of Deobandism influenced the majority of the Afghan clergy, particularly in the areas bordering Pakistan, as most mullahs had been trained in Pakistani madrasas aligned with this fundamentalist-leaning school (Dorronsoro 2000; Roy 2000; 2002). The other main source of recruits for the Taliban came from disenfranchised and alienated communities and individuals who, even if they had not supported the Taliban initially, saw their tribal enemies turn the government and the foreign contingents against them.The Taliban then appeared as the only protection available (Daniel 2006; Rohde 2004; Stormer 2004; Walsh 2007).[5] In other terms, bad governance seems to have been the key factor in driving these people into the hands of the Taliban, because in 2002 dubious characters had been appointed by Kabul as governors and chiefs of police. The corruption and ineffectiveness of the judiciary also contributed to the problem. These communities were mainly concentrated in the south, where interim president Hamid Karzai's associates and allies, with their militias, had driven their local rivals over to the opposition by systematically marginalizing them from all positions of power and then harassing them. The situation in the south was further complicated by the fact that in 2004–2005, in part because of the pressure of the international community to clean up his act, Karzai and his circle started dropping their local allies one by one. As a result, these strongmen stopped acting as a bulwark against the Taliban (Giustozzi 2007b).

In other parts of the country the penetration of the Taliban was patchier. Much of the southeast, for example, turned out not to be a very welcoming place for the insurgents, although by 2006 there were signs that the support of the tribal leadership for Karzai and the government was waning because of its inability to provide security. Within the southeast, the areas where the influence of the tribal leaderships was weaker and that of the clergy stronger, such as southern Ghazni, much of Paktika, and Zurmat of Paktia, saw a much more rapid expansion of Taliban influence (AFP 2003a; Trives 2006).[6] In the east the success of the Neo-Taliban was also modest. This was due to the fact that here too tribal structures maintained a high degree of cohesion and an ability for self-rule and self-governance. In addition, the Taliban had always had weak roots in this area. In Nangarhar, the presence of a relatively strong intelligentsia with at least some tribal connections, and with strong nationalist (anti-Pakistani) feelings, played against an insurgency widely seen as a Pakistani stooge. A mix of Taliban and other insurgents found more support in Kunar, Nuristan, and northern Laghman, where tribal structures are stronger and tribal governance weaker.[7] In the rest of Afghanistan, recruitment among disenfranchised communities at different times achieved success in some isolated pockets of territory, such as Bala-i Murghab and Ghormach of Baghdis or Tagab of Kapisa.

NATO sources acknowledged a dramatic increase in the number of locally recruited fighters during 2006, even though in September 2006, it was estimated that still 40% of insurgents were coming straight from Pakistan. Forced recruitment was probably the most extreme form of local community involvement in the Taliban war effort; even in communities that sided with the Taliban, some families would be reluctant to contribute their sons, and even when recruitment was endorsed by local notables, the line between voluntary and forced enlistment (enforced mainly through intimidation) must have been a thin one (Cooney 2005; *Pajhwok Afghan News* 2006a).

It would be a mistake to see the Neo-Taliban insurgency as a tribal revolt, dominated by the Ghilzais, one of the two largest Pashtun tribes (with the Durrani). The Rahbari Shura (Leadership Council), which includes the main political military leaders of the Neo-Taliban, was never dominated by the Ghilzais: If anything, the Durrani tribes were better represented (Giustozzi 2007a). No strict tribal logic dictated which local communities divided up into pro-government and pro-Taliban elements. The Taliban were ready to accept anybody who shared their views and accepted their rules, regardless of ethnicity and tribe and regularly mixed together individuals with different tribal backgrounds. Clearly, the Taliban did not want to present themselves as aligned with a particular tribe or community. This made it easier for them to move across tribal territories without antagonizing the locals, but at the same time it was also a way of advertising their movement as above intercommunity rivalry. Those who had supported the Taliban regime and had been marginalized afterwards were prime targets for recruitment, regardless of their tribal background, even though an estimated 95% of the members were Pashtuns. It is true, however, that the distribution of pro-Taliban communities was very uneven among the tribes. Many were found among the western Ghilzais, who felt marginalized by the scant resources they received for reconstruction. Other southern tribes with widespread support for the Taliban included the Kakar and the Tarin, but many communities belonging to the Durrani tribes were also drawn toward the insurgency, first and foremost the Noorzais of Kandahar. The uneven participation of the tribes in the insurgency was the result of the tribal politics of the government and local authorities, rather than a conscious targeting on the side of the Taliban (Giustozzi 2006; Rahimullah Yusufzai, quoted in *PakTribune* 2006; Smith 2006b).[8]

There is some evidence that at least in some areas of Afghanistan, elders and secular notables welcomed the Taliban in order to gain support in local struggles against communities connected to the government and old-time rivals. In general, however, relations between elders and the Neo-Taliban have not been good. Indeed, strong elders remaining in control usually worked to prevent the infiltration of the Taliban, as they did in much of the southeast (Burke 2003a; McGirk 2005; Trives 2006; Wright 2006b). The Taliban would first of all approach the elders and ask for the right to enter tribal territory and the villages. If successful, they would establish themselves in the villages and then either work with the elders or gradually marginalize them. In certain areas and on certain issues, such as the opposition to foreign presence or to the eradication of the poppies, the elders were aligned with the Taliban. In areas like these, the Taliban allowed them a voice (Leithead 2006a; Shahzad 2006a; 2006d). If the Taliban were not allowed into a village's territory or faced resistance from a section of the elders, they would start targeting the notables in a campaign of intimidation and murder, usually accusing the victims of being American spies. The elders often found it difficult to oppose the Taliban's onslaught once they became able to concentrate a large number of their men in a small area. On the whole, it seems that the Taliban's carrot-and-stick tactics in bringing the elders in line were successful (Gall 2006b; Perreaux 2006; Rubin 2006a; Watson 2006; *Xinhuanet* 2005).[9]

As the conflict progressed, victims of abuses by both Afghan and foreign troops, and of the side effects of US reliance on air power, began to represent another important source of recruits for the Taliban. Large numbers of displaced people sought refuge in camps around the provincial centres, or Kandahar city itself, where they often struggled to make a living. These internal refugee camps then turned into recruitment grounds for the insurgents. However, the main boost to the Taliban probably came not from the bombardment per se but from the revelation that the weak government was supported by foreign contingents that were stretched thin and had a limited capability to control the country. To Afghan villagers, the ability of NATO and coalition forces to win battles brought little comfort, as the Taliban's ability to roam around the villages remained unchallenged. Nor were their mountain strongholds eliminated. The expectation that the Taliban would eventually emerge as the winners of the conflict, or at least force a compromise favourable to them, also pushed villagers toward them. Even where the Taliban had little direct support, the unpopularity of the government and what was perceived as the "disrespectful" behaviour of the foreign troops, fuelled by lack of understanding for the local culture, had the effect of dividing and demoralizing the opposition to the insurgents and creating some nostalgia for the time when the Taliban were in power (AFP 2006b; Gannon 2006; *Pajhwok Afghan News* 2006b; Rohde and Risen 2006; Sands 2006; Stormer 2004; Wright 2006b).[10]

The other components of the ongoing insurgency are marginal compared with the Taliban. Hizb-i Islami has been in a loose alliance with them since 2002, but its military force is modest. In 2006 there were signs that Hizb-i Islami was trying to mark its identity as separate from the Taliban by claiming military actions for itself. It is not clear whether the leadership of the party is trying to increase its value in the eyes of the Taliban and of external sponsors, in order to attract new funds, or whether the move precedes the start of negotiations with the government (Eghraghi 2004; MEMRI 2003; Munsif and Basharat 2006; Ratnesar 2002; Shahzad 2006b; 2006d).

How Are They Funded?

Given the amount of cash they paid to their fighters and the type and quantity of equipment they used, the Taliban may have spent between US$25 million and $40 million in 2006 to fund the conflict. According to sources inside the Taliban, in 2002 Mullah Omar started raising funds for the new jihad within his network of contacts in Pakistan and the Gulf, composed of "Karachi businessmen, Peshawar goldsmiths, Saudi oil men, Kuwaiti traders and jihadi sympathizers within the Pakistani military and intelligence ranks" as well as, presumably, Pakistani Islamic militants. Support from Afghan traders was also claimed, from as far away as the Gulf. The exact role of "Al-Qaeda" in funding is not clear, although it might have contributed too, at least in channelling the funds. As the general population perceived the chances of the insurgency to succeed to be growing, support from local traders seemed to grow too. The Taliban's fundraising campaign does not seem to have been done directly by field commanders; instead, appointed "officials" in charge of such logistics presumably reported back to the Pakistani-based *Shuras*. This way the leadership prevented field commanders from establishing their own independent sources of revenue (Bergen 2007; Rubin 2006a; Shahzad 2007a; Shahzad 2006c; Smith 2006a).

There are clear signs that the Taliban exploited the opportunity created by the government's half-hearted effort to eradicate the opium poppies, despite their earlier opposition to the growing of poppies in 2000–2001. In Helmand, they appear to have offered protection to the farmers targeted by eradication. However, how important the revenue from the narcotics trade is to the Taliban is not clear. I am inclined to think that drugs remain a secondary source of revenue for the Taliban and that there is little evidence of them stimulating the farmers to grow poppies or of their direct involvement in the trade. There are a number of reasons for this, including the competition from corrupt police officers and, increasingly, even ANA troops (Jelsma, Kramer, Rivier 2006, 7; Leithead 2006b; Walsh 2006a; Wright 2006a).

The Taliban have no qualms in admitting that they receive money from Arab sympathizers, while at the same time claiming that such financial support is not sufficient to acquire sophisticated anti-aircraft and other weaponry. Pakistani Islamic parties and groups like Jamaat-i Islami, Jamaat-al Ulema and others are very vocal supporters of the Taliban insurgency, and rank-and-file Taliban have admitted to journalists to having received direct support from them, even though the Pakistani government has banned raising funds for jihadi activities (AFP 2004; Baldauf and Tohid 2003). The question of whether the Pakistani authorities provide material help remains open, but what matters most is how external funding is channelled to the

Taliban. Although no information is available in this regard, the fact that such disparate sources of funding did not lead to the permanent splitting of the Neo-Taliban suggests that support must be channelled directly to the top leadership. It might be that the Pakistani authorities imposed a degree of control over revenue as a condition for letting the Taliban operate from their country and then channelled it directly to the top leaders.

The Strategy of the Neo-Taliban

To the extent that the Neo-Taliban have a strategy, it seems unlikely that, given their limited intellectual resources and flexibility, they conceived their goals without a major contribution from the Pakistani Inter-Services Intelligence (ISI) and the Arab jihadists. Certainly the Taliban's activities show consistent patterns and seem to hint at the existence of clear strategic aims. Due to the Neo-Taliban's initial poor organizational state, their military activities in 2002 were limited to cross-border raids and the harassment of US garrisons, mainly through long-distance launches of rockets. However, small teams of ten to twenty insurgents were already infiltrating the Afghan countryside with the purpose of identifying villages that could provide hospitality and support. Groups of Taliban were able to cross the Pakistani border undetected throughout 2002–2007, although they had to downsize from 100 to sixty members in 2003 to five or less in 2005 as interdiction efforts by the coalition strengthened. The strategic task of these "vanguard" teams was to prepare the ground for a later escalation of the insurgency. The teams would visit the villages and carry out propaganda actions such as handing out or posting leaflets or talking to people, as well as threaten elements of the local population who were deemed to be hostile to them. Occasionally they would carry out terrorist or guerrilla actions such as targeted assassinations, attacks on police posts, ambushes, or bombings, mostly aimed at reinforcing the threats against anti-Taliban elements and destroying whatever little presence the Afghan state had in the countryside. The vanguard teams identified people and communities who could be trusted and who could provide shelter, supplies, and intelligence. Suitable locations for ammunition and weaponry stockpiles would also be identified to allow the insurgents to later infiltrate the region without carrying weapons or using the main roads. As a result, the insurgents were able to amass large numbers of fighters over short periods of time in any of their strongholds (Australian Department of Defence 2006; Franco 2007; Gall 2005; Graveland 2006; McGirk 2005; RFE/RL 2006).

As important to the Taliban as identifying sympathizers and potential supporters was identifying and eliminating or rendering inoffensive government workers and supporters. The assassination campaign targeted at "collaborationists" affected from the beginning even areas that were not, or not yet, the object of intense Taliban military activities. The targets included senior clerics, doctors, teachers, judges, policemen, National Security Directorate officials, NGO workers and anybody co-operating with the government (Rohde 2006; Walsh 2006b; Wright 2006b). A key aspect of their strategy was a focus on psychological more than military achievements, probably meant in part to make up for the limited military skills of their guerrilla army. They deliberately tried to demoralize their enemies through relentless attacks, often against the same targets and regardless of their own casualties (Rohde and Risen 2006; Schiewek 2006).[11] The strategy of repeatedly attacking enemy posts was successful (apart from its heavy price), and gradually the Taliban achieved the demoralization of several pro-government militias and most of the police force. Possibly sensing an opportunity to deal the final blow to the "collaborationists," during 2006, the Taliban further shifted the focus of their military activities against Afghan forces, against which attacks increased fourfold (Cordesman 2007; Shahzad 2003b; UNDSS 2007).[12] The adoption of suicide attacks was yet another aspect of the strategy of demoralization, decided upon relatively early in May 2003, but its effective implementation was slowed by the difficulty of finding sufficient recruits. With the help of large numbers of foreign volunteers, suicide bombings increased in 2005 and most of all in 2006, when they reached an average of around ten a month (Associated Press 2007; Peterson 2006; Shahzad 2003b; Straziuso 2006; Tohid 2003a).

In order to develop a base of popular support and to exploit the foundering of the state under their attacks (or because of its own inherent contradictions), the Taliban started setting up their own "no-frills" administration. It was centred on the judiciary, whose services were in high demand in the countryside because of the total failure of the central government to establish a reasonably reliable judicial system. At the same time, the Taliban tried avoiding antagonizing potential constituencies by accommodating demands such as participation in the presidential and parliamentary elections of 2004–2005. They also attempted (often clumsily) to manage violence and carefully target it. Although there are many examples of atrocities carried out by the insurgents, there seems to have been a clear effort to focus the violence on whomever the Taliban considered a collaborator of the government and of the "occupiers" (Kemp 2007). Reports from the field show that the Taliban were not taxing travellers at the check posts, contrary to what government militias, police, and army were doing. They also were not looting the harvest of the farmers when crossing a field (Espinosa 2006; Gall 2005; Gannon 2006; Grant 2006; Smith 2006a; Wright 2006b). Of course, in the case of IEDs (improvised explosive devices) and suicide

bombings, unwanted civilian casualties were unavoidable, not least because of the weak technical proficiency of the insurgents. However, even
in these cases, the Taliban sometimes presented excuses for their mistakes,
confirming the existence of a serious concern for their image among the population. Conflict within the leadership about the use of suicide bombing was
also reported (Reuters 2004; Watson 2006).

Until 2006, there was little that could be described as a Taliban attempt
to launch a large scale attack. Even though at the beginning of 2004 they
had announced their intention to attack and take a major city and to attack
US military bases, they were largely busy infiltrating the territory and establishing infrastructures. By 2006, the situation had changed, and they were
ready to pursue those ambitious plans. It is possible that the Taliban might
have been under pressure from their Arab, Pakistani, and other "donors"
to deliver a steady pace of advancement and some high-profile victories. It
is also possible that the leadership of the Taliban might have planned to escalate its military operations well in advance as a move toward a new stage
of the insurgency, taking on US and allied military forces in larger-scale
engagements. A fourth hypothesis is that the replacement of US troops
with Canadian troops in Kandahar in the spring of 2006 might have been
seen by the insurgents as an indication that the US intended to withdraw
from the country and as a golden opportunity to score easy victories, boosting the morale of the insurgents and possibly forcing a hasty retreat of the
Canadians from Kandahar.[13] Whatever the immediate reason was for the decision to escalate, and whatever term is used to describe the escalation,
there is no question that 2006 marked the first time the Taliban had openly
challenged the foreign contingents in a large battle (Pashmul near Kandahar) since what the US military calls Operation Anaconda in March 2002.[14]

The Taliban also seem to have planned for late 2006, early 2007 major
operations around Lashkargah in Helmand and were reportedly planning
to move the focus of their military activities closer to Kabul, as suggested
by their build-up in Tagab and the infiltration of Kabul's southern surround-
ings. However, their objectives were confounded by the defeat suffered in
Pashmul in September 2006 and by the fact that their adversaries were
now actively trying to disrupt the Taliban's capability to escalate military
activities by raiding their mountain strongholds (*Afghanistan* 2007; Burke
2006; Leithead, 11 February 2007; Lobjakas 2007; *Reuters*, 22 November
2006; Shahzad 2007b; *Spiegel Online*, 4 December 2006; Wood 2007;
Yousafzai and Moreau 2007).[15]

There are some indications that the Taliban entertained negotiations
with Kabul, which would seem to be at odds with its transformation as a
component of the international jihadist movement. Talks with Karzai had
been going on at least since 2003, although it is not clear how far up the

Taliban leadership were Karzai's contacts. It appears that the Taliban con-
tacted Kabul through UNAMA and that Kabul agreed to negotiate one
month later after receiving the green light from the US embassy. US military authorities officially endorsed the possibility of talks with "moderate
members" of the Taliban in December of that year (Burnett 2003; Shahzad
2003a).[16] The actual content of the negotiations, however, is not known, nor
is it clear whether the "moderate Taliban" were testing the ground for the
leadership of the movement or were acting autonomously. After a period
of apparent suspension, negotiations were resumed, as admitted by President Karzai himself in 2007 (Faiez 2007). One might speculate that until
2005 or 2006, the Taliban were not as confident about their ultimate victory and thought that their only chance was to find an accommodation
with Kabul. It is also possible that they were forced by the Pakistani authorities to include negotiations in their agenda. The demands of the Taliban include a withdrawal of the foreign troops, even gradual, and the introduction of "Islamic elements" into legislation and the system of government
(Abrashi and Straziuso 2006).[17]

Tactics of the Neo-Taliban

Throughout 2002–2006, the weapons used by the Taliban were usually the
Kalashnikov assault rifle (AK-47, -74, AKM) and the RPG-7 rocket launcher,
as well as primitive models of field rockets (BM-1) and machine guns, including a few heavy DShK. By the standards of the early twenty-first century, these are quite obsolete and inadequate weapons when confronting
a state-of-the-art Western army, especially since, for the most part, only
standard ammunition was available to the insurgents. Some improved penetration bullets, better able to pierce bullet-proof vests, were reportedly
found in the Taliban's hands in a few occasions, but the ability to inflict mor-
tal wounds on foreign troops seems to have been only marginally affected.
In engagements taking place over large areas, the gap in communications
technologies was also a major handicap for the Taliban (*AFP*, 22 July 2006;
Allen 2006; Rohde, 30 March 2004).

During the conflict, the Taliban managed to introduce two new weapons
onto Afghanistan's battlefields, IEDs, and suicide bombers, and continued
to improve their ability to manage the technology. The source of the technology and know-how is clearly Iraq, as acknowledged by the insurgents
themselves. A small number of Taliban reportedly travelled to Iraq to learn
the techniques (Daniel and Yousafzay 2005; MEMRI 2006; Rubin 2006a).
Although the Taliban always lagged behind the sophistication of their Iraqi
colleagues in the manufacturing of IEDs, the gap was estimated to have
narrowed from an initial twelve months to six months during 2006, despite

the alleged capture of 250 bomb makers by foreign and government forces. In the spring of 2006, the Taliban were already experimenting in stacking anti-tank mines together, and throughout 2006 linking together IEDs to improve the targeting of moving vehicles became common. At the same time, government and foreign forces were also improving their skills. Similarly, the technology used in suicide bombings improved, as did the skills of the suicide bombers. In 2004, suicide attacks were still estimated to have a failure rate of around 60–70%. In 2005, the failure rate was down to 10–15%, showing a dramatic improvement in the skills of the Taliban's "bomb craftsmen" and of the suicide volunteers. The Taliban also claim to have received help from networks of Arab sympathizers, starting around 2004. Certainly some technology seems to have come from abroad (ANSO sources, quoted in Chipaux 2005; Badkhen 2006; Dougherty 2007; *Jane's Intelligence Review* 2006; MEMRI 2006; Reuters 2007; Rubin 2006a; UNDSS 2007).[18]

The use of mortars was reported as early as 2002 in attacks against US and Afghan bases. Since mortars require relatively high degree of training to be used effectively and are rather cumbersome on the battlefield for non-motorized infantry, it is perhaps not surprising that they started being used in open engagements only in 2006 and even then they played a relatively limited role. In general, NATO officers had disparaging views of the Taliban's ability to use mortars effectively (Bergen 2006; Lamb 2006; McGirk and Ware 2002; Roggio 2006b; Synovitz 2006). By 2006, the Taliban's difficulty in dealing with armoured vehicles was proving to be a major shortcoming, as they had started closing in on Kandahar and had made the decision to contest the mainly flat ground surrounding the city. The Taliban apparently referred to armoured vehicles as "monsters" or "beasts." Although they started using recoilless guns in July 2006, these were so cumbersome that they were only used in engagements fought within the Taliban's strongholds of Helmand and Zabul and were not reported to have been used against armour. Anti-tank mines have been used by the Taliban since at least 2003 (Tohid 2003), but these were old models and often ineffective. More effective types were reportedly in use in 2005, but only occasionally. Moreover, the impact of mines on the battlefield is limited only to defensive operations or to occasional ambushes. The Taliban tried to cope with the problem by organizing ambushes in which salvos of several RPG grenades were fired at a single target (or kill zone), but again there are obvious limitations to the impact of these tactics. Foreign advisors to the police and officers of various foreign military contingents acknowledged that the Taliban were actively seeking heavier anti-tank weapons with little success (Afghana.org 2006; Albone 2006; Bergen 2006; *Jane's Intelligence Review* 2006; Meo 2005).

There were some other efforts by the Taliban to upgrade the technology of their arsenal, but these too were limited. They first obtained anti-aircraft guided missiles in 2005, but they faced serious difficulties training their fighters to use them and only toward the end of 2006 started using them, but to little effect. The aiming and success rate of the field rockets undoubtedly improved between 2002 and 2006, but this appears to have been due to the greater skills of those firing them than to the adoption of more advanced models (AFP 2007; Baldauf and Khan 2005; Roggio 2006a; Shahzad 2007c; Smith 2006b).[19] Given the features of the Afghan conflict and the low marksmanship levels of the Taliban rank-and-file, an obvious option for improving the ability to inflict casualties would have been the widespread deployment of snipers, but despite some reported attempts to train snipers, little of this activity was seen on the battlefield (Coghlan 2006).

Some of the most important innovations in the Taliban's arsenal were not weapons. Motorcycles started to be used extensively inside Afghanistan for purposes of transport, reconnaissance, communications, and battlefield coordination and also to carry out attacks against road blocks. Substantial resources were also invested in improving telecommunications, with the purchase of large numbers of satellite phones, presumably for long-distance communications. Field radios made their first appearance during the summer of 2005, although it was not until 2006 that the Taliban started using them proficiently on the battlefield to coordinate groups of more than a hundred combatants. However, the radios used by the Taliban to the end of 2006 were always commercial types, not frequency-hopping military models. Precise US artillery and air bombardment, combined with advanced radio monitoring techniques, often resulted in the quick elimination of Taliban scouting teams. After some disastrous incidents involving radios and satellite phones, the Taliban became increasingly aware that their enemies were constantly monitoring their communications and started using them more carefully, resorting to coded messages or even dropping radios in favour of low-technology techniques like torch-signalling (AFP 2003b; Baldauf and Khan 2005; Maykuth 2003; Naylor 2006a; Rashid 2003; Rubin 2006b; Stormer 2004; Wright 2006b). The use of Icom scanners to monitor radio and phone calls has also been reported (Wright 2006b; Zabriskie 2006).

Despite these limitations, the Neo-Taliban showed some success in improving their tactical skills. NATO and US sources tend to agree that by 2005–2006, the ability of the Taliban to rapidly gather large numbers of men and the rapidity of the response on the battlefield improved considerably. The insurgents also demonstrated an ability to split into small groups of four or five, to scatter when ambushed, and then reorganize (AFP 2006a; Coghlan 2006; Franco 2005; Lamb 2006; Naylor 2006a; Wright 2006b).

The Taliban also placed a great emphasis in establishing a thick network of informers, able to inform them of the movements of the enemy and enabling their forces to set up ambushes quickly.

On the whole, the tactical proficiency of the Taliban left much to be desired, and ideological training was often given priority over technical training in the training camps based in Pakistan. This did not always have negative repercussions on the tactical ability of the fighters, because it at least helped the Taliban instill a strong determination in their fighters. In a number of fights in 2005 and 2006, the Taliban did not even break contact after having been targeted by two-thousand-pound bombs and often fought to the last man, not a common tactic in guerrilla warfare. However, the focus on ideological indoctrination and on the formation of group comradeship came at the expense of tactical skills. Often, in the early period of the insurgency, little military training was imparted at all, resulting in disastrous outcomes on the battlefield. Although this problem was resolved to some degree, others were not. Particularly in the south, the aiming skills of the insurgents were very bad, as they often missed their targets even at very short distances of ten to fifty feet. Another outcome of poor training was weak radio discipline. This occurred despite the awareness that NATO and US forces were constantly monitoring the insurgents' communications (Baldauf 2005a; 2005b; Lamb 2006; Naylor 2006a; 2006b; Walsh 2006c; Zoroya 2005). Training was imparted to a few Afghans in Iraq, but it mainly focused on handling explosives and remote control detonators. While this might have improved the insurgents' skills with IEDs, it is unlikely to have significantly affected their battlefield performance (Daniel 2006).

The biggest tactical problem for the Taliban was avoiding air strikes. They identified three basic options. The first was to split into small groups and flee, but that would have amounted to forsaking any major offensive operation. Moreover, splitting into small groups and disappearing into the countryside was not always easy for non-local guerrillas who did not know the region in which they were operating. A source close to the US military alleges that most losses among the Taliban ranks in the summer of 2006 occurred among Pakistani volunteers, who were unable to melt into an unknown countryside (Dunnigan 2007). The second option was to seek cover where available, refusing to engage when aircraft were present on the scene. Whenever possible, the insurgents exploited the rugged terrain to avoid the superior firepower of US and NATO troops (Wright 2006b). The Taliban developed the ability to calculate the exact flight time of helicopters from their bases to the target area, preparing themselves to go into hiding when necessary. However, the use of unmanned aerial vehicles (UAVs) meant it was possible for the alliance to surveil an area of suspected Taliban concentration virtually indefinitely, often without the insurgents even realizing it.

Nonetheless, during the first few months of 2007, signs emerged that the Taliban were becoming increasingly proficient in avoiding air attacks. The US and allied air forces were increasingly forced to rely on expensive guided missiles to eliminate small teams of insurgents, often as small as two or three individuals (Loyd 2007).[20] The third option, adopted when it was deemed necessary to confront the adversary in the open ground or attack its bases, was to carry out human wave attacks, closing in as rapidly as possible and saturating enemy defences. This tactic was first used as early as 2005 in the southeast, where the level of training and the skills of Taliban cadres were higher. They usually abstained from resorting to this tactic in flat areas or where the enemy had strong artillery support, or whenever the target was not deemed worth the risk. It later spread to the south, but was used parsimoniously. Using human waves at no time allowed the Taliban to succeed in taking any objective defended by foreign troops, or inflict large casualties on the foreigners, despite costing high casualties. The intense battles of 2006 had a political impact, however, contributing to doubts in the minds of many Afghans about the portrayal of the conflict by the government and its international allies (Associated Press 2006; Greenberg 2006; Meo 2005; Senlis Council 2006, 32, 37).

From late 2006, the Taliban began paying much greater attention to fighting off attempts at infiltration by intelligence agencies of both the government and its external allies. As the insurgents moved closer to the cities, and with their increased recruitment inside Afghanistan, they became increasingly vulnerable to enemy information gathering. Although Western officials recognized that penetrating the core of the Taliban remained almost impossible, Taliban presence in many inhabited areas and the travels of their leaders across vast regions offered the opportunity for villagers to supply key information to their enemies. Searching individuals, particularly "strangers," became a routine for the Taliban, and executions of "informers" and "spies" were constantly reported in early 2007 (IWPR 2007).

Conclusion

By 2006 there were clear signs that the Taliban were becoming an integral part of a wider supra-national jihadist movement, to a much greater extent than the "old Taliban" ever were. They increasingly appeared to believe that the decisive factor in winning the war would not be Western public opinion, as those who describe the conflict as fourth-generation warfare argue (see Hammes 2006), but the support of their Muslim brethren. If this is true, some apparent irrationality in the Taliban's strategy and goals could be explained: their priority would be to mobilize Muslim opinion worldwide as a source of funding, moral support, and volunteers (see MEMRI 2006). Ultimately, the belief is that victory will come with the overstretching of the enemy through the creation of "one, ten, a hundred Iraqs," rather than with country-specific strategies. Since there is little evidence that the leadership of the Neo-Taliban held this view already in 2002 when they started the insurgency, it is likely that this strategic view emerged gradually under the influence of external advisors, financial contributors, and allies.

What can we expect from the Taliban next? On one hand, their strategy seems to be focused on bringing a collapse of Afghan pro-government forces, so that in the future the fighting could be more convincingly described as one of pitting Afghans against foreigners. To some extent they have scored a few successes already, considering that from 2006 a much bigger international force had to be mobilized to fight against them. The future of NATO is at stake now, and the "Western alliance" is now fully committed to the theatres of Iraq and Afghanistan, with virtually no reserves left for a possible third front. This strategy seems to derive from the Taliban's new global jihadist "soul," and it does not have tight deadlines for success. In fact, in principle, and subject to the ability to maintain the mobilization of the fighters, the longer the war lasts, the better, because chances of a new front opening in a third country increase over time. Given the growing reservoir of xenophobic sentiment in Afghanistan and the large potential for external funding, the Neo-Taliban might well keep going for several years. The government-sponsored Peace Strengthening Commission, which is trying to attract individual Taliban by offering reconciliation with Kabul, does not appear a serious threat to the viability of the insurgency. Although by 2007 more than 4,000 opponents of the government were claimed to have joined it, only a small minority were genuine insurgents. Direct negotiations with the leadership of the Taliban have also taken place, but with little progress being made. On the other hand, it is not clear whether the Pakistanis will allow the Neo-Taliban a free ride toward their pan-jihadist aims. During 2006 and 2007, signals emerged that the Pakistanis are manoeuvring for a political deal,[21] possibly because they judged that the insurgency had grown sufficiently to give them the leverage for pushing forward a settlement in their own terms, that is, one that would guarantee a strong Pakistani patronage over Kabul. The twin movements in Afghanistan and the Pakistani North-West Frontier province are likely to be a source of worry in Islamabad. Should a political deal involving the Pakistanis, but not the Neo-Taliban, be made, the viability of the Neo-Taliban would be seriously endangered, and the movement could be condemned to a slow but irreversible decline.

Notes

This chapter is based on my book *Kuran, Kalashnikov and Laptop: The Neo-Taliban Insurgency in Afghanistan, 2002–2007* (Giustozzi 2007a).

1 See also the interview with a pro-Taliban Mawlawi in Anne Nivat (2006), pp. 89–91.
2 Also interview with UN official, Herat, April 2004.
3 Also personal communication with foreign diplomat, Kabul, March 2007.
4 Interviews with police officers and UN officials in Takhar and Kunduz, May 2006. See also for example Halima Kazem, "U.S. Thins Taliban's Ranks, but Their Ideological Grip Remains Strong," *Christian Science Monitor*, 18 September 2003.
5 Also interview with Afghan security officer, Kandahar, January 2006.
6 Interview with Massoud Kharokhel, 1 October 2006, Tribal Liaison Office, Kabul; interview with Tribal Liaison Office official in Gardez, October 2006; interview with UN official, Gardez, October 2006.
7 Interview with UN official, Jalalabad, February 2006.
8 Also interview with security officer, Kandahar, January 2006.
9 Also interview with UN official, 2006.
10 Also interview with Afghan journalist returning from the south, Kabul, October 2006; personal communications with Afghan MPs, tribal leader and notables, Kabul and Gardez, October 2006.
11 See the example of Lizha (Khost) in Watson 2006.
12 Also personal communication with UN official, Kabul, October 2006.
13 This hypothesis is favoured by some high-ranking UN officials (personal communication, Kabul, October 2006).
14 During "Anaconda," an estimated 500–700 Taliban remnants and foreign volunteers chose to stay and fight it out with the US forces (McGirk 2005; AFP 2004).
15 Also personal communication with ISAF source, Kabul, 7 December 2006; personal communication with Niamatullah Ibrahimi, Crisis States Research Centre, Kabul, January 2007.
16 Also personal communication with UN official, Kabul, October 2003.
17 Also interview with Zaif, ex ambassador of Taliban in Pakistan, Kabul, October 2006.
18 Also personal communication with UNAMA official, Kabul, May 2005.
19 Also personal communication with UN official, Kabul, March 2007.
20 Also personal communication with Declan Walsh, who was embedded as a journalist with British forces in Helmand, April 2007.
21 Such signals include contacts with groups formerly opposed to the Taliban in Northern Afghanistan, a rather open sponsorship of Hizb-i Islami and its leader Gulbuddin Hekmatyar, and repeated statements of President Musharraf and high-rank Pakistan officials in favour of a political settlement.

References

Abrashi, Fisnik and Jason Straziuso. 2006. "Deepening Insurgency Puts Afghanistan on Brink." Associated Press. 8 October.
Afghana.org. 2006. "Les talibans cherchent à se procurer des armes plus puissantes." 8 May. http://www.afghana.org/html/article.php?sid=2092.

Agence France-Presse (AFP). 2003a. "Sud-est de l'Afghanistan: 'Ici, c'est la guerre!'" 20 September.

———. 2003b. 21 September.

———. 2004. "Menace taliban dans le Sud." 20 February.

———. 2006a. "Taliban Fighting with More Sophistication: U.S.-Led Coalition." 22 July.

———. 2006b. "In Kandahar, the Taliban Are Not a Bad Memory." 8 December.

———. 2007. "Coalition Strikes Taleban Linked to Anti-Aircraft Weapons." 10 March.

Albone, Tim. 2006. "Pathfinders On a Four-Day Mission Fight Off Eight-Week Taliban Siege." *The Times*. 27 September.

Allen, Nick. 2006. "Sticks and Carrots Sway Wayward Afghan Town." Deutsche Presse-Agentur (DPA). 18 December.

Ansari, Massoud. 2003a. "Almost Two Years after They Were Defeated, Thousands Join the Taliban's New Jihad." *The Telegraph*. 7 September.

———. 2003b. "On the Job with a Taliban Recruiter." *Asia Times Online*. 27 November. http://www.atimes.com/atimes/South_Asia/EK26Df03.html.

Associated Press. 2006. "Afghan Firefight Kills 55 Militants." 30 October.

———. 2007. "New U.S. Commander in Afghanistan Predicts More Suicide Attacks this Year." 30 January.

Australia Department of Defence. 2006. "Socaust Media Briefing Post Op Slipper." 27 September.

Badkhen, Anna. 2006. "Foreign Jihadists Seen as Key to Spike in Afghan Attacks." *San Francisco Chronicle*. 25 September.

Baldauf, Scott. 2005a. "Taliban Play Hide-and-Seek with U.S. Troops." *Christian Science Monitor*. 12 October.

———. 2005b. "Small US Units Lure Taliban into Losing Battles." *Christian Science Monitor*. 31 October.

Baldauf, Scott and Owais Tohid. 2003. "Taliban Appears to Be Regrouped and Well-Funded." *Christian Science Monitor*. 8 May.

Baldauf, Scott and Ashraf Khan. 2005. "New Guns, New Drive for Taliban." *Christian Science Monitor*. 26 September.

Bergen, Peter. 2006. "The Taliban, 'Regrouped and Rearmed.'" *Washington Post*. 10 September.

———. 2007. Afghanistan 2007: Problems, Opportunities and Possible Solutions, Testimony to the House Committee on Foreign Affairs. 15 February.

Burke, Jason. 2003. "Stronger and More Deadly, the Terror of the Taliban Is Back." *The Observer*. 16 November.

———. 2006. "Taliban Plan to Fight through Winter to Throttle Kabul." *The Observer*. 29 October.

Burnett, Victoria. 2003. "U.S. Backs Afghan Proposal to Woo Moderate Taliban." *Financial Times*. 31 December.

Cheragh, 19 April 2007.

Chipaux, Françoise. 2005. "En Afghanistan, des rebelles mieux organisés infligent de lourdes pertes aux forces américaines." *Le Monde*. 22 August.

Clark, Kate. 2006. "Cash Rewards for Taliban Fighters." *File On 4*, BBC Radio 4. 28 February.

Coghlan, Tom. 2006. "Taliban Train Snipers on British Forces." *Daily Telegraph.* 23 July.

Collett-White, Mike. 2003. "Les taliban ne manquent pas de recrues." Reuters. 23 August.

Cooney, Daniel. 2005. "General: Hard-Hit Taliban Recruiting Kids." Associated Press. 24 July.

Cordesman, Anthony. 2007. *Winning in Afghanistan: The Challenges and the Response.* Washington, DC: Center for Strategic and International Studies.

Daniel, Sara. 2006. "Afghanistan: 'Résister aux talibans? A quoi bon!'" *Le Nouvel Observateur.* 10 August.

Daniel, Sara and Sami Yousafzay. 2005. "Ils apprennent en Irak les secrets du djihad technologique." *Le Nouvel Observateur.* 3 November.

Dorronsoro, Gilles. 2000. *Pakistan and the Taliban: State Policy, Religious Networks and Political Connections.* Paris: Centre D'études et De Recherches Internationales (CERI). October. http://www.ceri-sciencespo.com/archive/octo00/artgd.pdf.

———. 2005. *Revolution Unending.* London: Hurst.

Dougherty, Kevin. 2007. "NATO and Afghanistan: A Status Report." *Stars and Stripes* (Mideast Edition), 18 February.

Dunnigan, James. 2007. "The Secret War in Afghanistan." *Strategy Page.* 1 January.

Eghraghi, Shahin. 2004. "Hekmatyar: The Wild Card in Afghanistan." *Asia Times.* 7 January. http://www.atimes.com/atimes/Central_Asia/FA07Ag01.html.

Espinosa, Ángeles. 2006. "La OTAN lucha en territorio talibán." *El País.* 14 September.

Faiez, Rahim. 2007. "Karzai Says He Has Met with Taliban." Associated Press. 6 April.

Franco, Claudio. 2005. "Islamic Militant Insurgency in Afghanistan Experiencing 'Iraqization.'" *Eurasianet.* 8 November.

———. 2007. "In Remote Afghan Camp, Taliban Explain How and Why They Fight." *San Francisco Chronicle.* 21 January.

Gall, Carlotta. 2005. "Despite Years of U.S. Pressure, Taliban Fight On in Jagged Hills." *New York Times.* 4 June.

———. 2006a. "Taliban Continue to Sow Fear." *New York Times.* 1 March.

———. 2006b. "Taliban Surges as U.S. Shifts Some Tasks to NATO." *New York Times.* 11 June.

Gannon, Kathy. 2006. "Taliban Comeback Traced to Corruption." Associated Press. 24 November.

Giustozzi, Antonio. 2006. *"Tribes" and Warlords in Southern Afghanistan, 1980–2005.* Working Paper Series 2 no. 7, London: Crisis States Research Centre.

———. 2007a. *Kuran, Kalashnikov and Laptop: The Neo-Taliban Insurgency in Afghanistan, 2002–2007.* New York and London: Columbia University Press/Hurst.

———. 2007b. "The Inverted Cycle: Kabul and the Strongmen's Competition for Control over Kandahar, 2001–2006." *Central Asian Survey*, no.3.

Grant, Greg. 2006. "Emboldened Taliban Emerging." *Army Times*. 3 July.

Graveland, Bill. 2006. "Les talibans: un ennemi difficilement saisissable." Associated Press. 27 December.

Greenberg, Lee. 2006. "Renewed Afghan Fighting Comes amid Signs of Taliban Buildup." *Ottawa Citizen*. 30 October.

Hammes, Thomas X. 2006. *The Sling and the Stone.* St. Paul, MN: Zenith Press.

Institute for War and Peace Reporting (IWPR). 2007. "Informer Killings Show Growing Taleban Control." *Afghan Recovery Report*, no. 243. 26 February. http://www.iwpr.net/?p=arr&s=f&o=333561&apc_state=henh.

Jane's Intelligence Review. 2006. "Increasing Afghan IED Threat Gives Forces Cause for Concern." 1 August.

Jelsma, Martin, Tom Kramer, and Cristian Rivier. 2006. *Losing Ground: Drug Control and War In Afghanistan.* Debate Papers no.15. Amsterdam: Transnational Institute. December.

Kazem, Halima. 2003. "U.S. Thins Taliban's Ranks, but Their Ideological Grip Remains Strong." *Christian Science Monitor*. 18 September.

Kemp, Robert. 2007. "Counterinsurgency in Eastern Afghanistan." In *Countering Insurgency and Promoting Democracy*, ed. Manolis Priniotakis. Washington, DC: Council for Emerging National Security Affairs.

Lamb, Christina. 2006. "Have You Ever Used a Pistol?" *The Sunday Times*. 2 July.

Leithead, Alastair. 2006a. "Can Change in Afghan Tactics Bring Peace?" *BBC News*. 17 October.

———. 2006b. "Unravelling the Helmand Impasse." *BBC News*. 21 December.

———. 2007. "Helmand 'Seeing Insurgent Surge.'" *BBC News*. 11 February.

Loyd, Anthony. 2007. "It's Dawn, and the Shelling Starts. Time to Go into the Taleban Maze." *The Times*. 14 February. http://www.timesonline.co.uk/tol/news/world/asia/article1381532.ece.

Lobjakas, Ahto. 2007. "Afghanistan: NATO Seeks to Preempt Taliban Offensive in Helmand." RFE/RL. 31 January.

Maley, William. 1998. "Interpreting the Taliban." Introduction in *Fundamentalism Reborn? Afghanistan and the Taliban*, ed. W. Maley. London: Hurst.

Maykuth, Andrew. 2003. "An Afghan Rebuilding Takes Shape." *Philadelphia Inquirer*. 6 October.

McGirk, Tim. 2005. "The Taliban on the Run." *Time Magazine Online*. March 25. http://www.time.com/time/magazine/article/0,9171,1042511,00.html.

McGirk, Tim and Michael Ware. 2002. "Losing Control? The U.S. Concedes It Has Lost Momentum in Afghanistan, while Its Enemies Grow Bolder." *Time*. 11 November.

Meo, Nick. 2005. "In Afghanistan, the Taliban rises Again for Fighting Season." *The Independent*. 15 May.

Middle East Media Research Institute (MEMRI). 2003. "Interview with Afghan Islamist Leader on Jihad against U.S." *MEMRI Special Dispatch Series*, no. 455. January 6.

———. 2006. "Taliban Military Commander Mullah Dadallah: We Are In Contact with Iraqi Mujahideen, Osama bin Laden & Al-Zawahiri." *MEMRI Special Dispatch Series*, no. 1180. June 2.

Mir, Hamid. 2005. "The Taliban's New Face." *Rediff* (India). 27 September.

Morarjee, Rachel. 2006. "Taliban Goes for Cash over Ideology." *Financial Times*. 25 July.

Munsif, Abdul Qadir and Hakim Basharat. 2006. "Conflicts Keep away Taliban, Hizb-i-Islami." *Pajhwok Afghan News*. 12 December.

Naylor, Sean D. 2006a. "The Waiting Game. A Stronger Taliban Lies Low, Hoping the U.S. Will Leave Afghanistan." *Army Times*. February.

———. 2006b. "Outnumbered and Surrounded by Taliban, the Spartans Came out on Top in 54-hour Fight." *Army Times*. 26 June.

Nivat, Anne. 2006. *Islamistes: comment ils nous voient*. Paris: Fayard, 2006.

Pajhwok Afghan News. 2006a. "Taliban Start Recruiting Fighters in Ghazni." 7 August.

———. 2006b. "Civilian Casualties Trigger Anti-govt Sentiments." 21 August.

PakTribune. 2006. "Senate Body for Launching Pak-Afghan Inter-Parliaments Dialogue." 15 December.

Perreaux, Les. 2006. "NATO Urges Afghans to Vacate Volatile Panjwaii District." Canadian Press. 31 August.

Peterson, Scott. 2006. "Taliban Adopting Iraq-style Jihad." *Christian Science Monitor*. 13 September.

Radio Free Europe/ Radio Liberty. 2006. "NATO in Afghanistan: NATO Plans to Go beyond Peacekeeping." *RFE/RL Afghanistan Report*, Vol. 5, no. 20. 1 August. http://www.rferl.org/reports/afghan-report/2006/08/20–010806 .asp.

Rashid, Ahmed. 2003. "Safe Haven for the Taliban." *Far Eastern Economic Review*. 16 October.

Ratnesar, Romesh. 2002. "In the Line of Fire." *Time*. 8 September.

Reuters. 2004. "Excuses des talibans pour une 'petite erreur' ayant fait 16 morts." 6 January.

———. 2006. "Les taliban annoncent une offensive de printemps en Afghanistan." 22 November.

———. 2007. "Taliban Seen Adjusting Tactics." 13 February.

Roggio, Bill. 2006a. "Observations from Southeastern Afghanistan." Counterterrorism Blog. June 18. http://counterterrorismblog.org/2006/06/observa tions_from_southeastern.php.

———. 2006b. "Taliban Losses in Afghanistan, Gains in Pakistan." Blog appeared in *The Fourth Rail*. 25 June. http://billroggio.com/archives/2006/06/ taliban_losses_in_af.php.

Rohde, David. 2004. "G.I.'s in Afghanistan on Hunt, but Now for Hearts and Minds." *New York Times*. 30 March.

———. 2006. "Afghan Symbol for Change Becomes a Symbol of Failure." *New York Times*. 5 September.

Rohde, David and James Risen. 2006. "C.I.A. Review Highlights Afghan Leader's Woes." *New York Times*. 5 November.

Roy, Olivier. 1998. "Has Islamism a Future in Afghanistan? In *Fundamentalism reborn?* ed. W. Maley. London: Hurst & Co.

———. 2000. *Pakistan and the Taliban*. Paris: CERI. October. http://www.ceri -sciencespo.com/archive/octo00/artor.pdf.

———. 2002. *Islamic Radicalism in Afghanistan and Pakistan*, Writenet Paper no. 06/2001, Geneva: UNHCR.

Rubin, Elizabeth. 2006a. "In the Land of the Taliban." *New York Times Magazine*. 22 October.

———. 2006b. "Taking the Fight to the Taliban." *New York Times Magazine*. 29 October.

Sands, Chris. 2006. "Afghan MPs Predict Very Big War." *The Dominion*. 19 December.

Schiewek, Eckart. 2006. "Efforts to Curb Political Violence in Afghanistan." In *Political Violence and Terrorism in South Asia*, 150–71. Ed. Pervez Iqbal Cheema, Maqsudul Hasan Nuri, and Ahmad Rashid Malik. Islamabad: Islamabad Political Research Institute.

Sand, Benjamin. 2006. "Afghanistan's Taleban Insurgency Fueled by Drug, Terrorist Money." *Voice of America*. 22 August.

Senlis Council. 2006c. *Canada in Kandahar: No Peace to Keep. A Case Study of the Military Coalitions in Southern Afghanistan*. London: Senlis Council.

Shahzad, Syed Saleem. 2001. "Taliban's Trail Leads to Pakistan." *Asia Times*. 13 December. http://www.atimes.com/ind-pak/CL13Df01.html.

———. 2003a. "U.S. Turns to the Taliban."*Asia Times Online*. 14 June. http://www .atimes.com/atimes/Central_Asia/EF14Ag01.html.

———. 2003b. "Taliban Raise the Stakes in Afghanistan." *Asia Times Online*. 30 October. http://www.atimes.com/atimes/Central_Asia/EJ30Ag01.html.

———. 2006a. "Taliban Deal Lights a Slow-Burning Fuse." *Asia Times Online*, 11 February. http://www.atimes.com/atimes/South_Asia/HB11Df04.html.

———. 2006b. "Afghanistan Strikes Back at Pakistan." *Asia Times*. 9 November. http://www.atimes.com/atimes/South_Asia/HK09Df02.html.

———. 2006c. "How the Taliban Prepare for Battle." *Asia Times Online*, 5 December. http://www.atimes.com/atimes/South_Asia/HL05Df01.html.

———. 2006d. "Taliban line up the heavy artillery." *Asia Times Online*. 21 December. http://www.atimes.com/atimes/South_Asia/HL21Df01.html.

———. 2007a. "How the Taliban Keep their Coffers Full." *Asia Times Online*. 10 January. http://www.atimes.com/atimes/South_Asia/IA10Df02.html.

————. 2007b. "Afghanistan's Highway to Hell: The Winter of the Taliban's Content." *Asia Times Online.* 25 January. http://www.atimes.com/atimes/South_Asia/IA25Df02.html.

————. 2007c. "Pakistan Makes a Deal with the Taliban." *Asia Times Online.* 1 March. http://www.atimes.com/atimes/South_Asia/IC01Df03.html.

Smith, Graeme. 2006a. "Inspiring Tale of Triumph over Taliban Not All It Seems." *Globe and Mail.* 23 September.

————. 2006b. "The Taliban: Knowing the Enemy. Graeme Smith Ventures into the Infamously Lawless Pakistani Province of Baluchistan to Meet Foot Soldiers of the Taliban." *Globe and Mail,* November 27.

Spiegel Online. 2006. "A Growing Threat In Afghanistan: The Taliban Gets Closer to Kabul." 4 December. http://www.spiegel.de/international/spiegel/0,1518,452290,00.html.

Stormer, Carsten. 2004. "Winning Hearts, Minds and Firefights in Uruzgan." *Asia Times Online.* 6 August. http://www.atimes.com/atimes/Central_Asia/FH06Ag01.html.

Straziuso, Jason. 2006. "Outgoing Gen. Sees more Afghan Battles." Associated Press. 30 December.

Synovitz, Ron. 2006. "Taliban Launches 'Spring Offensive' with Attack on Helmand Base." *RFE/RL.* 30 March.

Tohid, Owais. 2003. "Taliban Regroups—On the Road." *Christian Science Monitor.* 27 June.

————. 2003. "Arid Afghan Province Proves Fertile for Taliban." *Christian Science Monitor.* 14 July.

Trives, Sébastien. 2006. "Afghanistan: réduire l'insurrection. Le cas du Sud-Est." *Politique étrangère* 1: 105–18.

UNDSS. 2007a. Weekly presentation, 26 January–1 February. Unpublished internal report, Kabul.

————. 2007b. Weekly reports, February. Unpublished internal reports, Kabul.

Walsh, Declan. 2006a. "Better Paid, Better Armed, Better Connected—Taliban Rise Again." *The Guardian.* 16 September.

————. 2006b. "Kandahar under Threat, War Raging in Two Provinces and an Isolated President. So what went wrong?" *The Guardian.* 16 September.

————. 2006c. "In the Heartland of a Mysterious Enemy, U.S. Troops Battle to Survive." *The Guardian.* 5 December.

————. 2007. "Special Deals and Raw Recruits Employed to Halt the Taliban in Embattled Helmand." *The Guardian.* 4 January.

Ware, Michael. 2002. "Encountering the Taliban." *Time.* 23 March.

Watson, Paul. 2006. "On the Trail of the Taliban's Support." *Los Angeles Times.* 24 December.

Wood, David. 2007. "Afghan War Needs Troops." *Baltimore Sun.* 7 January.

Wright, Joanna. 2006a. "The Changing Structure of the Afghan Opium Trade." *Jane's Intelligence Review.* 9 September.

———. 2006b. "Taliban Insurgency Shows Signs of Enduring Strength." *Jane's Intelligence Review.* October.

Xinhuanet. 2005. "Afghanistan : un responsable tribal pendu par des talibans." 16 July.

Yousafzai, Sami and Ron Moreau. 2007. "The Mysterious Mullah Omar." *Newsweek.* 5 March.

Zabriskie, Phil. 2006. "Dangers Up Ahead How Druglords and Insurgents Are Making the War in Afghanistan Deadlier Than Ever." *Time.* 5 March.

Zabriskie, Phil and Steve Connors. 2002. "Where Are the Taliban Now?" *Time.* 24 September.

Zoroya, Gregg. 2005. "Afghanistan Insurgents' Extremely Resolute and Fought to the Last Man." *USA Today.* 16 November.

7

Mark Sedra

Security Sector Reform and State Building in Afghanistan

As many observers of Afghanistan have recognized in 2006 and 2007, the Afghan state building process faces a "tipping point" (Rubin 2007; Patel 2007). Over the past two years, security conditions in the country, particularly in the south and east, have deteriorated to a point where the post-Taliban political order appears at risk. Many Afghans have yet to receive the peace dividend that they were promised by Afghan and international leaders following the collapse of the Taliban regime. Ordinary Afghans were buoyed by talk of a Marshall Plan for the country that would bring hope and a break with the violence and endemic poverty that has characterized life for most Afghans over the past three decades. However, by 2008 the most noticeable change in the lives of most Afghans has been a rise in insecurity and the growth of a public administration increasingly seen as predatory, obtrusive, and corrupt. This has fed a growing sense of pessimism and disillusionment that has only emboldened spoiler groups such as the Taliban. Today, many Afghans from Kabul to Kunduz to Kandahar assume that the Taliban will return to power, not because of a renewed belief in the Taliban fundamentalist ideology, but due to a feeling that momentum is on their side, that international actors are losing interest, and that the Karzai regime is weak and faltering. As the media coverage of Afghanistan clearly shows, the security situation now defies classification as a post-conflict environment. One need only glance at recent statistics regarding the insurgency to grasp the extent of the problem. By September 2007, an average of six hundred security incidents—including bombings, fire fights, and intimidation—were occurring on a monthly basis, a 20% rise from 2006 (Rohde 2007). There were 160 suicide bombings in 2007, a tactic largely unknown in Afghanistan prior to 2001, a significant increase from the twenty-seven that occurred in 2005 (UNSG 2008, 5). Finally, there were more than eight thousand conflict-related fatalities in 2007, 1,500 of which were civilian, a figure almost eight times greater than that of 2005 (SRSG 2008, 4; Afghanistan 2006b, 2). The Taliban do not just control districts by night in many areas of the south as seen in 2006; they now brazenly control them by day as well.

Whether Afghanistan will tip toward state consolidation and development or state failure and internecine conflict will depend to a great extent on the outcome of security sector reform (SSR), the process to remake the security architecture of the state. It provides the only means for the Afghan government to achieve a central prerequisite for statehood, a monopoly over the use of coercive force, and the only viable exit strategy for the international community. Although this became obvious in 2007, donors and the Afghan government alike did not always grasp the centrality of the process. The 2001 Bonn Agreement addressed the security sector only superficially, featuring vague provisions on the extension of state authority over armed militias and the establishment of a Judicial Reform Commission. The steady rise of insecurity and the growing awareness that development and reconstruction would be forestalled until the security situation had stabilized elevated the SSR process to the forefront of the state building process. President Karzai would refer to the SSR process in the summer of 2003 as the "basic pre-requisite to recreating the nation that today's parents hope to leave to future generations."[2] Despite this recognition, the process has laboured to build momentum and has been hindered by a series of chronic problems ranging from resource shortfalls to coordination deficits.

Many of the problems afflicting the Afghan SSR agenda centre on the framework established to support it (see Sky 2006). At a G8 security donors' conference held in Geneva in April 2002, the SSR agenda was formally set with the establishment of the lead nation donor support framework. The plan divided the security sector into five pillars and appointed a lead nation to oversee reforms in each. The five pillars were: military reform (United States); police reform (Germany); judicial reform (Italy); demilitarization (Japan); and counter-narcotics (United Kingdom). By tying individual donors to specific areas of the reform agenda, the system was meant to assure balanced distribution of resources and durable donor engagement. However, the system failed to establish a mechanism to harmonize the activities of the lead nations or build synergies among them, undercutting one of the core precepts of the SSR model, which advanced a holistic approach to reform. Some donor actors assumed that the Afghan government would take on this coordination and oversight role, but acute shortfalls in capacity prevented it from doing so. While the system succeeded in firmly affixing the lead donors to their pillars, it also served to territorialize the process. Donors were often more concerned with protecting their turf than advancing the wider SSR agenda.

Moreover, the system did not adequately consider differences in donor competencies or the resource levels that they could provide. This contributed to wide imbalances, with massive resource disparities between the pillars. As a result, the pace and achievements of reform have differed significantly across the process, with the military reform and demilitarization pillars severely outperforming their counterparts. What became clear by the beginning of 2007 was that the integrated nature of the different pillars of the security sector made such differentiation counterproductive. Sustaining achievements in one pillar is contingent on a degree of parallel progress in the remaining four. For instance, as this chapter will show, advancements made in deploying newly trained police have been undermined by the lack of progress to strengthen the judicial system. In early 2006 at the London Donor Conference, the international community recognized the problematic nature of the lead donor system, and emphasized the importance of stronger Afghan ownership and leadership. However, the failure to formally scrap the system meant that it would continue to cast a long shadow on the process.

This chapter will not seek to deconstruct the entire Afghan SSR process (see Sedra 2006). Rather it will identify and analyze four key factors that have hindered it. They are: the short-term approach to SSR, which can be conceptualized as a "slide toward expediency" in the process (ibid.); the failure to prioritize police reform at the outset of the process; the under-funding of the justice sector; and the lack of political will. The analysis will centre primarily on the impact of donor policies and assistance. Although significant steps had been taken by early 2008 to address these challenges, they remain the pre-eminent obstacles to achieving the goals of the SSR agenda, and by extension the entire state building process in Afghanistan.

The Slide toward Expediency

SSR does not merely entail the training and equipping of security forces, the most common form of Western security assistance to developing states during the Cold War. Rather, it embraces a holistic vision of the security sector that balances the need to enhance the operational effectiveness of the security forces with the imperative that they be subordinated to democratic civilian authority and conform to international norms of human rights.

Moreover, this model of security assistance expanded the boundaries of the security sector, recognizing the symbiotic relationship between the security forces and the judicial system. A product of the growing awareness of the nexus between security and development that materialized in the wake of the Cold War, SSR is intended to advance the security of people rather than regimes, reflecting the emergent human security agenda.

While the SSR model was well developed and endorsed as a staple of state building practice by government agencies, intergovernmental bodies, and NGOs by the time of the Taliban's fall in 2001 (see Chanaa 2002; UNDP 2003; Wulf 2000), its influence over the actual implementation of Afghanistan's SSR process was short-lived. Initial planning of the process reflected SSR doctrine, but over time it regressed into a Cold War–era train and equip program. This stemmed largely from the failure of international military forces to provide an adequate security buffer for the state building project, which impelled the government and donors to see the SSR process, particularly the nascent Afghan security forces, as the principal mechanism to address immediate security threats. The resulting focus on improving the operational effectiveness of the security forces stripped the process of its holistic focus, drawing resources away from judicial reform and initiatives to establish effective management and governance structures. Many of the imposing problems that confronted the SSR process in the beginning of 2007 can be traced to this slide toward expediency in its implementation (Sedra 2006).

In many respects, the SSR process has been driven by short-term thinking, which has sacrificed the long-term sustainability of the Afghan security sector to address the immediate security threats of the post-Taliban era. The task of training and equipping the army and police has been elevated above the imperatives of building oversight and management structures to govern them and ensure that they are situated within a sound legal framework. While such an approach may seem justified by the acute security crisis that faces Afghanistan, it has distorted the process and created new obstacles to change. For instance, as the next section will show, the failure to dedicate enough attention to restructuring the Ministry of Interior, responsible for domestic security, slowed the remaking of the police service. Moreover, the failure to adequately empower the Office of the National Security Council (ONSC) of Afghanistan, mandated to coordinate national security policy and provide a degree of oversight over the sector, has undercut Afghan efforts to assert ownership of the process and synchronize the many actors and interests involved in it. The absence of robust parliamentary and executive oversight and accountability structures has left the sector without mechanisms to counter the culture of impunity in the security forces and judicial apparatus that has had such a corrosive impact on public perceptions of the government.[3] Paradoxically, the great innovation of the SSR concept—its focus on fostering effective governance of the security sector—is accorded little attention in the Afghan context.

A telling example of the short-term outlook of the SSR process relates to the fiscal sustainability of the security forces. According to the World Bank, in fiscal year 2004/2005 security expenditures equaled almost 500% of domestic revenues and 23% of GDP (World Bank 2005, 42–43). In contrast, the global average for defence expenditures hovers at about 4% of GDP (Rubin 2006, 181). Even if the government meets its target of raising domestic revenue to 8% of GDP by fiscal year 2010/11 it will still not be able to sustain such expenditures (Afghanistan 2006a, 56). The Interim Afghan National Development Strategy (I-ANDS), released in early 2006, admitted that "the international community has imported models of security forces that impose costs Afghanistan may not be able to sustain," but it does not offer a strategy on how to address this urgent dilemma (Afghanistan 2006a, 27). Without a change in approach that could involve downsizing segments of the security forces, the Afghan government will remain dependent on international budgetary support for the foreseeable future. Considering the limitations on raising domestic revenues, the Afghan government will be unable to pay the wage bill of the Afghan security forces at their expected force levels and salary scales without international assistance. It is worth remembering that in the history of the modern Afghan state the failure to pay salaries has been one of the main determinants of indiscipline, corruption, factionalization, and eventual collapse of the Afghan security forces. At its current fiscal trajectory there is a significant chance that this pattern could be repeated, as the inevitable downsizing of international aid could create resource pressures that could again lead to the breakdown of the security forces and a resumption of civil conflict (see Sedra 2007).

Another example of the myopia that has characterized Afghanistan's SSR process relates to the formation of the Afghan National Auxiliary Police (ANAP), a militia force intended to complement and reinforce the regular police. In late May 2006, the Afghan government announced that the President had approved a plan to mobilize militia forces to address the growing security crisis caused by the upsurge of insurgent activity. After acrimonious debate, a plan was introduced that called for 11,271 Auxiliary Police to be mobilized and deployed in 124 districts of 21 provinces, mainly in the south and east (Afghanistan 2006a; ICG 2007b). The purpose of the force was to secure static checkpoints and play a community policing role, freeing up the regular police to support counter-terrorist and counter-insurgency operations. Recruits for the force received ten days of training in makeshift camps, covering operational police techniques, as well as firearms and tactics. They also received classroom instruction on the Afghan constitution, ethics, and morality. Each camp was capable of producing 200 ANAP recruits every two weeks, with 8,331 having completed the basic training course by July 2007 (ICG 2007b, 13).[4] Once their basic training was completed, ANAP personnel received firearms, police uniforms and salaries identical to those of the ANP. It was envisaged that the ANAP would receive additional training every quarter, which, by the end of their first year on the job, would have left them with the same level of training as rank-and-file ANP patrolmen. This would have permitted the ANAP's integration into the regular police, enabling the ANP to meet its force target of 82,000.[5]

Considering that ANAP units were recruited, trained and deployed locally, they were extremely vulnerable to factional control and manipulation. There were no clear accountability mechanisms to monitor and curb factional influence, let alone Taliban infiltration.[6] Although all recruits were vetted using the same system employed by both the Afghan National Army (ANA) and Afghan National Police (ANP), US trainers still suspected that as many as one in ten of the ANAP recruits were agents of the Taliban (Sand 2007).[7] US military officials were never enthusiastic about the program, often referring to it as a "temporary" or "stop-gap" measure. Their reservations were well-founded as the incompetence and ineffectiveness of the force led to its disbandment by early 2008.[8]

Despite the failure of the ANAP experiment those who advocated greater reliance on informal security structures were not deterred. It would not take long for the successor program to the ANAP, the Afghan Social Outreach Program (ASOP) to take form. Framed more as a governance than a security initiative, the ASOP calls for the creation of a *shura* or traditional local council to oversee the mobilization of community resources to respond to security threats. According to the program, which had entered a pilot phase by the spring of 2008, the *shuras* are to receive a stipend or grant to underwrite their efforts to enhance local security. The rationale behind the program is to empower local communities to assume responsibility for their security and to foster greater communication and collaboration with the government. Militia or self-defence forces raised through the scheme will, unlike the ANAP, not be provided with uniforms, weapons, or salaries, making the structure much more informal in nature than the ANAP. The concept is inspired by the traditional *arbacki* model, a community-led self-defence structure indigenous to certain areas of eastern Afghanistan. Although far more nuanced in its design than its ANAP predecessor, the ASOP faces the same drawbacks.

While the notion of exploiting traditional security structures to fill the prevailing security vacuum is surely compelling, such an approach is problematic in three ways: First, the mobilization of militias runs contrary to the government's demilitarisation process, sending a powerful signal that the government is not committed to the process. Second, the provision of special dispensation to re-arm and re-mobilize militias in insecure Pashtun areas, where much of the focus of ASOP will be placed in its initial stages, will create resentment among the northern ethnic factions, the majority of which disarmed, at least partially, under the DDR program.[9] Many warn of the prospect of tit-for-tat re-militarization.[10] Third, without establishing robust vetting, oversight and accountability structures, the sub-national militias could become a reservoir for factionalism and corruption. It could also serve as a convenient façade for factional commanders to maintain the integrity of their militias and legitimize their de facto authority in the periphery.[11] The ANAP and ASOP experiments reflect a fundamental problem of the SSR process; it has been geared more to getting 'Afghans into the fight' than it has to building rights-respecting and accountable security forces.

A False Start for Police Reform

At 8 a.m. on 29 May 2006, a large cargo truck leading a US military convoy into Kabul from the Khair Khana Pass north of the city experienced a "mechanical failure" and crashed into twelve cars, killing five civilians (Gall 2006a). The rioting that ensued across Kabul resulted in a least seventeen more deaths, over 190 injuries, and millions of dollars in damage (Gall 2006c). As rumours spread that the crash was deliberate and that US soldiers fired into angry crowds at the scene, hundreds of men and boys, some brandishing assault rifles, formed roving mobs that attacked offices of international organizations, guesthouses, restaurants and government buildings. It took the mobs two hours to reach the city centre, home to most international offices, foreign embassies, and government offices (Murray 2007). Not only did the police fail to halt the rioters from reaching the centre of Kabul, but many fled checkpoints in the path of the mobs. Others took off their uniforms and joined the rioters. According to a representative of CARE International, the international humanitarian NGO, police were involved in the looting and torching of their country office.[12] A representative of another international NGO ransacked during the riots claimed that police demanded payments to protect their premises.[13] When police did stand their ground against the rioters, they proved to be woefully trained and equipped to confront the situation. Most of the police had not received any training in crowd control and lacked non-lethal equipment like riot gear, water hoses, and tear gas (Murray 2007). As a result, the police violated basic internationally accepted crowd control protocols by using their guns to disperse crowds, which in many cases only served to escalate the situation.

Whether the riots were spontaneous or well orchestrated, they showed the ineptitude of the police and the failure of four years of police reform to change the culture of the force. Tom Koenig, the then Special Representative of the UN Secretary General in Afghanistan, characterized the police response to the riots as "weak and disappointing" and called on the government to accelerate reforms (Morarjee 2006). The president's Chief of Staff issued an even sterner condemnation, calling the police reaction "really shameful" (Gall 2006b). That the episode occurred in Kabul, whose police have received a disproportionately large share of resources and attention, accentuated the deep flaws in the reform process, which from its outset has been under-resourced, poorly planned, and plagued by problems of coordination and capacity deficits.

Since 2002, the Afghan National Police (ANP) has been a source of insecurity for communities across the country. A significant proportion of Afghans view the police with fear and resentment. The only exposure many Afghans have to the police is to pay them bribes or illegal taxes. Police increasingly commit crimes, from kidnappings for ransom to bank robberies, which have fuelled a rising crime rate across the country (Rubin 2007). In November 2004 a spokesperson of the Afghan Independent Human Rights Commission (AIHRC) claimed that 15% of all human rights violations reported over the previous six months were perpetrated by police. The most common offences reported were torture, forcible theft of property, and the failure to prosecute murder cases (IWPR 2004). Such trends have continued unabated in 2007. Corruption is rampant throughout the police, with up to 80% of the force allegedly involved in the drug trade.[14] The amount of money generated from corruption ranges from $200 a month for a patrolmen to $30,000 a month for a police general.[15] A majority of the police are loyal to regional commanders rather than the Ministry of Interior, a byproduct of the heavy factionalization of the force. In a telling expression of the depth of corruption and factionalism in the police, one senior Afghan police official claimed in June 2006 that he trusted less than thirty of the approximately 1,500 police in Helmand province.[16] As of early 2007, the police reform process had only scratched the surface of these problems.

In the spring of 2006, former Interior Minister Ali Jalali, who served in the post from January 2003 to September 2005, claimed that "the ANP continues to be ill-trained, poorly paid, under equipped, and inadequately armed" (2006). Because the police represent one of the principal interfaces between government and society, the failure to address the clear deficiencies of the force—its corruption, culture of impunity, and lack of effectiveness—has in turn eroded the legitimacy of the state.

Despite the acute problems of the police, they have been at the frontlines of the counter-insurgency campaign. The ANP have suffered the brunt of the casualties in engagements with the Taliban. Between May 2006 and May 2007, 406 ANP were killed, more than twice that of the Afghan National Army (ANA) in the same period (ICG 2007b). The inability of NATO and Afghan government forces to hold territory in the south following military operations has been attributed to the incompetence of the police. Lightly armed, poorly trained police have been shown to be no match for the Taliban, which have specifically targeted ANP convoys, checkpoints, and bases. NATO and the Afghan government depend on the ANP to hold territory that has been secured through military operations. The inability of the police to do so has hamstrung NATO's counter-insurgency strategy (Rohde 2007).

One of the principal reasons for the deplorable state of the police in 2008 was the slow start that the reform process received in the immediate post-Taliban period. The government of Germany, which became the lead donor for police reform under the G8 SSR donor support framework, lacked the resources or the ambition to meet the daunting demands of the process. Its rehabilitation of the National Police Academy, intended to train upper-level officers for the force, was an important achievement, but it ignored the critical need to address the rank-and-file patrolmen. The bulk of the police in the country are former militiamen who lack any semblance of formal training and bring a "militiamen's mentality" to the job that is not conducive for community policing (Sedra 2002). The failure to address their needs from an early stage in the process not only inhibited the force from fulfilling its duties but enabled the entrenchment of people and practices that would subsequently serve as a major obstacle to reform.

Concerned with the slow progress of police reforms, and how this affected the entire security sector, the United States entered the process in early 2003. Through that year and the next, US support resulted in the establishment of a constabulary training system intended to rapidly train the country's regular police. The US program succeeded in greatly accelerating the pace of training; by the end of 2004, over 32,000 police had been trained in a Central Training Centre (CTC) in Kabul and seven Regional Training Centres (RTCs) in key hubs across the country, and this number swelled to 71,147 by July 2007 (GAO 2005; O'Toole 2007). However, the bulk of those who graduated from the US training program received training of questionable quality. The three core courses offered by the program are: a five-week course for illiterate officers, a nine-week course for literate officers, and a fifteen-day Transition Integration Program (TIP), which provides training for "veteran police" (GAO 2005, 20). Considering that more than 70% of ANP recruits are illiterate, the proportion of officers who graduate from the nine-week program, which comes closest to meeting basic international standards for police education, are highly limited. According to US Department of Justice statistics, only 10% of the graduates from these three courses had completed the nine-week program by June 2006. More than 40% had completed only the fifteen-day TIP program. In the light of these statistics, it is not surprising that in June 2006, the Combined Security Transition Command Afghanistan (CSTC-A) reported that only 30,395 of the police that had received training met basic readiness criteria.[17] By mid-2007, only one out of the seventy-two police units deployed could lead security operations with coalition support, let alone conduct independent missions (Cordesman 2007, 7).

The lack of in-service training or mentoring for the ANP has also been a major obstacle to the creation of an effective, accountable, and rights-respecting force. Police mentors were not deployed in Afghanistan until 2005, and even by the beginning of 2007 the number in the country was insufficient. By early 2007, the US had deployed approximately five hundred mentors in the country, the bulk of them under contract with the US private security company DynCorp International, and the majority deployed to the restive southern provinces (ICG 2007b, 7).[18] Considering that over eight hundred mentors had been embedded with the ANA—a number widely seen as inadequate for the 40,000 troops that had been trained by late 2007—a significant increase in police mentors is required to meet the needs of the more than 70,000 ANP personnel who had completed training by the fall of 2007. Even if the training received through the National Police Academy and the RTCs is sufficiently rigorous, police will invariably regress into undesirable patterns of behaviour if they do not have ongoing training and observation. US military officials have indicated that 2,350 embedded trainers are needed to prepare the ANP for service.

In February 2007, the European Union (EU) announced that it would deploy 195 police advisors, mentors, and trainers, a move long urged by both Germany and the United States (Lobjakas 2007; Nicola 2007). By June 2007, the European Policing Mission to Afghanistan (EUPOL) was operational and had brought the bulk of the non-US policing personnel in Afghanistan under its umbrella, including non-European actors. However, while this was an important step that should give the police reform process a significant boost, EUPOL was already mired in controversy by late 2007. In early September 2007, the commander of EUPOL, Friedrich Eichele, resigned only three months after assuming the position, allegedly as a result of an internal clash with the EU's special envoy to Afghanistan, Francesc Vendrell. Further compounding the problems of the mission, only sixty of the 195 mission contingent had arrived on the ground by mid-September, with many member states balking at earlier commitments of personnel and resources (Nicola 2007). Considering that the size of the EUPOL mission was already considered insufficient to meet the resource gap in the process, particularly in terms of the number of police mentors deployed, these setbacks could prove particularly damaging.

While it is clear that Afghanistan will need intensive donor engagement in the police reform process for up to a decade, the form it will take will determine the success of the project. The process has never had a clear strategic plan and since the United States entered it in 2003, donor coordination has been a significant problem. Tensions between the US and German police missions stemmed from two sources: First, the differing policing and legal traditions of Germany and the United States have fostered different reform approaches and mindsets that have clashed at times. The German police project emanates from a highly centralized police tradition and a civil code legal system, while the US system is decentralized and rooted to common law. The second source of tension has been the G8 lead nation framework itself. US funding to the police from 2002 to 2006 was $2.1 billion. In May 2007, the US government committed an additional $2.5 billion to be spent by September 2008 (ICG 2007b, 8–9; Wilder 2007, 19–20). By contrast, Germany contributed a total of $80 million from 2002 to 2006. The massive disparity in spending between the two donors, incommensurate with Germany's lead-nation status, contributed to tensions between them. These were allayed somewhat following the 2006 London Donor Conference, when Germany relinquished its lead-nation status in favour of the title of "key partner," a symbolic gesture intended to emphasize Afghan ownership over the process. Germany would pass on this key partner role to the EUPOL mission upon its inauguration in June 2007 (ICG 2007b, 8).

Coordination between the German and US police missions improved markedly in late 2006 and early 2007. This came after a meeting of police advisors in Dubai in April 2006, in which both missions resolved to work more closely together.[19] In the months following the meeting, the CSTC-A accepted two embedded advisors from the German police project.[20] Another important development that indicated a more co-operative approach by the two donors was the initiation of steps to coordinate the lesson plans of the National Police Academy and the US-sponsored training centres.[21]

One of the most debilitating problems afflicting the development of the police is a lack of leadership both in the senior ranks of the ANP and in the Ministry of Interior. The focus of the reform process was on training and equipping the police, not building the capacity of the Ministry of Interior, the central government institution intended to manage it. This permitted corruption and factionalism to spread and permeate every organ of the ministry, thereby hindering efforts to change the culture of the police. One cannot effectively reform the body of an institution if the head is in a state of disarray.

Reforming the Ministry of Interior became a secondary priority to the task of overhauling the police at the outset of the reform process. This was exemplified by the fact that the German police project had embedded only one senior advisor in the ministry with the mandate to advance administrative and personnel reforms by late 2003 (Sedra 2004). After the Bonn conference, the Panjshiri faction[22] of the Northern Alliance entrenched its control over large parts of the ministry, integrating their militias into the police and insulating their activities in the illicit economy. Former Interior Minister Ali Jalali was able to weaken the factional hold over the ministry but not remove it. Furthermore the ministry lacked even the most basic administrative systems such as personnel and procurement, undermining its ability to assert effective command and control over the force.

The apparent reticence to advance reforms in the Ministry of Interior began to change slowly with the entrance of the US into the police reform process in 2003. One of the most significant achievements of this expanded reform effort was the launch of the pay and rank reform process in 2006. It had three primary objectives: to rationalize and restructure the police rank system (which was extremely top heavy) by reducing the senior ranks of the force; to introduce a transparent, merit-based recruitment and promotion system to supplant hiring and career advancement based upon bribery and the leveraging of personal and factional connections; and to increase the pay scale to militate against corruption and promote recruitment and retention. The aim of the process was to achieve a 75% reduction in the number of police officers in the ranks of generals through captains and nearly a 30% increase in the number of lieutenants, sergeants, and patrolmen. By the spring of 2008, the highest ranks of the force (generals and colonels) down to the captain and lieutenant levels had been reformed, leaving only the lowest ranks of sergeants and patrolmen. All rank reforms were earmarked for completion by the end of 2008. The process had also achieved the overhaul of the wage scale, increasing the ratio of lowest to highest monthly salaries from about 1:1.5 ($70:$107) to 1:10 ($70:$750) (Wilder 2007). The program is a major milestone for the wider police reform process, as it represents the most important step undertaken to date to mitigate the two most acute problems facing the police: factionalism and corruption. However, the program has not been without setbacks, ranging from government interference in the appointment process at the higher rank levels, and corruption compromising vetting and selection procedures in the reform of the lower ranks. While the problem of government interference was largely resolved due to stringent pressure from the international donor community, the challenge of corruption lower down in the reform process remained unrecognized and unaddressed by the spring of 2008. In the final months of the program steps should be taken to redress irregularities and breakdowns in the vetting process and establish rigorous oversight and accountability mechanisms to monitor its implementation.

The Afghan government and international community are attempting to compensate for the false start experienced by the police reform process in the aftermath of the Taliban's fall, which cost it two years and set back the entire SSR agenda. Some observers argue that one of the biggest mistakes made by the international community, and more specifically the US, in the wake of the Taliban's fall was to invest heavily in the army at the expense of the police.[23] It is conceivable that an effective countrywide police force with some paramilitary capacity could have more effectively provided an enabling environment for reconstruction and protected communities from the threat of spoilers, warlords, and basic criminality. The obvious desire of some donors to drastically accelerate the process and institute quick fixes to compensate for its false start—demonstrated by the ANAP experiment—exemplifies growing donor awareness of the centrality of the project and the need for more intensive engagement in it, but such steps should not be taken at the expense of long-term sustainability. The uncomfortable truth that donors are facing is that the ANP will require intensive donor support for a decade before it reaches self-sufficiency.

Ignoring Justice

At the core of the endeavour to establish the rule of law in post-conflict societies are "the legal norms and institutions necessary for the creation, interpretation, and application of the law" (Tolbert with Solomon 2006, 44–45). Although the police play an indispensable role in enforcing the law, "without functioning courts and a judiciary system, there can be no rule of law" (45). In Afghanistan, the international community and the Afghan government failed to heed this axiom. Although the Bonn Agreement called for the appointment of a Judicial Reform Commission "to rebuild the domestic justice system in accordance with Islamic principles, international standards, the rule of law and Afghan legal traditions," judicial reform was from the outset a secondary objective to training and equipping the country's security forces (Bonn Agreement 2001). The wide disparity in international assistance provided to the security force train and equip program as compared to efforts to reconstitute the judicial system exemplify this prioritization of reforms. According to the World Bank, only 3% of expenditures in the security sector were allocated to justice institutions in fiscal year 2003–2004 (World Bank 2005, 50). Considering its decrepit state following the collapse of the Taliban, this level of assistance was grossly inadequate to restore the judicial system in much of the country.

In 2004, J. Alexander Thier affirmed that "every aspect of a functioning judiciary is presently absent" in Afghanistan (Thier 2004, 2). At the time, the sector lacked courthouses, law libraries, correctional facilities, and office buildings for prosecutors and attorneys. Adequately trained jurists were in short supply; the majority of judges in the country lacked any formal legal training. Finally, a complete record of the law had not been assembled and disseminated widely, fostering variations in the nature and application of legal statutes. Despite programs to address each of these areas, the situation had not changed dramatically by the beginning of 2008. The courts are barely able to function in some parts of the country. There is abundant anecdotal evidence of criminals being apprehended by the police only to be released shortly thereafter due to the corruption and incompetence of local justice operators and the lack of adequate detention facilities. A survey by the Asia Foundation in 2006, the largest ever undertaken in Afghanistan, found that only 16% of Afghans take their disputes, whether criminal or civil, to government courts (Asia Foundation 2006, 59). More than 90% of "legal matters" in the country are taken to the informal or traditional legal system rather than to state courts (Afghanistan 2005, 14). Average Afghans see the courts as expensive, corrupt, and out of touch with local realities.

Close scrutiny of the judicial reform process in early 2008 showed that the obstacles to change continued to outweigh reform achievements. Foremost among these obstacles is coordination. There have been coordination breakdowns at every level of the process, between the main donors, between the government and the donors, and between the main government judicial institutions. The resulting lack of consensus on even the most fundamental aspects of the reform process fostered duplication and hindered the formation of a coherent strategy.

Perhaps the most problematic coordination failure pertains to the relationship between the two principal donors to the process, Italy and the United States. Relations between the Italian Justice Project and the USAID Rule of Law Project were openly strained in mid-2006. The differing legal traditions of the two donors—Italy featuring a civil code system and the United States common law—largely accounts for the persistent tensions between them and complicated the reform process. Reforms of the Supreme Court exemplify how the two traditions have clashed. The Afghan constitution adopted the US Supreme Court model, featuring nine Supreme Court justices and thirty-six advisors, dispensing with the French Civil Code model of the previous constitution, which entailed forty Supreme Court Justices and hundreds of advisors. The implementation of the new model has been problematic because the courts have continued to operate in a manner consistent with the previous system, in which the Court of Cassation falls under the remit of the Supreme Court. This has placed a huge burden on the new, more compact Supreme Court (Afghanistan 2005).[24] The US is working to alleviate the burden on the Supreme Court by devolving responsibilities to provincial courts. By contrast, the Italians have argued for the restoration of elements of the civil code system.[25] The divergence in approaches of the two donors sent confusing and contradictory signals to Afghan actors.

Another obstacle from the outset of the process was the lack of an overarching reform strategy, a by-product of the coordination deficits that existed among the main actors engaged in it. Italy designed a strategy early in the process, but the other stakeholders did not endorse it due to a lack of adequate Afghan input. It was not until late 2005 that a coherent reform vision materialized. In August of that year a three-day conference called *Justice for All* was held in Kabul to consult all the main stakeholders in the process—including the three permanent Afghan justice institutions,[26] Afghan legal scholars, UN agencies, donors, NGOs, and civil society groups—"on the dimensions of reform, benchmarks and timelines" (Afghanistan 2005, preface). The result of the conference was a ten-year strategic vision of the same name released on 25 October 2005. It divided the judicial reform process into five dimensions: reforming the laws; making institutions work; reaching out to the people; consulting with the community on traditional justice; and co-operation with other government programs (ibid. 3). For each dimension, the framework identified broad goals to be achieved in three time horizons: one to three years, four to five years, and five to ten years.

While the "Justice for All" paper provided for the first time a unified strategic vision for the judicial reform process, a succinct justice sector implementation strategy was still lacking. An important step toward elaborating this strategy was taken at a two-day conference in Rome on 2–3 July 2007. The Rome Conference on Justice and the Rule of Law in Afghanistan, co-hosted by the government of Afghanistan, the government of Italy, and the United Nations, assembled experts and practitioners working on every aspect of the Afghan judicial system. It resulted in fresh pledges of $360 million to underwrite reforms and a commitment by the Afghan Government "to finalize a national justice sector strategy" under the auspices of a new National Justice Program (Rome Conference 2007). If the dialogue at the Rome Conference is able to translate the reform vision of "Justice for All" into a succinct reform strategy, it will have been a watershed for the judicial reform process.

A commonly overlooked aspect of the judicial reform process is corrections reform. The rule of law system can be conceptualized as a triad whose three points are the police, the judiciary, and corrections. Corrections is clearly the most under-resourced of the three in Afghanistan. The omission is perhaps not surprising as corrections systems are characteristically not an attractive target for donor funding in any post-conflict context. In fact, many donors place restrictions on their aid that prevent its use on prisons. However, in light of the decrepit state of the Afghan corrections system, such shortfalls in funding have been particularly conspicuous and debilitating, obstructing progress in all points of the triad. Two country-wide surveys of the corrections system, conducted by the International Committee for the Red Cross (ICRC) and the US-led coalition, concluded that the majority of the country's prisons could be classified as "uninhabitable" by international standards (quoted in UNAMA 2006, 16). Without adequate facilities to hold prisoners the police and judiciary cannot perform their respective functions. Corrections is in a sense the missing link of the SSR process. Although it is formally viewed as an element of judicial reform—corrections falls under the mandate of the Ministry of Justice—no donor has come forward to champion the issue.

By 2008, there was almost universal recognition among Afghan and international actors of the deleterious impact of the slow pace of judicial and corrections reform on the SSR and wider state building processes. While several donors have augmented their support to the judicial sector, their contributions remain incommensurate to the scale of the challenges. The Afghan government estimates that process could face a shortfall of $1 billion over the coming decade (Afghanistan 2005, 5). Compared to the vast sums being spent to train and equip the army and police this is a modest sum, and must be met by the international donor community if the rule of law is to be restored across the country.

The Political Will Problem

The Afghan government has not always demonstrated the political will to undertake the difficult reforms necessary to advance the state building process. This is most clear in relation to corruption and the drug trade. It is widely known which government officials, some up to the level of minister, have links to the drug trade, yet they remain in office. A similar problem is apparent in the demilitarization process, where a lack of political will has crippled the Disbandment of Illegal Armed Groups (DIAG) program, the successor to the disarmament, demobilization, and reintegration (DDR) program. Whereas DDR targeted the formal units of the Afghan Military

Force (AMF), the makeshift force consisting largely of Northern Alliance militias established to fill the security vacuum until the ANA could be trained and equipped, the DIAG process aims to disarm the remaining illegal militias outside of government control, ranging from tribal self-defence forces to criminal gangs. The program estimates that there are 1,870 of such illegally armed groups comprising roughly 129,000 militiamen.[27]

At the second Tokyo conference on demilitarization, titled Consolidation of Peace in Afghanistan and held on 5 July 2006, President Karzai reiterated the government's "strong commitment to stand firm on DIAG and accomplish it at any cost despite the difficulties and challenges lying ahead" (Government of Japan 2006). Unfortunately, political rhetoric has not met reality. In its initial stages, the DIAG program targeted the removal of government officials with links to illegal armed groups. High-profile government ministries, even those directly involved in the DIAG program, obstructed and even subverted this effort. The executive branch, rather than championing the program across the government, has sought to provide protection for government officials targeted by it. According to an official of the Joint Secretariat, the Afghan institution that manages and directs the DIAG program, it was instructed by the government not to pursue officials at the governor or cabinet level.[28] The names of several cabinet ministers, governors, and parliamentarians appear on the list of the top ten illegally armed in the country compiled by the Joint Secretariat. Until serious effort is made to persuade these figures to disarm, the process may remain paralyzed. It is not a matter of resources or technical expertise, but politics.

According to a senior ANBP official, the first mistake of the entire demilitarization process was not to target the thirty highest profile commanders in the country at its outset. Had it done so, "the rest would have rolled over."[29] However, such an approach ran contrary to the accommodationist approach of President Karzai and the United States; it risked unravelling the fragile coalition of commanders and powerbrokers they had constructed. Countervailing logic affirms that this fragile coalition, while assuring a degree of stability in the short term, has hindered the state building process. The power of many of these commanders or warlords, whom the government appeases, is overstated. For instance, the removal of Marshall Mohammad Qasim Fahim, viewed as the most powerful warlord in the country, as defence minister in October 2004 did not trigger the coup d'état that many had predicted. Similarly, the transfer of Ismail Khan from the governor's post in his regional stronghold of Herat to a ministerial post in Kabul in September 2004 only aroused a minor anti-government outburst. These incidents showed that the government has more scope for action against regional commanders, some of whom could be described as "paper tigers," than it has employed. As time passes and these commanders are able to consolidate their positions, that scope decreases. Many of the commanders who could have been sidelined in 2002–2003 with relative ease now require the threat or even the use of force to contain. The dichotomy that the Karzai administration has advanced between accommodationism and instability is a false one. Quite to the contrary, the government will only be able to assure the long-term stability of the country by confronting recalcitrant warlords and commanders who challenge the sovereignty of the government.

Of course, as Giustozzi states, the "good state, bad warlord" dichotomy is also too simplistic. In a country where power is already highly decentralized, the state has proven unable to deliver core services in many areas of the country and is itself viewed as predatory by many Afghans, a perception engendered by high levels of government corruption and police heavy-handedness (Giustozzi 2004). This has created space for warlords to consolidate their constituencies through the provision of basic public goods such as security. The results of the presidential and parliamentary elections, in which armed powerbrokers fared extremely well, show that warlords have a high degree of political legitimacy and deserve to be engaged in the political process. Transforming warlords into legitimate politicians and business people is the key to the success of any post-conflict transition; you cannot sideline all such figures, nor is it wise to do so. However, many of these former commanders are so deeply entrenched in the illicit economy and dependent on the persistence of instability to maintain their power bases that they are beyond rehabilitation. In such cases the credibility of the post-conflict state depends on its ability to confront such actors. For the Afghan state to successfully extend its writ across the country, counter corruption, and establish a monopoly on the use of force, it must take a resolute stand against those predatory figures who continue to act with impunity and exploit the state administration to expand their own interests. President Karzai cannot risk alienating all of Afghanistan's former commanders, but by the same token he subverts the state by reaching out to those who have shown little respect for the rule of law or the sovereignty of the state. Bringing everybody under the tent can be as destructive as excluding too many.

Although support for the DIAG process within the executive branch has been tepid, it has verged on collapse in the parliament. In late May 2006, the upper house of the parliament, the *Meshrano Jirga*, unexpectedly approved a resolution calling for the temporary halt of the DIAG process on the grounds that the adverse security environment demanded that Afghans be allowed to maintain their weapons for self-defence.[30] This is perhaps unsurprising considering the high proportion of members of parliament with links to armed elements. For the DIAG process to recover from its significant early setbacks President Karzai must not only convince the international donor community of the government's resolve and dedication to realizing the goals of the process; he must also impress upon his own government the need to adopt them as well. The muted donor reaction to the intra-governmental divisions over the DIAG program can be attributed to an unwillingness to place undue pressure on President Karzai and to avert the perception that the program is being imposed externally. Unlike the DDR program, which was undertaken under the auspices of the UN-operated Afghan New Beginnings Programme (ANBP), the DIAG program was to be fully government-owned and directed, with only technical support from the donor community and UN.

The key to advancing the demilitarization process and expanding the state's legitimacy in the eyes of the people is to go after some of the "big fish" or high profile targets tied to the government, officials who continue to maintain militia forces, are corrupt and/or involved in the narcotics trade. When President Karzai has removed corrupt or ineffectual leaders in the past, he has tended to shift them to different positions in the state rather than remove them outright, merely displacing the problem. There is scope for the international community to demand more of President Karzai's government (Goodhand and Sedra 2007). Aid and assistance to Afghanistan has largely come unconditionally; it could be conditioned in a manner that will promote difficult reforms, such as the removal of corrupt or criminal state officials, and ensure greater adherence to democratic principles. It is not only wasteful but counterproductive to dedicate vast resources to a process where the political leadership shows only a tenuous commitment to reform.

Conclusion

Considering that in 2008 security sector reform in Afghanistan is widely seen as the key to the success of the state building project, it is easy to forget that in 2001 few viewed the process with particular urgency. The international community and the Afghan government failed to grasp the extent and complexity of the security dilemma in Afghanistan following the Taliban's fall, with severe consequences for the security situation and state building process. International assessments that informed initial planning for SSR "naively assumed an improvement in security which has not materialized" (Afghanistan 2004, 15). Attempts to compensate for this lost time further skewed the SSR agenda. With donor states unwilling to contribute the international troop numbers needed to stabilize the country,

SSR increasingly came to be seen as the panacea to stem the rising tide of insecurity, whether in the form of warlords, the insurgency, or general criminality. Training and equipping the security forces to fill the security vacuum and relieve pressure on international military forces came to supersede all other priorities, particularly the "soft" security elements such as judicial reform and security sector governance. Rather than jumpstarting the process, this approach created new obstacles to reform that have slowed it considerably.

By 2006, donors had recognized many of the gaps and problems in the process—from the acute under-resourcing of judicial reform to the need to overhaul the Ministry of Interior. However, despite increased donor investment in these priority areas, primarily from the United States, the process continues to be characterized by short-termism. This is exemplified by the introduction of the Afghan Social Outreach Program (ASOP)—an initiative that could serve to undermine both the demilitarization and police reform processes over the long term—and the failure to address the looming issue of fiscal sustainability. The critical balance between short- and long-term initiatives is lacking, as shown by the governance gap afflicting the process. Issues like governance, so crucial for the effective functioning of a security sector in a democratic polity, is treated like a long-term issue only to be meaningfully addressed when the security forces are competent and the security environment stabilized. Such logic ignores the interconnected nature of the security system, the fundamental principle upon which the SSR model is based. This is not to say that security force operational effectiveness is not important. It should be the central focus of the process in the immediate aftermath of a conflict, but not at the complete expense of efforts to reform its "soft elements" as seen in Afghanistan.

The lead nation framework for the SSR process had ostensibly been rendered irrelevant with the formation of the Afghan-led Joint Coordination Monitoring Board (JCMB) at the London Donor Conference, a development that most stakeholders welcomed. The JCMB has the potential to fill a glaring hole in the SSR process, a mechanism to ensure Afghan ownership of it. More than the creation of the JCMB, however, US control over the process rendered the lead nation system obsolete. By early 2007, the US was the largest financial contributor to four out of the five pillars, vastly outspending the existing lead donors in each. While increased US engagement has given the process a major boost, its penchant for quick fixes, achieved by throwing vast amounts of money at problems, could prove counterproductive in some areas.

Insufficient resources are not the only problem afflicting the process. The Afghan president has not always shown the necessary political will to address the rampant factionalism and corruption in the security institutions, a by-product of his accommodationist leadership approach. Karzai's big-tent policy, intended to advance political inclusiveness and reconciliation, has had the effect of paralyzing reforms. Channelling increased funds into unreformed institutions can drive corruption, which will in turn encourage a culture of impunity and alienate the local population. Only genuine local commitment to reform, to de-factionalizing and de-politicizing the security system, can halt this cycle. That commitment still appears tenuous. The increase in attention and resources to the SSR process, particularly the security forces, over the past two years, may succeed in covering some blatant weaknesses, but durable and sustainable change can only be achieved through the adoption of a holistic approach that aims to change the culture and ethos of the system. Achieving that change in culture requires a long-term approach by donors and Afghan stakeholders and a genuine domestic political commitment to change.

Security sector reform is both a microcosm of the state building process and the key to its success. Many of the same challenges that have afflicted the SSR process encompass the entire state building project, whether it is in the area of coordination or ownership. The stakes for SSR are particularly high, as development, reconstruction, and institution building in Afghanistan will be hard pressed to move forward until a secure environment is provided. The population will question the legitimacy of the state unless the government can provide that most basic public good: security. Some progress has been made in the past two years to place the SSR process back on track, after several years of neglect and wrong turns. That momentum must be maintained, for it is the Afghans, not NATO, the coalition, the UN, or any other external actor, that holds the solution to the Afghan security crisis.

Notes

1 Two hundred and twenty-five Afghans, the majority civilians, died in suicide attacks in the first eight months of 2007, as compared to 305 who lost their lives in 2006; United Nations Assistance Mission in Afghanistan (UNAMA), *Suicide Attacks in Afghanistan (2001–2007)*, (Kabul: UNAMA, 9 September 2007).

2 Opening Address by President Hamid Karzai to the National Symposium on Security Sector Reform, 30 July 2003.

3 Although three committees have been established in the Afghan legislature that deal directly with the security sector—the Committee on Defence, the Committee on Internal Security, Local Administration, Municipal and Territorial Affairs, and the Committee on Legal Affairs and Human Rights—their capacity to provide effective oversight remains severely limited.

4 The camps were overseen by the Combined Security Transition Command Afghanistan (CSTC-A), the Coalition body mandated to oversee US support to the reform of the Afghan security sector. Camps were established in Farah, Helmand, Uruzgan, Zabul,

Ghazni, and Kandahar as of January 2007; Capt. Greg Hignite, "On patrol: Newest ANAP graduates provide security in Kandahar," CSTC-A, *Defense and Security Highlights Afghanistan* (CSTC-A: Kabul, 7 January 2007).

5 Although the original force ceiling for the ANP, officially approved by the Afghan government in 2005, was 62,000, it was elevated by 20,000 in late 2006 to meet deteriorating security conditions.

6 Personal communication with Western donor official, Waterloo, Canada, 19 December 2006.

7 The Government in conjunction with the Coalition have introduced a "vouching system" to vet candidates for the ANA and ANP. According to this system, any individual wishing to join the army or police must have a tribal or village elder vouch for their integrity and commitment to the government of Afghanistan. They are then required to sign an oath of loyalty to the government.

8 US Department of Defense, News Briefing with Maj. Gen. Robert Durbin and Deputy Minister Abdul Hadir Khalid from the Pentagon, transcript, 9 January 2007.

9 These include the Tajiks, Uzbeks, and Hazarra.

10 Interview with Ustad Mohammed Mohaqqeq, Kabul, 16 June 2006; Interview with Vice President Abdul Karim Khalili, Kabul, 18 June 2006.

11 Interview with senior UNAMA official, Kabul, 17 June 2006.

12 Interview with CARE Afghanistan Representative, Kabul, 24 June 2006; Police reportedly donned Salwar Kameezs in an attempt to conceal their uniforms. Others took off their uniforms altogether in favour of civilian clothing.

13 Interview with NGO representative, Kabul, 25 June 2006.

14 Interview with senior Interior Ministry official, Kabul, 23 June 2006; Scott Baldauf, "Inside the Afghan Drug Trade," *Christian Science Monitor*, 13 June 2006.

15 Interview with senior Interior Ministry official, Kabul, 23 June 2006; Interview with international police advisor, Kabul, 20 June 2006.

16 Interview with senior ANP official, Kabul, 19 June 2006.

17 The three criteria used were: training received, unit staffing levels, and equipment status. Inspectors General of the US Department of State and the US Department of Defense, *Interagency Assessment of Afghanistan Police Training and Readiness* (Washington, DC: Department of State and Department of Defense, November 2006), p. 15.

18 Some mentors will also come from the military and the private military company Military Professional Resources Inc. (MPRI). Inspectors-General of the US Department of State and the US Department of Defense, *Interagency Assessment of Afghanistan Police Training and Readiness*, p. 25.

19 Interview with German Police Project Office (GPPO) official, Kabul, 14 June 2006.

20 The rationale behind this interagency decision was that the military could transfer its success in standing-up the ANA to the police.

21 Interview with German Police Project Office (GPPO) official, Kabul, 14 June 2006.

22 This primarily consists of Tajiks from the Panjshir Valley, situated North of Kabul.

23 Interview with senior Interior Ministry official, Kabul, 23 June 2006.

24 Italy has 200 judges for Cassation alone.

25 Interview with USAID official, Kabul, 14 November 2005; Interview with senior Italian Justice Project official, Kabul, 22 June 2006.

26 The three permanent justice institutions are the Supreme Court, the Ministry of Justice and the Office of the Attorney General.

27 Interview with ANBP official in Kabul, 23 May 2005.
28 Interview with official from the DIAG Joint Secretariat in Kabul, 24 June 2006.
29 Interview with senior ANBP official in Kabul, 13 June 2006.
30 Interview with senior UNAMA official in Kabul, 17 June 2006.

References

Agreement on Provisional Arrangements in Afghanistan Pending the Re-establishment of Permanent Government Institutions (The Bonn Agreement). 2002. http://www.unama-afg.org/docs/_nonUN%20Docs/_Internation-Conferences&Forums/Bonn-Talks/bonn.htm.

Asia Foundation. 2006. *Afghanistan in 2006: A Survey of the People.* Kabul: Asia Foundation.

Baldauf, Scott. 2006. "Inside the Afghan Drug Trade." *Christian Science Monitor.* 13 June.

Chanaa, Jane. 2002. *Security Sector Reform: Issues, Challenges and Prospects.* New York: Oxford University Press.

Combined Security Transition Command Afghanistan (CSTC-A). 2007. *Defense and Security Highlights Afghanistan.* Kabul: CSTC-A. 7 January.

Cordesman, Anthony H. 2007. *The Missing Metrics of "Progress" in Afghanistan (and Pakistan).* Working Draft. Washington, DC: CSIS. November.

Gall, Carlotta. 2006a. "Anti-U.S. Rioting Erupts in Kabul; at Least 14 Dead." *New York Times.* 30 May.

———. 2006b. "After Riots End, Kabul's Residents Begin to Point Fingers." *New York Times.* 31 May.

———. 2006c. "Afghans Raise Toll of Dead from May Riots in Kabul to 17." *New York Times.* 8 June.

Giustozzi, Antonio. 2004. "Good State" vs. "Bad Warlords"? A Critique of State-Building Strategies in Afghanistan, Working Paper 51. London: LSE Crisis States Programme.

Goodhand, Jonathan and Mark Sedra. 2007. "Bribes or Bargains? Peace Conditionalities and 'Post-Conflict' Reconstruction in Afghanistan." *International Peacekeeping* 14 (1): 41–61.

Government of Japan. 2006. *Co-chairs' summary: The second Tokyo conference on Consolidation of Peace in Afghanistan (DDR/DIAG),* 6 July. Accessed at http://www2.reliefweb.int.

Inspectors General of the US Department of State and the US Department of Defense. 2006. *Interagency Assessment of Afghanistan Police Training and Readiness.* Washington, DC: Department of State and Department of Defense.

Institute for War and Peace Reporting. 2004. *Afghan Press Monitor* 51. 25 November.

International Crisis Group (ICG). 2007a. Afghanistan's Endangered Compact, Asia Briefing no. 59. Brussels: ICG. 29 January.

————. 2007b. Reforming Afghanistan's Police. Asia Report no. 138. Brussels: ICG. 30 August.

Islamic Republic of Afghanistan. 2004. *Security Sector Paper.* Kabul: Islamic Republic of Afghanistan. 1 April.

————. 2005. *Justice for All: A Ten-Year Strategy for Justice Reform in Afghanistan.* Kabul: Islamic Republic of Afghanistan, Ministry of Justice. October.

————. 2006a. *Afghanistan National Development Strategy Summary Report: An Interim Strategy for Security, Governance, Economic Growth & Poverty Reduction.* Kabul: Islamic Republic of Afghanistan.

————. 2006b. *Implementation of the Afghanistan Compact: Bi-Annual JCMB Report.* Kabul: Islamic Republic of Afghanistan. November.

Jalali, Ali A. 2006. "The Future of Afghanistan." *Parameters.* (Spring).

Lobjakas, Ahto. 2007. "Afghanistan: EU Aid Targets Justice System." Radio Free Europe/Radio Liberty. 12 February.

Morarjee, Rachel. 2006. "Call to Speed Afghan Police Reform." *Financial Times.* 6 June.

Murray, Tonita. 2007. "Police-Building in Afghanistan: A Case Study of Civil Security Building." *International Peacekeeping* 14 (1): 122–23.

Nicola, Stefan. 2007. "Analysis: EU Police Mission Troubled." *United Press International (UPI).* 14 September.

O'Toole, Pam. 2007. "Afghan Police 'Under-equipped.'" *BBC News·Online.* 13 July. http://news.bbc.co.uk/go/pr/fr/-/1/hi/world/south_asia/6897051.stm.

Patel, Seema. 2007. *Breaking Point: Measuring Progress in Afghanistan.* Washington, DC: Center for Security and International Studies.

Rohde, David. 2007. "Afghan Police Are Set Back as Taliban Adapt." *New York Times,* 2 September.

Rome Conference on Justice and Rule of Law in Afghanistan. 2007. Chair's Conclusions. 2–3 July.

Rubin, Barnett R. 2006. "Peace Building and State-Building in Afghanistan: Constructing Sovereignty for Whose Security?" *Third World Quarterly* 27 (1): 175–85.

————. 2007. "Saving Afghanistan." *Foreign Affairs,* January/February.

Sand, Benjamin. 2007. "Afghan Government Recruiting Thousands of Auxiliary Police to Battle Insurgents." *Voice of America.* 10 January.

Sedra, Mark. 2002. *Challenging the Warlord Culture: Security Sector Reform in Afghanistan,* Paper 25. Bonn: Bonn International Center for Conversion.

————. 2004. *Securing Afghanistan's Future: Accomplishments and Strategic Pathway Forward—National Police and Law Enforcement Technical Annex.* Kabul: Islamic Transitional State of Afghanistan.

————. 2006. "Security Sector Reform in Afghanistan: The Slide Toward Expediency." *International Peacekeeping* 13 (March): 94–110.

————. 2007. "Security Sector Reform in Afghanistan: An Instrument of the State-Building Project." In *Fragile States and Insecure People? Violence,*

Security, and Statehood in the Twenty-First Century, ed. Louise Andersen, Bjørn Møller, and Finn Stepputat, 151–76. London: Palgrave-Macmillan.

Sky, Emma. 2006. "The Lead Nation Approach: The Case of Afghanistan." *RUSI Journal.* December.

Thier, Alexander J. 2004. "Re-establishing the Judicial System in Afghanistan." CDDRL Working Paper no. 19, Stanford: Stanford Institute for International Studies.

Tolbert, David with Andrew Solomon. 2006. "United Nations Reform and Supporting the Rule of Law in Developing Countries." *Harvard Human Rights Journal* 19 (Spring): 29–62.

United Nations Assistance Mission for Afghanistan (UNAMA). 2006. Afghanistan Justice Sector Overview, unpublished. June.

——. 2007. *Suicide Attacks in Afghanistan (2001–2007).* Kabul: UNAMA. 9 September.

United Nations Development Programme (UNDP). 2003. *Security Sector Reform and Transitional Justice: A Crisis Post-Conflict Programmatic Approach.* New York: UNDP.

United Nations Secretary-General (UNSG). 2008. The Situation in Afghanistan and its Implications for International Peace and Security, A/62/722-S/2008/159. New York: United Nations. March 6.

United States Department of Defense. 2007. News Briefing with Maj. Gen. Robert Durbin and Deputy Minister Abdul Hadir Khalid from the Pentagon, transcript. 9 January.

United States Government Accountability Office (GAO). 2005. *Afghanistan Security: Efforts to Establish Army and Police Have Made Progress, but Future Plans Need to Be Better Defined.* Washington, DC: GAO.

Wilder, Andrew. 2007. *Cops or Robbers: The Struggle to Reform the Afghan National Police.* Kabul: AREU.

World Bank. 2005. *Afghanistan: Managing Public Finances for Development—Improving Public Finance Management in the Security Sector.* Washington, DC: World Bank.

Wulf, Herbert. 2000. *Security Sector Reform in Developing Countries.* Eschborn, Germany: Deutsche Gesellscaft für Technische Zusammenarbeit (GTZ).

8

Husain Haqqani

Insecurity along the Durand Line

As 2006 drew to a close, violence spiraled in Kabul and the Afghan countryside. Afghanistan's president, Hamid Karzai, stepped up his criticism of Pakistan's role in supporting a resurgent Taliban. "Pakistan hopes to make slaves out of us, but we will not surrender" (*International Herald Tribune* 2006), Karzai declared in a statement that marked the end of quiet diplomacy between two Western allies and the beginning of more public condemnation of Pakistan by Afghanistan.

NATO and UN officials indicated that they sympathized with Karzai's view with diplomatically worded expressions of concern about Pakistan's policies. But most Western governments, notably that of the United States, remained unwilling to publicly put pressure on Pakistan's military ruler, General Pervez Musharraf, or to acknowledge that the roots of Afghanistan's security problems lie in Pakistan.

Musharraf responded by recounting the many ways he has assisted the United States in the war against terrorism and insisted that the Afghans should "avoid the blame game" and work with Pakistan in dealing with a shared problem. One of Musharraf's cabinet ministers, Sheikh Rashid Ahmad, went further. He told a public rally, "This person [Karzai] spent his exile days during the Soviet invasion of Afghanistan, enjoying the lavish hospitality of Pakistan, and who also won his presidency due to favour and intimation of President Musharraf. While today he has the temerity to indulge in a free blame game about Taliban intrusion into Afghanistan" (*Pak-Tribune* 2006).

It is true that Pakistan cannot fully control its complex 1590-mile (2450-kilometre) border with Afghanistan. Equally true are credible reports of Pakistan's tolerance and, in some cases, active support for its former Taliban protégés. Pakistan's powerful security services, notably the Inter-Services Intelligence (ISI), have never liked the idea of removing the Taliban from power.

In the aftermath of the 9/11 attacks, Pakistan became a reluctant US ally, and the ISI took some action against al-Qaeda. But Pakistan did little to fight the Afghan Taliban. Pakistani efforts against pro-al-Qaeda tribesmen were undermined by divisions within Musharraf's government and the presence of a strong faction that seeks accommodation with pro-Taliban Pashtun tribes on the Pakistani side of the Pakistan–Afghan border.

The military operations conducted by the Pakistani army in the traditionally autonomous tribal areas straddling the border have negatively impacted the social and power structures among the tribes. The failure to succeed militarily in the South and North Waziristan tribal regions led the Musharraf regime to seek ceasefire agreements and peace deals with tribal elders that have ended up empowering and legitimizing the local Taliban and religious leaders (mullahs) that back them. These operations have also been criticized as being excessive in their use of force and viewed as a betrayal by the local tribal leaders.

The Pakistani army seems too focused on technological enhancements (like artillery, precision-guided munitions) rather than on enhancing its human element while engaging in the Federally Administered Tribal Areas (FATA). The region has become a "state within a state," with the local Taliban and tribal leaders having a separate system of taxation and justice. The Pakistani federal government has been unable to reverse this.

The Pakistan–Afghan relationship has, to a large extent, been shaped by the historic legacy of the British Raj in India and the insecurity of the Pakistani state since its emergence from the Raj as an independent country in 1947. Pakistan's role, with US help, as the staging ground for guerilla war against the Soviet Union in Afghanistan is widely known. After the withdrawal of Soviet troops, Pakistan continued to support hard-line Islamist *Mujahideen* in the ensuing civil war, leading to the rise to power of the Taliban. But Pakistan's involvement in Afghanistan was not just the inadvertent consequence of America's proxy war against the Soviet Union. Pakistan was concerned with extending its influence into Afghanistan long before the arrival of Soviet troops in Afghanistan.

The Pakistan–Afghanistan border was demarcated in 1893 as the frontier of the British Raj in India. After independence, Pakistani leaders had assumed that Pakistan would inherit the functions of India's British government in guiding Afghan policy. But Afghanistan responded to the emergence of Pakistan by questioning its rationale. Afghanistan voted against Pakistan's admission to the United Nations. It argued that the treaty that demarcated Afghanistan's current border with Pakistan was no longer valid because a new country had been created where none existed at the time the treaty was signed under British coercion.

Afghanistan's initial reluctance to recognize Pakistan and the Afghan claim on Pakistani territory inhabited by Pashtun tribes along their border added to the psychological insecurity of Pakistani leaders, who already believed that India sought to undo partition. The prospect of Afghanistan stirring the ethnic cauldron in Pakistan, with Indian backing, became part of the list of challenges that had to be dealt with in forging Pakistan's identity as an independent state. Pakistan emphasized its Islamic ideology in the hope of blunting the challenge of ethnic nationalism supported by Afghanistan, tied Afghan aspirations in relation to "Pashtunistan" with an Indian plan to break up Pakistan, and sought US assistance in pursuing an agenda of regional pre-eminence.

Since its independence, Pakistan has been fearful of Afghan officials collaborating with India to squeeze Pakistan, through a kind of pincer movement. Even now, Pakistani support or tolerance for the Taliban is often privately justified by Pakistani officials as being connected to pre-empting an Afghan–Indian threat to Pakistan's existence.

Pashtunistan

Afghanistan's frontier with British India was drawn by a British civil servant, Sir Mortimer Durand, in 1893 and agreed upon by representatives of both governments. The border, named the Durand Line, intentionally divided Pashtun tribes living in the area to prevent them from becoming a nuisance for the Raj. On their side of the frontier, the British created autonomous tribal agencies, controlled by British political officers with the help of tribal chieftains whose loyalty was ensured through regular subsidies. The British used force to put down the sporadic uprisings in the tribal areas but generally left the tribes alone in return for stability along the frontier.

After the partition of India, Afghanistan supported the calls for creating "Pashtunistan," which would link the Pashtun tribes living in Afghanistan with those in the North-West Frontier Province (NWFP) and Baluchistan. There were also ambiguous demands for a Baluch state "linking Baluch areas in Pakistan and Iran with a small strip of adjacent Baluch territory in Afghanistan" (Cordovez and Harrison 1995, 14). The most outspoken advocate of this irredentist claim was Sardar Mohammad Daoud, cousin of

King Zahir Shah, who also served as his prime minister for several years before becoming president of Afghanistan in a coup d'état in 1973.

From Pakistan's perspective, demands for Pashtunistan amounted to demanding the greater part of Pakistan's territory and were clearly unacceptable. The Afghan demand failed to generate international backing, and Afghanistan did not have the military means to force Pakistan's hand.

At the time, Afghanistan had a population of twelve million and a small military, which could not constitute a threat to Pakistan. The international community generally backed Pakistan. Britain insisted that its treaties with Afghanistan remained valid for the lawful successor state, Pakistan, and Afghanistan did not formally take its claim to the United Nations. But, given the overall feeling of insecurity felt by Pakistan's leadership about the future of their fledgling state, Afghanistan and its demand for Pashtunistan became part of the combination of perceived security threats that required Pakistan's military build-up backed by great power alliances.

Although India did not publicly support the Afghan claim, Pakistan's early leaders could not separate the Afghan questioning of Pakistani borders from their perception of an Indian grand design against Pakistan. Ian Stephens, a pro-Pakistan British author, explained Pakistani fears when he wrote, "if on Pakistan's birth coordinated movements opposed to her could be produced in Kashmir and Afghanistan, both of them predominantly Muslim territories and near to one another, the new state might be still-born, sort of crushed by a sort of pincer movement" (Stephens 1953, 108). Pakistan's military adopted the doctrine of "dual containment," which meant guarding against possible Indian military invasion as well as against Afghan subversion.

In addition to the Pashtunistan issue, Pakistan's pursuit of alliance with the United States during the 1950s also had a bearing on its relations with Afghanistan and on Afghanistan's own subsequent direction. The lure of Pakistan as a security partner in Cold War containment strategy led to the neglect of Afghanistan in US diplomacy and foreign assistance. The Pakistanis developed an interest in painting a menacing picture of Soviet influence in Afghanistan to bolster their own position as the first line of defence against Soviet expansion into South Asia.

The early view of Pakistan's military–bureaucratic leadership toward Afghanistan was summarized by Aslam Siddiqi, an official with Pakistan's Bureau of National Reconstruction (established by Pakistan's first military regime as a think tank closely associated with the intelligence services) in a policy book published in 1960:

> Afghanistan...has a very great and special importance for Pakistan...the safety of the Indo-Pakistan subcontinent has depended on the degree of in-

fluence, which its rulers could wield on the areas round about the mountains of the Hindukush.... Mr. Fraser Tytler is so much impressed by the danger from beyond the Hindukush that, in his opinion, nothing but concerted action by Afghanistan and Pakistan can prevent it. He writes: "the remedy is the fusion of the two states of Afghanistan and Pakistan in some way or other. It may be argued that, given the differences in mental and political outlook of the two states, such fusion is impossible. This may be so. But history suggests that fusion will take place, if not peacefully, then by force." ... Fusion by force will mean confusion, which will inevitably lead to the ruination of both the states. Such possibilities in fact are tied up with the controversy of racialism versus ideology within the Islamic civilization. If Islam is again to become a force, Islamic ideology must triumph over racialism. (52)

The Pakistani response to fears of India and Afghanistan working together to pose an existential threat to Pakistan was a forward policy aimed at the fusion of Pakistan and Afghanistan. Given that secular Pashtun and Afghan nationalism was not favourably disposed to the idea of Pakistan, the two states fusion could only be possible under an Islamic banner.

Development versus Strategic Depth

Afghanistan's elite was searching for international partners for development just as Pakistan sought strategic depth for security. While Pakistan portrayed itself as the first line of defence against Soviet expansion into South Asia to win over the United States, Afghanistan was engaged in clumsy diplomacy of its own, seeking an external patron to substitute the British.

The British Indian Empire had helped Afghan rulers maintain control and manage what little development Afghanistan had seen in the first half of the twentieth century. With Britain's withdrawal from South Asia, Afghanistan's royal family needed someone else to carry the burden of military and economic assistance.

The Afghan search for an alternative foreign source of support was partly undermined by Afghanistan's confrontation with Pakistan and partly by inadequate attention from Washington. The United States, seeking alliance with much larger Pakistan, chose to neglect Afghanistan and "inadvertently pushed Afghanistan towards rapprochement with the U.S.S.R." (Roberts 2004, 165).

The Afghan leader accepting Soviet assistance was none other than Sardar Mohammad Daoud, who became prime minister in 1953. Daoud had emerged as the principal advocate of Pashtunistan. It was easy, therefore, for Pakistan to claim that the demand for Pashtunistan and Soviet penetration were interlinked. Pakistan had already positioned itself as the critical American ally in the region, and its perceptions of Afghanistan began to influence the US view of developments there.

Pakistan's military elite saw Afghanistan as a potential Pakistani sphere of influence. Instead of helping to roll back Soviet influence in Afghanistan by befriending its royalist regime, Pakistan's security services highlighted Soviet inroads into Afghanistan to prove Pakistan's usefulness in American containment strategy.

Securing US assistance was not the only reason for Pakistan's early focus on Afghanistan. Soon after independence, Pakistan's military had become concerned about the lack of depth in Pakistan's land defences. Pakistan's early military leaders were trained as part of the British Indian army, with strategic doctrines that suited the Raj. The British Empire was global and plans for its defence could rely on one part of the empire springing into action to protect the other. Furthermore, the Empire's defence strategy for India envisaged a single unit stretching from the frontier with Afghanistan in the west to Burma in the east.

From 1958 onward, Pakistan's generals became the country's rulers, independent of civilian oversight. They applied their training in defending the empire to defend a much smaller country, divided until 1971 in two wings, and threatened from what was originally the heartland of the British Empire—the post-partition state of India. The Pakistani generals' notion that East Pakistan could be defended against India with a strong and impregnable base in West Pakistan proved deeply flawed, especially when put to the test during the India–Pakistan wars of 1965 and 1971. Their other strategic belief about the fusion of the defence of Afghanistan and Pakistan led to Pakistan's complicated role in Afghanistan, beginning well before the Soviet invasion of 1979 or through the rise and fall of the Taliban.

It is commonly believed that Pakistan developed an interest in creating a client regime in Afghanistan after playing a key role in the anti-Soviet *Jihad* during the 1980s. But Pakistan's pursuit of "strategic depth" in Afghanistan began soon after independence. Pakistan clashed with Afghanistan sporadically from 1947 over Afghan propaganda on behalf of Pashtunistan.

Episodic tribal insurgencies in Baluchistan and NWFP provided Afghanistan with an opportunity to create difficulties for Pakistan and, instead of dealing with the local factors giving rise to the revolts, Pakistan put the blame for these insurgencies on India and Afghanistan. In Pakistan's tribal regions, Pakistani officials emphasized Islam as the unifying force "in spite of foreign attempts at subversion" (Siddiqi 1960, 45), deploying *Ulema* (clerics) and *Mashaikh* (hereditary spiritual leaders) to combat tribal sentiment among the Baluch and the Pashtun. Pakistani repression drove

Baluch and Pashtun nationalists to align with left-wing intellectuals and activists, gradually making Pakistani claims of Communist influence along the Durand line a self-fulfilling prophesy.

In addition, Afghanistan's acceptance of greater levels of Soviet aid and inclusion of Afghan Communists in its government alarmed the United States. Soon the CIA, ISI, and the secret service of the Shah of Iran, SAVAK, were running clandestine operations in Kabul, making it an arena for Cold War rivalries and intrigue. In the words of Selig Harrison, "As factionalism, corruption, and political uncertainty grew, externally backed forces began to jockey for position in preparation for the power struggle expected to follow the elderly Daoud's death" (1994, 14).

Pakistan Plays the "Great Game"

Pakistan's allies or instruments of influence in this new "great game" of intrigue were Afghan Islamists. Religious sentiment had always been strong in Afghanistan and had been a crucial factor in the opposition to British influence through much of the nineteenth century. Among the political factions that emerged in Afghanistan with the introduction of an elected parliament in the 1960s were the communist People's Democratic Party of Afghanistan (PDPA) and Islamist groupings that "set out to establish a political movement that would work for the creation of an Islamic state based on Sharia law" (Harrison 1995, 15).

In 1972, Jamiat-i Islami Afghanistan (Islamic Society of Afghanistan) emerged from the informal Islamist groupings that had existed since the 1960s. Led by Burhanuddin Rabbani, a professor of theology at Kabul University, Jamiat-i Islami Afghanistan was closely linked to Pakistan's Jamaat-e Islami. Rabbani was an ethnic Tajik. His Pakistani supporters considered him suitable not only for influencing Afghanistan but also for igniting the flames of Islamic revolution among fellow Tajiks inside the Soviet Union. Rabbani's early followers included two Kabul University students, Ahmed Shah Massoud and Gulbuddin Hekmatyar, both of whom played a significant role in subsequent events in Afghanistan.

After the 1973 republican coup that brought Sardar Muhammad Daoud to power, Jamiat-i Islami questioned Communist influence in the Afghan Republic and resisted Daoud's secular orientation. Daoud ordered the arrest of Rabbani, who fled to Pakistan with most of his key supporters. In Pakistan, Rabbani's group was initially hosted by the Jamaat-i Islami. Soon after their arrival in Peshawar in 1973, Rabbani and his associates were provided financial support by the Inter-Services Intelligence (ISI), and some of his associates were given military training. To maintain deniability in case the Pakistan army and the ISI were blamed for destabilizing

Afghanistan, management of the covert operation was initially assigned to the paramilitary Frontier Scouts. After arriving in Peshawar and signing up for Pakistani support, the Afghan Islamists found dissension in their ranks. In 1976, Hekmatyar split off from Jamiat-i Islami Afghanistan to form the Hizb-i Islami (Islamic Party), which also operated from Pakistan.

Between 1973 and 1977, Afghanistan and Pakistan fought what can best be described as a low-intensity proxy war. Daoud supported Baluch rebels in Pakistan, while Pakistan backed the Afghan Islamist insurgents based in Peshawar. In the aftermath of the Soviet invasion of Afghanistan in 1979, the Pakistan-sponsored Islamist rebellion became the American-backed *Jihad* against Soviet occupation. The massive covert operation in support of the Afghan *Mujahideen* enhanced Pakistan's value as an American ally. Brigadier Mohammad Yousaf, who ran ISI's Afghan operation between 1983 and 1987, later explained that General Zia-ul Haq's motives in agreeing to make Afghanistan a Soviet Vietnam were not exclusively related to global security. Regime survival and Pakistan's traditional policy paradigm of seeking leadership in the Muslim world, securing national unity through Islam, and obtaining Western economic and military assistance were also factors that weighed in his decision (Yousaf and Adkin 1995, 25–26).

By the end of 1980, almost one million Afghans had come to Pakistan as refugees. By 1988, the number of refugees reached three million. These refugees had fled Afghanistan because of the upheaval following the Soviet invasion. As the *Mujahideen*'s guerilla attacks made Afghanistan unsafe for Russian and Afghan Communist forces, security in small towns and the countryside became fragile. Some of the refugees were religiously minded subsistence farmers escaping the godlessness of Communism at the urging of village clerics. Middle-class professionals, landowners, small shopkeepers, civil servants, royalist military officers, and businessmen also joined the flood of refugees headed toward Pakistan and Iran.

Pakistan housed Afghan refugees in tented villages, mainly in the NWFP and Baluchistan. Their expenses were paid for primarily by the United Nations High Commissioner for Refugees. A Pakistani civil servant was also appointed Commissioner for Afghan Refugees to administer the provision of basic services to the refugees. Pakistani officials gave the *Mujahideen* groups an unofficial role in registering refugees upon their arrival in Pakistan. This created a linkage between access to refugee aid and membership in one of the seven *Mujahideen* parties that Pakistan recognized.

In addition to the Jamiat-i Islami and Hizb-i Islami, which had already been active since 1973, two other fundamentalist parties had emerged by the time US and Arab aid started flowing through Pakistan. One was the Ittehad-i Islami (Islamic Union) led by the Wahabi cleric Abdur Rab Rasool Sayyaf. The other was a faction of Hizb-i Islami led by an elderly Pashtun theologian, Yunus Khalis, who broke away from Hekmatyar's group in 1979. In addition, there were three moderate groups led by conservative leaders who did not share the radical worldview of the Islamists.

Although Pakistan allowed all seven groups to operate, it clearly favoured the two factions it had worked with the longest—Jamiat-i Islami and Hekmatyar's Hizb-i Islami. Over time, Pakistani officials set up the education system for refugees in a manner that converted young Afghans to the cause of *Jihad* and the Islamist worldview. Zia-ul Haq also encouraged Islamist charities from Saudi Arabia and the Gulf to invest in building mosques and *madrasas* (seminaries) both for Afghan refugees and Pakistan's own population.

As the scope of the Afghan *Jihad* expanded, so did the influence of Islamist ideology in Pakistan. Ever mindful of the need to retain control, Zia-ul Haq made sure that Jamaat-e Islami was not the only Pakistani party involved with the Afghan refugees and militants. A faction of the Jamiat Ulema Islam (JUI—Society of Islamic Scholars) comprising clerics from the influential Deoband School joined in the distribution of charity received from Arab countries to set up madrasas. In his Pan-Islamic zeal, Zia-ul Haq allowed volunteers from all over the world to come and train alongside the Afghan *Mujahideen*.

The most significant arrival in Pakistan at the time was that of the Palestinian scholar Abdullah Azzam, who created the Maktab al-Khidmaat (services bureau) to facilitate the participation of foreign *Mujahideen* in the Afghan Jihad. Azzam cited the Quran and Hadith to remind Muslims of their obligation to assist the *Jihad*. Osama bin Laden, scion of a prosperous Saudi business family, was one of many moved by Azzam's call. He moved to Pakistan in 1984 and started funding the Services Bureau. His contributions increased the number of foreign recruits for *Mujahideen* activities.

Once the United States decided to supply sophisticated ground-to-air missiles to the *Mujahideen* in 1986, airpower—the Soviet Union's one major advantage against the *Mujahideen*—became ineffective. The *Mujahideen* were described as "freedom fighters" in the international media and their successes were a symbol of Soviet humiliation. By 1987–88, the Americans had achieved their objective in Afghanistan and the Soviets, now led by the reformer Mikhail Gorbachev, were willing to negotiate a way out of their Afghan quagmire.

Pakistan's prime minister, Muhammad Khan Junejo, encouraged by US diplomats, accepted in April 1988 a deal negotiated through the United Nations for the withdrawal of Soviet troops from Afghanistan. Zia-ul Haq and the ISI insisted that any agreement for Soviet withdrawal should also address the issue of who would rule Afghanistan after the departure of the Soviets. The accords signed at Geneva, however, left that question unresolved. American officials maintained that the PDPA regime in Kabul would fall to the *Mujahideen* within weeks of the withdrawal of Soviet military protection. Zia-ul Haq was certain that the *Mujahideen* would end up fighting among themselves.

At the heart of Zia-ul Haq's objections was the fear that once Soviet military presence was gone, the United States would no longer support his vision of an Islamic fundamentalist Afghanistan closely tied to Pakistan. Zia-ul Haq had "hoped to force a political settlement while the superpowers were still engaged" (Kux 2001, 287). He wanted the Americans to pay Pakistan its due for helping defeat the Soviets by installing his preferred Afghan leader, the Islamist Gulbuddin Hekmatyar, at the head of an Afghan *Mujahideen* coalition government. The Americans wanted to do no such thing and were content with declaring victory now that the Soviets were leaving Afghanistan.

On 17 August 1988 General Zia-ul Haq and several of his key generals died in a mysterious plane crash. With the death of Zia-ul Haq, Pakistan's military and the ISI did not give up *Jihad* or the pursuit of strategic depth in Afghanistan. Islam as a factor in Pakistan's national security policy grew significantly during the period of *Jihad* against the Soviet Union. The much enlarged ISI—its covert operations capability enhanced ten-fold—became a greater factor in Pakistan's domestic and foreign policies. Pakistan's military and security services were deeply influenced by their close ties to the Islamist groups.

Enter the Taliban

Following Zia's death in 1988, Pakistan had eleven years of chaotic democracy. The ISI played a role in making and breaking civilian governments led alternately by Benazir Bhutto, daughter of the prime minister Zulfikar Ali Bhutto—the man Zia-ul Haq had overthrown and executed—and Nawaz Sharif, a Zia protégé who developed an independent power base over the years. The Bhutto and Sharif governments essentially followed the military's lead in dealing with Afghanistan and India. When Bhutto, in her first term (1988–90) and Sharif during his second stint in office (1997–99) attempted to mend fences with India, the military orchestrated their removal from office.

The collapse of the Soviet Union was followed in 1992 by the collapse of the Najibullah regime in Afghanistan, paving the way for a civil war between *Mujahideen* factions for the control of Kabul. Pakistan's efforts to secure a leading role for its protegé Hekmatyar failed, and Hekmatyar did not advance his cause with his reckless rocket attacks on Kabul's inhabitants. Hekmatyar mobilized support on the basis of his Pashtun ethnicity, while his rival, Commander Ahmad Shah Massoud of Jamiat-i Islami, ended up rallying non-Pashtun groups including Tajiks, Uzbeks, and Hazaras.

By 1994, the Afghan civil war had devastated Kabul and driven the Afghan countryside into anarchy. The central government existed only in name and Afghanistan was divided into the domains of various warlords. At this point, former students of religious seminaries in Pakistan organized themselves into the Taliban movement and launched a *Jihad* ostensibly to restore order to Afghanistan. Pakistan's ISI backed the Taliban with arms, training, and money, and enabled them, by 1996, to take control of Kabul. Pakistan also persuaded Saudi Arabia and the United Arab Emirates to recognize the Taliban regime, which had failed to secure much international support because of its obscurantist stance and human rights violations. Pakistan served as the Taliban's principal backer until it was forced into alliance with the United States in the aftermath of the 11 September 2001 terrorist attacks in New York and Washington, DC.

In his memoir, General Musharraf makes it clear that Pakistan's decision to abandon the Taliban was made after the US threatened that Pakistan "should be prepared to be bombed to the Stone Age" (2006, 201). Pakistan has co-operated extensively with the US and other Western nations in detaining alleged members and leaders of al-Qaeda and its associated terrorist groups. But its attitude toward the Taliban has remained sympathetic if not outright supportive. By allowing the Taliban to regroup and mount insurgent attacks across the border, Pakistan hopes to make it clear to the Afghan leaders such as Hamid Karzai that they cannot stabilize their country without Pakistan's help.

At the same time, Pakistan does not want the situation to reach the point of inviting US reprisals. In addition, Pakistan continues to use FATA as its base for building influence in Afghanistan. Pakistani policy appears to be that there is no need to revisit the legitimacy of the Durand Line. In addition, Pakistan wants to continue using FATA as a semi-settled, partially autonomous region not fully controlled by Pakistani central authorities.

In order to maintain its influence in Afghanistan, Pakistan has over the years relied on networks built by its Inter Services Intelligence (ISI) directorate. Even after Pakistan reversed its support for the Taliban, many pro-Taliban officials in the ISI, some serving and many retired, continued to be the conduit for support to the Taliban. ISI is believed even today to view the Taliban as their "best bet" to achieve "strategic depth" in the region.

Afghanistan has regularly accused Pakistan of tolerating militant recruitment and training camps within its territory. Top Taliban commanders find sanctuary within Pakistan, and Islamabad's efforts to prevent infiltration by these elements are often seen as insincere by their neighbour. Taliban leaders roam freely in Quetta, Baluchistan, and their fighters often find shelter in the border areas of Pakistan–Afghanistan after fights with coalition forces in Afghanistan (United States, White House Fact Sheet 2007).

In September 2006, after NATO forces had fought the bloodiest battle in five years with the Taliban in Afghanistan (codenamed Operation Medusa), several NATO commanders demanded that their governments get tough with Pakistan over the support and sanctuary the ISI was providing the Taliban. NATO reportedly believes that there is an entire Taliban support structure in Baluchistan. The ISI support is said to run the gamut from training camps to ammunition dumps, meeting places of the Quetta *Shura*, and arrival points for new weapons. According to General Rahim Wardak, Afghanistan's defence minister, "Taliban decision making and all its logistics are all inside Pakistan" (Rashid 2007).

In November 2006, some Pakistani officials even urged NATO countries to accept the Taliban and to work toward a new coalition government in Afghanistan inclusive of the Taliban. Lt. Gen. Ali Mohammed Jan Orakzai, governor of the North Western Frontier Province, has told several reporters that to him the Taliban represent the Pashtuns, Afghanistan's largest ethnic group, and all they are doing is leading a resistance movement against foreign occupation forces.

A large part of the funding for the Taliban comes from the illegal but booming opium trade along the Pakistan–Afghanistan border. They have been able to buy sophisticated arms and even surface-to-air missiles to increase their fighting capabilities. Their most important leadership council is the *Shura* (consultative body) based in Quetta. It reportedly oversees the insurgency in the Taliban heartlands of Kandahar, Uruzgan, and Helmand. Three members of the Taliban *Shura*, Mullah Dadullah Akhund, Mullah Akhtar Usmani, and Qari Faiz Mohammad, have been killed in the last two years while on their way to or from Pakistan.

The death in May 2007 of Taliban commander Mullah Dadullah in Afghanistan during a coalition raid set in motion a major change within the Taliban's command structure. In June 2007 Mullah Omar laid down new guidelines that forbade members of the Taliban central military command from operating in southwestern Afghanistan and gave group commanders control of specific districts to develop their own decentralized military strategy. According to one account, Mullah Omar outlined the new chain of command to comprise the district committees, Taliban-appointed provincial "governors," and the Taliban's central command council. The Taliban are also said to have decided to discourage personality cults like Dadullah's, as the death of a "hero" demoralizes his followers. Omar has also appointed four spokesmen to decentralize the Taliban's media-information wing. Each spokesman would look after only a specific zone so that in case of his arrest, only information about that zone would pass on to the Afghan government or NATO. Each of the spokesmen will also use the same name, currently Qari Yousuf Ahmedi (Shahzad 2007).

Pakistani Taliban

As a result of decades of Islamist activity along the Pakistan–Afghan border, groups with ideological affinity with the Afghan Taliban and al-Qaeda have organized themselves on the Pakistani border. These Pakistani Taliban have set up a parallel administration in some parts of the tribal area, enforcing Sharia rule. They also impose taxes on certain businesses in return for protection. Taliban *Shuras* have been set up in different Pakistani tribal agencies and districts. Under US pressure, Pakistan conducted military operations against the Taliban, especially those offering protection to foreign fighters from al-Qaeda. After heavy casualties among government troops, peace agreements were signed with tribal elders and Taliban leaders, as a result of which Pakistani Taliban have consolidated themselves in both South and North Waziristan and have spread to other FATA agencies as well as adjoining towns like Tank, Dera Ismail Khan, Bannu, Kohat, and the Dir and Malakand region.

The first Pakistani peace accord signed in 2004 was aimed at neutralizing Maulvi Nek Muhammad and his Taliban forces in South Waziristan. Nek Muhammad was, however, killed in a missile attack by either the United States or Pakistani forces, leading to the breakdown of the ceasefire. Then, after renewed fighting that resulted once again in heavy losses for both sides a new peace accord was signed on 7 February 2005 between the government and Baitullah Mehsud, who succeeded Nek Muhammad as the Taliban's main backer among the Mehsud tribe. Under this agreement, Mehsud and his followers laid down their arms in a tribal jirga meeting, pledging not to provide any assistance to foreign (i.e., non-Pakistani) militants and promising not to launch any operations against the government forces.

On 5 September 2006 a separate peace agreement was signed by the government and the insurgent militants, this time in the North Waziristan tribal area. The peace agreement pledged to halt cross-border movement of fighters into Afghanistan and to end attacks on government installations and security forces. The three-page agreement contained sixteen clauses and four sub-clauses. One of the clauses read: "There shall be no cross-border movement for militant activity in neighbouring Afghanistan"

(Gul 2006). The government, for its part, pledged to resolve issues through local customs and traditions and also promised not to undertake any ground or air operation against the militants.

The Pakistani government insisted that the agreement would secure the help of the tribesmen against al-Qaeda. The agreement provided that foreigners living in North Waziristan would have to leave Pakistani territory, or if they could not leave then they could live peacefully by respecting the law of the land and the agreement. The terms laid down also said that the Pakistan army would no longer man the checkposts in the region and would be replaced by the tribal militias known as the *khasadars* and *Levies*. Both the army and the militants agreed to return each other's weapons, vehicles, and communication tools seized during previous military operations.

The government undertook to pay compensation for seized weapons and ammunition and promised to release prisoners caught during its military action. Payment was also approved to compensate for the loss of life and property of any innocent tribesmen killed by the military. In return, the pro-Taliban tribal leaders agreed that militants would not enter any settled districts adjacent to the agency. The tribal leaders also promised that there would be no attack on state property or law enforcement personnel. According to the wording of the agreement, "There will be no target killing and no parallel administration in the agency. The writ of the state will prevail in the area" (Gul 2006). Quite clearly, Pakistani authorities had accepted to ignore past challenges to the writ of the state and agreed to pay huge sums of money in compensation to secure the tribes' vague commitment to formally remain part of Pakistan.

The tribal people saw the peace accords as a victory for the Taliban. Instead of taking a back seat and letting central government representatives exercise the writ of the state, Pakistani Taliban continued to roam in open trucks solving the day-to-day problems of the people and bypassing administration officials appointed by the central government. The Waziristan region, especially North Waziristan, has become a very strong base for al-Qaeda and Taliban fighters on the run also due to the large number of *madrassas* in the region.

Spoilers in Afghanistan

Gulbuddin Hekmatyar, who had moved to Iran while the Taliban ruled Afghanistan, has resurfaced as the leader of the anti-Western resistance in some provinces of Afghanistan. He has given interviews on Pakistani television and issued statements claiming that he is based inside Afghanistan. In one interview, Hekmatyar took credit on behalf of his Hizb-i Islami for helping Osama bin Laden escape from his mountain redoubt at Tora Bora soon after the fall of Kabul to the Northern Alliance. The ease with which

Hekmatyar's faction of Hizb-i Islami manages to orchestrate publicity in Pakistan suggests that he might be located in Pakistan, as Afghan officials claim. In the summer of 2007, Hekmatyar announced that he would be willing to negotiate with the Karzai government provided the focus of talks was on re-establishing Afghan sovereignty and the complete withdrawal of foreign forces.

Another former Pakistani protégé, Jalaluddin Haqqani, is also believed to operate his own insurgent network against NATO troops and the Karzai regime. Haqqani was a major commander of the Hizb-i Islami faction led by Maulvi Yunus Khalis during the war against the Soviets. He is influential in the provinces of Paktia and Paktika bordering Pakistan, and his network draws strength from his Jadran tribe. Haqqani was educated at a Pakistani madrassa and is believed to retain significant contacts both within Pakistan's religious political parties and the security establishment. He served as a minister in the last days of Taliban rule in Afghanistan but now operates independent of them. Jalaluddin Haqqani maintains close ties with Pakistani Taliban leaders from Waziristan, Bajaur, and Kurram.

The major spoilers in Afghanistan are, however, still the Taliban. After being toppled from power in the aftermath of 9/11, the Taliban have reconstituted in parts of the Afghan countryside as an insurgent force. In October 2005, after the death of eighty-four American soldiers and 1,400 Afghans since the beginning of the year, Pakistani authorities announced the arrest in Quetta of Taliban spokesman Abdul Latif Hakimi. Officials in Afghanistan were not impressed. They wondered why it had taken the Pakistanis so long to silence Hakimi when he had operated freely in Pakistan for over two years. Pakistan's decision to arrest the Taliban spokesman was attributed to relentless US pressure. Western and Afghan officials realize that it will be difficult to bring lasting peace to Afghanistan if the Taliban and other enemies of President Hamid Karzai's government continue to find sanctuary in Pakistan. But it is difficult to prove official Pakistani support for Afghan insurgents. The rise of the Pakistani Taliban, and the difficulties they pose for their own country, provides Pakistani officials the argument that Pakistan lacks the capacity but not the will to restrain infiltration across the border into Afghanistan.

During the war against the Soviets, Pakistan's military leader General Zia-ul Haq had adopted a policy that would bleed the Soviets without goading them into direct confrontation with Pakistan. Pakistani intelligence officers then used the metaphor "the water must not get too hot" to describe that policy. It is plausible that Pakistan is pursuing a similar policy in relation to Afghanistan today. By allowing the Taliban to regroup and mount insurgent attacks across the border, Pakistan hopes to make it clear to Afghan leaders such as Karzai that they cannot stabilize their country without Pakistan's help. At the same time, Pakistan does not want the situation to reach the point of inviting US reprisals.

Pakistan's attitude toward Afghanistan was formed largely by historic developments of the nineteenth century, when Britain and Russia competed for influence in Central Asia in what came to be known as the "Great Game" of espionage and proxy wars. Resurgent Taliban, now willing to conduct suicide bombings, continue to threaten the security of Afghanistan and few people are convinced that Pakistan is not involved in their resurgence. For their part, Pakistani officials have called for the fencing of Pakistan's border with Afghanistan, claiming that it would be the ultimate solution to the problem of infiltration by Taliban and other terrorists. In 2005, Pakistani foreign minister Khurshid Mahmud Kasuri said, "Pakistan can do nothing more than that [building the fence] to prevent incursions. We are fed up of people who say we have to do more" (CNN 2005).

It is not clear how successful this fence would be in stopping the flow of human traffic across the Pakistan–Afghan border, if it is built at all. Ostensibly, the proposed fence would start from the point of convergence of the frontiers of Pakistan, Iran, and Afghanistan and extend to Pakistan's border with the Chinese territory of Xinjiang, passing on the way the Wakhan Corridor where the Hindu Kush and the Pamirs meet. Building a 2500 kilometre–long fence along a forbidding mountainous terrain would be expensive. Apart from the terrain and expense, the proposal to build a fence would also have to take into account the division of Pashtun tribes that live on both sides of the Durand line.

Different approaches to the Durand Line remain a cause of disagreement between Pakistan and Afghanistan. Accepting the fencing would mean the Afghan government's final acceptance of the border. From Pakistan's point of view, the border is already settled, and the only problem remaining is the Afghan insinuation that it might not be legitimate, in view of the colonial legacy. In April 2007, when the Pakistani government tried to fence thirty-five kilometres of the 2500-kilometre border, official Afghan and Pakistani troops exchange fire. The governor of Paktika province of Afghanistan, Mohammad Akram Khpalwak, said, "First of all, we cannot accept the [Durand] line." He added, "It is not demarcated and not clear where the border is. So [the Durand Line] is the basic issue. For solving the Durand Line issue, the problems of [ethnic-Pashtun] tribes living on both sides should be considered and they must be consulted. So it is [a] very complicated issue and must be determined by the [ethnic-Pashtun] tribes living on both sides of the line" (*Radio Free Europe/Radio Liberty* 2007).

In addition to proposals for building a fence, Pakistani officials also claim that it is the presence of large numbers of Afghan refugees (rather than considered Pakistani policy) that is responsible for the Taliban resurgence in Pakistan. It is estimated that of the over three million Afghan refugees that have lived in Pakistan in the almost twenty-five years since the Soviet military intervention of 1979, almost two million are still living there.

Since 2002, the United Nations High Commissioner for Refugees (UNHCR) has helped repatriate Afghan refugees in Pakistan. A tripartite agreement signed between UNHCR and the governments of Pakistan and Afghanistan governs the voluntary repatriation process that started in 2002. The underlying principle was voluntary and gradual return so as to ensure that those who go home can be absorbed into Afghanistan and do not flow back into Pakistan. Many refugees, however, do not want to go back to a war-ravaged country, and Pakistan remains reluctant to absorb them into its own population.

In 2006, Pakistani Foreign Minister Kasuri asked for the creation of a multi-billion dollar fund to help repatriate and rehabilitate the remaining Afghan refugees. He said, "We've suggested to the Americans that they are spending so much money, maybe it would cost $4–5bn to create the right conditions for these people to go back to Afghanistan. If you take the refugees away, let's say, in two or three years, then at least once these people go away, there will be no easy refuge [for Afghan insurgents in Pakistan]" (BBC News 2006).

Continuation of Forward Policy?

Afghan leaders and Pakistani critics of official Pakistani policy do not accept official rationalizations for why Afghan Taliban continue to find safe haven in Pakistan and about the rise of Pakistan's own Taliban. From the critics' point of view, Pakistan still continues to pursue its "forward policy" of penetrating Afghanistan with the purpose of pre-empting a Pashtun nationalist challenge to Pakistani nationhood. Pakistan started supporting Islamist ideologues in the hope of weakening Pashtun ethnic identity and substituting it with an Islamic one. In the process, an Islamist Pashtun identity has been born, and although some Taliban periodically threaten Pakistani authority, Pakistani officialdom (notably the ISI) is unwilling to change the basic premises of Pakistan's policy toward Afghanistan.

Pakistani efforts to stem the Taliban tide have been half-hearted at best. In the six years since 9/11, Pakistan has arrested only one principal Afghan Taliban leader and has summarily dismissed reports of Taliban leaders moving around freely in the country. Mullah Obaidullah Akhund, the Taliban No. 3 who was detained in the Pakistani city of Quetta in February 2007, freely gave interviews to Pakistani and international media for over three years before being caught during US vice-president Dick Cheney's visit to Pakistan (Roggio 2007).

Pakistani officials concede privately that Pakistan does not want to be left without an option in Afghanistan in case the Karzai government fails. Pakistan has voiced concern about close relations between Afghanistan and India, an echo from the past when Pakistan's Afghan policy was originally shaped. For his part, Karzai argues that Afghanistan has no reason to ignore India, a rising global power and one that gives as much as $260 million annually in aid to Afghanistan. Publicly, Musharraf expresses his willingness to work with Karzai in controlling the Taliban and including "moderate Taliban" in the Afghan government.

Officials in Islamabad say they would like to work with the government in Kabul to resolve differences. But the covert option, developed and consistently pursued since the 1960s, has not been given up. Even the deterioration in Pakistan's control over its own Pashtun tribal regions does not seem to have altered Pakistan's ambition of maintaining influence inside Afghanistan. From Pakistan's point of view, a friendly government in Kabul would only be one that excludes Indian influence. Even under the leadership of an ostensibly secular Musharraf, Pakistan trusts Islamist Pashtuns more than secular ones. Secular Pashtuns remain suspect in Pakistan's strategic thinking because of fears that they might revive the ideas of a "Greater Afghanistan" or "Pashtunistan."

Pakistan's policy toward Afghanistan remains rooted in British forward policy and the great game of the nineteenth and early twentieth centuries. Pakistan remains insecure about the Durand Line and, in an effort to forestall an Indian-backed effort to support Baluch and Pashtun irredentism, continues with efforts to have power over Afghanistan's external relations. Only when the international community addresses Pakistan's insecurity, and Afghanistan's concerns, in relation to the Durand Line will the two countries be able to find a basis for a stable, good neighborly relationship.

References

BBC News. 2006. "Afghan refugee return fund sought." June 24. http://news.bbc .co.uk/2/hi/south_asia/5113448.stm.

CNN. 2005. "Pakistan proposes Afghan border fence: Musharraf, Rice discuss measure to block extremists." September 12.

Cordovez, Deigo and Selig S. Harrison. 1995. *Out of Afghanistan: The Inside Story of the Soviet Withdrawal*. New York: Oxford University Press.

Gul, Pazir. 2006. "Waziristan accord signed." *Dawn*. September 6.

Harrison, Selig S. 1995. "How the Soviet Union Stumbled into Afghanistan." In *Out of Afghanistan: The Inside Story of the Soviet Withdrawal*, by Diego Cordovez and Selig S. Harrison, 13–44. New York: Oxford University Press.

International Herald Tribune. 2006. "Frustrated or Seeking Attention? Karzai Lashes out at Pakistan Again." December 13.

Kux, Dennis. 2001. *Disenchanted Allies: The United States and Pakistan 1947–2000.* Washington, DC: Woodrow Wilson Center Press.

Musharraf, Pervez. 2006. *In the Line of Fire.* New York: Free Press.

PakTribune. 2006. "A former Pakistani Dependent Karzai Daring Pakistan: Sheikh Rashid." December 15. http://www.paktribune.com/news/index.shtml ?163115.

Radio Free Europe/Radio Liberty. 2007. "Afghan, Pakistani Troops Battle over Border Fence." April 20.

Rashid, Ahmed. 2007. "NATO Commanders Demand Pakistan Close Taliban Sanctuary." *Eurasia Insight.* September 19.

Roberts, Jeffery J. 2004. *The Origins of Conflict in Afghanistan.* Westport and London: Praeger.

Roggio, Bill. 2007. "Mullah Obaidullah Akhund Arrested in Pakistan." *The Long War Journal.* 1 March. http://www.longwarjournal.org/archives/2007/03/m.

Shahzad, Syed Saleem. 2007. "Taliban a Step Ahead of US Assault." *Asia Times.* August 11.

Siddiqi, Aslam. 1960. *Pakistan Seeks Security.* Lahore: Longmans Green.

Stephens, Ian. 1953. *Horned Moon.* London: Chatto and Windus.

United States of America, White House. 2007. "Fact Sheet: The Terrorist Threat to the US Homeland; What the Administration Is Doing to Protect America from the Persistent, Evolving Threat from Al-Qaeda." July 17. http://www.whitehouse.gov/news/releases/2007/07/20070717–2.html.

Yousaf, Mohammad and Mark Adkin. 1992. *The Bear Trap: Afghanistan's Untold Story.* Lahore: Jang Publishers.

The Canadian Case

9

Nipa Banerjee

Peace Building and Development in the Fragile State of Afghanistan

A Practitioner's Perspective

This chapter offers a practitioner's perspective on the role of the international community in the development and reconstruction of Afghanistan. The evidence considered here suggests that despite certain notable successes in social and economic sectors, Afghanistan remains a fragile state appropriately categorized as a "low income country under stress" (LICUS) due to the failure to build strong state institutions.

A great deal of attention has been focused on fighting terrorism and resisting the Taliban challenge to the democratically elected Afghan government. However, military action cannot address the root causes of the conflict, such as widespread poverty, inequity in the distribution of income, and the weakness of state institutions that lack authority and legitimacy in much of the country.

The essential ingredients for a durable and sustainable turnaround of a fragile post-conflict state are economic growth that can support investment in poverty reduction, human security build-up with the related social and economic development, and a state with efficient and effective institutions to serve as the custodian of such advances (François and Sud 2006). An equally important non-military component of building a durable peace is the need to give opposition groups a stake in the post-conflict political order (Lemarchand 2004). These components, central to the planning of post-conflict strategies for development and peace building, integrate the three spheres of defence, development, and diplomacy (3D).

Between 2002 and 2005, when the international community faced a relatively peaceful and secure situation, the opportunity to sow the seeds for longer-term development was largely missed. The international community neglected to attend to the needs of the south, the heartland of the Taliban. More serious, what initial investment the international forces made in the southern region, mainly through Provincial Reconstruction Teams (PRTs), turned out to be neither strategic nor visionary.

There were several problems. The PRT investments in the south did not necessarily focus on locations that indicated signs of tension as early warnings of the re-emergence of conflict. The PRT projects did not help the central government gain a presence in the south, because the design and delivery of reconstruction was not undertaken through the government but through parallel structures set up by individual donors, intergovernmental organizations, and NGOs. The initial PRT investments also concentrated on civil–military co-operation activities like well-digging, road construction, and cash handouts. These activities came at the expense of longer-term development initiatives in basic education and health, youth training, or agriculture, which could have produced sustainable results. The short-term measures also failed to address the longer-term development needs for building a rudimentary justice system and a functioning police force to ensure minimum physical security for citizens.

For the international community, meeting the conditions of the Bonn Agreement—an election and establishment of democracy—became priorities. Little attention was paid to the fact that democracy could not be firmly grounded in the absence of appropriate governance structures. This generated both a security and a governance vacuum (Foot 2007). While the government of Afghanistan and the international community moved haphazardly without a strategic plan, the Taliban regrouped, taking advantage of the security vacuum and the absence of the central government (Blanchfield 2007). The international security forces were not deployed in sufficient numbers (Paris 2006/2007). Apart from a US base in Kandahar and several other smaller bases, there was virtually no military presence in three of the four southern provinces (Uruzgan, Helmand, and Zabul). While the Taliban flourished, coalition forces failed to secure even the major cities and highways in the south. The lack of security in the south meant that the UN agencies and the international and Afghan aid organizations could not deliver reconstruction and development assistance efficiently or effectively. The vital agricultural sector was neglected. Inadequate investment in agriculture, on which 70% of the population depends, led to a massive return to poppy cultivation by destitute farmers in the south, with the danger of a quick spread over the rest of the country.

Between 2001 and 2005, the 3D approach to peace was not followed in southern Afghanistan. The foreign troops could not bring security, and development investment was inadequate and un-strategic. Diplomacy, required for mediation and de-escalation of conflicts, post-conflict management, and promotion of inter-ethnic and inter-cultural dialogue, hardly played a role.

Ineffectiveness of Premature Liberalization before Institutionalization

The current situation in Afghanistan reflects classic problems resulting from the premature introduction of political liberalization, democratization, and an economic liberalization process. Afghanistan is a typical fragile state where the economy is ruined, the legitimacy of the government is continually challenged, and where warlords, terrorists, and drug lords exert inordinate influences. Attempts to liberalize markets in Afghanistan were not accompanied or preceded by serious attempts to combat corruption, create clean and efficient judicial systems, or introduce any institutional infrastructure required for a fair and thriving market economy (Patterson, Blewett, and Karimi 2006). The negative manifestations of unregulated economic liberalization are, thus, quite visible. Monopolistic forces have violated free and open market principles, which likely exacerbated economic inequalities and have the potential to increase societal tensions and disrupt a fragile peace process. Indications are that three vital industries—carpet, vine, and construction—are under monopolistic controls (ibid.).

Between 2002 and 2005, the international community and the Afghan government addressed the elections—the democratic development benchmark of the Bonn Agreement—without paying adequate attention to consolidating the state and its institutions. When the state apparatus was too weak to govern, to provide security and protection to the citizens, or to satisfy basic needs, the democratization process, advanced with millions of dollars of investment in elections, exacerbated the existing social and ethnic cleavages. The political mobilization process unleashed destructive political competition, with opportunists manipulating and exploiting inter-communal distrust and disillusionment (Rosser 2006).

According to Holtz (2003), true state consolidation comprises three elements: the control of violence through reforms of the security sector (including disarmament, demobilization, and reintegration (DDR) of regular and irregular militia, police reforms, and trained national armed forces); the development of an independent judiciary; and the reform and strengthening of the bureaucracy for delivery of basic services to citizens.

To what extent have the international community and the Afghan government addressed these core elements required for state consolidation?

Disarmament, Demobilization, and Reintegration (DDR) of the Regular Militia Forces

The DDR program demobilized sixty-five thousand soldiers. Canada's 3D co-operation was best exemplified in the demobilization exercise, under the leadership of Chris Alexander, Canada's first ambassador to Kabul. The reintegration aspect proved less successful because of a dubious strategy of supply-driven training provided to the demobilized soldiers. It failed to integrate the demobilized and decommissioned soldiers into society and provide them with alternative means of livelihood (UNDP May 2005; CIDA May 2007; Chrobok 2005). No large-scale survey has yet been undertaken to confirm the numbers not integrated; however, several scholarly papers refer to demobilized soldiers taking up arms again, joining irregular militia groups and working for warlords(Hashemi 2007; Rubin 2007).

Disbandment of Illegal Armed Groups (DIAG)

With the support of Canadian Overseas Development Assistance (ODA), the Canadian embassy took a strong lead in planning and launching a multi-donor DIAG program. However, DIAG proved to be a non-starter due to resistance from the groups and a lack of government commitment. Although a substantial tonnage of weapons and ammunition was collected, the groups did not disarm fully (D&R Commission 2006).[1] A relatively smaller project for Heavy Weapons Cantonment, another example of successful 3D co-operation under the leadership of the Canadian ambassador, produced results that surpassed the investment made (ANBP 2005).

Police

The major means for strengthening the police were training programs created by the United States and Germany and a Law and Order Trust Fund (LOTFA, under UNDP) to which Canadian ODA contributed substantially. LOTFA had mixed results at best. A LOTFA evaluation (UNDP 2005) confirmed that it made little contribution to strengthening and improving the functioning of the police or the management capacity of the Ministry of Interior. A lack of coordination between Germany and the US, inadequate length and questionable quality of training, and a lack of mentoring were identified as major weaknesses in the police reform process. The US State Department's assessment of the US-financed police training indicates serious failures (Glanz and Rohde 2006; Rubin 2007).

Afghan National Army

Better results have been achieved in strengthening the armed forces (using some Canadian defence resources but no ODA funds). The number of troops is increasing, and corruption does not appear to be a problem. Nonetheless, the Afghan National Army continues to be of variable quality. The army training must be accelerated and the troop numbers expanded to help the Kabul government establish its presence and legitimacy across the country and provide security against insurgents (Paris 2007; Rubin 2007). Fiscal considerations, however, must guide any such expansion program.

Counter-Narcotics

Increased acreage for poppy cultivation and a significant rise in production, especially in the southern provinces (UNODC 2005; 2006a; 2006b; 2007), are indicators of an unsuccessful strategy for poppy elimination. The planners made eradication their top priority, with secondary attention given to development and implementation of Alternative Livelihood Programs. Regrettably, proper understanding of an appropriate "alternative livelihood" concept never took root. Small and fragmented livelihood projects cannot produce revenues to compete with the income that poppy earns. Alternative livelihood programming must embrace integrated rural/community development (Mansfield and Pain 2005), aimed at improving a community's quality of life through alternative cropping, agricultural extension, and improved varieties of seeds, fertilizers, and irrigation facilities. Such development would also improve access to markets, health services, water, sanitation facilities, and basic education. Progress like this cannot occur overnight and will not eliminate poppy within a year. However, experience shows that farmers would rather not grow an illegal crop if they have indications that such interventions are planned and will be delivered. This type of programming has been successful in Thailand, India, Pakistan, Bolivia, and Peru (Ward and Byrd 2004). Of the 3Ds, it was the Canadian development wing that had advocated most strongly the adoption of true alternative livelihood programming in Afghanistan.[2]

There is concern that Canadian ODA funding of the alternative livelihood program under the Counter-Narcotics Trust Fund (CNTF), managed by UNDP, may not yield the desired results. While successful alternative livelihoods delivery requires community-based integrative and comprehensive programming that is coordinated under a single line ministry, the trust fund promotes projects from multiple ministries in multiple sectors, with no coordination facility. Such a fragmented approach to the delivery of alternative livelihoods for poppy elimination purposes is unlikely to be successful. The lack of progress made by the CNTF in disbursing funds effectively has prompted the UK, the strongest supporter of the CNTF, to consider pulling out its financial support (Loyn 2007).

Most international development experts oppose the legalization of poppy cultivation and the utilization of poppy for medicinal purposes as advocated by the Senlis Council. Licensed poppy cultivation can be controlled only under a very strict surveillance and monitoring system where the rule of law prevails. Such controls are close to non-existent in Afghanistan; thus, legalization of poppy growing would have a counterproductive impact and result in uncontrolled and increased poppy cultivation (Byrd, quoted in Drohan 2007).

Jonathan Goodhand has noted elsewhere in this volume that a focus on drug traffickers is required rather than eradication, which negatively affects poor farmers' livelihoods. If the heroin-consuming countries of the north, mainly the UK and the US, took stronger measures to curb demand at home, it would have a significant impact on the supply side (i.e., cultivation), but measures to achieve this have failed to gain support.

Other factors necessary for sustained poppy elimination are political stability, strong governance, and leadership. The northern provinces, which are no more developed than the southern provinces, are almost free of opiate cultivation because they are relatively stable politically. A solution for poppy, thus, can be found in good governance and the rule of law (Walters, quoted in Butler 2007).

Mine Action

Afghanistan contains the most landmines in the world, so demining is a priority. Canada assumed a significant role in the mine action program through the UN Trust Fund by taking a leadership role in donor coordination. Demining and, to a lesser extent, mine victim assistance have been unqualified success stories. Lives have been saved, more land is available for development, and mine victims' quality of life has improved. Despite pressure from the international community, the UN dragged its feet for several years in promoting the transfer of ownership of this program to the Afghan government. Recently, however, the UN has initiated some required actions to help facilitate this process.

Rehabilitation of Refugees and Internally Displaced People (IDP)

Primarily undertaken as a measure of humanitarian assistance, the rehabilitation program for refugees and internally displaced people makes a major contribution to security building in a post-conflict fragile state by settling and reintegrating groups that may otherwise join fractious elements in society (IDMC 2005). Many refugees have returned and settled peacefully. As opposed to demobilized soldiers, many of whom are alleged to be involved with criminal activities, no evidence exists that the IDPs and returned refugees have disrupted social peace in Afghanistan. Thus, the security benefits of these multi-donor programs (led by the UNHCR) are enormous. Canadian ODA provided major financial support to these programs.

Justice Sector

The Aghan government must address the need for the creation and maintenance of a functioning legal order for establishing its legitimacy, protecting the rights of the people, and earning their support. Afghanistan has a reputation for judicial corruption. The appointment of the highest officials in justice institutions reflected little political will for judicial reform, and the international community did not raise its voice loud enough to reverse the situation. In the years following the Bonn Agreement, donor investments in the justice sector produced little change. Italy took the lead in the justice sector and made substantial investments, as has the US, with the dollar value of its contribution surpassing that of Italy. Canadian ODA funds were invested in legal training though the International Law and Development Organization and in support of the justice sector reform process (CIDA, *Strengthening the Rule of Law*). However, in the absence of real judicial reform by the Afghan government, international investment in the sector produced few visible results.

Institutions for Public Service Delivery

A theory that promotes institutionalization before liberalization emphasizes the need to establish a network of domestic institutions with the capacity to plan, launch, and manage reforms (François and Sud 2006). In Afghanistan, strengthened institutions in the Ministries of Finance, Health, Rural Rehabilitation and Development, Defence, and most recently Education have managed reforms that have generated long-term development results.

In April 2007, the IMF and the World Bank decided to include Afghanistan in the Heavily Indebted Poor Countries (HIPC) list based on its good economic performance. Despite the difficult security environment Afghanistan has achieved strong and continued progress toward macroeconomic stability under the leadership of successive finance ministers Ashraf Ghani and Anwar-ul Ahady. As William Byrd has detailed elsewhere in this volume, it has attained double-digit GDP growth, stabilized its currency, and met its revenue collection targets. Wide-ranging structural reforms have also been put in place (IMF 20007). Despite many challenges, clear signs of health sector recovery and progress are emerging. A health facility assessment commissioned by the Ministry of Public Health indicates a 25% improvement in overall quality of health services since 2004. A Johns Hopkins University assessment found improvements in virtually all aspects of health care in almost every province. Maternal and infant mortality have been reduced as well.[3]

The Ministry of Rural Rehabilitation and Development, led by successive Ministers Haneef Atmar and Ehsan Zia, is credited with extending successful and innovative community development programs and microfinance dispensation for income generation across the country. Efforts at a wider spread of basic education, attempts at replacing foreign-implanted *madrassas* with home-grown *madrassas* offering a mix of religious and secular curriculum, and community primary schooling with preferences given to girls are indicators of a strengthened Ministry of Education under the competent leadership of Minister Haneef Atmar. In contrast, the Ministries of Agriculture, Counter-Narcotics, Public Service Reform, Commerce, Interior, and Justice have been unable to manage extremely needy sectors. Canadian ODA has helped strengthen the Ministries of Rural Rehabilitation and Development, Finance, Defence, and Education.[4] Canadian support for programs of the Ministries of Counter-Narcotics and Interior, and to the justice sector, met with little success. Recently Canada has supported the health-delivery program led by Minister Amin Fatimie, which is known to yield excellent results.

Infrastructure for Quick/Visible Results

Promises of rehabilitation and the construction of infrastructure to produce quick and visible results often fail as a confidence-building measure and may instead generate unrealistic expectations, which, if unfulfilled, will result in a loss of faith in the government (Suhrke el al. 2002; François and Sud 2006). School construction without teachers and supplies, electricity generation and supply without cost recovery mechanisms, and wells that adversely affect water tables and water supply damage the credibility of the provider, be it the international community or the government.

Rather than creating unrealistic expectations with promises of quick results, the government should devote time to manage people's expectations and involve them in a demand-led participatory process of development (Strand et al. 2003). The National Solidarity Program (NSP),[5] which was designed and implemented by the Afghan government, is evidence of successful confidence-building through a demand-led process that has the potential of meeting some of the expectations related to human security, including economic, political, and social security. While the NSP does address individual communities' infrastructure needs, it is largely the participatory process that earns the people's trust in the government. With improvements in lifestyle over the longer term, the trust relationship is expected to be strengthened. This program has effectively improved state–citizen relationships and created Community Development Councils (CDCs) that can foster reconciliation in fractious local settings. The CDCs can and have played a role integrating refugees, internally displaced people, and former combatants. A similar process for strengthening governance and solidarity at the district level has been launched through the National Area Based Development Programme, which is also supported with Canadian ODA funds. Currently, twenty thousand CDCs cover 33,800 villages out of a target of 38,579 Afghan villages. To date, 282 District Development Assemblies have been established, out of a target of 364 (CIDA National Area Based Development Programme). The Afghan government's efforts to strengthen subnational governance is proceeding well.

Technical Assistance/Capacity Building (TA)

In the past, a massive influx of expatriate technical assistance (TA) to fragile states with weak capacity have failed to produce the desired result (Michailof 2007). Classic random and fragmented approaches are reflected in the international community's financing of TA in Afghanistan. With an expenditure of over $6 billion in six years, little capacity-building is visible. For security reasons, recruitment of quality TA workers for fragile states has been difficult, and placements of inexperienced and under-qualified staff have resulted in little actual capacity building. Many of the TA programs have turned into individual donor and UN-driven high-cost service provisions (2007) through temporary installation of expatriate personnel in line ministry staff positions. Such technical assistance performs no capacity building function, nor transfers skills to locals.

The Afghan government has frequently commented on the high salary and benefits earned by expatriate advisors. The culturally insensitive operational styles of many such advisors hamper amicable co-operation with Afghan staff and slow the smooth transfer of skills (Michailof 2007). Canadian experience showed that placement of Afghan expatriate advisors (presumably better attuned to local conditions) is also costly and does not necessarily produce the intended result.

The practice of supporting line ministries to hire comparatively better trained and competent local Afghans at a salary higher than what is paid locally but lower than that of expatriate advisors, is considered more effective and less costly. Canada, as a donor, has tried this approach; however, there is little indication yet that this practice has helped to extend and expand capacity in the Afghan government. It is also doubtful that these better-paid Afghan staff would ever join the government and accept civil service salaries once donors stop subsidizing their earnings. Utilization of these Afghan nationals might be possible when the salary scales are raised in the Afghan civil service structure (Michailof 2007).

To date, the enormous gap between the salaries of public service workers and expatriate advisors has generated disaffection among local public servants. Such salary differences undermine the civil service and the process of public service reform. Linked to this is the issue of financing staff of extra-governmental units, such as the Afghanistan National Development Strategy (ANDS) Secretariat, a UNDP Project, not officially a part of any Afghan government ministry. The unit is resourced with overpaid contracted personnel. Many of the ANDS sector strategies have been written by expatriate consultants. This practice is counterproductive, because it separates the advisors from the ministries whose capacity should be the first order of business. Such extra-governmental units, not functioning under government budgets and not nationally executed, severely undermine government ownership principles.

Canada has supported programs that have helped the government successfully address some of the issues identified above. The National Area Based Development Programme strengthened the provincial directorates of the Ministry of Rural Rehabilitation and Development through staff placement in the provincial governors' offices across the country and provided the opportunity for on-the-job training.

Also worth mentioning is the contribution made by Canada through the placement of a Strategic Advisory Team (SAT-A) from the Department of National Defence. Members of this team are placed within operational program units of the Government of Afghanistan to provide planning support to the Afghan government (DND 2007). Because of its demand-driven services and low-key approach, SAT has earned a fair amount of success, but it is yet to be proven whether SAT will leave a permanent imprint on the building of sustainable capacity.

Alternative/Parallel Delivery Mechanisms

Because of institutional weaknesses in fragile states, peace building operations often use alternative channels of aid delivery outside the government machinery, such as non-governmental organizations and private sector firms. However, such practices have pitfalls. The delivery of services through external agencies undercuts the state building agenda and ignores opportunities for capacity building in government institutions. The international community will not be able to improve the government's performance if ministries are not allowed to coordinate development programming and implementation and be accountable for the resources invested (François and Sud 2006; Nixon 2007). When the government only serves as a spectator in a donor-driven show, the opportunity to build credibility with citizens is lost. In addition, programming and large-scale delivery through external agents generates resentment among citizens because ODA funds diverted through foreign agencies and non-governmental organizations are delivered at a higher cost. In 2006–2007, the Afghan government controlled only 30% of the total development funds; 70% was invested through parallel mechanisms (JCMB 2007). According to the former finance minister, Ashraf Ghani, the business practices of many international partners (including the UN) result in higher transactional and delivery costs and other problems (2005). In practical terms, service delivery through parallel mechanisms in Afghanistan undermines the Afghan government's authority and visibility as the primary service provider. It also prevents the international community from demanding accountability from the Afghan government (Schetter and Wimmer 2002). Parallel service delivery further makes financial planning unpredictable, because the government faces the risk of programs under external budgets suddenly shifting to the limited core budget if donors terminate financing.

Too many development projects have failed because of parallel resource transfer and delivery mechanisms. It is no wonder that bypassing the government system results in little capacity growth despite a $6 billion investment. Nor should it be surprising if donor-constructed schools remain unused, with no teachers or supplies, because Ministry of Education officials did not know that the buildings exist. Similarly, infrastructure may be built but deteriorate rapidly because the relevant ministry was not consulted and therefore failed to include the maintenance costs in its budget (World Bank 2007).

In contrast, many successful government projects, such as the Water and Sanitation Program, Micro Finance Program, the National Solidarity Programme, and the National Rural Access Program have been financed through the Afghanistan Reconstruction Trust Fund (ARTF), which transfers donor finances to the central budget for execution by the government. The National Solidarity Programme (NSP) best exemplifies how national programs can have a massive state building impact. Officials noted that of the 170 schools burned in Afghanistan in 2006, not one of them was sponsored by the National Solidarity Programme. The point is that projects owned by the community gain legitimacy (Patel, World Bank 2007).

Reconciliation as a Component of Peace Building

The Afghan government and the international community have neglected the need to give opposition groups a stake in the post-conflict order. To exploit all opportunities for peace building and stabilization in a post-conflict country, talks with all groups is essential (Holtz 2003). The Taliban is a movement that includes terrorists, but it is also known to have a political foundation. Fractious groups in the Taliban include Islamic fundamentalists and drug dealers but also young people who are frustrated with a lack of life opportunities: no education, no employment, and little income. Tom Koenig, a former Special Representative of the UN Secretary-General in Afghanistan, has said it is nonsensical to consider killing all members of these groups to end the conflict: "The answer to the conflict cannot only be based on the military solution or on development policies and programming but must be comprehensively political" (*Ottawa Citizen* 2007).

The Afghanistan Compact

The Afghanistan Compact was adopted in London in 2006 as a joint commitment between the Afghanistan government and the international community. The compact launched a multifaceted process, integrating all pillars of Afghan development on the basis that "security cannot be provided by military means alone. It requires good governance, justice and rule of law reinforced by reconstruction and development" (ICG 2007). Conceptually, the compact suits Afghanistan's context and needs. Full donor support to the compact subsumed under the Afghanistan National Development Strategy is essential to move Afghanistan from the transitional framework to a long-term development framework. However, the specific provisions, included as "benchmarks" in the compact were rushed and hurriedly agreed upon, largely at the political level, in Kabul. The benchmark development process was not inclusive and did not undertake appropriate consultation with the international development community. Stronger collaboration/coordination with the development community would have been more strategic as this would have drawn donor commitments at an early stage.

An analysis of the benchmarks and the indicators exposes flaws and identifies misplaced priorities. The international community has repeated the mistakes of the Bonn process and is chasing dubious indicators of progress, neglecting longer-term needs. A realistic question to ask would be, even if all the benchmarks of the Afghanistan Compact were attained, would Afghanistan become a more stable state? Benchmarks are not ends in themselves but are only the means to measure progress toward results. Chasing the benchmarks with inadequate attention to the results is eroding the usefulness of the compact, which should be realistically placed within a larger framework of sequenced priorities and final results (ICG 2007).

Decentralization

The potential contribution of decentralization to increase citizen participation is getting increasing recognition. However, decentralization by accentuating ethnic, political, and geographic divisions in a fractious society with weak state machinery might lead to further conflict as well (Wimmer and Schetter 2002; Suhrke et al. 2002). Joseph Siegle found that the effect of decentralization on conflict mitigation has been variable. His conclusion is that if decentralization promotes local governance, functions through elected leaders, allows increased local expenditures based on a participatory process, and generates employment, it is less likely to succumb to ethnic conflict (2007). Decentralization, encompassing a number of these elements, is typified in the National Solidarity Programme, which allows decision making to be decentralized to the local level with accountability to the central government. This is perhaps better defined as deconcentration, which is more suitable in a fragile state situation (Strand et al. 2003). In Afghanistan, deconcentration to the district and provincial levels would also be possible, but not without full control of revenues. The elements that can be decentralized are decision making for resource allocation within government-set agendas and budgets. Encouraging any further regional autonomy in a fragile state context would further weaken the central government's control in the regions and threaten its legitimacy. Ashraf Ghani argues that any attempt at decentralization in fragile states should be accompanied by good governance principles with a balanced distribution of decision-making rights and accountability between central and subnational levels of government (2007). It is yet to be seen if the government program of strengthening governance at the subnational would address these objectives.

Donor Coordination

Better than average donor dialogue, through various consultative mechanisms, exists in Afghanistan, and attention is paid to the pursuit of multilateralism. Yet, competition among donors to gain higher profiles and outperform each other continues to hamper development and benefits neither the government nor the international community. The lead donor/agency concept has dominated the scenario in Afghanistan since the Bonn Agreement in 2001. Although the concept is useful, a lack of flexibility and an unwillingness of some donors to compromise have been counterproductive. The donors have no shared vision, much less a common strategy. Two-thirds of foreign assistance continues to bypass the Afghan government and undermine its role in state and institution building.

Assistance to Southern Afghanistan (including Kandahar)

The US, UK, the Netherlands, and Canada have substantial investments in the south. Given Canada's troop deployments in Kandahar and the recognized need to address the perceived causes of conflict, millions of dollars have already been invested by Canada in this province and more have been promised. The funded programs range from Kandahar-focused national programs (such as the National Solidarity Programme, National Area-Based Development Programme, National Rural Access Programme, and Mine Action) to assistance for strengthening the justice system and the police, basic needs assistance for vulnerable rural families, polio eradication, maternal health, emergency food assistance, and infrastructure development. The current assessment is that to generate concrete outcomes the south needs to be politically stable and the Ministry of Interior and the justice institutions reformed. The troop-contributing countries' development investments have often been ineffective because they lacked strategic counterinsurgency planning; under pressure from strong constituencies at home, longer-term sustainability issues have often been overlooked. Investments have often been made on the basis of what is believed to be good development practice but in reality are only short-term measures intended to achieve quick and visible results (ICG 2007).

Women's Development

Except perhaps in the southern provinces, indications of some progress since the Taliban times are present in most major cities. Such changes could be simply the direct result of the absence of Taliban repression. It is yet to be assessed how strategic some of the donor-assisted women's programs are, especially in the absence of appropriate donor coordination in this programming area. Evidence exists of positive results generated by well-coordinated programs, such as micro-credit for women and attention to maternal health.

While raising women's rights awareness has its value, its effectiveness should not be overestimated. In the absence of a supportive society, "aware" women can do little to change their own position, let alone the position of others. The use of Gender Funds financing to promote small, specific projects often have little value.

Regrettably, no national programs have been developed to integrate the priority issues affecting women's position in society. The priorities are: *income generation* for women that will elevate women's position in the family and society as the best means to achieve financial empowerment; *women's access to education* can raise awareness, not of "rights" issues alone but of societal issues and development needs, making them effective participants in the development process and ensuring women a fairer share of development dividends; *access to health services* in a country with one of the world's highest maternal mortality rates; and *access to justice* with assurance of physical security. Without any serious violation of social, cultural, and religious sensitivities, the government can execute a national program addressing these important elements.

An Assessment

How much has Afghanistan gained from the human and financial (as opposed to the military) investment of Canadian resources? Although human resources investment was minimal in the first two years after the establishment of the Canadian Embassy in 2003, Afghanistan gained the status of the largest recipient of Canadian ODA. Interestingly, these two years were equated with the highest achievements attained by Afghanistan in the post-Taliban period. Canada's contribution, well recognized by Afghans themselves, is attributable to several factors, including the strong leadership provided by Canada's ambassador, Chris Alexander, to the Canadian 3D team and the international community. Circumstances also promoted Canadian investment in the most needful national programs, designed, owned, and implemented by the Afghan government. Canada is one of the lead donors that uses the government's budget process for resource transfer and refrains from using parallel processes for planning and execution of programs. Although working with government structures was initially prompted by the difficult security situation that prevented private sector firms and NGOs from operating in Afghanistan, the national programs financed by Canada serve as flagships exemplifying not only the Afghan success story but also Canada's commitment to the March 2005 Paris Declaration principles.[6] Canadian diplomacy and development officials in the field undertook and, in certain instances, led useful coordination and policy dialogue functions. Canadians, for example, chaired the External Advisory Group of the Afghanistan National Development Strategy, and the Ammunition Steering Committee.

Canadian experience shows that disjointed, uncoordinated responses to issues in any sector fail to achieve the results contemplated and are not useful for stabilization purposes. Canadian support of capacity-building (TA program) has had mixed results at best. Without supporting regulatory and enforcement institutions, Canadian private sector investment could not have effectively contributed to any sustainable private sector development. Investment in democratic development and governance materialized during the elections but failed to secure full democratic rights for the people in the absence of a fair judicial system and the rule of law. Canadian leadership in security sector programs such as heavy weapons cantonment, ammunitions destruction, and the demobilization of regular militia groups was commendable. However, the absence of appropriate reintegration of demobilized soldiers left the work of demilitarization incomplete. Results from a substantial Canadian investment in the DIAG program are yet to be realized. Canada's investment in the Law and Order Trust Fund will not attain its objective of securing the rule of law until an appropriately trained and corruption-free police force provides the necessary services and required protection to citizens. In the absence of reforms of the justice institutions, further investment in the justice sector is not likely to be productive. Strong diplomatic intervention will be required to push justice sector and police reforms. The detainee crisis,[7] for instance, could have been avoided with appropriate monitoring and an earlier intervention.

Certain investments through Canadian NGOs failed to produce sustainable results. Investment in women's radio stations hardly addressed the concept of value for money and left little useful sustainable benefits. The Kabul Widows Program conducted by CARE Canada supported a large number of widows at a critical time but failed to provide sustainable income opportunities in the earlier years. Some measures have since been introduced to address the needs of widows in a sustainable way (see Care Canada 2006; Foot 2006).[8] Funding provided to local NGOs with the objective of raising women's awareness produced small-scale impact at best. In general, programming to effectively benefit women's advancement in society should avoid small scale but administratively costly programs. Other more recent development program investments and Kandahar-specific programming have yet to be evaluated.

Canadian ODA investment in core development sectors, such as rural development and local governance (NSP/NABDP), mine action, and microfinance programs, etc., generated positive results that contributed to peace building and further helped state consolidation by building confidence in and loyalty to the government. Canada's support to refugee and internally displaced people's resettlement successfully addressed these objectives as well. The security sector investments, except for those in Heavy Weapons Cantonment, displayed weaker indicators of success. In fact, the security sector reform agenda of the international community has achieved little except for some strengthening of the Afghan National Army.

Afghanistan's transition continues to be under threat. A window of opportunity was lost to launch a comprehensive peace-building process in the most conflict-prone region of the country—the south, the home of the Taliban. Comprehensive engagement of the international community in southern Afghanistan from the start could have averted the insurgency now encountered.

The classic pitfalls of past peace-building exercises were all repeated in Afghanistan: liberalization before institutionalization; rushed and unstrategic investment in infrastructure development for quick and visible results; uncoordinated and fragmented donor-driven Technical Assistance programs; and parallel structures for resource transfer and project delivery at a higher cost, which undermined government ownership and leadership of critical development programs in violation of aid effectiveness principles. Overall, inadequate attention was devoted to the construction of a functioning Afghan state that would establish the government's legitimacy and authority.

A fundamental problem remains the lack of state institutions capable of implementing a monopoly on power and a unitary legal order. These are the preconditions for security and also for social, economic, and political development. Pressures from the troop-contributing countries to invest in short-sighted quick fixes have not made development happen instantly. Even urgently required short-term measures should be considered within the context of longer-term strategic planning. The international community can enhance the effectiveness of its interventions by functioning from a strong knowledge base and the application of lessons learned. Strengthened linkages of planning and programming with the existing body of research would tie the strategies to ground realities. After the 2001 war, the international community did not deploy enough staff. This was reflected in inadequate authority given to the field staff and inadequate headquarters' support to field missions.

In all fragile states, the transition from fragility to stability requires development, defence, and diplomacy interventions. Development interventions should not be consistently overshadowed by so-called "political considerations." Although weight must be given to the principle of making programming interventions politically acceptable, it is important to underline that "good development" is essentially "good politics." Similarly, while accountability requirements should not be overridden, performance and development results on the ground should ultimately define accountability. In real terms, "effective development" equals "good accountability." The failure to achieve the desired turnaround in Afghanistan is in part due to conflicts between short-term political agendas and long-term state building processes. Such conflicts must be transcended if Afghanistan is to move from being a fragile to a stable state.

Notes

1 Also a series of verbal report presentations at DIAG Steering Committee Meetings in Kabul 2005–2006.
2 "The project works towards preventative alternative development in three provinces (Bamiyan, Baghlan and Parwan) where poppy cultivation is on the rise or at the risk of starting." See CIDA, "Alternative Livelihoods Program in Northeastern Afghanistan."
3 Johns Hopkins University study results released through *Joint Statement* from World Bank and Afghan Minister of Public Health, Reported by the Associated Press in the *Edmonton Journal*, 28 April 2007.
4 See the list of current CIDA projects in Afghanistan online at http://www.acdi-cida .gc.ca/ CIDAWEB/acdicida.nsf/En/JUD-12514940-QGL (accessed November 2007).
5 National Solidarity Program, http://www.nspafghanistan.org/content/index_eng .html (accessed 15 August 2007).
6 For details on the Paris Declaration, see http://www.oecd.org/document/18/0,2340 ,en_2649_3236398_35401554_1_1_1_1,00.html.
7 On the prisoner detainee crisis, see Geoffrey Hayes's chapter in this volume.
8 Media reports suggest that CIDA was not going to renew funding for the program, but public pressure in Kabul forced a renewal for one year.

References

Afghanistan New Beginnings Programme (ANBP). 2005. *Final Report for CIDA Grant*. February.
Barakat, Sultan, et al. 2006. Mid-term Evaluation Report of the National Solidarity Programme (NSP). Afghanistan Post-war Reconstruction and Development Unit (PRDU), University of York and Ministry of Rural Development, Islamic Republic of Afghanistan. May.

Blanchfield, M. 2007. "Taliban Exploited Vacuum." *Ottawa Citizen*. 8 April.
Butler, Daren. 2007. "Stability Cuts Afghan Opium Output in North." Reuters. 10 May.
Canadian Department of National Defence. 2007. "Canadian Forces in Afghanistan." Backgrounder. 14 August. http://www.forces.gc.ca/site/newsroom/view_news_e.asp?id=1703.
Canadian International Development Agency (CIDA). Alternative Livelihoods Program in Northeastern Afghanistan. http://www.acdi-cida.gc.ca/CIDAWEB/acdicida.nsf/En/JUD-12515510-RKA. Accessed August 2007.
———. Strengthening the Rule of Law. http://www.acdi-cida.gc.ca/CIDAWEB/acdicida.nsf/En/JUD-12610180-KXT Accessed November 2007.
———. National Area Based Development Programme—National Program including Kandahar Province. http://www.acdi-cida.gc.ca/CIDAWEB/acdicida.nsf/En/JUD-125161243-SVH Accessed November 2007.
Care Canada. 2006. "CIDA Renews Funding to Help Afghanistan's Widows." 10 March. http://care.ca/press/press_e.asp?pressID=204.
Chrobok, Vira. 2005. *Demobilizing and Reintegrating Afghanistan's Young Soldiers: A Review and Assessment of Project Planning and Implementation*. Bonn International Centre for Conversion.
D&R [Disarmament and Reintegration] Commission. 2006. *A Review of Disbandment of Illegal Armed Groups in Afghanistan*, 25 November.
Drohan, Madelaine. 2007. "Opium Economics: Ending Illegal Opium Production in Afghanistan: Why There Are No Silver Bullets." *CBC News*. 5 July. http://www.cbc.ca/news/viewpoint/vp_drohan/20070705.html.
Foot, Richard. 2006. "Widows Shame Canada into Restoring Food Aid: Silenced by Taliban, Women Reclaim Their Voice." *Montreal Gazette*. 6 March. Accessed on Widows' Rights International: http://www.widowsrights.org/afghancanada.htm.
———. 2007. "Taliban Flourishes in Power Vacuum." *Ottawa Citizen*. 23 March.
François, Monika, and Inder Sud. 2006. "Promoting Stability and Development in Fragile and Failed States." *Development Policy Review* 24 (2): 141–60.
Ghani, Ashraf. 2005. *Closing the Sovereignty Gap: An Approach to State Building*, Working Paper no. 253. Overseas Development Institute, London. September.
———. 2007. *Relationship between Good Governance and Decentralization*. World Bank South Asia Decentralization Series. Paper presented, 7 March. Washington, DC: SAR Multilateral Decentralization Group.
Glanz, James and David Rohde. 2006. "Panel Faults US-Trained Afghan Police." *New York Times*. 1 December.
Hashemi, Z. 2007. "Former Afghan Official Says Country Lacks Adequate Security, Governance. Transcript of interview with former Minister of Interior of Afghanistan. March. Reprinted in CIDA's media survey report, April 3.
Holtz, U. 2003. Foreword to *Fragile Peace: State Failure, Violence, and Development in Crisis Regions*, ed. Tobias Debiel and Axel Klein. London: A. Zed Books.

International Crisis Group (ICG). 2007. "Aiding the State: Afghanistan's Endangered Compact." Policy Briefing, Asia Briefing No. 59. Kabul/Brussels. 29 January. http://www.crisisgroup.org/home/index.cfm?id=4631&l=1.

Internal Displacement Monitoring Centre. 2005. "Who are the IDPs in Afghanistan?" September. http://www.internal-displacement.org/idmc/website/countries.nsf/(httpEnvelopes)/0309A0348FF994B9802570B8005 A71DB?OpenDocument.

International Monetary Fund (IMF). 2007. "Islamic Republic of Afghanistan Added to the List of Countries Eligible for Assistance Under the HIPC Initiative." Press Release No. 07/75. 21 April 21. http://www.imf.org/external/np/sec/pr/2007/pr0775.htm.

Johnson, Harley, and Dale Posgate. 2007. *Ongoing Review of CIDA Afghanistan Program.* Reports July 2005, February 2006, August 2006, May 2007. http://www.acdi-cida.gc.ca/CIDAWEB/acdicida.nsf/En/ANN-6513594-P4G.

Lemarchand, René. 2004. "The Politics of Turnaround in Burundi." Paper prepared for the Low Income Countries Under Stress (LICUS) Initiative, The World Bank. 2 December. Unpublished manuscript.

Loyn, David. 2007. "Aid Failings 'Hit Afghan Progress.'" *BBC News.* 26 June 26. http://news.bbc.co.uk/2/hi/south_asia/6764345.stm.

Mansfield, D., and A. Pain. 2005. *Alternative Livelihood: Substance or Slogan?* Briefing Paper. Kabul: Afghanistan Research and Evaluation Unit (AREU). October.

Michailof, Serge. 2007. *Review of Technical Assistance and Capacity Building in Afghanistan.* Discussion paper for the Afghanistan Development Forum. World Bank.

Nixon, H. 2007. *Aiding the State? International Assistance and the Statebuilding Paradox in Afghanistan.* Briefing Paper Series. Kabul: Afghanistan Research and Evaluation Unit (AREU). April.

Ottawa Citizen. 2007. "UN Envoy Calls for Dialogue with Taliban in Afghanistan." from Berliner Zeuter, April 13, 2007. May. Available at http://afghanistan newscenter.com/news/2007/april/apr132007.html#1.

Pajhwak Afgan News. 2007. "JCMB Finds Afghanistan Compact on Track." Report of the Berlin meeting of the Joint Monitoring and Coordination Board on 30 April 2007. May 1. http://www.afghanistannewscenter.com/news/2007/may/may32007.html#17.

Paris, Roland. 2006/2007. "Nato's Choice in Afghanistan: Go Big or Go Home." *Policy Options* December/January: 26–43.

Patel, Praful. 2007. Remarks at Afghanistan Development Forum. World Bank South Asia. Kabul, April 29–30. http://www.adf.gov.af/src/speeches/world%20bank.pdf.

Patterson, A., J. Blewett, and A. Karimi. 2006. *Putting the Cart Before the Horse: Privatization & Economic Reform in Afghanistan.* Briefing Paper Series. Kabul: Afghanistan Research and Evaluation Unit (AREU). November.

Rosser, A. 2006. Foreword in *Achieving Turnaround in Fragile States, IDS Bulletin* vol. 37, no 2, March.

Rubin, B. 2007. "Saving Afghanistan." *Foreign Affairs* 86 (1): 57–78.

Schetter, Conrad, and Andreas Wimmer. 2002. State-Formation First: Recommendations for Reconstruction and Peace-Making in Afghanistan. Discussion Paper on Development Policy No. 45. Bonn: Centre for Development Research (ZEF-Bonn). April.

Siegle, J. 2007. *Assessing Decentralization as a Conflict Mitigation Strategy*. World Bank South Asia Decentralization Series. Paper presented. 9 April. Washington, DC: SAR Multilateral Decentralization Group.

Strand, A., H. Toje, A. M. Jerve, and I. Samset. 2003. "Community driven development in contexts of conflict." Commissioned by World Bank in Report R-2003:11 Chr Michelsen Institute Development Studies and Human Rights.

Suhrke, Astri, with Kristian Berg Harpviken, Are Knudsen, Arve Ofstad, and Arne Strand. 2002. "Peacebuilding: Lessons for Afghanistan?" Report R 2002-9 Chr. Michelson Institute Development Studies & Human Rights. http://www.cmi.no/publications/publication/?831=peacebuilding-lessons -for-afghanistan.

United Nations Development Program (UNDP). 2005. *Evaluation Mission of UNDP LOTFA Project, Final Report.* May-June.

United Nations Office on Drugs and Crime. (UNODC). 2005. *Afghanistan Opium Survey.* November.

———. 2006a. *Afghanistan Opium Rapid Assessment Survey.* February.

———. 2006b. *2006 Annual Opium Poppy Survey in Afghanistan.* September.

———. 2007. *2007 Annual Opium Poppy Survey in Afghanistan.* September.

Ward, C., and W. Byrd. 2004. Afghanistan's Opium Drug Economy. South Asia Poverty Reduction and Economic Management Working Paper. Washington, DC: World Bank.

10

M.D. (Mike) Capstick

Establishing Security in Afghanistan

Strategic and Operational Perspectives

Missed Strategic Opportunities

The international effort to bring stability and security to Afghanistan has been characterized by a growing list of missed strategic opportunities. Driven by "transformational imperatives," the US strategy to depose the Taliban regime depended on a unique combination of airpower, special forces, and local militias. However, the unintended, but totally foreseeable, consequence of the American reluctance to deploy major ground forces was that the power and prestige of some problematic warlords and commanders was reinforced. This was then exacerbated by American insistence that the United Nations–mandated International Security Assistance Force (ISAF) limit operations to Kabul. The ostensible reason for this was to allow US (Operation Enduring Freedom) forces to pursue counter-terrorist operations in the rest of Afghanistan. This "dual" chain of command persisted, in violation of well-established military principles and common sense, until late 2006 when NATO assumed command of operations throughout the entire country. During this entire period, the term "economy of force" best described US strategy. The number of "boots on the ground" was never sufficient to establish the level of security necessary to permit substantive development, and the tactics employed failed to provide the population with a basic level of security. Further, the consequent security vacuum provided many warlords the opportunity to consolidate their regional power and to tighten their grip on poppy cultivation and other criminal enterprises.[1]

At its core, this failure to translate a tactical victory against the Taliban regime into strategic victory for the future of Afghanistan is the result of international incoherence and a failure to understand that winning battles is simply not enough to ensure strategic success. Despite the overwhelming historical evidence that military force alone cannot defeat an insurgency or stabilize a failed state, the international community's efforts in Kabul have been characterized by an apparent lack of strategic vision. Although the Bonn process succeeded in its aim of establishing the building blocks of statehood, there was no agreed international strategy that linked the essential security, governance, and development aspects of nation building until the Afghanistan Compact was approved at the London Conference in February 2006.

From the military perspective, much of this lack of coherence results from one basic but critical mistake: the collective failure of American and NATO leaders to understand the true nature of conflict in failed and failing states. This failure led to the application of military force using concepts, doctrine, tactics, and equipment optimized for "state-on-state" conflicts, but not well-adapted to the realities of warfare "among the people" (Smith 2005, 394–98).

The Operational Concept

The American-led attack against the Taliban regime was initially characterized as a validation of the Pentagon's transformational vision of warfare. High technology, precision weapons systems, satellite communications, and sophisticated command and control networks all permitted the American military to prevail without committing large numbers of ground troops. In December 2001, it seemed that the concepts and technologies that characterized the "Revolution in Military Affairs" had proven their worth and rendered large ground forces irrelevant. Despite the popularity of military transformation in the Pentagon and in the military debates of the first post-Cold War decade, some soldiers and the United States Marine Corps held to the idea that "boots on the ground" remain the most essential military capability.

General Charles C. Krulak, the 31st Commandant of the United States Marine Corps, first coined the term "three block war" in a speech to the National Press Club in Washington in December 1997. General Krulak was among the most colourful Marine officers of his generation and is also credited with developing the phrase "strategic corporal" to capture the intellectual and ethical demands that even the most junior levels of leadership face in the "postmodern" battlespace. Krulak described the three block war as follows:

...our enemies will not allow us to fight the Son of Desert Storm, but will try to draw us into the stepchild of Chechnya. In one moment in time, our service members will be feeding and clothing displaced refugees, providing humanitarian assistance. In the next moment, they will be holding two warring tribes apart—conducting peacekeeping operations—and finally they will be fighting a highly lethal mid-intensity battle—all on the same day, all within three city blocks. It will be what we call the "three block war." In this environment, conventional doctrine and organizations may mean very little. It is an environment born of change. (1997)

Though Krulak never formally developed the concept in any rigorous fashion, the three block war metaphor seized the imagination of "land-centric" military analysts and intellectuals and, like most metaphors, it has been abused ever since. It is important to place Krulak's imagery in the context of the times. In 1997, the US military establishment was still basking in the glow of the 100 hours of ground combat in Iraq that ended in victory in Operation Desert Storm. The "Revolution in Military Affairs"—precision weapons, information superiority, and concepts like "network-centric warfare" and "rapid decisive operations dominated American military thinking" (Corum 2007, 51–52). The Marine Corps was the only service to resist this latest, high-tech interpretation of the attritional "American Way of War." Officers like Krulak and General Anthony Zinni understood that war is an essentially human event and that people—soldiers, political leaders, the affected population, and the citizenry of our own nations—are far more important than technology as determinants of victory. Before most other military leaders and analysts, they also understood that the dominance of state-on-state warfare was in decline. In the aftermath of the Cold War, there was no competitor with enough military power to challenge the United States in any conventional military sense. They understood that, in the absence of direct military threats to the survival of Western states, most future conflicts would be "wars of choice" and the enemy would have to adopt "asymmetrical" strategies and tactics in the face of the "overwhelming force" represented by American military power. In short, while the rest of the US military establishment was building on the legacy of Desert Storm, Krulak and the Marines saw the future in the streets of places like Grozny and Mogadishu and they intended to be ready. The three block war idea was the shorthand that Krulak chose to describe this crucial philosophical fault-line in American military thinking.

Like most shorthand, the term "three block war" cannot convey the full range of meaning intended by its author. The kind of conflict envisioned by General Krulak has been actualized in Afghanistan, Iraq, Lebanon, and in the persistent civil wars in parts of Africa. Current military theory refers to this type of conflict as Fourth Generation Warfare

(4GW). One of the leading theorists in the field, retired Marine Colonel Thomas X. Hammes, describes 4GW as an "advanced insurgency" that uses "all available networks—political, economic, social, and military—to convince the enemy's decision makers that their strategic goals are either unachievable or too costly for the perceived benefit" (Hammes 2004, 2).

At its core, fourth generation warfare is strategic as it targets the political will of its adversaries. Three block war imagery is, on the other hand, a tactical image of small tactical units engaged in combat, peacekeeping, and humanitarianism in a defined geographical area. This picture is further reinforced by Krulak's idea of the "strategic corporal" and the reality that small unit actions can have serious strategic consequences. In my view, the tactical imagery of the three block war idea is one of the main conceptual obstacles that has led to a lack of clarity at the strategic level.

It is clear that the Taliban's pursuit of fourth generation warfare in Afghanistan today has achieved a degree of strategic success in Kabul, in NATO capitals and, most critically, in the minds of the people of troop-contributing nations and Afghan citizens. Until now, the government of Afghanistan and NATO nations have often ceded the information advantage to the Taliban and have failed to apply a strategic level three block war approach to the international effort. That said, the Afghanistan Compact provides an excellent strategic framework and a common language that should now be used to bring essential coherence to that effort. The remainder of this chapter will describe how the compact reflects Krulak's "three block war" shorthand at the strategic level. In addition, I will make some comments concerning the reality of the insurgency and the problematic relationship between the military and development aspects of state building.

Fourth-Generation Conflict in Afghanistan

Some media and civil society groups have been critical of a perceived shift in Canadian strategy resulting from the move to Kandahar in late 2005. Some commentators have concluded that it represents a strategic shift from state building and reconstruction toward a purely military counter-insurgency role.[2] This conclusion can only result from a fundamentally flawed understanding of the insurgency itself, exacerbated by the failure of successive Canadian governments to communicate a clear and coherent strategic vision. The Taliban-led terror campaign in the south and east is not a classical anti-colonial struggle, nor is it a simple battle of competing political ideologies. It is, instead, a battle between the forces of tradition and the advocates of modernity. The Taliban's objective is not mere territorial control or political power—it is control of the population and the re-establishment of the perverse theocracy that ruled until late 2001 (Hsu and De-Grasse 2006). To that end, they have formed financial and other alliances with local drug lords and other criminals who profit from instability, and with international and national networks that share a common interest in ensuring that the rule of law remains weak. This amorphous coalition of groups is more than willing to use extreme violence to achieve their aims and has demonstrated repeatedly that development in the absence of basic security is futile. Finally, the fact that the insurgent coalition is a collection of groups with different motivations and interests renders discussion of a "comprehensive peace process" moot. It is true that the Afghan government's National Reconciliation Program has brought some moderate Taliban into the political process, and NATO forces understand the vital importance of providing alternatives to young Afghan men who fight on a part-time basis for pay. Still, there is little coherent insurgent leadership with which to negotiate, especially the hard-core leadership in their Pakistani sanctuary.

In short, the war in Afghanistan is an "advanced insurgency" that meets the definitional standard of a fourth generation conflict. Two elections and extensive social science research provide ample evidence that the majority of Afghans reject the insurgents' world-view.[3] The UN Security Council's endorsement of the Afghanistan Compact (including the Security Pillar) represents explicit approval of both the ongoing American-led counter-insurgency operations and the ISAF transition concept (Afghanistan 2006, 6).[4] Further, the compact and Afghanistan's National Development Strategy explicitly address the social, political, and economic aspects of state building—an effort that must continue even while the security situation remains contested. In short, the international community through the authority of the UN Security Council has chosen not to remain neutral or impartial but to support the Afghan government in a battle that continues to put the future of the country in jeopardy.

The Afghanistan Compact's Strategic Three "Blocks"

Almost three decades of insurgency, invasion, resistance, civil war, and, ultimately, the American-led attack on the Taliban, have left Afghanistan shattered. Despite this legacy of violence, the progress made since 2001 has been nothing short of spectacular. The Bonn Agreement formed a political roadmap that has allowed Afghans to take control of their own future. Even with the pressure of an ongoing insurgency, Afghanistan has promulgated a constitution, held two very successful elections, opened the

Parliament, and restored a sense of normalcy in most of the country. Major problems persist—insurgency, opium, criminality, and, most importantly, grinding and endemic poverty. Determined to overcome these obstacles, the government of Afghanistan, in partnership with the international community, is ready to take the next steps.

These steps are mapped out in two crucial documents, the Afghanistan Compact and Afghanistan's National Development Strategy (ANDS), both presented and approved at the London Conference in January and February 2006. With an immediate unanimous endorsement by the UN Security Council (1659/2006), the compact became the political "deal" between Afghanistan and the international community that sought to achieve the Afghan government's vision "to consolidate peace and stability through just, democratic processes and institutions, and to reduce poverty and achieve prosperity through broad based and equitable economic growth" (ANDS 2006, 3). This mutual commitment is best expressed in the compact itself: "The Afghan Government hereby commits itself to realizing this shared vision of the future; the international community, in turn commits itself to provide resources and support to realize that vision" (2006, 2).

Both the compact and ANDS are built around three "blocks" or "pillars." The first is *security*. This includes the international military contribution to help defeat the insurgency, reform the National Army (ANA) and police (ANP), and disband illegal armed groups. The second is *governance, rule of law, and human rights*. It encompasses reform of the machinery of government, revitalization of the civil service, justice reform, the fight against corruption and the poppy economy, and making the institutions of the state work for the people. The third pillar, *economic and social development*, is the real heart of the compact. It is under this pillar that the bulk of the reconstruction effort falls and it is, in essence, the real objective of the ANDS. In addition to the pillars, both documents describe gender equity, counter-narcotics, regional cooperation, anti-corruption, and the environment as "cross cutting themes," because these issues need to be dealt with in the context of all three pillars and at the societal level (see Hamees 2004; Regehr 2006).

The result of extensive consultation and a very concerted effort by both the international community and, most importantly, all elements of the Afghan government, the Afghanistan Compact and ANDS received an extraordinary degree of consensus at the London Conference. Together, these documents map the future of Afghanistan and, if properly implemented, they will establish the conditions necessary for Afghans to achieve their vision of a peaceful, just, democratic, stable, and prosperous Islamic state. At the strategic level, the compact's pillars are, in essence, analogous to Krulak's "three blocks" at the tactical level. The security pillar covers the war-fighting and peacekeeping aspects of his concept. Peacekeeping is also part of the governance pillar, and the economic and social development pillar is an expanded version of the humanitarian aid block. This construct is a more appropriate conceptualization at the strategic level, because it avoids both the tactical imagery and the spatial limitations of the original expression by Krulak and could well serve as a model for any future international intervention in failed and failing states.

There should be no doubt—the future of Afghanistan is still in the balance. Although a reasonable degree of security exists in most of the country, there are areas in the south and east where the insurgency has prevented major development projects. The institutions of the state are, for the most part, still weak, and the government is not yet capable of protecting the population. The outcome is by no means guaranteed. Achieving the vision will require a cohesive, coherent and sustained international commitment to the compact and to the ANDS. Canada and the Canadian Forces (CF) have a vital role to play in this commitment, as these documents represent a significant step forward in dealing with the fourth generation warriors currently terrorizing the people of Afghanistan and preventing development work in large parts of the country.

The Canadian Forces and the Afghanistan Compact

The three pillars of the Afghanistan Compact suggest that there is a neat division of labour among the three lead Canadian government departments and agencies in Afghanistan with respect to their engagement. This is true in broad terms: Defence and the CF lead on security issues, the Department of Foreign Affairs and International Trade (DFAIT) leads on governance, rule of law, and human rights and the Canadian International Development Agency (CIDA) is the focal point on the economic and social development front. Other departments and organizations also contribute. For example, the Royal Canadian Mounted Police (RCMP) has officers in the Kandahar Provincial Reconstruction Team (PRT) and in the United Nations Assistance Mission Afghanistan (UNAMA) headquarters, as does Corrections Canada. Despite this apparent clarity, the reality is more complex, and no Canadian government agency can operate strictly in one pillar or another. Although not necessarily obvious, the Canadian Forces play a role in each of the three pillars as part of the cohesive "whole of government" approach that Canada is trying to apply as a means of achieving the best effects on the ground. In turn, DFAIT and CIDA both have significant influence on, and are active in, the security sector. For example, the ambassador and the head of aid played key roles in the disarmament, demobilization, and reintegration (DDR) program, a function of the security pillar.

The remainder of this section will describe how the CF support each of the pillars of the ANDS. This discussion will be through a CF lens, and it must be borne in mind that each of the other committed departments and agencies has a vital role to play in the efforts of the others.

The CF have been engaged in Afghanistan since the deployment of a combat unit to Kandahar in late 2001 as part of the American-led coalition (Operation Enduring Freedom/OEF). They have participated in the International Security Assistance Force (ISAF) and assumed the command of ISAF V under then Lieutenant-General Rick Hillier, who later served as Chief of the Defence Staff. Although the number of troops has varied, the CF have made major contributions to both, mutually supporting multi-national forces in the country (Department of National Defence 2007). From 1 March until 1 November 2006, Canada assumed lead-nation status in Regional Command (South) (RC(S)). This region includes some of the most unstable provinces in the country, including Kandahar, Uruzugan, Helmand, Nimroz, and Kunduz. The commitment included the lead of the Multinational Brigade Headquarters that exercises command over Canadian, British, American, Romanian, Australian, and Dutch units in the region. The Canadian commitment includes an infantry battle group in Kandahar Province, the Kandahar PRT and an Operational Mentor and Liaison Team (OMLT) embedded with Afghan National Army units in the province. This commitment was initially part of OEF and as a result became conflated in some quarters with the less popular aspects of US foreign policy. The Canadian mission (and Regional Command South) came under the command of ISAF at the end of July 2006, and the Canadian-led command structure was instrumental in establishing the conditions for the successful transition from US to NATO command.

In addition to the troops in RC(S) and Kandahar, the Canadian Forces have a strong presence in Kabul. Canadian staff officers serve in both ISAF and the coalition headquarters, and a fifteen-soldier training team works with ANA units to prepare them for deployment to the provinces. In addition, a small military–civilian team of planners (Strategic Advisory Team–Afghanistan/SAT-A) works directly with Afghan government agencies to assist in the development of the strategic plans necessary to achieve the objectives of the compact.

The Canadian Forces and the Security Pillar

It is clear that security is the prerequisite for the success of the Afghanistan Compact. In the absence of security, economic and social development is almost impossible. In addition, the insurgency presents a direct threat to the development of good governance structures and practices. For example, in the months before the September 2005 parliamentary elections, a number of candidates were murdered, others were threatened and forced to withdraw, and approximately fifteen religious leaders were assassinated in the south. As a result, the security pillar will continue to be the focus of CF effort in Afghanistan for some time to come. Despite this emphasis, the Canadian Forces Campaign Plan for Afghanistan and the Multinational Brigade Campaign Plan both have three lines of operation that mirror the ANDS pillars.[5]

The battle group in Kandahar is organized and equipped to assist the provincial governor and the Afghan National Army and Police in their efforts to establish the legitimate government's "monopoly on the use of lethal force" in the province. The PRT, with military members, diplomats, and CIDA development specialists, is also heavily engaged in the security pillar. The PRT "reinforces the authority of the Afghan government in and around Kandahar and helps local authorities stabilize and rebuild the region. Its tasks are to monitor security, promote the policies and priorities of the national government with local authorities, and facilitate reform in the security sector" (Department of National Defence 2007). Analysis of this mandate reveals that the PRT concept is illustrative of the reciprocity between security, governance, and development.

With the exception of the Strategic Advisory Team–Afghanistan (SAT-A), almost every other CF member in the Kabul area is engaged in the security pillar. Canadian staff officers and troops at ISAF and various coalition headquarters are fully integrated into those organizations. The ANA training team and the OMLT are also fully committed in this pillar as their work involves hands-on tactical training of Afghan soldiers at the small-unit level.

Canadian Forces Support to Governance, the Rule of Law, and Human Rights

In this ANDS pillar the most obvious examples of CF support are found in the PRT and SAT-A. The PRT is, by its mandate, intended to "reinforce the authority of the Afghan government" (Department of National Defence 2006). Although its focus has been on security because of the prevailing situation in Kandahar province, it has provided significant support to the provincial governor, the ANA, and ANP and, by virtue of its development work, the line ministries of the central government. This level of support will continue to grow, because the intent is to co-locate part of the PRT headquarters in the governor's office. It must be noted here that Afghan provincial governors are agents of the central government, appointed by the president and reporting to the Minister of the Interior. PRT security sector reform activities strongly emphasize the rule of law and respect for human rights as basic operating principles for security forces. In addition, CIDA funds and conducts a "confidence in government" strategy, intended to involve Afghan Government authorities in the delivery of local development projects.

SAT-A has a direct role in the governance pillar as its planning team directly supports the Independent Administrative Reform and Civil Service Commission. This body is charged with achieving the ambitious benchmarks for Public Administrative Reform set out in both the compact and ANDS. A team of planners are also working in the Ministry of Rural Rehabilitation and Development (MRRD, the main Afghan government agent for reconstruction outside of Kabul) to help develop the MRRD strategic plan. This includes the strategy for the establishment of the comprehensive governance structure for development that extends from the village to the national level. At all levels, the team has formed working partnerships with international organizations such as the World Bank and the United Nations Development Program. These bodies bring to the table expertise in governance, while SAT-A provides the skills to integrate their input and assist Afghan managers in the formulation of a coherent strategy. SAT-A insists on working directly with Afghan government counterparts to ensure that its work is true capacity building at the working level, and not "capacity replacement," as is so often the case. This work is a clear demonstration of the potential of military staff "skills transfer" to the civil sector in a post-conflict society that has had little time to develop viable public institutions and a culture of good governance.

Canadian Forces Support to the Economic and Social Development Pillar

Within the security envelope provided by the Battle Group in Kandahar Province, the PRT is focused on development and reconstruction. This includes support to alternative livelihood programs, rural rehabilitation, and any number of public infrastructure projects. At the same time, ISAF in general, and the PRT in particular, have renewed their emphasis on good governance. Working with the MRRD, the PRT has initiated a variety of CIDA programs designed to increase confidence in the government and to deepen the roots of the nascent Afghan democracy. The PRT will also provide direct support to the newly-established Provincial Development Councils and their district and village level equivalents. The unit is, by far, the best example of a "whole of government" concept at the tactical level because it includes a senior diplomat, CIDA expertise (augmented by both the British Department for International Development and USAID), and RCMP officers. It is the CIDA component, not the military, that plans and coordinates development activities, while the CF provide the basic security and the essential support framework.

The Canadian Battle Group and PRT in Kandahar have a vital role. Simply put, unless the security situation is stabilized, the south will be left out of the national reconstruction and development effort. As a result, it will remain a "festering sore" and a fertile ground for the growth of an insurgency (Barton, Crocker, and Morgan 2005). Underlying the Canadian military campaign in Kandahar is the clear understanding that sustained economic development is the most effective way of defeating the insurgency.[6] Plans, tactics and techniques are shaped accordingly. In essence, the combined effect of the Battle Group and PRT in Kandahar is to create the security environment necessary to permit development—a direct contribution to Canadian and international objectives in Afghanistan.

In addition to the Kandahar focus in the Economic Development pillar, SAT-A in Kabul is directly involved with a planning team supporting the Afghan-led ANDS Working Group. This small group of military officers and civilians works alongside the Afghan staff of the senior economic advisor's office and a number of international consultants. Under Afghan leadership, this diverse group formulated the interim ANDS and facilitated the broad consultative process and is poised to develop the full-scale implementation plan. Similar to the effort in MRRD, the ANDS Working Group and international experts provide the substantive and technical content, while SAT-A applies military strategic planning to ensure coherence, synchronization and sequencing in the same way that it would for a military campaign.

Some have questioned the legitimacy of using military planners in this role, and there have been suggestions that other agencies would be better suited to the task. Although this concern is understandable, there are practical advantages to using the CF as the basis of the SAT. In addition to the obvious education, training, and experience in strategic planning techniques that military officers bring, the CF are really the only arm of the Canadian government that can quickly and continually generate the requisite numbers of trained people with the will to work in an austere and, at times, unstable environment. Most importantly, the SAT-A initiative is explicit recognition that the character of armed conflict has undergone a major transformation since the end of the Cold War and that traditional concepts for the use of armed force are insufficient to establish a lasting peace.

Security and Development

The original articulation of the three block war concept used tactical level language and imagery to make a very specific point about the changing character of "post-modern" conflict. General Krulak was concerned about the US military's intense focus on high-tech solutions, and his aim was to restore the soldier and small unit to their rightful place on the battlefield. In that the three block war is most often discussed at the tactical level, the idea of soldiers delivering humanitarian aid is the most contested part of the concept. Much of this discussion is a "dialogue of the deaf" and is rooted in military and humanitarian values that were developed and practiced in a far simpler world than the one that we face today.

Recent operations in Afghanistan and Iraq have demonstrated that the three block war concept is not as simple as Krulak's original articulation. In any conflict, there is a moral duty for military forces to care for the population remaining in the combat zone and ensure that no further harm comes to innocent civilians. But humanitarian aid delivered by fighting military forces must be limited to the life-saving essentials demanded by the principle of the "duty of care." In reality, tactical combat units have very little capacity in this area and will remain focused on fighting the battle or maintaining a tenuous security situation. As soon as there is sufficient security in a specific area, traditional humanitarian organizations will commence operations and will likely provide the vast majority of aid using the values and principles espoused in the Humanitarian Charter, the Code of Conduct[7] and individual organizational guidance.

Although this traditional construct carries risks; in that humanitarian organizations could find themselves providing medical care and food to the insurgents who are threatening the very same population the organizations are trying to protect, military forces should still support this model because humanitarian NGOs are far more proficient and efficient in delivering this type of aid.

Colonel Joseph Collins of the US Army War College has referred to this phase as "part one" of the "Humanitarian Assistance and Economic Development" block of the three block war concept (Collins 2004, 70–72). In essence, it deals with the immediate humanitarian requirement to alleviate human suffering and, at least in my view, should be both impartial and independent as far as the security situation permits. Collins defines "Economic Development, or "political reconstruction" as "part two" of the "block." Given the UNSC endorsement of the Afghanistan Compact, programs and projects under the "Economic and Social Development" pillar cannot be considered impartial humanitarian aid. In short, the international community has chosen to support the government of Afghanistan and has endorsed a comprehensive plan that is intended to secure the future of the country. That said, it is in part two that the military–development interface has become problematic. There are any number of contentious issues in this regard, and most are the result of a lack of role clarity and questions of professional jurisdiction—on both sides of the relationship.

Without a doubt, the PRT concept is a work in progress. Until 2006, NATO and American PRTs operated with very different guidance. National caveats have detracted from the ability of ISAF Headquarters to coordinate PRT activities at the national level and, most importantly, a number of well-intentioned PRT commanders have initiated projects that do not reflect Afghan priorities and are of questionable sustainability. On the positive side, the political/military chain of command in Afghanistan has recognized all of these issues. In recent months the joint Afghan–International PRT Executive Steering Committee has been rejuvenated. ISAF Headquarters hosted the first NATO–US PRT Commanders Conference in the summer of 2006 and has issued the first draft of a PRT handbook intended to provide more precise guidance. Crucially, ISAF and the coalition have been making a strenuous effort to align PRT activities with Afghanistan's National Development Strategy.

At the same time, there appears to be some unresolved issues over the appropriate roles of official development agencies and NGOs. As arms of their parent governments, official development agencies must support national strategies and objectives. In other words, CIDA cannot and must not be viewed as either impartial or independent, as its activities form an integral part of Canada's overall strategy. However, most agencies, CIDA included, contract the delivery of programs to private contractors or NGOs. This, in effect, makes the involved NGOs agents of the contracting government and cannot help but place their traditional impartiality in question. Only the NGO community can resolve the issues of principle that arise from this practice but, as a minimum, they cannot claim that their traditional impartiality applies when they are acting on behalf of a national government or international organization.

These issues are often discussed at the tactical level. However, it is at the international and national levels that coherence and the coordination of military and development efforts is most crucial. The Fourth Generation" adversary uses "all available networks—political, economic, social, and military" (Hammes 2004, 2), and it is clear that the government of Afghanistan and the international community must seize the initiative and use the strategic framework provided by the Afghanistan Compact and Afghanistan's National Development Strategy to counter those networks.

The international community must also ensure that the correct diplomatic, developmental and military tools are being used to attain the ambitious vision of the compact. It is clear that there is a certain degree of international incoherence in both the diplomatic and developmental aspects of the Afghan mission. By late 2006, and into 2007, it also became evident that the security effort suffered from a degree of incoherence and that both international and Afghan military forces have been slow to adapt to the realities of "war among the people."

Adapting Military Force

The primary role of military forces within the broader effort required to stabilize a failed or failing state must be to establish a level of security sufficient to provide the local population with a basic level of individual (or human) security. Although it is difficult to establish objective criteria to define the meaning of a "basic level of security," in most cases security means that people feel free to go to work, till their fields, and go to school with a degree of confidence that they and their families will not come under attack by insurgents. Of equal importance, they must also be confident that international or government forces will not harm them, or their property, in the course of military and security operations.

To be effective in the "war among the people" that is ongoing in parts of Afghanistan, military forces must adapt their structures, equipment, tactics, and most importantly, their attitudes and military culture to the new reality. Unfortunately, in the Afghan conflict most have not. The lack of "boots on the ground." has led to a continuing over-reliance on airpower, with inevitable and tragic consequences for the civilian population. Weak human intelligence has contributed to this situation, as the insurgents have adapted their tactics to defy the high-tech surveillance platforms on which Western armies have come to depend. National caveats have constrained the freedom of action that NATO commanders need to respond to the changing threats around the country, and radical force protection policies have alienated much of the population and, even worse, created political tensions and divisions within NATO.

Some individual nations and armies have done a good job adapting their tactics to local conditions and have begun to develop more effective human intelligence networks. NATO has made some progress in aligning national PRTs and is pressuring troop contributors to eliminate non-essential caveats. In short, efforts are being made to adapt while engaged in combat with the insurgents. On the other hand, dichotomies in national attitudes and military cultures continue to contribute to "a combustible and confusing mix of doctrine and tools" that can "begin to feel like terrorism to ordinary Afghans" (Sewall 2007).[8]

Some commentators claim that the American military is culturally predisposed to a "methodical and high-tech approach to war" that has become "extreme" (Corum 2007, 117). Sarah Sewall, an astute student of counter-insurgency, has described the contradictions between the NATO and US military approaches and concludes that the US reliance on airpower, combined with poor targeting information and excessive civilian casualties will continue to erode public support in Afghanistan and in NATO nations and, thus, render the Afghan mission untenable (2007). Dr. James S. Corum of the US Army Command and General Staff College is even more critical, describing the American approach as a "highly flawed model when confronted with the realities of Afghanistan" (2007, 75).

Based on my observations in Afghanistan, other armies have taken on some aspects of this American military mindset that is bound to be counterproductive in the face of mounting civilian casualties. It is clear that all of the military forces engaged in counterinsurgency operations in Afghanistan—both international and ANA—must adapt their structures, tactics, and operating cultures to meet the complex challenges of fighting a "war among the people." To accomplish this, NATO and US forces must become more cognizant of protecting the Afghan population. Air strikes should be limited to well-defined targets with little risk of collateral damage, and both special forces and regular infantry should be the instruments of choice in attacking confirmed insurgent positions. Finally, the shortage of international troops must be offset with a more robust mentoring and training program for the ANA.

Conclusion

Despite the pessimistic tone of much commentary, Afghanistan has seen some remarkable progress in the past six years. As part of the Bonn Process, the roadmap that established the basic political framework necessary for good governance, Afghans agreed to a constitution, held very successful presidential elections in October 2004 and parliamentary elections on 18 September 2005. These achievements should not be underestimated. Thirty years of conflict had not only destroyed the basic structures of the state and much of the physical infrastructure, it had also inflicted serious damage to the social fabric of the country. This kind of damage is almost impossible to see, but it is probably more significant than the kind of damage that can be photographed and measured. Massive population movements have all but destroyed many of the traditional methods of social regulation and conflict resolution, and constant fighting has left the population with a collective case of psychological disruption. The success of the Bonn process, in effect, signalled the collective commitment of the Afghan people to democratic processes over the power of the gun. In addition to this impressive political process, Afghans and the international community have established basic security in about three-quarters of the country. Hundreds of thousands of children, including girls, have returned to school. Clinics, roads, irrigation systems, and countless other development projects have been completed, much with little fanfare or media attention.

The Afghan state building project is extremely complex. The chronic criminality, corruption, poppy, poverty, and weak state institutions cannot be "wished away." Instead, they can only be resolved by the concerted joint Afghan–international effort that was committed to at the London Conference. State building is a long and arduous process. Canada is one of thirty-six nations with military forces on the ground—even more countries are involved in development. Patience, resolve, and perseverance are essential if the people of Afghanistan are to see the results of the promises made in the past four years. We should have no illusions. Much remains to be done in Afghanistan, and the future of the country is by no means assured.

One of the major lessons of the Afghan experience is that good governance and economic development are essential elements of security and stability. Most military professionals have long recognized that military force alone is insufficient to defeat a determined insurgency and that security without sustained development and good governance will inevitably be transitory. Although Canada's "whole of government" strategy reflects this reality (as do the strategies of several other nations), establishing security and accomplishing the vision of the Afghanistan Compact demands that all of these strategies be unified at the international level in Kabul.

Notes

Reprinted with permission from the *Journal of Military and Strategic Studies* 10, no. 11 (Fall 2007).

1 See Hy S. Rothstein, *Afghanistan and the Uncertain Future of Unconventional Warfare* for a comprehensive discussion of the numerous strategic errors that have led to many of the problems faced by the Afghan Government in 2005 and 2006.

2 For example, Linda McQuaig's polemic in the 12 February 2006 edition of the *Toronto Star* is a particularly ill-informed critique of CF operations in Afghanistan. A more balanced view is offered in the Project Ploughshares Briefing #06/01, titled *Afghanistan: Counter-insurgency by Other Means*. Ernie Regehr asks a number of valid questions that should be resolved by a careful reading of the *Compact, ANDS,* and Canadian Forces statements. The UNSC endorsement in its resolution 1659 (2006) should satisfy those who question the legitimacy of the Canadian commitment to the Afghanistan Compact. See http://www.nato.int/isaf/topics/mandate/unscr/resolution_1659.pdf.

3 Charney Research, *ABC Poll: Life in Afghanistan*, 7 December 2005. Available at: http://www.charneyresearch.com. This poll found that 77% of Afghans support the current government's "direction" for the future and that 88% consider the US overthrow of the Taliban a "good thing." Similar findings were made by the Center for Strategic and International Studies. See Frederick Barton, Bathsheba Crocker, and

Morgan L. Courtney, *In the Balance: Measuring Progress in Afghanistan*, Center for Strategic and International Studies (Washington, 2005)

4 The compact is very specific in terms of the role of the government and all international forces in securing the security and stability of the country. UNSC endorsement is a clear expression of support.

5 Personal communication with Brigadier General David Fraser (CA), Comd RC(S), 11 February 2006.

6 Dr. Ghani (former Afghan Finance Minister and now Chancellor Kabul University) is one of the most articulate Afghan advocates of economic development as a weapon in the battle against the insurgency.

7 See http://www.sphereproject.org/ for the Humanitarian Charter and the Code of Conduct. These documents detail the principles that NGOs aspire to in the conduct of their operations in humanitarian disasters and emergencies. Impartiality and independence are at the heart of these principles.

8 Sarah Sewall, the director of the Carr Center for Human Rights at Harvard, has worked extensively with General David Patreaus (the current coalition commander in Iraq and the driving force behind the new US Army counter-insurgency doctrine).

References

"Agreement on Provisional Arrangements in Afghanistan Pending the Re-establishment of Permanent Government Institutions" (The Bonn Agreement). 2002. Available online at http://www.unama-afg.org/docs/_nonUN%20 Docs/_Internation-Conferences&Forums/Bonn-Talks/bonn.htm.

Barton, Frederick, Bathsheba Crocker, and Morgan L. Courtney. 2005. *In the Balance: Measuring Progress in Afghanistan*. Washington, DC: Center for Strategic and International Studies.

Canada, National Defence Backgrounder. 2007. *Canadian Forces Operations in Afghanistan*. 14 August. http://www.forces.gc.ca/site/newsroom/view _news_e.asp?id=1703.

Collins, Joseph. 2004. "Afghanistan: Winning a Three Block War." *Journal of Conflict Studies*. Winter: 70–72.

Corum, James S. 2007. *Fighting the War on Terror: A Counterinsurgency Strategy*. St. Paul, MN: Zenith Press.

Ghani, Ashraf and Clare Lockhart. 2006. "Rethinking Nation Building." *Washington Post*. 1 January.

Hammes, Thomas X. 2004. *The Sling and Stone: On War in the 21st Century*. St. Paul, MN: Zenith Press.

Hsu, Emily and Beth DeGrasse. 2006. *Afghan Insurgency Still a Potent Force*. USI Peace Briefing. Washington, DC. February.

Islamic Republic of Afghanistan. 2006. *The Afghanistan Compact: A Strategy for Security, Governance, Economic Growth and Poverty Reduction*. Kabul. http://www.ands.gov.af/ands/I-ANDS/afghanistan-compacts.asp.

———. 2006b. *Afghanistan National Development Strategy, Summary Report*. Kabul. http://www.ands.gov.af/ands/I-ANDS/summary-report.asp.

Krulak, Charles C. 1997. "The Three Block War: Fighting in Urban Areas." *Vital Speeches of the Day* 64 (5): 139–42. 15 December.

McQuaig, Linda. 2006. "Is Our Mission about Preserving Our Way of Life, or Helping U.S. Extend its Supremacy?" *Toronto Star.* 12 February.

Regehr, Ernie. 2006. *Afghanistan: Counter-insurgency by Other Means.* Project Ploughshares Briefing no. 06/01.

Rothstein, Hy S. 2006. *Afghanistan and the Uncertain Future of Unconventional Warfare.* Annapolis, MD: Naval Institute Press.

Sewall, Sarah. 2007. "A Heavy Hand in Afghanistan." *Boston Globe.* 15 June.

Smith, Rupert. 2005. *The Utility of Force: The Art of War in the Modern World.* London: Allan Lane.

United Nations Security Council. 2006. Resolution 1659/2006. 15 February. http://daccessdds.un.org/doc/UNDOC/GEN/N06/244/81/PDF/N0624481.pdf?Open Element.

11

Geoffrey Hayes

Canada in Afghanistan
Assessing the Numbers

The Canadian mission in Afghanistan was by far the top Canadian news story of 2006 (*Toronto Star* 2007) and with good reason, for not since the Korean War have so many Canadians died in an overseas conflict. Thirty-six Canadian soldiers and one diplomat were killed in Afghanistan through the year. Sixteen more Canadian soldiers died in Afghanistan in the first half of 2007. In July 2008, the Canadian death toll in Afghanistan reached eighty-eight.

Perhaps we need look no further than these figures to explain why Canadians are so divided over our role in Afghanistan. Polls show a substantial decline in support for the Canadian military mission, from 75% in favour in 2002 to 50% as of October 2006. A poll commissioned by the CBC, the national public broadcaster, in November 2006 found 59% "wanted Canadian troops out of Afghanistan before 2009." When asked how they thought the Canadian mission to Afghanistan would end, "58% [of respondents] said it would not be successful, while 34 said it would be."[1] In April 2007, a slim majority (52%) of Canadians supported the role of Canadian troops in Afghanistan. But two-thirds wanted Canadian troops to come home when Canada's current commitment ends in February 2009.[2]

These polls prompted campaigns to shore up support for the Afghan deployment by the Minister of National Defence and Brigadier-General David Fraser upon his return from Regional Command (RC) South, where in 2006 he commanded some six thousand NATO troops in southern Afghanistan, including some 2,300 Canadians (Martin 2006).

We might conclude that Canadians simply are ill-informed about the Afghan enterprise. But this chapter begins with the assumption that we cannot view the Afghan mission in a vacuum but rather as part of a fluid and often contradictory view of how Canadians understand their place in the world, their relationship with the United States and their Allies, and the role of the Canadian Armed Forces (CF). In light of their changing roles in Afghanistan, Canadians are also concerned about whether they can make a difference without sacrificing Canadian lives or Canadian values. In short, Canadians are uncertain about the prospects of their mission to Afghanistan.

This chapter begins by examining a Canadian strategic culture and how it may have informed Canadians about the mission to Afghanistan. It then explores Canada's various roles in Afghanistan in light of changing politics at home. A combat role in 2002 was followed by a three-year stint in which Canadians played a considerable military, but also diplomatic and development role in Kabul. In the political climate of the time, what might be called Canada's "3D" phase (disarmament, development, and democracy) appeared as a popular and relatively inexpensive way of balancing our commitments. The decision to return to southern Afghanistan in mid-2005 came just as a new, more fragile domestic political climate was emerging. As Canadian casualties mounted in 2006, and questions grew about the mission's prospects, the domestic political consensus quickly evaporated. By 2007, the government's appeals to lofty notions of internationalism and human rights no longer carried as much weight as they once had. Indeed, in the fall of 2007 the current government faced a political dilemma over extending the Canadian commitment past February 2009.

Perhaps Kim Nossal's historical view of Canada's perceptions abroad is a good starting point to understand a Canadian view of itself in the world. He argues that Canadians initially defined the "realm," the parts and peoples of the world that Canadians needed and wanted to defend, as the British Empire. Nossal maintains that a vocal isolationism limited the realm after 1919, but that it still extended across the Atlantic in 1939 when Canada entered the Second World War. After 1945, the realm expanded, Nossal argues, both in Canada's commitment to Western Europe through its NATO membership and by its continental security agreements (NORAD) with the United States. Even though Canadian government support for NATO and NORAD declined through the 1970s and 1980s, Nossal argues that "public support for the idea of a wider definition of the Canadian "realm" persisted" (2004, 515).

One of the ways Canada sought to influence a wider realm was through its support of the United Nations generally, and UN peacekeeping specifically. For many Canadians the United Nations represents an important counterweight to our economic, political, and military relationship with

Washington. Canada's golden age of foreign policy reached a zenith when diplomat and future prime minister Lester Pearson organized the United Nations Emergency Force (UNEF) during the Suez crisis in 1956. Pearson won the Nobel Peace Prize for his efforts. Successive Canadian governments (including Pearson's) found peacekeeping missions problematic, but until the Cold War ended, many Canadians came to identify closely with Canadian peacekeepers wearing the blue helmets of UN-sanctioned missions in places like Egypt, the Golan Heights, or Cyprus. Despite its ad hoc nature, peacekeeping held a wide symbolic appeal, especially among those who held suspicions of American influence. UN peacekeeping helped define a Canadian place in the world where the United States could not go. Many Canadians came to believe that "Canadians keep the peace; Americans fight wars" (Granatstein 2007).

As Nossal notes, the end of the Cold War only confused Canada's place in the world. And no wonder: as it pulled its forces from Europe, the government of the day reduced the size of the Canadian Forces. While the number of Canadian peacekeepers on UN operations also declined, Canada's overseas deployments increased through the decade, often within peace-enforcement operations in places like Somalia, Bosnia, Croatia, and Kosovo. Canadians soon realized that these were not "traditional" peacekeeping missions. The death of a young Somali detained by Canadian troops in 1993 prompted a public inquiry that shattered public confidence in the CF.[3] The mass slaughter of Rwandan Hutus in 1994 while a small, Canadian-led peacekeeping force stood helplessly by further undermined a well-established understanding that Canadian peacekeeping efforts saved lives.[4] These episodes point to the paradox of which Nossal speaks. On one hand, Canadian governments in the 1990s showed a concern for "human security," a principle advanced by Lloyd Axworthy, who was the foreign affairs minister between 1996 and 2000. But as Canadian officials tried to broaden Canada's international "realm," Nossal argues that Canadians tended to "narrow their perimeter of concern." Where once Canadians were willing to defend Western Europeans against Soviet attack, Nossal maintains that Canadians in the 1990s appeared indifferent to the plight of "Kosavar Albanians, or Timorese, or Bosnian Muslims" let alone the hundreds of thousands who died violently in Africa (2004, 517). Some might well ask if the Canadian "realm" includes the people of Afghanistan.

Canadians showed little confusion in the aftermath of 11 September 2001. Backed by United Nations Security Council resolutions 1368 and 1373, as well as NATO invocations of its collective security arrangements, the Canadian government announced in October 2001 that it would "contribute air, land and sea forces to the international force being formed to conduct a campaign against terrorism." Canadian ships were the first

Canadian forces deployed as part of Operation Apollo in support of the US-led Operation Enduring Freedom (OEF) in Afghanistan (DND 2004).

In January 2002, a 750-soldier Canadian battle group joined American, Australian, and British forces in Paktia province to search out and destroy small groups of al-Qaeda and the Taliban (AQT). On 17 April 2002, four Canadian soldiers near Kandahar were killed and eight others wounded when American aircraft accidentally bombed their training area outside of Kandahar. The public shock across the country was matched only by the outrage that American pilots had mistaken Canadian night-fire exercises for Taliban targets (Brown 2002; DND 2004). A month later, the Canadian government announced that Canadian forces were to leave southern Afghanistan by July.

We have seen elsewhere in this volume that the Americans initially had little desire to undertake a broad-based state building project after the Taliban were driven from Kabul in 2001. In December 2001, the UN authorized the International Security and Assistance Force (ISAF) to assist the Afghan Transitional Authority (ATA). ISAF was a compromise intended to provide a security buffer for the Bonn Agreement. In the eyes of Canadian commentators, however, ISAF was also "designed to get the international community to buy into Afghanistan reconstruction under international, not American auspices" (Maloney 2006/ 2007, 25). In the aftermath of the Canadian "friendly fire" incident, and with the Americans preparing for its invasion of Iraq through the fall of 2002 (Ricks 2006), ISAF offered an increasingly attractive alternative to the Canadian government.

By the timing alone, Canada's commitment in February 2003 to the ISAF mission in Kabul appeared tied to its decision a month later not to commit troops to the American-led war in Iraq. As Simeon McKay recently noted, Canada's decision not to participate in the Iraq war divided the governing Liberal party by forcing it to choose between the United States and the United Nations. Indeed, Canada spent a great deal of diplomatic capital when Canada's ambassador to the UN Paul Heinbecker tried to persuade the Americans to delay the Iraqi invasion until UN inspectors had completed their search for weapons of mass destruction. The Canadian initiative failed, but it reflected how important it was in Ottawa to reconcile the "two important pillars of Canadian foreign policy" (McKay 2006, 882).

Canada's commitment to ISAF in Kabul (Operation Athena) was another attempt to bridge our precarious international position, for by contributing to the UN-sanctioned mission in Kabul, the government hoped it had found a way to reconcile our faith in the UN with the strategic interests shared with Washington. Soon the government presented our new role as part of a "3D" approach, one that merged defence, diplomacy, and development (Pratt 2004). The policy reflected a growing international consensus on how to rebuild post-conflict and failed states, but the balance implicit in "3D" also appealed to a range of Canadian opinion. Canadians deployed two thousand troops to Kabul in the first half of 2004, making them one of the largest of twenty-six national contingents in the capital. But the military's job was not to hunt down al-Qaeda and the Taliban in the hills of eastern Afghanistan; rather it was to assist the Afghan Transitional Authority to maintain security. A Canadian, General Rick Hillier, was then the ISAF commander, while another Canadian, Brigadier-General Jocelyn Lacroix, headed the Kabul Multi-National Brigade (KMNB). In Camp Julien, built in the city's southern outskirts between the ruins of the King's and Queen's Palaces, the Canadians could boast of facilities and resources that were the envy of the other military forces.

But it was not only Canadian soldiers who were then providing leadership. From the Canadian embassy that opened in Kabul in September 2003 came energetic and influential counsel to the highest levels of the Afghan government. And from the Kabul offices of the Canadian International Development Agency (CIDA), Canadian humanitarian and development aid began to flow at unprecedented levels. After the Tokyo Conference on Afghan Reconstruction in January 2002, Afghanistan became Canada's largest recipient of bilateral aid (CIDA 2007).

Between 2003 and 2005, Canadian troops conducted thousands of patrols on Kabul streets, often in the company of Afghan police. To many Canadians these patrols appeared consistent with our peacekeeping legacy. It was also relatively safe: just four Canadian soldiers were killed in Afghanistan between 2003 and 2005. We were "punching above our weight" because of our military commitment, the money we had to spend, and the leadership and advice we had to offer. We had also earned strategic influence, for Canadian military planners were then creating an investment management framework that identified for the Afghan government specific areas for unified action. With the invitation of interim president Hamid Karzai, Canadian planning staff began to consider longer-term areas of concern. A Canadian strategic planning role continues through a Strategic Advisory Team for Afghanistan (SAT-A) that began its work in 2005.

Although Canada's commitment to Kabul was important and popular back home, a critical strategic window of opportunity was already closing by 2004. Concerned about draining resources from its operations in Iraq, the American administration prevented ISAF from moving operations beyond the Afghan capital until the fall of 2003. William Maley has called this delay "one of the worst blunders in post-Taliban Afghanistan" for it prevented the Afghan central government from extending its presence and legitimacy outside of Kabul (2006, 65). It was a delay for which Canadians have paid dearly.

When General Hillier moved from his ISAF command to become Chief of the Defence Staff (CDS) in February 2005, he emerged as a far more public military leader than Canadians have known for a long time. General Hillier also has no trouble describing the mission in Afghanistan in direct and often indiscreet terms (Murphy 2006b).[5] It was General Hillier and foreign affairs officials who lobbied to deploy the bulk of Canadian military operations in Afghanistan from Kabul to Kandahar. This redeployment also took the Canadians away from the NATO-led ISAF command and back under the US-led Operation Enduring Freedom, a move that may have assuaged Washington's disappointment in Ottawa's decision in February 2005 not to take part in its missile defence program.[6]

This third phase of Canada's involvement in Afghanistan was marked by little public debate, as it was overshadowed by the attempts of Paul Martin's Liberal minority government to stay in power. The Canadians officially took up their duties in early 2006 amid a federal election campaign that won Stephen Harper's Conservative Party a minority government, forcing the Liberals from office after thirteen years. That election campaign stood in sharp contrast to the one in the Netherlands, where the Dutch government nearly fell over the decision to send Dutch troops to Afghanistan's southern provinces (*CBC News* 2006).

The new Canadian prime minister (who in opposition had supported a Canadian role in Iraq and missile defence) came out strongly in support of the Afghan mission. A Parliamentary consensus appeared firm at a time when the Afghanistan Compact (signed in London in January–February 2006) signalled a revived international commitment to Afghanistan. But events beyond Canadian control again intervened. Through the summer of 2005, the Canadians set up a Provincial Reconstruction Team (PRT) in Kandahar. Made up of military, diplomatic, development, and police officials, the PRT concept is seen by NATO as a means of extending the 3D approach beyond the Afghan capital. On 15 January 2006, Glyn Berry, the political director of the Canadian PRT, was killed by a suicide bomber. With Canadian civilians at increased risk, Ottawa promptly withdrew civilian officials from Kandahar to reassess the security situation. To counter the impression that the development and diplomatic components of Canada's new "whole of government" approach were in eclipse, the new government pledged in February an additional $200 million for "reconstruction and development activities" (CIDA 2007).

When the prime minister visited the troops and met with Afghan officials in March 2005, he commented that Canada "would not cut and run." One commentator noted that it was a clever phrase, for "instead of actually explaining to Canadians why our soldiers were fighting and dying in a remote corner of the world, Harper simply appealed to ... [Canada's] ... latent macho pride" (Taylor 2007, 12). The prime minister employed more lofty rhetoric when Parliament met in May to debate whether to extend the mission to 2009. The government emphasized Canada's "important contribution" to the United Nations and NATO but then referred to a set of higher values like "reducing poverty, enhancing human rights and gender equality, strengthening civil society, and helping to build a free, secure and self-sustaining democratic state for all Afghan men, women and children." Finally, the government noted that "Canada's commitment in Afghanistan is consistent with Canada's support of freedom, democracy, the rule of law and human rights around the world" (Canadian Parliamentary Debates 2006).

If the government's intention was to embarrass and divide the opposition, it succeeded, but the debate also signalled a shifting political landscape. The Liberal opposition questioned whether the commitment to Afghanistan prevented deployments to other potential trouble spots such as Haiti or Darfur. Members from the sovereigntist Bloc Québécois (BQ) were mindful that a Quebec-based battle group was preparing for an Afghan deployment in 2007. Bloc leader Gilles Duceppe asked about the nature of the Canadian military commitment: "Is there a specific schedule and a withdrawal plan should the situation become uncontrollable?" Several members from the left-wing New Democratic Party (NDP) were concerned that Canada was no longer taking part in traditional peacekeeping operations and were too closely supporting the Bush administration under Operation Enduring Freedom. According to member of Parliament Bill Siksay, "We are there to deliver development aid, but not to deliver it by the military. That is not the Canadian way of doing development work. We are there to do democratic development, but not to do it at the end of the barrel of a gun. That is not the Canadian way." In the end, the Liberal opposition, who had made the original commitment to Afghanistan, were divided over extending the mission, while the BQ and the NDP were solidly opposed. The motion passed by just four votes. Parliamentary consensus on the Afghan mission had evaporated by the early summer of 2006 (ibid.).

The divisions apparent in the Parliamentary debate were widened when the Senlis Council reported to Canadian audiences in June 2006. In language reflecting the subtle balances of Canadian strategic culture, the council maintained that "confusion over objectives" in Kandahar not only went against Canada's peacekeeping tradition, but that Canadians were then "bearing the brunt of America's mission failures" and not addressing the crises of poverty, opium and security (Senlis Council 2006a).

Though some question the Senlis Council for its campaign to encourage the purpose of poppy production in Afghanistan,[7] its report highlighted the growing confusion among Canadians about Canada's role in Afghanistan. Were Canadians fighting a war on terror, on narcotics, or for the security of the Afghan people? In the summer and early fall of 2006, the Canadian battlegroup unexpectedly fought a series of pitched battles as the Taliban attempted to take back their strongholds in the south. Brigadier-General David Fraser led those operations and has argued since that that kind of fighting gave the Canadians influence, presumably in Kabul, NATO headquarters, and Washington (Staples 2007).[8] But that influence came at a cost that not all Canadians were comfortable paying. Between May and August 2006, eleven Canadian soldiers were killed in Afghanistan; another forty-one were wounded.[9] As Canadians watched firefights play out on YouTube.com (see, for example, Kesterson 2006), it was becoming more difficult for some to distinguish between the Canadians fighting in Operation Medusa, the growing American and British quagmire in Iraq, and Israel's failed attempts to rid southern Lebanon of Hezbollah strongholds.

The Canadian political divisions over Afghanistan only widened as a result. In September, the New Democratic Party urged again that Canada's commitment be reconsidered. "This is not the right mission for Canada," argued the NDP leader (Fitzpatrick 2006). Concerns also emerged from the Liberal Party, which had made the first military commitments back in 2001. Some of the candidates vying to become Liberal leader through the fall of 2006 began to question the military orientation of the mission. Among them was Stéphane Dion, who won the Liberal leadership in December from front-runner Michael Ignatieff, a well-known early supporter of both the Afghan and Iraq endeavours. Days after becoming the leader of the opposition, Dion called for "a kind of Marshall Plan" that would emphasize economic development rather than combat operations: "There's no use for us to try to kill the Taliban in every corner of every mountain and to risk the lives of our soldiers in this way" (Clark and Laghi 2006, A5).

Dion's comments may hold little appreciation of the conditions in Afghanistan, but that is beside the point. Dion's intended audience was largely in Quebec, where support for the mission remains consistently weaker than in the rest of Canada. Not to be outdone, BQ leader Gilles Duceppe threatened to defeat the government in a Parliamentary vote of confidence unless it "rapidly and profoundly change[d] the Canadian mission in Afghanistan, which in a few months will be made up of men and women from Valcartier [Quebec]." Duceppe proclaimed that "we will not be accomplices of an obtuse government who would stubbornly maintain the current course" (*Globe and Mail* 2006).

It was difficult to find much optimism about the Afghanistan enterprise from any international observers toward the end of 2006. In October, the Senlis Council again urged Canadians to take a "new strategic approach" within NATO to provide food and medical supplies; to help "establish political structure in communities" by organizing emergency *Jirgas* or Afghan assemblies; and to find "science-based" alternatives to opium production and eradication (Senlis Council 2006b, 4). The International Crisis Group (ICG) was also pessimistic. Its November 2006 report praised the countries that had stood up to the Taliban, but maintained that there were no "quick fixes." The ICG report emphasized widespread corruption in the country, a flourishing drug trade, and an increasingly bold insurgency that was partly coming across the porous border between Afghanistan and Pakistan (2006). Few Canadians were reading this kind of material, but such reports influenced the Canadian media (see, for example, *New York Times* 2006). When such reports were set against the fifteen Canadian fatalities suffered between September and November 2006 (each well covered in the press), Canadian support for the mission declined even further. In November 2006, just 44% of Canadians polled supported the role of Canada's troops in Afghanistan.[10]

Poignant Christmas stories about troops away from home reflected an admiration that Canadians hold for their troops overseas (Blatchford 2007a). But "bumper-sticker patriotism" was becoming more difficult to reconcile against a wide, complex, and seemingly unsolvable series of crises over which Canadians have little control (Simpson 2007; Travers 2007). The NATO summit late in 2006 did little to satisfy a growing Canadian sense that other countries needed to "step up" and assist in southern Afghanistan. Only Poland offered troops for the south, while Canadians learned with some frustration that other NATO nations had imposed caveats on their NATO deployments to avoid casualties. It seemed strange indeed to see Canadians at the forefront of the NATO alliance, bolstering a mission that some quarters consider a crucial test of the alliance.[11]

The problems within NATO were just one of thirteen major issues identified in a report by the Standing Senate Committee on National Security and Defence in February 2007. Seeking to replace "emotional" with "intellectual" patriotism, the senate committee visited Afghanistan to assess the chances and costs of Canadian success. The report was blunt, noting that the Taliban "have time and geography on their side." Against them is a government in Kabul known for its corruption, supported by an alliance that Afghans too often associate with civilian deaths. The committee met with one Afghan police colonel who, "after he said all the proper things in a speech he had clearly memorized, became more animated and more frank when he claimed that Canada has no chance of winning the support of the people of Kandahar as long as so many innocent Afghans were dying as a result of NATO air strikes" (Senate Committee 2007). The committee also criticized Canada's development efforts, arguing that CIDA's focus on funding central governing institutions was appearing to do too little immediate good for the people in Kandahar.

Canadian senators are not elected, so they can ask some provocative questions: "Are Canadians willing to commit themselves to decades of involvement in Afghanistan, which could cost hundreds of Canadian lives and billions of dollars with no guarantee of ending up with anything like the kind of society that makes sense to us?" (ibid.). A prominent Canadian historian was equally blunt in his answer. Desmond Morton wrote in the journal *Policy Options* that "we are spending human lives and billions of dollars to sustain a war effort with no prospect of success. Since most NATO members realize this and refuse troops for a hopeless commitment, the alliance is stressed to a breaking point" (2006/2007, 20).[12] Morton might not be right in his assessment, but the tone of his remark pointed to a sobering realism about the Afghanistan mission. In September, a national columnist known for her support of the mission echoed a general frustration as she described how Canadians fight for ground they had won the year before, but which was lost "in a stew of corruption, ineptitude and tribal quarrels" (Blatchford 2007b).

This frustration comes in response to a mission that has come to dominate our Canadian defence and foreign policy. In 2005, the total regular force strength of the Canadian Forces was 62,181: 9,954 in the Navy, 13,547 in the Air Force and just 20,458 in the Land Forces. A senate committee maintained in 2005 "that the Canadian Forces are operating at a personnel level approximately 40–45% below what they require to perform the types of duties they have been ordered to perform over the past decade" (Senate Committee 2005).[13] Canada's increased tempo of operations since 2005 holds enormous implications for the men and women of the Canadian Forces, especially the foot soldiers who form the bulk of the Canadian battlegroup.

The Afghanistan mission has also come at the expense of almost all of our other overseas military commitments. Of the 2,907 members of the CF deployed in July 2007 on overseas missions, some 2545 (88%) are serving in Afghanistan: 2,500 under ISAF command, thirty under American command to help rebuild and train the Afghan National Army and the Afghan Police, while another fifteen personnel form the Strategic Advisory Team in Kabul. In contrast, sixty-four Canadian personnel serve in four missions in Africa, while eight are in the Balkans, and just four serve in Haiti. Except for a Canadian vessel deployed on NATO operations, the largest Canadian overseas deployment outside of Afghanistan consists of just twenty-eight personnel in the Sinai.[14] Canada has limited options should demands be made to deploy in other parts of the world. In the longer term, a "Canada First" defence policy announced in 2006 calls for more CF personnel, but these priorities will also have to be balanced against the need to replace aging ships and aircraft to defend Canada's borders, especially its claims in the Arctic (DND 2006).

The senators' report also asks Canadians to consider how the Afghan mission is consistent with Canadian values. Few Canadians seek to impose their beliefs on an Islamic state, but on some moral issues Canadians hold strong feelings. Supporters of the mission, for example, often cite the increased numbers of young women in school as a measure of progress in Afghanistan after the fall of the Taliban. But this "values-based" defence of the mission can cut both ways. A story in March 2006 related how Afghan authorities allegedly threatened an Afghan man with death for converting to Christianity. It prompted a visceral reaction among many Canadians. One eloquent Canadian commentator concluded on national television at the time:

> Are Canadians to fight and die for the right to execute recent converts? There is nothing that will more toxify the morale of Canadian troops than the idea that they are risking their lives to support a government that believes in hanging people for what they believe. That's not democracy. That's barbarism, and it surely is not worth fighting and dying for in Afghanistan or anywhere else. It is, however, very much worth fighting against. (Murphy 2006a)

The treatment of Afghan prisoners has also left successive Canadian governments seeking to reconcile Canadian values with Afghan justice. The issue was first raised late in 2001 when the first Canadians were deployed to the region, and it has dogged successive governments ever since. A sustained attack on the Harper government began in April 2007 when *The Globe and Mail* reported that Afghans detained by Canadian soldiers and handed over to Afghan police officials were "beaten, whipped, starved, frozen, choked and subjected to electric shocks during interrogation" (Smith 2007). The editors accused key Canadian military and political leaders (including the Defence Minister and the Chief of Defence Staff, who signed the original detainee agreement in December 2005) of providing false assurances that prisoners were being monitored. The editorial noted that such revelations were that much more "shattering" after a public inquiry in September 2006 explored how American authorities detained a Canadian citizen, Mahar Arar, in September 2002 and deported him to his native Syria where he was imprisoned and tortured for over a year (*Globe and Mail* 2007a).

Against these revelations and discussions came more Canadian casualties. On 8 April 2007, six Canadian soldiers were killed when their armoured vehicle struck an improvised explosive device outside of Kandahar City; three days later, two more died and three more were wounded in roadside bombings.[15] Some keen observers claim that the Canadian mission is finally making progress after the fighting of 2006. They cite as evidence the growing numbers of Afghans who have returned to their homes in Kandahar province after they were driven out last year. Supporters also see progress in the growing outreach of the revived Provincial Reconstruction Team, as well as the expanding numbers of community development councils that allow Afghans to set local priorities and gain access to funds through the National Solidarity Programme (Maloney 2007).[16] Despite further casualties, Canadian public support for the mission in early 2007 rose slightly from the fall of 2006, but only to 52%. Polls suggest that almost two-thirds of Canadians (63%) want the troops home when our current commitment ends.[17] With Canada having lost sixty dead in Afghanistan by late June 2007, the mission had reached a tipping point. As a contingent drawn from Quebec prepared for its deployment to Kandahar, NATO Secretary-General Jaap de Hoop Scheffer came to Quebec City to see them off.

Canada is an important measure of NATO's strength, but the domestic political factors described here forced the government to reconsider its policy. After conceding the need for a Parliamentary consensus to extend the Canadian presence in Afghanistan beyond 2009, the Conservative prime minister commissioned an independent panel in October 2007 to explore "Canada's Future Role in Afghanistan." Led by former Liberal cabinet minister John Manley, the panel consulted widely and recommended in January 2008 that Canada rebalance what was once known as the 3D approach. The panel called for "a stronger and more disciplined diplomatic position regarding Afghanistan and the regional players." It also concluded that Canada should remain in Kandahar past February 2009, but only if another country sent an additional one thousand soldiers to the south, and only if the Canadian Forces placed "increasing emphasis" on training the Afghan National Security Forces. On development funding, the panel maintained that Canada give grater priority to "direct, bilateral project assistance," which should include at least one "signature project (a hospital, for example, or a major irrigation project) identified with Canada and led by Canadians." Better measures of Canadian contributions against the goals of the Afghanistan Compact were also recommended. The panel also called for a new Canadian government message on Afghanistan, one that was "franker and more frequent" and that gave "greater emphasis to ... [Canada's] diplomatic and reconstruction efforts as well as those of the military" (Independent Panel on Canada's Future Role in Afghanistan 2008, 37–38).

The panel sent two signals at once. First, it signalled NATO allies that Canada could withdraw in 2009 if no further international support came to Afghanistan's south. But the report also offered a compromise to Canada's opposition parties, who since 2006 had opposed what some considered Canada's purely "military" mission. By these measures, the panel's signals were heard. In March 2008, soon after a Parliamentary compromise agreed to extend the Canadian mission to 2011, France confirmed a promise to send troops to eastern Afghanistan so that more American troops could move south. Days later, prime minister Stephen Harper agreed that the international community had met Canada's conditions for extending the mission (Simpson 2008; Agence France Presse 2008b; 2008c; Dow Jones International News 2008).

The Canadian case is not unique, for each of Canada's allies within the NATO-led mission considers its role in Afghanistan through its own political lenses. The Dutch military has been in Afghanistan's Uruzgan province since 2006, at a cost of fourteen Dutch soldiers and a divisive political debate that has, at times, spilled over onto Afghan streets. After postponing a parliamentary debate in the fall of 2007, the Dutch cabinet decided to reduce its deployment in Uruzgan after August 2008, and to end its "military responsibility" in that province after 1 August 2010. According to the Dutch cabinet decision, "by then [the Netherlands] will have borne its burden as a NATO partner" (Dutch Ministry of Foreign Affairs 2008; Agence France Presse 2008a).

Then there is the case of Germany, which in 2008 deployed over three thousand soldiers to Afghanistan as part of its NATO commitment. It has led the reform of the Afghan police, and it maintains a PRT in Kunduz province in the country's north. But the Germans do not take part in combat operations, for as one German commentator noted in May 2007:

> Until recently there was a clear division of labor in Afghanistan within the International Security and Assistance Force. The British, Canadians, Americans and Dutch were responsible for the dangerous south, and the Germans took care of the far less dangerous north. Put coarsely—fighters at the bottom, construction helpers at the top. That was a concession to the Germans, though not one that was publicly expressed. Because (Germans) used to be state terrorists, and then turned into exceptionally peaceful world citizens, one didn't want to force them to take on tough foreign jobs. (cited in Spiegel Online International 2007a)

This unflinching assessment came after three German soldiers were killed by a suicide bomber in the increasingly unstable province of Kunduz. The deaths of three German soldiers in August 2007 raised the German death toll in Afghanistan to twenty-one and sharpened political debate over extending the German mandate (*Spiegel Online International* 2007b). In March 2008, the Canadian foreign affairs minister urged Germany to do more by extending its deployment to southern Afghanistan (*Spiegel Online International* 2008). But so far, the German chancellor has resisted such pressure. German public opinion polls show that more than half of German respondents want to withdraw their troops from Afghanistan completely (Saunders 2007; Dempsey 2007b).

It may be that the Canadian government has been more adept than some of its NATO partners at negotiating the many uncertainties of the Afghanistan mission. Since 2001, Canadian military personnel have taken part in a wide spectrum of activity. Canadian combat operations in support of the US-led "war on terror" in 2002 were followed by almost three years under ISAF command in the relative calm of Kabul. When Canadians returned to the volatile Kandahar province in 2005, the rising casualty rate forced apart the Canadian political consensus. With the possibility of an election looming over Canada's mission to Afghanistan, the government sought the advice of an independent panel that called for a tough stand on Canada's NATO allies while offering Canadians a higher profile for Canadian diplomatic and development efforts. The government won significant compromises abroad and at home, ensuring a Canadian presence in Afghanistan until at least 2011.

But uncertainty over the future of Afghanistan will continue to drive the debate in Canada. Some commentators will urge that our support of the mission is essential to our well-being as a nation, especially in our relationship with the United States. Those who still understand Canada's international role through peacekeeping will insist that there is no peace to keep in Kandahar.[18] Others will question a military role that threatens to over-stretch the capabilities of the Canadian Forces, but which holds little strategic effect in a war that has no reasonable chance of success in the foreseeable future. For many, the Canadian realm may not include Afghanistan if it costs too many Canadian lives. Or, as one recent *Globe and Mail* (2007b) byline noted grimly: "As death toll rises, support wanes."

Notes

1 CBC-Environics Public Opinion Poll, November 2006, http://www.cbc.ca/news/background/afghanistan/afghanistan-survey2006.html.
2 Ipsos-Reid Poll, 24 April 2007, http://www/ipsos-na.com/news/pressrelease.cfm?id=3454.
3 The Report of the Somalia Commission of Inquiry was released on 2 July 1997. It is available online at http://www.dnd.ca/somalia/somaliae.htm.
4 On the Rwandan genocide from the perspective of the Canadian peacekeeping commander, see Romeo Dallaire with Brent Beardsley, *Shake Hands with the Devil: The Failure of Humanity in Rwanda* (Toronto: Random House Canada, 2003).
5 Hillier once commented that the Taliban "are detestable murderers and scumbags. I'll tell you that right up front. They detest our freedoms, they detest our society, they detest our liberties" (CBC News, "Helping Afghanistan Will Protect Canada, Says Top Soldier," 15 July 2005). http://www.cbc.ca/canada/story/2005/07/15/hillier-attack050715.html.

6 See Janice Gross Stein and Eugene Long, *Unexpected War: Canada in Kandahar* (Toronto: Viking Canada, 2007).

7 See for example, the Canadian Government's official stand against legalizing opium production in Afghanistan, "Legalizing Opium Production in Afghanistan? Not the Answer." http://www.canada-afghanistan.gc.ca/cip-pic/afghanistan/library/opium_prod-en.asp.

8 David Staples, "Paying top dollar for poppies; Coaxing Afghan farmers to plant crops other than poppies has been tried before. As the ultimate incentive, a Canadian general is advocating buying those alternative crops for the same price as opium" 23 June 2007, *Edmonton Journal*, A17. General Fraser argues in that article that a "poppy for medicine" campaign of the kind endorsed by the Senlis Council is not viable because of the weaknesses of the Afghan government.

9 CBC, "In the Line of Duty: Canada's Casualties" http://www.cbc.ca/news/background/afghanistan/casualties/total.html (last checked 21 May 2007).

10 Ipsos-Reid Poll, 24 April 2007. http://www.ipsos-na.com/news/pressrelease.cfm?id=3454. Accessed 17 May 2007.

11 On the NATO alliance and the stakes in Afghanistan, see Bruce Riedel, "Afghanistan: The Taliban Resurgent and NATO."

12 Morton's solution is to try to bring the Chinese into Afghanistan.

13 Force strength figures are drawn from Appendix VI, "Current Manning Levels." These figures do not exclude those in training, secondments, administrative appointments, etc., who are not otherwise available for overseas deployment.

14 CF International Operations as of 20 July 2007. http://www.forces.gc.ca/site/operations/current_ops_e.asp (last checked 6 September 2007).

15 CBC, "In the Line of Duty: Canada's Casualties."

16 On the National Solidarity Programme, see http://www.nspafghanistan.org/content/index_eng.html.

17 Ipsos-Reid Poll, 24 April 2007, http://www.ipsos-na.com/news/pressrelease.cfm?id=3454#.

18 Asked "When it comes to Canada's role in the world, some people say that Canada should focus on a peace-building role in the world. Others say that Canada should focus on active combat roles with our allied countries. Which view is closer to your own?" Eighty per cent of respondents preferred that Canadians pursue a peace-building role. CBC-Environics Poll, November 2006.

References

Agence France-Presse. 2008a. "Afghan Protests against Dutch, Danish 'Insult' Spread." 5 March.

———. 2008b. "Canadian Troops to Stay in Afghanistan." 13 March.

———. 2008c. "France to Send Force to East Afghanistan: NATO." 2 April.

Blatchford, Christie. 2007a. "My Most Meaningful Christmas." *Globe and Mail*. 6 February: A17.

———. 2007b. "Not a waste of time, but close to it." *The Globe and Mail*. 1 September: A1.

Brown, DeNeen L. 2002. "Afghan Deaths Stir Debate on Canada's Role; Ottawa Orders Inquiry." *Washington Post*. 19 April. Final, A14. [Corrected 5 July].

Canadian Department of Foreign Affairs. "Legalizing Opium Production in Afghanistan? Not the Answer." http://www.canada-afghanistan.gc.ca/cip-pic/afghanistan/library/opium_prod-en.asp (last updated 17 October 2007).

Canadian Department of National Defence. 2004. "Backgrounder: The Canadian Forces' Contribution to the International Campaign Against Terrorism." 7 January. http://www.forces.gc.ca/site/Newsroom/view_news_e.asp?id=490.

———. 2006. Message from the Minister. Budget 2006. http://www.dnd.ca/site/Reports/budget06/message_e.asp.

Canadian International Development Agency (CIDA). 2007. "Funding: Canada's Commitment to Afghanistan." (Accessed 26 June 2007) http://www.acdi-cida.gc.ca/CIDAWEB/acdicida.nsf/En/JUD-12514411-QD6.

Canadian Parliamentary Debates. 2006. 39th Parliament, 1st Session, Edited Hansard, Number 025, 17 May. http://www2.parl.gc.ca/HousePublications/Publication.aspx?Language=E&Mode=1&Parl=39&Ses=1&DocId=2215122.

Canadian Senate Committee on National Security and Defence. 2005. "WOUNDED: Canada's Military and the Legacy of Neglect. Our Disappearing Options for Defending the Nation Abroad and at Home." Interim Report. September. http://www.parl.gc.ca/38/1/parlbus/commbus/senate/Com-e/defe-e/rep-e/repintsep05-e.htm#_ftnref11.

———. 2007. "Canadian Troops in Afghanistan: Taking a Hard Look at a Hard Mission." Interim Report. February. http://www.parl.gc.ca/39/1/parlbus/commbus/senate/com-e/defe-e/rep-e/repFeb07-e.pdf.

CBC News. 2006. "Dutch Debate Sending Troops to Afghanistan." 30 January. http://www.cbc.ca/world/story/2006/01/30/dutchafghan060130.html.

Clark, Campbell and Brian Laghi. 2006. "Afghanistan Mission Must Show Results, Dion Warns; He Says Allies Should Build Marshall Plan because Focus on Combat Is Not Working." *Globe and Mail*. 6 December: A5.

Dallaire, Romeo with Brent Beardsley. 2003. *Shake Hands with the Devil: The Failure of Humanity in Rwanda*. Toronto: Random House.

Dempsey, Judy. 2007a. "Cracks Appear in Allied Coalition in Afghanistan." *International Herald Tribune*. 13 September. http://www.iht.com/articles/2007/ 09/13/healthscience/coalition.php.

———. 2007b. "Germany Wrestles with Keeping Its Soldiers in Afghanistan." *International Herald Tribune*. 16 September. http://www.iht.com/articles/2007/09/16/europe/germany.php.

Dow Jones International News. 2008. "France to Send More Troops to Afghanistan—Pres. Sarkozy." 26 March.

Dutch Ministry of Foreign Affairs. 2008. *Summary. Dutch Cabinet's Decision on Contribution to ISAF*. April. http://minbuza.nl/binaries/afbeeldingen-nieuw/themas/dossiers/kern-art-100-besluit_eng_021207.pdf.

Fitzpatrick, Meagan. 2006. "Withdraw from Afghanistan: Layton." *National Post.* 1 September: A4.

Globe and Mail. 2006. "Bloc Issues Ultimatum on Afghan Mission." 12 December: 1.

———. 2007a. "The Truth Canada Did Not Wish to See." 23 April: A18.

———. 2007b. "Troops won't stay unless all parties agree, PM says." 23 June: A17.

Granatstein, J.L. 2007. "The Peacekeeping Myth." *National Post.* 31 January, A19.

Independent Panel on Canada's Future Role in Afghanistan. 2008. Final Report. Ottawa. http://www.independent-panel-independant.ca/main-eng.html.

International Crisis Group (ICG). 2006. "Countering Afghanistan's Insurgency: No Quick Fixes." *Asia Report* no. 123. 2 November.

Kesterson, Scott. 2006. "Canadian Ambushed in Afghanistan. Video, 15 July, [uploaded 3 August 2006]. http://youtube.com/watch?v=qaC-w2dIxZc&mode=related&search=.

Maley, William. 2006. *Rescuing Afghanistan.* London: Hurst & Co.

Maloney, Sean M. 2006/2007. "Canada, Afghanistan and the Blame Game." *Policy Options.* December/January: 25.

———. 2007. "Winning in Afghanistan." *Maclean's.* 23 July: 25.

Martin, Don. 2006. *National Post.* December 14.

McKay, Simeon. 2006. "The Limits of Likemindedness." *International Journal* 61 (4): 875–94.

Morton, Desmond. 2006–2007. "Afghanistan, Famously Inhospitable to Foreigners." *Policy Options.* December/January: 17–20.

Murphy, Rex. 2006a. "Hanging People for What They Believe." CBC News, *The National.* 22 March. http://www.cbc.ca/national/rex/rex_060322.html.

———. 2006b. "A General Who Is Allergic to B.S." CBC News. *The National.* 20 April. http://www.cbc.ca/national/rex/rex_060420.html.

New York Times. 2006. "Losing the Good War." 5 December.

Nossal, Kim Richard. 2004. "Defending the 'Realm': Canadian Strategic Culture Revisited" *International Journal* 59 (3): 503–20.

Pratt, David. 2004. "The Way Ahead for Canadian Foreign and Defence Policy." Keynote Address at the 20th Annual Conference of Defence Associations Institute Seminar. 26 February. http://www.cda-cdai.ca/seminars/2004/pratt.htm.

Ricks, Thomas E. 2006. *Fiasco: The American Military Adventure in Iraq.* New York: Penguin.

Riedel, Bruce. 2006. "Afghanistan: The Taliban Resurgent and NATO." Washington, DC: Brookings Institution. 28 November. http://www.brookings.edu/views/op-ed/fellows/riedel20061128.htm.

Saunders, Doug. 2007. "Berlin Begs Ottawa to Stay Past 2009." *Globe and Mail.* 7 September: A1.

Senlis Council. 2006a. "Canada in Kandahar: No Peace to Keep. A Case Study of the Military Conditions in Southern Afghanistan." London: Senlis Council. June. http://www.senliscouncil.net/modules/publications/013 _publication.

———. 2006b. "Losing Hearts and Minds in Afghanistan: Canada's Leadership to Break the Cycle of Violence in Southern Afghanistan." Policy Paper. Ottawa: Senlis Council. October.

Simpson, Jeffrey. 2007. "A Bad End Looms over Canada's Afghan Mission." *Globe and Mail.* 6 January: A19.

———. 2008. "Manley Wants Us to Play a Game of Chicken with NATO." *Globe and Mail.* 28 January: A17.

Smith, Graeme. 2007. "From Canadian Custody into Cruel Hands." *Globe and Mail.* 23 April: A1.

Spiegel Online International. 2007a. "Germany Must Stay the Course in Afghanistan." 21 May. http://www.spiegel.de/international/germany/0,1518,483993 ,00.html.

———. 2007b. "Roadside Mine Kills 3 Security Offices in Afghanistan." 15 August. http://www.spiegel.de/international/germany/0 ,1518,500086,00.html.

———. 2008. "Germany Can Do More." 26 March. http://www.spiegel.de/inter national/world/0,1518,543480,00.html.

Staples, David. 2007. "Paying Top Dollar for Poppies." *Edmonton Journal.* 23 June: A17.

Taylor, Scott. 2007. "Canada's Mission in Afghanistan: Beyond the Rhetoric." In *Canada in Kandahar,* ed. John Ferris and James Keeley. Calgary Papers in Military and Strategic Studies, vol. 1: 11–18.

Toronto Star. 2007. "Hope Fading among Afghans." 16 January: A18.

Travers, James. 2007. "Harper Should Pray for Longshot in Afghanistan," *Kitchener-Waterloo Record.* 17 May: A7.

Nipa Banerjee worked for thirty-three years for the Canadian International Development Agency (CIDA), serving both at the headquarters level and in the field. She represented CIDA in Bangladesh, Indonesia, India, Thailand, Cambodia, Laos, and Afghanistan. Her most recent posting, in Kabul (2003–2006), was as CIDA's head of aid for Afghanistan. In July 2008, she joined the Graduate School of Public and International Affairs at the University of Ottawa, where she lectures on international development. Her research interests include development in post-conflict countries and aid coordination and aid effectiveness, with a focus on Afghanistan.

William A. Byrd is currently serving in the World Bank Headquarters in Washington, DC, as adviser in the Poverty Reduction and Economic Management Unit of the South Asia Region. Until recently he was the bank's senior economic adviser in Kabul, Afghanistan, where he helped to develop the World Bank's strategy for Afghanistan's reconstruction effort. He led the team that produced the first World Bank economic report on Afghanistan in a quarter-century. He has been with the World Bank for more than twenty years, during which time he has worked on China, India, Pakistan, and Afghanistan. His publications include six books on China and numerous articles, including several on Afghanistan. He has been responsible for reports on Afghanistan's public finance management, economic co-operation in the wider Central Asia region, and Afghanistan's drug industry. Most recently he co-authored a joint report of the World Bank and the UK Department for International Development titled

Afghanistan: Economic Incentives and Development Initiatives to Reduce Opium Production.

Colonel **Mike Capstick** retired from the Canadian Armed Forces (Regular) in late 2006 after thirty-two years of service. His final appointment was as Commander of the first deployment of the CF Strategic Advisory Team – Afghanistan from August 2005 until August 2006. This unique unit, a mixed military–civilian team, provided strategic planning advice and capacity building to development-related agencies of the government of the Islamic Republic of Afghanistan. He was awarded the Meritorious Service Medal for his leadership of this team and is currently an associate at the Centre for Military and Strategic Studies, University of Calgary.

Antonio Giustozzi is a research fellow at the Crisis States Research Centre at the London School of Economics, where he runs a research project on contemporary Afghanistan. He is the author of *War, Politics and Society in Afghanistan, 1978–1992* (2000) and *Koran, Kalashnikov and Laptop: The Neo-Taliban Insurgency in Afghanistan* (2007) as well as several papers and articles on Afghanistan.

Jonathan Goodhand teaches in the development studies department of the School of Oriental and African Studies at the University of London. His involvement with Afghanistan dates back to the late 1980s, when he was an aid worker based in Peshawar, Pakistan. Since then he has conducted research and published widely on issues related to civil wars, war economies, international aid, and post-conflict peacebuilding. His most recent publication is *Aiding Peace? The Role of NGOs in Armed Conflict* (2006).

Husain Haqqani is Pakistan's ambassador to the United States. Prior to taking this post he was the Director of Boston University's Center for International Relations and co-chair of the Islam and Democracy Project at the Hudson Institute in Washington, DC. He has served as an adviser to Pakistani prime ministers Nawaz Sharif and Benazir Bhutto and as Pakistan's ambassador to Sri Lanka. His most recent book is *Pakistan between Mosque and Military* (2005).

Geoffrey Hayes is an associate professor in the department of history at the University of Waterloo and is the associate director of the Laurier Centre for Military, Strategic and Disarmament Studies at Wilfrid Laurier University, both of which are based in Waterloo, Canada. His work on contemporary defence issues has appeared in such journals as *War and Society: An Interdisciplinary Journal* and *Behind the Headlines*. Most recently he co-edited, with Mike Bechthold and Andrew Iarocci, *Vimy Ridge: A Canadian Reassessment* (Wilfrid Laurier University Press, 2007).

Ali A. Jalali was the interior minister of Afghanistan from January 2003 to September 2005. He is currently serving as both a distinguished professor at the Near East South Asia Center for Strategic Studies and a researcher at the Institute for National Strategic Studies, both of which are based at the National Defence University in Washington, DC. His areas of interest include reconstruction, stabilization, and peacekeeping operations in Afghanistan and regional issues affecting Afghanistan, Central Asia, and South Asia. He has published widely on Afghanistan.

William Maley is a professor and the director of the Asia-Pacific College of Diplomacy at the Australian National University. He has served as a visiting professor at the Russian Diplomatic Academy, a visiting fellow at the Centre for the Study of Public Policy at the University of Strathclyde, and a visiting research fellow in the refugee-studies program at Oxford University. A regular visitor to Afghanistan, he is the author of numerous books on Afghanistan, including *Rescuing Afghanistan* (2006) and *The Afghanistan Wars* (2002).

Seema Patel is an independent consultant whose focus is on market-led economic development in fragile environments. She is currently a consultant to the Afghan–American chamber of commerce and the Global Development Alliance at USAID. She recently left the Post-Conflict Reconstruction Project at the Center for Strategic and International Studies, where she served as a business development advisor for the project. From 2006 to 2007 she led a comprehensive CSIS field-based study on reconstruction in Afghanistan. The final report for the project was titled *Breaking Point: Measuring Progress in Afghanistan*.

Mark Sedra is a research assistant professor in the department of political science at the University of Waterloo and a senior fellow at the Centre for International Governance Innovation, both of which are based in Waterloo, Canada. He currently leads CIGI's research program on global and human security. He has regularly served as a consultant to governments, intergovernmental organizations, and NGOs on security issues in Afghanistan and has published widely on the country. His most recent publications are: *The Search for Security in Post-Taliban Afghanistan* (2007), co-authored with Cyrus Hodes, and *Afghanistan, Arms, and Conflict Armed Groups, Disarmament and Security in a Post-War Society* (2008), co-authored with Michael Vinay Bhatia.

Books in the Studies in International Governance Series

Alan S. Alexandroff, editor
Can the World Be Governed? Possibilities for Effective Multilateralism /
2008 / vi + 438 pp. / ISBN: 978-1-55458-041-5.

Geoffrey Hayes and Mark Sedra, editors
Afghanistan: Transition under Threat / 2008 / xxxiv + 314 pp. /
ISBN-13: 1-55458-011-1 / ISBN-10: 978-1-55458-011-8

Paul Heinbecker and Patricia Goff, editors
Irrelevant or Indispensable? The United Nations in the 21st Century /
2005 / xii + 196 pp. / ISBN 0-88920-493-4

Paul Heinbecker and Bessma Momani, editors
Canada and the Middle East: In Theory and Practice / 2007 /
ix + 232 pp. / ISBN-13: 978-1-55458-024-8 / ISBN-10: 1-55458-024-2

Yasmine Shamsie and Andrew S. Thompson, editors
Haiti: Hope for a Fragile State / 2006 / xvi + 131 pp. /
ISBN-13: 978-0-88920-510-9 / ISBN-10: 0-88920-510-8

James W. St.G. Walker and Andrew S. Thompson, editors
Critical Mass: The Emergence of Global Civil Society / 2008 /
xxviii + 302 pp. / ISBN-13: 978-1-55458-022-4 / ISBN-10: 1-55458-022-6

Jennifer Welsh and Ngaire Woods, editors
*Exporting Good Governance: Temptations and Challenges in Canada's
Aid Program* / 2007 / xx + 343 pp. / ISBN-13: 978-1-55458-029-3 /
ISBN-10: 1-55458-029-3